Collected Works of Professor B.R. Grover
Vol. III

Indian Agrarian Structure – Ancient to Early British: Elements of Continuity and Change

Collected Works of
Professor B.R. Grover
Vol. III

Indian Agrarian Structure—
Ancient to Early British
Elements of Continuity and Change

Edited by
Amrita Grover
Dr. Anju Grover Chaudhary
Dr. J C Dua

Originals
Delhi-110052

Collected Works of
Professor B.R. Grover
Vol. III

Indian Agrarian Structure – Ancient to Early British:

Elements of Continuity and Change

Edited by
Amrita Grover
Dr. Anju Grover Chaudhary
Dr. J C Dua

Originals
Delhi-110052

First Published 2007

ISBN 81-88629-63-4 (Vol. 3)

Published by
Originals
A-6, Nimri Commercial Centre,
Near Ashok Vihar Phase-IV, Delhi-110052
Phones: 27302453
e-mail: lpp@nde.vsnl.net.in
visit us at: www.lppindia.com

Printed at
D K Fine Art Press P Ltd.
Delhi-110052

PRINTED IN INDIA

Dedicated to the Memory of my Esteemed Brother Professor B.R. Grover

Amrita Grover

Table of Contents

About the Author

(b. 1923- d. 2001)

Professor B.R. Grover, former Chairman of the Indian Council of Historical Research, with an academic and administrative career spanning more than 55 years, has left an indelible mark as one of India's most eminent and dedicated historians. He has left behind a massive wealth of historical research based on original Persian, Urdu, Ottoman Turkish, Punjabi and English sources. Known for doing intensive research in the archives and libraries of India, several European countries and the United States of America, Professor Grover had carved out a distinct position for himself as a moving encyclopaedia of source material on agrarian history of the Mughals, especially the land revenue administration.

Upon his death on May 10, 2001, the then Prime Minister Atal Behari Vajpayee paid him a rich tribute, stating: "He would always be remembered for his formidable legacy of excellence, erudition, and dedication to historical research and academic administration." Dr. Murli Manohar Joshi, then Minister of Human Resources and Scientific Research, paid him a personal homage and called him a real "Karma Yogi". He said, "He lived like a Yogi and died like a Yogi." Former Vice President of India, Justice Hidayatullah, had also applauded him for his research. His colleagues described him as "a man of sterling qualities of head and heart"; and "a dynamic and objective head of country's premier historical Institute who has left a rich legacy of his outstanding achievements in the world of historical research," among other things.

Born on February 10, 1923, Professor Grover started his career in teaching in 1946 in Lahore and later taught at the University of Punjab and various universities in Delhi until 1974, including Delhi University, Jawahar Lal Nehru University and Jamia Milia Islamia, where he also served as head of the Department of Indian History and Culture. In 1974, he was called upon to join as Director cum Member-Secretary of the newly established Indian Council of Historical Research (ICHR), a premier historical research Institute, where he served from 1974 to 1985 as Director and was later appointed as Chairman in 1999. For his long association with ICHR, his colleague, Prof. A.R. Khan, wrote in his obituary: "On account of his long association with the Council and the services rendered by him to it, Professor Grover became an institution by himself and he and the Council became a synonymy, as the latter came to be identified, both in India and abroad, with Professor Grover, even when he was not holding any office in the Council."

Initially having received training at Paris under the auspices of UNESCO for the promotion of history as a means of international understanding, Professor Grover wrote and published books in British history. Later, because of his deep interest in the study of original sources and his proficiency in Persian language, his research interests shifted to the medieval period of Indian history. His interest later widened to the study and research in regard to the social, cultural and economic impact of the Indian immigrants in West Asia and East European countries. As an avid researcher, Professor Grover wrote and published copiously on various aspects of the Mughal Agrarian System, Patterns of Rural Trade, The Concept of Village Community and a host of other topics. His writings, mostly published in prestigious journals, like the journals of the Delhi School of Economics and the proceedings of various conferences, became nodal points for the scholars of his generation. His published writings in *The Indian Economic and Social History Review, Proceedings of the Indian Historical Records Commission, Indian Archives, Proceedings of the Punjab History Conference, Punjab Past and Present* and *The Proceedings of the Indian History Congress,* among others, brought him national and international recognition. At an early stage of Professor Grover's career, Prof. M.M. Pearson of Pennsylvania University, U.S.A., wrote about his Mughal Agrarian writings as "...an impressive start...brilliant, which makes fundamental contribution in this area." Prof. C.A. Bailey of Cambridge University, complimented him for "comprehensive listing of materials" and "excellent bibliographies."

Because of his expertise in historical manuscripts/documents and objects, Professor Grover was nominated by the Government of India for several honorary positions such as member of the Indian Historical Records Commission, member of the Historical Documents Purchase Committee of the National Archives of India, member of the Committee on Preservation and Development of Cultural Heritage of Delhi, and an expert member of the Verification Committee of National Museum, India. Professor Grover was also a member of the Publication Committee of the "Comprehensive History of India". For the Indian History Congress, he served intermittently as a Joint Secretary, a Treasurer and Sectional President (Medieval India). Professor Grover also edited the well-known Time Capsule in 1978, and advised the Government to display it in the National Museum instead of inserting it again underground. He also served on the Editorial Board constituted by the Government of India for the production of documentaries on "Freedom Struggle for India's Independence, 1984-2001." Under this scheme, more than 75 documentaries were published by the Films Division, Ministry of Information and Broadcasting.

Professor Grover represented India at several international organizations, including UNESCO in 1951; Indian delegate to West Germany, 1957; delegate to the International Conference in History, Bucharest, 1980; delegate to the International Conference on the Bulgarian Studies, Sofia, 1986; and delegate to the World Archaeological Congress, Croatia, 1998, among others. Besides participating in numerous Indo-European cultural exchange programmes, presiding over innumerable regional/national/international seminars and conferences and contributing papers to various national/ international seminars and conferences, he also lectured widely in West Germany (1957), Bulgaria (1986), Zagreb (1998), UK (1998), Holland (1998), and United States (1998 and 2000).

Professor Grover received several honours and awards for his historical research. For his writings on Georgi Dimitrov, the "Role of the Indian Immigrants in the Culture and Economy of the West Asian and East European Countries During the Medieval Age," and "The Social, Religious and Agrarian Aspects in East Europe, especially Bulgaria under the Ottoman-Turkish Rule (14th-19th centuries)," he was awarded Georgi Dimitrov Gold Medal by the Peoples Republic of Bulgaria. For his work on Punjab History, Professor Grover was awarded Saropa Roll of Honour by the Punjabi University, Patiala, in 1996. A life-long scholar of medieval and Islamic India, Professor Grover again came in limelight in 2001 when (upon the demolition of Buddhist statues at Bamiyan by the Taliban government), his expert opinion was sought by the Indian media to determine whether there was any parallel between Bamiyan and Ayodhya.

As a distinguished historian and a scholar with an integrated and scientific approach to the analysis of the historical process, Professor Grover, being a liberal thinker, was a great believer in the social cohesion and national integration in India and made an immense contribution in this regard.

Introduction

Professor B.R. Grover, an eminent scholar of medieval Indian history, was one of the few historians of India who prompted agrarian history. His meticulously researched papers published in the 1960s added to our knowledge and understanding of pre-colonial rural society and economy. His findings are based on his indepth study of original Persian sources. While going through his collection of historical documents, it was a revelation to me that as far back as 1950s, he had consulted the 17th and 18th century *pargana* and village level records— the *arhasatta* and *jamabandi*—pertaining to Sarkar Rewari of the Mughal suba of Delhi.

During the period that Professor Grover was carrying on his research, the major trend was to attempt to make a systematic study of the ruling class and nature of interaction between its two constituents—the zamindars and the nobility. The other major concerns were to examine the working of land revenue system, agrarian economy and rural social structure. Many Indian historians rejected the colonial constructions of pre-colonial state, society and economy in India. Professor Grover researched the subject in the various libraries of India and abroad also contributed immensely in the area of agrarian history and his writings were widely appreciated by the scholars.

Professor Grover consulted a large number of primary sources in Persian, English and vernaculars and collected a great deal of information on the nature and working of land revenue system in India. Without subscribing to any particular ideological bias in history writing, he objectively analysed facts and figures contained in the original sources and placed them in historical perspective.

Many of the studies that have dealt with the relations between the state and rural society in pre-colonial India have tended to focus on the magnitude of agrarian taxation and the administrative assignments for its assessment and collection. While an understanding of the complexities surrounding revenue collection and the functional responsibilities of various administrative officials provide useful information, the institutional emphasis in these studies has generally kept them from examining the interaction between the state, its taxation policy and agricultural productivity. Professor Grover, in his writings, attempted to relate the logic and principles of taxation adopted by the state to its objectives and role in agricultural production.

Professor Grover's historical work on land revenue system in India will be appreciated by the scholars as it goes beyond the rigid periodization of Indian history. It covers the entire range of land revenue systems starting from ancient India to early phase of British rule in India. This approach is useful as it enables us to grasp the evolution of land revenue system over a long period of time and highlights elements of continuity and change from one regime to another. Professor Grover probed into several interrelated issues concerning land revenue systems such as the nature of land revenue, its social justification, the primary objectives and methods of land revenue assessment, the choice excercised in maximization of revenue between the two alternatives of progressive increase in demand and expansion of rural economy, the social impact of land revenue, the correlation between rate of assessment and actual payment in practice, changes, if any, in the level of real taxation and its relationship to peasant produce. Professor Grover further took care to highlight regional and local features of land revenue system in terms of variations in environmental features, social organization and customary practices. Here is an admirable attempt by a scholar to bridge the gap between the empirical evidence and theorisation.

It is partly due to the limitation of our sources and their overriding concern with revenue transactions that the relations between the state and the rural society figure so prominently in our discussion of the agrarian economy. Still more research is needed to understand the relationship between the state action and agricultural production. It is on this question that historians have offered diverse opinions.

The present work also contains a glossary of revenue and administrative terms used in the primary sources of the Mughal period. Professor Grover devoted much of his time in preparing this glossary and gave a precise meaning and definitioon of each of the term. In the glossary, he also explains the context in which a particular term occurred and its varying usages. This glossary will be very useful to the students and researchers of medieval Indian history.

History writing with regard to India's past has moved considerably over the last three decades. Priorities are rapidly changing. Despite a major shift in priorities, Professor Grover's work on land revenue remains distinctive and relevant for both students as well as researchers and he will always be remembered as a dedicated and distinguished scholar in the area.

At the end, I would like to congratulate the editors of this volume: Ms. Amrita Grover, Dr. Anju Grover Chaudhary and Dr. J C Dua in bringing together and presenting extremely valuable writings of Professor B.R. Grover on land revenue in India. The publication of this volume is a welcome addition to the existing corpus of historical writings on land revenue system.

Dilbagh Singh
Professor
Centre for Historical Studies
Jawahar Lal Nehru University
New Delhi

New Delhi
29th December, 2006

Preface

The peasantry has always formed the backbone of the Indian agrarian society. At the same time, income from land has been the financial mainstay of the medieval Indian State. The stability and solvency of the state has always depended upon the sound and well-balanced land revenue system. Hence, land revenue administration has been a perennial problem of the Indian administration and governance. The subject, therefore, is of tremendous importance to the social and economic historians.

The economic historians working on ancient, medieval and early British administration in India have dealt with many an aspect of the agrarian system but have primarily stuck to their fields relying on their limited, respective source material and accounts of foreign travellers. Earlier writers did not have much access to the Persian manuscripts and contemporary original records due to their limited knowledge of the Persian language and thus lacked an understanding of the exact nature of the working of the administrative history of the Mughal age. Moreover, the earlier writers did not try to bridge the gulf between the writings on ancient, medieval, the modern Indian history by highlighting the elements of continuity and change in the various aspects of agrarian system from the early history of India to the pre-industrialized phase in this country.

The papers presented in this volume of The Collected Works of Professor B.R. Grover contain the writings of Professor Grover on those aspects of agrarian system that especially highlight the continuity and change from ancient period of Indian history to the early phase of the English administration in India—a subject that remained largely untapped by previous historians due to their lack of accessibility to contemporary original records. Some original records of the Mughal government in Persian and Rajasthani became available to the research scholars only after the integration of the Indian states to the Union Government of India. Professor Grover examined these documents from

1972 onwards relating to the incidence of state share of agricultural produce, incidence of the various types of cesses, pattern of crops, methods of assessment, extent of cash nexus and units of land holdings of the varying classes of the agriculturists in different *parganas*. Specifically, he consulted various administrative manuals, literature and records; episcoplar collections; geographical and topographical works; dictionaries; private papers and personal collections of the Rajas, Thakurs and landed families of Rajasthan and Himachal Pradesh, among others; revenue papers; assessment reports; and the settlement reports at the Commissioner's offices, District Record offices and Tehsils as well as the village *tappah* and *pargana* records to fully ascertain the actual working of the land revenue system in various provinces. He consulted numerous Persian documents and manuscripts lying scattered in different Archives and libraries in India and abroad, such as The National Archives of India, New Delhi; State Archives, Allahabad; Bihar State Archives; *Daftar-i-Diwani* (new State Archives of Andhra Pradesh, Hyderabad); *Daftar-i-Diwani wa Hazuri*, Jaipur (now Rajasthan State Archives, Bikaner); Aligarh Muslim University Library; State Library Rampur (U.P.); Khuda Baksh State Library, Patna; Royal Asiatic Society Library, Calcutta; Asfia State Library, Hyderabad (Deccan); British Museum, London; India Office Library, London; Bodelin Library, Oxford; Edinburgh University Library, Edinburgh; Bibliotheqe Nationale, Paris; Bavarian State Library, Munich; State Library (Berlin East); and The University Libraries of Marburg and Tubingen (West Germany), among others.

Two of the articles – 'Organisation of the Agrarian Structure and Practices in North India from the Ancient to Medieval Age – Pre Mughal Era (Elements of Continuity and change)', presented at **The Symposium on Transition from Ancient to Medieval Period: Problems of Economic and Social Organization of the Society (India and the Territories of USSR)** and 'Elements of Continuity and Change in Land Ownership and Rights from the Mughal Age to the Early British Administration in India', presented as **Presidential Address, Medieval India Section, 37th Session of Indian History Congress, 1976,** especially trace the elements of continuity and change in specified aspects of agrarian system from ancient period to early British rule in India. Other writings included in this volume involve an elaborate and critical discussion on (i) Land Revenue System in Ancient and Early Medieval India under the Hindu Rule; (ii) Land Revenue Administration during the Sultanate

Period; (iii) Land Revenue Administration under Sher Shah (it also includes a detailed discussion on the Machinery of Collection of Land Revenue under Sher Shah); (iv) Land Revenue Administration During the Early Period of Akbar's Reign; and (v) A Note on An Integrated Agrarian Society during the Mughal age. All these writings are based on original source material in Persian, Urdu, Marathi, Sanskrit and English available in various Archives, Record Offices, and personal collections of erstwhile officials at different places in India and abroad. However, except the first two articles, since all the other writings were finalized during the late 1950s and early 1960s, the books published after that period have not been referred to or commented upon. Despite this lacuna, the writings throw a new light on the understanding of the subjects/aspects discussed since all these re-writings took into consideration practically all the secondary and primary source material then available.

In his writings, Professor Grover time and again stressed that ever since ancient times, India has been 'par excellence' an agricultural country. Therefore, its socio-economic structure, till at least the pre-industrialized phase in the recent past, has predominantly been governed by the agrarian economy. The role of cash nexus which was limited in character in the early phase got impetus from the Gupta period onwards, more especially for the valuation of the villages for the purposes of revenue assignment to the religious persons and institutions as well as to the state officials. By the 12th century A.D., it got wider operation, if not in the whole of India, at least in Marwar (Rajasthan) and Bengal. Both in ancient and medieval periods, rulers would make land grants and revenue assignments for secular and religious purposes and except when granted revenue from the villages of the crown lands, the grantee had no proprietary claim to the agrarian lands of the revenue paying peasant families who continued with their ownership rights over lands.

Professor Grover's writings also show that imposition and re-imposition of the intermediary rights of the conquering clans has been a recurring phenomenon throughout the medieval ages. In India, even after the Turkish conquest, the land owning communities, unless recalcitrant, retained their lands, privileges and rights so long as they continued to pay the required state demand. However, Persian terminology, which the Turkish ruling class was used to, came to be applied to various revenue practices and institutions. The assignation of the revenues of the villages and the revenue-free land grants on perpetual basis not only created hereditary landed class of priesthood, some parasitic attitude was also bound to develop and this remained a marked trait of this class throughout ancient and medieval ages. No doubt, the Delhi Sultanate laid considerable emphasis on the organization of the military-cum-revenue machinery for the collection of the land revenue from the conquered families in north India, but apart from this, it is very doubtful if the Sultanate rule (excepting Sher Shah's reign) brought about any fundamental changes in the existing pre-Turkish revenue practices and the Hindu principles of agrarian administration with regard to the incidence of state demand (excepting Alauddin Khalji's reign) or methods of assessment prevailing in different regions of north India. From the viewpoint of the state, Professor Grover maintained, Allauddin's attack on Hindu landed intermediaries who exempted their own agrarian lands from revenues and defied the revenue regulations can be well appreciated. But the heavy incidence of state demand and additional cesses must have been extremely harsh on the peasantry. As regards Sher Shah, Professor Grover has opined that no doubt his land revenue system as a continuation of the system as he found it and there was no basic break with the past, nor was any thing new introduced except that he picked and chose all that was of permanent value in the system. Nevertheless, as any stern rule naturally would, his reign witnessed radical modification in several aspects of that system resulting in the improvement of the condition of the raiyats, the efficiency of the administration and betterment of the financial conditions of the state. However, the initiation of the advancement of the *taqavi* to the agriculturists, especially since the Tughlaq period, is a distinct contribution in the formulation of the agrarian policy during the Sultanate period.

Without belittling the administrative achievements of Delhi Sultanate, Professor Grover held the view that the agrarian set up of north India in the pre-Akbar medieval age has to be viewed in the socio-economic background and the nature of political hold that the Turkish and Afghan rulers were from time to time able to exert on the local Hindu chiefs and the petty landed intermediaries (all designated as zamindars) who formed the backbone of the agrarian society during the medieval age. Throughout the Sulanate period, the prevailing Hindu revenue practices and the socio-economic structure based on landed intermediaries played a dominant role. In general, this is true not only of the Delhi Sultanate, but also of the contemporary Sultanate in Kashmir and other independent states like Gujarat, Malwa, Jaunpur and Bengal which sprang up from the late 14th century onwards on the disintegration of territories of the Delhi Sultanate.

By the time Mughal Empire was established, Professor Grover has opined, the agrarian structure in different regions was based on socio-economic pattern and polity inherent in the Indian situation. The Mughal state, having adopted the existing landed structure, was replenished further with new avenues for the realization of the revenues. However, it did not enunciate any theoretical claim to the state ownership of the land, nor did it make *shariat* as the basis of the property concept, land holding and revenue administration. The Indian Muslim jurists remained divided over the issue of the land property in India. Some scholars upheld the view that the landed in India being *Kharaji* was the property (*malkiyat*) of the existing possessors of lands (*maliks*) even though a major portion of land was possessed by the non-Muslims. Another school of thought considered that the land being the property of the *baitul mal* (Muslim state treasury), the state had further right to alienate it to the new grantees with proprietary rights. Professor Grover was of the view that the European travelers, who visited India during the 16th and 17th centuries, held that all the land was owned by the state. They evaluated the position of the *tankhwah jagirdars* of the Mughal nobility in comparison to the landed nobility in Europe. But, Professor Grover observed that the *tankhwah jagirdars* under the Mughal system were entitled only to the revenues of the assigned territories and were not the owners of land. The European travelers did not fully appreciate the institutional implications of this system against the agrarian and political set-up of the country but howsoever biased they may be in the evaluation of the Indian agrarian society as against the European society, it seems that in their erroneous judgement they were equally misled by the assertion of the paramount rights of the state in the effective control of the agrarian land. However, broadly speaking, there was two-fold division of lands, i.e., unappropriated state owned and appropriated lands vested with the *riaya* for the purposes of habitation and cultivation.

Another point raised by Professor Grover in the writings being published in this volume is that during the Mughal age, the maintenance grants by way of exemption of the revenues on the land, assignation of the revenues of the cultivated lands of cash grants were bestowed upon different kinds of beneficiaries. The 17th century chronicles refer to both *madad-i-maash* and *suyurghal* but in general use, they were considered as *aimma* grants. Technically, such grants were made for the personal life of an assignee but in practice, the hereditary claim for the renewal of grants which got established was conceded. All land grants, unless otherwise specifically mentioned in the original *Farmans,* which were rather rare, were subjected to periodical verification and confirmation by every succeeding monarch. After the assumption of Diwani rights by the East India Company in Bengal, Bihar and Orissa (1765), tremendous revenue literature was produced on the subject. It comprised not only the reports, memoranda and minutes of the English administrators but also commentaries in Persian by Indian revenue experts. However, this literature is full of contradictions. Though broad similarities could be drawn between the English pre-capitalist concept of property and the pre-British Indian concept of property, there are still marked differences based on the respective concept of land laws and practices in the agrarian life of the two countries. Even John Shore, who was the shrewdest of the administrators, could not easily trace any vital analogy between the English and Indian proprietary rights and he found the situation singularly confused. With the best of probing, John Shore and even other administrators were not able to understand the Indian concept of land ownership and comparative land rights of the state, the zamindars and other categories of the *riaya* in proper perspective. Professor Grover asserted that the introduction of Permanent Settlement (1793) in Bengal, Bihar and Orissa was as much influenced by the financial and political considerations on the part of the East India Company as the latter's policy of not ending the institution of *zamindari* and the usage of the realization of intermediate holders. Later on when the word 'rent' was broadly defined in the Tenancy Acts, then the relationship between the zamindars and the *riaya* was essentially as between the landlord and the tenant. The landlord or the rent receiver was the owner of the land and the rent payer, even when he was in occupancy, paid only for the use and occupation of the land. This implied a complete change from the Mughal concept of property and agrarian relations. Also, the growth of sub-infatuation and subdivisions of the lands in many a *zamindari* and *taaluqdari* was a new phenomenon in the agrarian structure of the permanently settled territories during the first half of the 19th century. At the same time, Professor Grover did concede that it was not intended to suggest that the creation of property in land was the British innovation because of the impact of the contemporary economic thought upon the administration of the East India Company in India. But under the British, a right holder (a person possessing permanent rights in the soil) entitled to engage for the payment of the land revenue would be deemed to have proprietary right in land. This was a clear English innovation in the concept of agrarian property which had far reaching effects upon the land owning classes.

Another important point raised by Professor Grover in his writings contained in this volume is that during the early 19th century, it was realized that the Permanent Settlement in Bengal had ignored the land rights of the cultivating *raiyats* and left them completely at the mercy of the zamindars. Accordingly, at the time of introducing the *rayatwari* settlement in the Madras Presidency, Thomas Munro believed that it was 'no innovation' and it was in continuation with the pre-British institution, customs and revenue practices of the people. But, Professor Grover held that in principle, the *rayatwari* system was not totally in continuation of the pre-British pattern which was essentially revenue, *i.e., Jama muqarari* or *Jama muqarari istamrari*. It is clear from the *zamindari* records that both according to the assertion of the zamindars and the English understanding, the above revenue terms, even though distinct from each other, were considered to be denoting permanently fixed revenue. However, unlike the British concept, in order to avoid discretionary and arbitrary fixation of rates upon the *raiyats* by the zamindars, the state reserved its right to regulate the terms by which the zamindar was to let his lands to the *raiyats*. In practice, however, such significant right was not exercised for a long time. All this implied a complete revolution in the agrarian structure and ownership of the estates which formed the subject of the Settlement.

From late 18th century to the middle of the 19th century, different patterns of land settlements were introduced in India. The English administrators and revenue officers surmised on the nature of land ownership and rights in regard to the various strata of the agricultural classes during the pre-British period. Notwithstanding the changes in land tenures brought about by them for many a region, they thought that they were mostly continuing the traditional pattern inherited from the pre-British era. However, Professor Grover stated that apart from other things, the application of British theory of rent equally affected the agrarian relations in India. The Regulations of Permanent Settlement claimed a revenue as the share of produce of every bigha of cultivated land in line with the Mughal practice. They did not use the word rent with reference to the annuity payable by the zamindars but used the word revenue. Later on, a distinction was made between revenue and rent. The term revenue was understood to mean the amount paid by the superior land owners to the state while rent was the amount payable to the superior land owners by those who held land under them whether they were the actual occupants or characterized by the landed intermediary classes. Professor Grover further stipulated that Munro himself conceded the existence of different categories of zamindars but he could not distinguish the nature of ownership rights and the *inam* lands held by virtue of being landed intermediaries. Moreover, the reshuffling of the nature of land rights and the high incidence of rent implicit in the *rayatwari* system caused severe socio-political strains and agrarian tensions in the territories of its operations. However, the maintenance land grants, *dharmadayam* (*khairati, bhattavritti*) as well as endowed grants (*devadayam*), which had acquired hereditary and transferable character were (in the early stages of English administration) continued and were considered as the private property of the assignees.

In brief, Professor Grover has made a scholarly contribution in tracing and connecting the elements of continuity and change in the various aspects of land revenue, land ownership, and land rights from the ancient period to the early British administration in India. The editors hope that these writings would not only be of great value to the historical world but would also be very useful to the scholars and students of economic history of India.

The editors are extremely grateful to Dr. Dilbagh Singh, Professor, Centre for Historical Studies at Jawahar Lal Nehru University, for having spared his precious time to write an Introduction to this volume.

The editors are highly obliged to Dr. Tasneem Ahmad, Deputy Director, Indian Council of Historical Research, for his very valuable assistance in checking the Persian quotes in this volume.

The editors are also very grateful to Shri Pradeep Mittal, Originals Publishers, for an excellent job in publishing this volume.

Ms. Amrita Grover
Dr. Anju Grover Chaudhary
Dr. J. C. Dua

Chapter 1

Land Revenue System in Ancient and Early Medieval India Under the Hindu Rule

I

In India, the state has always claimed land revenue as its share in the produce of land cultivated by the agriculturists. In the ancient and medieval periods of Indian History, the land revenue system was gradually evolved out of varying indigenous practices and notions of fiscal administration prevalent from time to time. The land revenue was always reckoned as a determinate share in the gross produce and it is very doubtful if the states ever regarded it as a land tax. For the known historical phases of ancient Indian polity, the earliest statement on land revenue comes from the *Rig Veda* when Gods are asked to compel the subjects of the king to make contributions (*Bali*) to the ruler to ensure the stability of his reign.[1] In the later Vedic polity, the monarchy with its civil and military establishment entrenched its position as a secular institution and claimed land revenue from the agriculturists as an obligatory contribution to the state revenues.

The exact incidence of state share for this period is not known. The term *bhaga,* meaning a share in the produce, came to denote the land revenue whereas *'bali',* originally known to the Rig Veda and Smirits as land revenue, came to be associated with periodical agricultural cesses.[2] By the Mauryan age, the agricultural economy and the land revenue system seem to have been at a fairly developed stage. Megasthenes puts 1/4th of gross produce as the land revenues.[3] Kautilya's *Arthasastra,* which has been generally associated with the Mauryan age[4], gives a more detailed picture of the land revenue practices. Kautilya draws distinction between the crown lands and the private owned lands.[5] The royal lands were either directly cultivated by slaves and laborers or were leased out to tenants on the basis of one half of the division of crops.[6] Some tenants would get 1/4th or 1/5th of the produce grown or some might pay as much as they could conveniently afford to give to the state.[7] It seems in this context that permanent and full time tenants wore entitled to 1/2 of the produce whereas some of the cultivators who possessed their own lands which were not very productive would supplement their income by working as tenants on the royal lands and would be required to pay 3/4th or 4/5th of the produce or as much they could conveniently afford to pay to the state.[8] The *Arthasastra* recommends that the land revenue assessment on the holdings of the cultivators should be based on the classification of agrarian lands viz. upland and low land soils and the available means of irrigation rendered through overflowing of rivers, river-channels, tanks and wells.[9] As such, the state demand could range between 1/5th to 1/3rd of the gross produce dependent upon the labour necessary for the cultivation of the particular crop.[10] Most likely, a further distinction was made between the grain crop assessed in kind and some of cash crop assessed basically on cash rates (*hiranya*) and there is every possibility that the incidence of state demand may have varied for these two categories of crops. Most of the scholars have associated the passage on the fixation of the varying revenue demand at 1/3rd, 1/4th or 1/5th with the water rates levied either exclusively on the crown lands[11] or on the privately cultivated lands.[12] In such a case, a cultivating family on the crown lands working on sharing basis at half the produce would have to part with 20% to 33% more depending on the means of irrigation leaving it hardly with 17% to 30% of the gross produce. Besides this those tenants who got only 1/4th or 1/5th of the produce would not be in a position to pay at all or would be left with nothing after having paid the water rates. In case of a privately owned land, a family paying the normal demand at 1/4th of the produce and the additional water rates mentioned above would have to part with 45% to 58% of the gross produce as the total state dues.[13] Neither of these versions is correct. In fact, the term *'udakbhagam'*[14] stands for the revenue assessed on the irrigated or wet- lands than a water rate. This is quite implicit in the text of the passage which asserts the principle of the fixation of the varying state demand in pre-portion to the physical labour involved in the different irrigational methods viz. by carrying water on shoulders by water lifts, by raising water from rivers, lakes, tanks and wells.[15] The ensuing passages are equally related to the fixation of the state demand.[16] The *Arthasastra* affords illustrations of the fact that certain crops were easy to grow (in relation to human labour and water supply) while others were comparatively difficult for growth. Thus the rice crop and the like (*i.e.,* millets etc.) were the easiest to grow, the vegetables etc. of intermediate nature and the sugar cane were the most difficult requiring much more care and expenditure. Further on, the *Arthasastra* explains that the varying nature of soils and irrigational methods were suited to the growth of varying special crops.

Thus, the lands on the river banks were suitable for growing pumpkin, gourd etc.; over flown lands (by rivers or rivulets) for growing long pepper grapes, and sugar cane; well irrigated lands for growing vegetables and roots; low grounds for green crops (*i.e.,* fodder etc.) and certain plants and herbs etc. which could be grown within the marginal furrows of the main crops in the cultivated fields. Thereafter, the *Arthasastra* gives the details of the seeds and the manuring methods to be adopted for various crops. It is thus evident that the state demand could have varied not only in accordance with the irrigational methods but also in relation to particular soils suited for particular crops and the labour involved in their cultivation. The vegetables and the expensive crops like sugar cane requiring more irrigation and human labour must have been assessed on lower rate and some of these in cash as well than the grain crops and the millets etc. All this is further confirmed by the *Arthasastra's* chapters on the colonisation of waste land and the state agricultural policy adopted during the emergency period.

For the purposes of colonisation of waste lands, the *Arthasastra* takes into consideration various factors viz. the qualities of the soil, the extent of labour required for cultivation, the degree of rainfall, the watery lands dependent upon artificial means of irrigation conducive to the growth of varying nature of grain and other crops.[17] For the emergency period, the *Arthasastra* recommends[18] the state share at 1/4th or 1/3rd of the grain produce on the fertile lands dependent on pure rainfall as well as colonisation of the wastelands by supplying grain and cattle to the pioneer cultivators. In case these measures failed to suffice the financial needs, the state would prevail upon the peasantry to resort to double cropping in the summer,[18] to be punctual in sowing the crops and to avoid any waste of grain at the time of harvesting. The state would claim 1/4th of the grain crops and 1/6th of the forest produce, cotton flowers, fruits and vegetables etc. It is not clear if these assessment rates applied only to the crops raised on fertile lands dependent only upon rainfall[19] and newly colonised waste lands or could be extended to all other peasants for their summer crops.[20] Though the summer crops would mostly subsist on rainfall, double cropping would be usually possible either by supplementing water by artificial means of irrigation or in the flooded areas overflown by the rivers and rivulets etc. Moreover, double cropping in the summer would be possible only by cultivating particular crops after having adopted a special pattern of crop sowing adaptable in a particular geographical region. Hence, it is possible that these assessment rates (of 1/4th of grain produce and 1/6th of vegetables etc.) either represent only the fertile lands dependent on simply sufficient rainfall or may even represent the reduced demand in comparison to the state share levied in irrigated areas even though the state would benefit through revenues accuring from two crops within the same summer season. At this same time, these assessment rates do not stand for the normal state demand levied on lands artificially irrigated in the winter season when more expensive grain and other crops are cultivated. This experiment of double cropping and raising revenues thereupon had an extremely limited scope as the *Arthasastra* gives only one chance to the state for such an administrative measure. However, the suggestion for distinction between the assessment rates on the grain crops and the other crops is quite significant and could as well have been applicable to the normal state demand levied both on the artificially irrigated areas and dependent on pure rainfall. This is further borne out by the later practice of assessing the cash crops based on the division of the produce (*bhaga*).[21]

It is also known from the *Arthasastra* that the cultivating families did own self-developed means of irrigation (dug out channels from rivulets, lakes and self constructed well etc.) and did possess even proprietary rights for mortgage or sale over such self- developed means of irrigation.[22] Such cultivators who did not possess personal means of irrigation could utilise water from the stored tanks of the owners on the payment of either fixed amount or annual rent or sharing portion of their produce.[23] They had also to help in the repair and maintenance of the tanks. It seems that even the owners of the tanks and lakes had to pay some water rate to the state though remission of water cess was afforded on the newly constructed or recently repaired tanks etc.[24] Apart from it, water rate had to be paid on the state owned reservoirs or lakes.[25] Land revenue remission was also given on the recently reclaimed areas.[26] The *Arthasastra* also mentions about the pasture lands on uncultivated tracts attached to the villages[27] but does not state if the cultivators were entitled to its free use. The fact that pasture grounds occur as one of the items of revenue sources shows that the cultivators had to pay some nominal cess for the pasture use.[28] With regard to the forests, the *Arthasastra* is quite particular that only the Brahmans would be sanctioned their free use for the Soma plantation, religious learning and other purposes mentioned therein.[29] Megasthenese's view of the state share fixed at 1/4th of the produce seems to be too rigid and perhaps was based on his general observation. Of the other Greek writers, Arrian does not mention the amount of state demand. Strabo maintains that the cultivators received 1/4th of the produce from the kind as payment.[30] Apparently, either Strabo confused the position of the land owing cultivators with a section of the tenant class working on the royal lands or else adopted a completely erroneous view that the former had to pay 3/4th of the produce as the state share. Diodorus makes distinction between the land tribute and land revenue and thinks that the cultivators had to pay both these charges to the state.[31] In fact, the Hindu polity never considered the state share in the produce as a tribute and evidently Diodorus confused the varying assessment rates on the agrarian lands and crops—both in kind or cash—with the land tribute and the land revenue.

The *Arthasastra* reveals a fairly developed stage of survey, assessment and collection of the land revenue in the settled villages. Based on a detailed topographical survey, full records of rights were maintained in respect of classification of agrarian land in the villages, their boundaries, the cultivated and uncultivated lands, agricultural fields, well irrigated lands, gardens, irrigation works and forests.[32] Possibly, such detailed records could not have been prepared without the process of indigenous methods of measurement of land. The assessment was based on actual measurement of the agrarian land. The survey and measurement of the revenue paying holdings of the cultivators was conducted by a state official.[33] As such, it is reasonable to presume that the revenue assessment was actually done directly by the state on the individual holdings of the cultivating families rather than as a lump sum fixation on the villages[34] even though the latter practice was equally known.[35] Besides this, regular census records were maintained in respect of the inhabitants in a village along with their castes, the revenue paying and the non-revenue paying house-holders, the exact number of cultivators, the cattle wealth, cow herds and the other professional classes.[36] The state also maintained regular information in respect of transfer of crown lands and land revenue remissions.[37] The villages were mainly divided into two categories, *i.e.,* the revenue free and the revenue paying. The latter were further classified into those contributing military service in lieu of taxes; paying revenue in kind by way grain, cattle, raw materials; and cash payment in gold; by supplying free labour and dairy produce in lieu of revenues.[38] This shows that varying modes of payment of revenues in kind or cash were prevalent in different villages. In the local administration, every village had a headman chosen from amongst the village elders. It is possible that in a large village, a headman was assisted by a council of elders and other subordinate officials for the revenue administration and the other problems of the village. Above the headman were the *Gopa* and *Sthanika* with a jurisdiction over five to ten villages.[39] The *Gopa* worked as revenue accountant. The *Sthanika* was the tax collector and worked directly under the *Pradesika* (incharge of district).[40] These officials were responsible to the *Samahartr* who was the Chief Collector (Commissioner) of the division.[41] All this emphasised direct contact between the state administration and the cultivators. Though land grants were given to regular officials,[42] the semi-official functionaries of the local administration may have been paid by a small percentage in the collection of revenues.

Megasthenes gives a favourable account of the state of agriculture with two annual harvests, the nature of crops grown, the fertility of the soil, the highly developed system of irrigation under the supervision of an official named *Agronomoi* and land measurement as the basis of assessment.[43] Megasthenes says that owing to developed irrigational methods, famines were quite unknown.[44] However, it is difficult to believe that drought was unknown to the vast territories of Mauryan empire though it is quite possible that no scarcity or famine occurred in the gangetic valley around the period that Megasthenes visited the Mauryan capital. Under Asoka, a local official named Prajuka assumed great importance and became the backbone of the rural administration.[45] He is known to *Arthasastra* and was probably the same official designated as *Agronomoi* of Megasthenes. He served as surveyor for measuring the lands and helped the assessment officer for the revenue assessment on the holdings of the cultivators. He had also the judicial powers in cases relating to land disputes, assessment matters, remission of land revenue, water disputes and grassing disputes etc. For all his functions, he was responsible to the *Pradesika* who possessed general powers of inspection and surveillance over the local administration. The assessment of land revenue was based on actual measurement of the holdings and strictly in accordance with the quality of the soil and other considerations of agrarian classification of land which have already been explained. The only reference to state demand under Asoka is known from 'Rmmindei' inscription which exempts the village of Lumbini, the birth place of the Buddha, from the payment of village tribute and the land revenue—which continued to be assessed—is put at 1/8th of the produce.[46] It cannot be said with certainty if this was a concessional state demand in the village of Buddha's birth-place or it was the normal state share levied in this region in accordance with the local practice and the classification of land.

The latter sources mention a lower rate of state share. Manu says that the land revenue was the main source of state revenues and underlines the principle of fixing the state share varying according to the soil and the labour necessary to cultivate it. According to him, in normal times the state share varied between 1/12th and 1/6th[47] but liable to rise even up to 1/4th of the gross produce in times of war and other public calamity.[48] The *Dharmasastra* puts the state share at 1/6th of the produce. Though some texts stick to the theoretical enunciation of 1/6th, others recommend varying rates at 1/6th, 1/8th, 1/10th or even 1/12th of the produce.[49] Later on for Harsha's reign, Hiuen Tsang mentions that the taxes on the people were light and the personal service required from them was moderate. Those who cultivated the royal lands paid 1/6th portion of the gross produce.[50] For the early medieval age, Al-Biruni mentions 1/6th of the produce as the state share under the Hindu rulers.[51] The *Shukraniti*, supposed to be a late medieval work, lays emphasis on the variation in the incidence of state demand governed by the nature of soil and means of irrigation, *i.e.,* 1/4th from the land irrigated by tanks, canals and wells and 1/2 from the land dependent on rainfall.[52]

The fact that the above-mentioned evidence drawn from *Arthasastra* and late sources disagree in the incidence of state share shows the variations in the critical concept of fiscal administration. It may be doubted if such a decline in the state demand came in actual practice in the source of the countries under the Hindu rule. However, it is reasonable to believe that variation in the incidence of state share was governed by the nature of soil and the means of irrigation along with the traditional concept of the regional practice. In a country like India with divergent physical and geographical features in respect of nature of the soil and means of irrigation, no uniformity of scheduled state demand could have been enforced in all the territories even under the centralised rule of the Mauryas or the early Guptas. On the basis of the contemporary evidence, it may be plausible to presume that in ancient and early medieval periods under the Hindu rule, the state demand varied from 1/12th to 1/3rd of the gross produce. All this was governed by various geographical, irrigational and regional factors as well as the fiscal policy of the kings in power from time to time. Apart from it, a peasant had to pay some extra local cessess (*kara, bali*) on cattle and other livestock and on dairy produce.[53] They had also to pay cessess for the use of the pasture land and piscary wherever ponds and lakes were available for this purpose.[54]

The direct evidence throwing light on the methods of assessment and the extent of the cash nexus for the revenue payment prevalent in the ancient and early medieval periods is rather meagre. However, some description is available from the *Jatakas, Arthasastra* and the later land grants. Varying methods of assessment seem to have been prevalent in different regions. The oldest and the most widely spread method is that of division of the produce on the thrashing ground (*Khalabhiksa*).[55] The *Jatakas* reveal the existence of appraisement of the standing crops (*Kankut*)[56] which must have been facilitated by the development of the practice of land measurement. Both the *Jatakas*[57] and the *Arthasastra*[58] point towards a regular method of land measurement with the help of a rope by a surveying staff. Such a process of measurement of the agricultural fields was based on regular indigenous unit areas and the application of the land rates to them. Later on, under the Guptas, the measurement of the unit areas became more systematic and came to be based on arithmetically calculated linear sized *reeds* (*Nala*).[59] A *reed* consisted of units of length called *hastas.* The units of length (*hastas*) might vary and the size of the *reed* was by no means uniform. In some regions, the size of the *hasta* measure was fixed and the area unit comprising eight *reeds* in length and nine in breadth (8 X 9 reeds) was standarised.[60] In the early medieval age, the Gujra-Prathihara kings adopted an improved standard *hasta* measure.[61] Still later in the 11th century, the Katachuri Rajput rulers of Awadh adopted a standardised measurement—(*devakutikastha*) and area unit (*naluka*).[62] In the 12th century, the Sena dynasty in Bengal restored the land measure according to *reed*-standard and the *drona* became the area unit.[63] Besides this, the land grants in some regions reveal the simultaneous existence of more primitive methods of measurement and assessment viz. ploughing capacity of the plough-oxen (*kula*) and the seed-capacity of the agricultural fields (*Kulyavapa*) in relation to the total respective yields of the crops. A *kula* comprised the area unit capable of being ploughed by twelve oxen[64] and a *kulyavapa* denoted an area capable of cultivation by a specified weight of seeds (*kulya*).[65] The total area capable of cultivation by plough-oxen or a certain specified weight of seeds and the approximate yield of the crops was always calculated having been based on experience.[66] Though these methods are known to have been applicable for the purposes of land assignments, there is every likelihood that they may have been equally correlated to the regular smaller land units in similar terms (*i.e.,* capacity of plough-oxen or weight of seeds) and that the assessment of the revenues of the cultivated fields could have been based on them. All the above-mentioned methods of assessment persisted in various regions throughout the medieval age though they acquired different nomenclatures.

Under the Hindu rulers, even though the assessment on the individual holdings of the revenue paying peasants acquired general practice, the mode of collective assessment (*pindakara, samksepa*) on the entire village was equally known.[67] In the latter case, the internal distribution of the assessed revenues of the village must have been done by the peasants themselves in proportion to their holdings. Such villages with collective assessment were clearly demarcated from those wherein assessment on individual peasants was done directly by the state.[68] As regards the mode of revenue payment, it was usually done in kind (*bhaga* varyingly known in different periods as *bhaga, bhagabhogakara, maya, dhanya*) and the role of cash nexus seems to have been of limited and of exceptional character. The cash revenue payment (*hiranya*) occurs in the *Smrtis,*[69] *Arthasastra*[70] and more so in the historical literature from the 4th to the 12th centuries A.D.[71] The available epigraphic evidence shows that in the 12th century it got wider operation in Marwar (Rajasthan)[72] and Bengal.[73] It is difficult to suggest as to how the cash revenue was assessed and it seems in the context that it was applicable only to particular crops.[74] Quite distinct from it, the cash assessment on the entire villages had been also known right from the period of *Jatakas,*[75] and was prevalent under the Mauryas.[76] The later land grants show the assessed cash valuation of the village for the purposes of revenue assignments.[77] The prevalence of cash valuation of the villages does not primarily show the co-existence of cash assessment on the cultivators. The assessed estimate in cash must have been worked out on the basis of the regional current prices of the crops only for the purposes of valuation and assignment. The fact that from the Gupta period onwards, apart from the religions grants, the revenue assignments to the civil and military officers became quite common,[78] must have accelerated the role of money-economy for the purposes of valuation. This equally affected the village wise preparation of the record of rights and all this was an important legacy to the medieval period of Indian History.

For the ultimate impact of the agrarian administration upon the peasantry, opposite views have been expressed. Some scholars assert that the imposition of revenues upon the peasantry was burdensome.[79] They refer to the stories in the *Jatakas* quoting harsh exactions on the part of the local officers and the 'en mass' emigration of the peasants from their villages to escape crushing taxation. This picture is considered to stand true for the entire Hindu rule. Other scholars maintain while the state demand in the pre-Mauryan and even in the Mauryan period was too high but in the later centuries it became extremely moderate and weighed lightly on the peasants.[80] Though exceptions can be made for any period under the rapacious local rulers and the periods of drought, the fact seems to be that with differential scale of state demand already explained, the paucity of agricultural labour and the viable holdings of the agricultural families, the latter could have led a substantial life so far as food is concerned. For want of contemporary evidence, it is difficult to work out the exact incidence of the additional agricultural cesses (*kara, bali*) but it seems that they constituted a nominal addition to the proper land revenue. The Hindu state not only remitted revenue in times of drought and bed harvests but afforded financial help to the peasants for the purchase of seed and plough oxen etc.[81] Even the cultivating families working on sharing basis either on the royal lands or private and landlords, led a fairly comfortable life. It is, of course, undeniable that in the periods of wars and conquest as well as the process of inroads and settlement of the dominant tribes and clans, it must have disturbed the agricultural economy of the affected villages and led to hardship on the peasant families.[82]

References

1. Rigveda, X, 173 f, *Atharvaveda III*, 3-5; VI, 86-88.
2. U.N. Ghosal, *The Agrarian System in Ancient India.* (Calcutta, 1930), pp. 6-7, 12. (Henceforth put as Ghoshal); 'Contribution to the History of Hindu Revenue System', *H.R.S.*, pp. 34-40, 59-60, 64-65.
3. J.W. McCrindle, *Ancient India as Described by Megasthenes and Arrian,* (Westminster, 1901), pp. 41-42.
4. For the date of the *Arthasastra,* see R. Shamasastry, *Kautilya's Arthasastra* (translation) Fifth Ed., 1956, Preface (Henceforth put as *Arthasastra*, Tr. S) pp. VII-XXXIII; For different opinions and discussion, also see Romila Thapar, *Ashoka and the Decline of the Mauryas,* OUP, Appendix I, pp. 218-225.
5. *Arthasastra* (tr. S), pp. 57-58, 127-51.
6. *Ibid.*, pp. 127-29.
7. *Ibid.*, pp. 128-29.
8. *Ibid.*, The passage runs, "....or those who live by their own physical exertion may cultivate such fields for 1/4th or 1/5th of the produce grown; or they may pay (to the king) as much as they can without entailing any hardship upon themselves, *with the exception of their own private lands that are difficult to cultivate*".
9. *Ibid.*, pp. 129-30.
10. *Ibid.*
11. Ghoshal, p. 12; Also C.H.R., pp. 30-31, 33.
12. Romila Thapar, *Ashoka and the Decline of the Mauryas,* pp. 66; B.K. Sarkar, *The Political Institutions and Theories of the Hindus,* (Calcutta, 1939), p. 124.
13. B.K. Sarkar (*Ibid.*) calculates the land revenue and irrigation charges at 40% to 57%. Romila Thapar (*Ibid.*) considers that a separate water rate ranging between 1/5th to 1/3rd was charged but still believes that the normal land revenue was fixed at 1/4th of the produce. Miss Thapar has not understood the proper position. A regular irrigation charge in addition to land revenue from all types of irrigational methods viz. channels from rivers lakes, tanks and wells, even though calculated separately, virtually becomes a part of the land revenue and the total dues that a cultivator would owe to the state. Miss Thapar's analogy that the normal demand of 1/4th of produce plus irrigation charges under the Mauryas was less than the state demand fixed at 1/3rd of produce under Akbar is rather fallacious. Under Akbar, the state demand at 1/3rd of produce was fixed for the grain crops whereas it was lower for the cash crops. Moreover, except for the canal irrigated lands, the Mughal government never charged any separate water rate for the well irrigated areas or such lands which were overflown by rivers or irrigated through regular water channels from the lakes and the ponds, etc.

14. *Arthasastra,* Sanskrit text, Book II, Chap. 24; The translation of '*Udakbhagam*' as water rate is too literal. Here, it stands for land revenue on irrigated and wet lands.

15. *Ibid.,* tr. S., p. 129.

16. *Ibid.*

17. *Ibid.,* p. 324.

18. *Ibid.,* pp. 271-272; Ghoshal, *op. cit.,* pp. 16-17.

19. *Ibid.,* p. 271. Shamasastry in his translation suggests the raising of the summer crops. The Sanskrit text, Book V, refers to the doubling of cropping during the summer. Also, see Romila Thapar, *op. cit.,* p. 66; Ghoshal (*Ibid.*) puts it as the compulsory raising of a second crop by the cultivators.

20. Romila Thapar, (*op. cit.,* 66) restricts the double cropping only to fertile lands dependent upon rainfall.

21. Ghoshal (pp. 16-17) considers it as a compulsory raising of the second crop by all the cultivators.

22. Ghoshal, pp. 38-46; W.H. Moreland, *The Agrarian System of Moslem India,* (Allahabad, 1929), pp. 5, 17, after having considered the varying incidence of state demand known from various ancient texts concludes that the differential scale of assessment within the same area was unknown to Ancient India and that a flat rate of demand was made. Ishwari Parsad states (*Medieval India,* p. 46) that a differential scales was introduced by the Arabs in Sindh during the 8th century but does not refer to any contemporary evidence. In view of the explanation offered above, both these views cannot be accepted.

23. *Arthasastra,* (tr. S.) p. 195.

24. *Ibid.*

25. *Ibid.*

26. *Ibid.,* p. 46-47.

27. *Ibid.,* p. 193.

28. *Ibid.,* p. 48.

29. *Ibid.,* pp. 58, 157.

30. *Ibid.,* pp. 48, 192.

31. Strabo, XV, pp. 1, 40.

32. Diodorus, II, p. 40.

33. *Arthasastra,* (tr. S), pp. 129-30, 158-59, 190-95.

34. *Ibid.,* p. 58 mentions a cess on land measurement (*rijju*). For land measurement in *Jataka* tales, Meyer, I, p. 366.

35. Also see Ghoshal, p. 43; Romila Thapar, *op. cit.,* pp. 67-68.

36. *Arthasastra* (tr. S.) p. 66; Ghoshal, pp. 17-18.

37. *Ibid.,* p. 159.

38. *Ibid.,* pp. 158, 192-93.

39. *Ibid.*, p. 158.
40. *Ibid.*, pp. 158-59.
41. *Ibid.*
42. For the Mauryan local administration, also see Romila Thapar, *op. cit.*, pp. 106-110.
43. *Arthasastra,* (tr. S) p. 46. Such grantees had no rights for further alienation by sale or mortgage.
44. See f.n. 3.
45. *Ibid.*
46. Romila Thapar, *op. cit.*, pp. 107-110.
47. J. Bloch, *les Inscriptions d'Ashoka,* (Paris, 1950), p. 157; Also, Ghoshal, p. 31; Romila Thapar, *op. cit.*, pp. 66-67. Ghoshal thinks that 1/8th was a reduced state demand from the normal demand of 1/4th. Thapar agrees that it was a concessional demand but asserts that the rate of reduction by 50% was too large and that the normal demand in this region would have been 1/6th of the produce; D.D. Kosambi, *An Introduction to the Study of Indian History,* (Bombay, 1956), p. 194, has also interpreted in the same manner.
48. Manu, Chapter VII, p. 139. Manu puts the normal demand at "an eight Sixth or Twelfth part of the grain according to the labour necessary to cultivate the land".
49. *Ibid.*, Chap. X, p. 118.
50. Ghoshal, pp. 7-12, 21, 30-33, 75-76; C.H.R., p. 58.
51. Beal 1. 215 (T. Watters, *On Yuan Chwang's travels in India,* ed. T.W. Rhys Davids and S.W. Bushell, 2 vols., (London, 1904-05), I., p. 176). According to Ghoshal (pp. 38-39, 48-49), the description about the royal land given by Fa Hian (399 to 414 A.D.) and then by Hiuen Tsang (629-645 A.D.) stands for the whole territory of the state and was not limited to the private lands of the king. As such, the state demand under Harsa stood at 1/6th of the produce in general.
52. *Kitab-ul Hind,* tr. Sachau, E.C. (Trubner's Oriental Series), London, 1914, Vol. II, p. 149.
53. *Sukraniti,* tr. B.K. Sarkar, (Allahabad, 1925), pp. 147-48. Sarkar has shown that *Sukraniti* belongs to late medieval period. Also Ghoshal, p. 25; C.H.R., pp. 66-67.
54. *Arthasastra,* (tr. S) pp. 57-58; Also A.L. Basham, *The Wonder That was India,* (London, 1954), pp. 107-108; Ghoshal, pp. 7, 12, 34, 77; C.H.R. pp. 59-60, 64-65.
55. *Arthasastra,* (*Ibid.*), pp. 43, 58, 158, 192-93; Ghoshal, *Ibid.*
56. Ghoshal, *Ibid.*, p. 55.
57. *Ibid.*, p. 26.
58. *Jatakas*, Vol. IV, p. 169; Meyer, *Jataka Tales*, Vol. II, p. 366.

59. *Arthasastra* (tr. S) p. 58.

60. Ghoshal, p. 41.

61. *Ibid.*

62. *Ibid.*, pp. 55-56.

63. *Ibid.*, p. 64.

64. *Ibid.*, pp. 71-72.

65. *Ibid.*, pp. 9-10. Compare it with the Qalba as an area unit during the Mughal age. Though the Mughal Qalba was a lesser area capable of cultivation by four plough oxen, the principle involved for the land measurement and the estimate of the yield of the crops is the same.

66. *Ibid.*, p. 41. Compare it with the Kharwar system in Kashmir under the Mughals. Here, too, the weight of Kulya varied from Khawar but the principle of land measurement is the same.

67. Though Dr. Ghoshal (*Ibid.*) considers these two methods for land measurement, he has not realised the fact these methods could be equally applied for calculating the approximate yield of the crops and the appropriation of the revenue could take place according to the sharing or any other method of assessment. It is interesting to note how the plough-oxen measurement and assessment methods developed in certain territories of North India in the early medieval period and the Mughal age. Compare it with the Nasq method of assessment under the Mughals. Similarly the procedure of estimate of the yield of the crops in relation to their respective seed weights has persisted in some portions of North India right till the 19th and the 20th centuries.

68. *Arthasastra* (tr. S), p. 36; Ghoshal (*Ibid.*), pp. 17-18.

69. *Ibid.*, The *Arthasastra* considers the practice of converting the villages assessed in lump sum into assessment based on individual holdings and vice versa as an illegal practice on the part of the revenue officials.

70. Ghoshal, pp. 76-77.

71. *Arthasastra* (tr. S), pp. 65, 158; Ghoshal (*Ibid.*), pp. 7-8, 76-77; Also, H.R.S., p. 58.

72. Ghoshal, pp. 76-77.

73. *Ibid.*

74. *Ibid.*

75. *Ibid.*, pp. 6, 16, 45; H.R.S., pp. 59-62. Based on *Smritis*, Ghoshal puts the cash charge (*hiranya*) at an extremely low rate of 1/50th of the value of the crops but has expressed his inability to explain as to how the assessment was determined. It seems that such a low cash rate could stand for either a cash cess or an assessment on a negligible and inexpensive cash crop. The vegetables and other expensive cash crops must have been assessed on higher rates.

76. *Ibid.*, p. 76.

77. *Arthasastra* (tr. S), p. 158.
78. Ghoshal (*Ibid.*), pp. 69-70, 76.
79. See f. n. 13.
80. Basham, *op. cit.*, pp. 107-109. For south India, Basham has referred to some later inscriptions giving the impression of rent-strikes and the imprisonment of the village council for the evasion of taxes. For the Chola Empire, an inscription shows the pillage of a defaulting village by the state order.
81. Ghoshal pp. 7-8, 30-34, 45-49, 75-80. Dr. Ghoshal thinks (*Ibid.*, p. 32) that the high state demand under Chander Gupta Maurya was perhaps not a legacy from the preceding period and was caused by the development of the administrative machinery. He also considers this as one of the eventual causes of the downfall of the Maurya Empire. Romila Thapar (*op. cit.*, pp. 65-67) however, puts the state demand at 1/4th of the produce only within the vicinity of Patliputra and postulates still lower rate in the outlying territories. She considers the revenue under the Mauryas, especially under Asoka, extremely moderate which would have been conducive to the welfare of the peasants. Dr. Ghoshal thinks that after the death of Asoka for nearly five and a half centuries, the historical records throw little light upon the land revenue practices in North India (*Ibid.*, p. 34). He also asserts that by the time of Harsa, the state demand became very light and that Hiuen Tsang's description of the cultivators under Harsa's empire paying only 1/6th of the produce and leading a fairly comfortable life is applicable to the peasantry in general rather than simply to the cultivators working on the privats lands of the king. (*Ibid.*, pp. 48-49). D.D. Kosambi, (*op. cit.*, p. 281) considers that in comparison to the Mauryan administration, the taxes under the Guptas were much lighter but quite paradoxically asserts that the very prosperity of the empire killed it. Kosambi also believes that the peasantry under Harsa was free from the oppression of the landlord. He further maintains that it is only after the disintegration of Harsa's empire and the growth of the feudal elements in the early medieval age that the peasant was subjected to higher land-rent, taxes and the cove and the force by the feudal barons. (*Ibid.*, pp. 288-89).
82. *Arthasastra,* (tr. S), pp. 46, 66, 193.

II

Land Assessments—Religious and Subsistence Revenue Grants

The Hindu state made assignments of land both for secular and religious purposes. It seems that during the Mauryan age (4th and 3rd centuries B.C.) and even under the early Guptas (5th century A.D.), the practice of making revenue assignments to the civil and the military officers in lieu of their salaries was much less in vogue. Megasthenes mentions that the military officers were paid in cash.[1] However, the *Smritis* and the *Arthasastra* do mention the assignments to the state officials but they seem to have been confined to the subordinate administrative and revenue staff of the local administration.[2] Such assignees enjoyed only the revenues and could not sell or mortgage the lands.[3] After the Mauryan period[4] and more so far in the later Gupta period onwards, the revenue assignments were made to the officers of all grades and this was a well-established practice by the reign of Harsa.[5] As explained later, large-scale assignments of the revenues of the villages were made by the Gujara—Pratihara rulers and more especially by the Rajput kingdoms from the 8th to the 12th centuries A.D. This was a deep-rooted practice under the Hindu polity on the eve of the Muslim conquest of North India.

As regards the religious rent-free grants of land, they were known throughout the ancient and early medieval periods of Indian History. They find occasional reference in the *Arthasastra*[6] and other ancient texts.[7] Moreover, the ever-increasing epigraphic evidence available from the Gupta period onwards sheds considerable light on the nature of such grants. These were, in fact, the maintenance grants bestowed on the priestly families as well as the religious institutions. Besides this, the donor always wanted to win religious merit for himself and his deceased parents and at the same time to win worldly glory and success.[8] The main beneficiaries of the rent-free grants were the Brahman families, the Hindu temple, Buddhist monasteries and the various priests and attendants attached to the latter. The rent-free grants could be made for the already settled villages or only for the waste culturable lands. A grant of a village meant the assignment of the state revenues from the granted village to the donee. Such grants were perpetual and hereditary in nature.[9] The revenue collection was done by the grantees themselves with the help of the local revenue machinery of the villages. The cultivators were ordered to obey and show full co-operation to the grantees.[10] Except when granted revenue-free villages from the Crown lands,[11] the grantee had no proprietary claim to the agrarian lands of the revenue paying peasant families who continued with their ownership rights over their lands.[12] The grantee may, however, cover the waste culturable land of the village and for this he was exempted from the land revenue due to the state.[13] In addition to the land revenue, the grantee was usually bestowed all other items of revenues due from the assigned villages. This is absolutely clear from the land grant made by Harsa in the 25th regnal year, 631 A.D. of his reign.[14] Such grants had many local variations. In some grants, the grantee may not be assigned all the revenues of the village and certain items of revenues may be reserved for the state.[15] Some of these grants were conditional in the sense that certain moral and political inhibitions were placed on the grantees who are required to remain peaceful, to do no wrong to other villagers and not to indulge in any recalcitrant activity against the state.[16] Some of the grants made by the Pala kings in Bihar are conspicuous by their detailed nature. The grantees were conferred the revenues of the villages including the income from the occasional markets, the fines form the specified offences and a right to the use of the wasteland.[17] The details of the grants mention not only the boundaries and pasture grounds of the villages but also the fruit trees (mango and mahua) and the reservoirs.[18] The underlying idea of giving such details was not to create any landed proprietary rights of the grantees but to underline the catastral survey of the village under assignment as well as to mention all pecuniary rights in addition to the land revenue viz. the cases imposed upon the fruit trees, pastures/grounds and reservoirs, if any.[19] A 7th century grant of a village in the Punjab given to temple priests mentions the bestowal of the village along with its residents[20] and some grants make a mention of the village workers[21] and some more. A few 11-12th century land grants (*Prasadapatta*) favour the assignees with cultivated fields, wells, houses and householders together with a village with its bipends, quadrupends, fileds and householders.[22] Such grants did not involve the transfer of the cultivating or working class resident to the assignees as the latter's slaves or serfs.[23] This implied the assignment of all income due to the state from the resident cultivators or working men in the villages and did not in any way involve either the person's or the landed and commercial rights of the residents of the villages. This was equally a matter of phraseology used in the grants which were invariably more detailed in description when granted by the local Chieftains, vassal states than the royal court. The Pala land grants show that in certain refractory areas, though very rarely, the grantees may also be given the right of punishing the thieves.[24] Thus, in certain cases, the assignees were granted not only usual fiscal rights but even a certain measure of administrative rights for the maintenance of law and order. The text of the land grants under the Pratiharas is not so detailed and followed the usual method of assigning the full or a part of the village or a part thereof, many a Brahman families were granted rent-free waste cultivable lands and the donees had the discretion either to cultivate the lands on their own or to get them cultivated by leasing out to the tenants on sharing basis or by employing hired labour.[25] The land grants of the Rajput kings in the 11th and 12th centuries usually followed the pattern of the Pratiharas.[26] As the grants were free of revenue and other cesses, the grantees could enjoy the income after having met the share of the tenants or the charges of the labour employed. In fact, by the early medieval age, the cultivation of the land on the part of the Pratihara families was an accepted social feature and, as such, Parasara, a law giver of the 8th century A.D., permitted Brahmanas to take to agricultural vocation.[27] But where the assignment of waste cultivable lands was too large or the reclamation of the waste lands attached to the assigned villages could not be covered by the families of the grantees, they could easily rent them out to the tenants. A fear of the early 7th century perpetual land grants in the region of Orissa forbid their further alienation[28] but this right seems to have been conceded more frequently under the Pratiharas and their Calukya feudatories in North India.[29] However, further transfers could be made only for religious purposes. As such, a mortgage or sale of the assigned territory would transfer only the rights over the collection of the revenues and their enjoyment rather than any title on the agrarian lands of the peasants. The fact that throughout ancient and early medieval ages, the assignment of the villages was done on the basis of assessed valuation in kind or cash[30] shows the right of the state to make direct assessment on the peasants and to transfer only the revenues to the assignees. The position was different in case of the self-developed rent-free waste culturable lands (*brahmadaya*) wherein the grantees exercised rights of ownership which they could also sell or mortgage.[31] Apart from the state land grants, the private philanthropists could also give gifts of waste cultivable lands to the Brahmana families after having got them demarcated by the state officials and paid off the state revenues in a compounded manner.[32]

The assignation of the revenues of village and the rent-free land grants on perpetual basis created a hereditary landed class of the priesthoods. It seems that from the Gupta age onwards, large-scale hereditary land grants were made to this class. Apart from the royal grants, numerous grants were made by the vassal states and the local Chieftains. Even though they were bestowed from the spiritual and philanthropic ends of the donor, looked at from the economic angle, the grants were intended for the maintenance of the priestly class, the renowned teachers, religious and educational institutions.[33] The grants could be made either to an individual family or as a collective one to numerous families or the institutions.[34]

Such grants were considered quite lucrative which is confirmed by the detection of a spurious copper plate land grant as early as in Harsa's reign.[35] Thus with the conferment of the fiscal and landed rights on the priestly class, some parasitic attitude was bound to develop and this remained a marked trait of this class throughout the ancient and the medieval ages. However, it is equally feasible that the Brahmanas, when assigned revenues or waste cultivable lands in the rural areas and more especially in the backward tracts or amidst the aboriginal tribes, carried on the civilising mission on behalf of both the Hindu religion and the state[36] and thereby became the main stronghold of Hinduism in the social life of rural India.

References

1. Dicdorus, II, p. 41.
2. Ghoshal, pp. 73, 74; *Arthasastra* (tr. S), p. 46.
3. *Arthasastra, Ibid.*
4. Basham, *op. cit.*, 96. Ghoshal (pp. 73-74) thinks that under the early Guptas, the practice of making assignments to the state officers did not exist and that it was not noticed by Fa Hian. But this view is not accepted by Basham and other scholars who refer to the authority of Fu Hian. See Charles Drekmeier, *op. cit.*, pp. 181-82.
5. Ghoshal, pp. 42, 74.
6. *Arthasastra,* (tr. S), pp. 48, 66, 158, 192, 194-195.
7. For *Smritis,* see Ghoshal, pp. 20; Pali Chronical Literature and *Jatakas*, *Ibid.*, pp. 27-28; Manu, Chap. VIII, p. 237.
8. Fleet, *Epigraphia Indica,* (E.I.) 7, 155-60 narrates Harsa's land grant in 25th R.Y; E.I. 15. 113-145. Sixth century copper plates mention grants of land by a merchant to a Brahmana family.
9. *Ibid.,* Also E.I., 11. 52-55 (A Pala grant in North Bengal). The land grants usually mention that they are given to the donee 'in the succession of the sons and son's sons, for so long as the moon, sun and earth shall endure'. It is interesting to compare the religious land grants under the Hindu rulers with the Mughal *Altamgha* and *madad-i-maash* grants. The Mughal grants did not concede such strong rights to the assignees as were in vogue during the Hindu rule. The Mughal *Altamgha* grants, though considered hereditary and perpetual, could be made both for secular and religious purposes. But in either case, they were not alienable in character. The *madad-i-maash* assignments were subject to periodical inspections and slashes on fresh renewals to the descendants. Neither the *Altamgha* nor the *madad-i-maash* assignees had any administrative jurisdiction. The *irrabdeya* grants under the Hindu rulers did create ownership rights in the agrarian lands. The *madad-i-maash* assignees did not claim such rights under the Great Mughals but definitely claimed a right of alienation of the assigned village and lands in the 18th century.
10. *Ibid.*, I. 45 (A Pala grant in Bihar).
11. Ghoshal, pp. 51-52. (Late 6th and early 7th centuries grants of the Gurjara dynasty in Gujrat; An 8th century grant of later Gupta dynasty in Gujrat).
12. Against this view, R.S. Sharma (vide 'Feudal Elements in the Pala and Pratihara Polity, 750-1000', *Asian History Congress,* New Delhi, 1961; Land Rights in Early Medieval India Circa A.D. 500-1200, *op. cit.*) maintains that till the Gupta age, only usufructuary rights over the villages were transferred to the donees but the post-Gupta grants of villages conferred full proprietary rights of the agrarian lands, the houses and wells etc. Such a distinction between the pre-Gupta and post-Gupta nature of land grants is not correct. In fact, Sharma seems to have been misled by the phraseology and the detailed

description of the land grants known from the epigraphic sources whereas the earlier legal texts make statements of the assignment of revenue-free villages to the Brahmans only in a general language. As explained further, the detailed description of the village never conferred the proprietary rights over the agrarian lands. Also see f.n. 19.

13. I A, V/VII, pp. 504 ff., 11. 39-46; I E, XXIX, No. 1, B. 11. 26-44 (Pala grants in Bihar and Bengal respectively).
14. E I. 7, 155-160; Also, a 9th century A.D. *Pratihara* grant. I A, XV, pp. 112-113, 11. 1-12.
15. E I., XXX No. 2. 11. 1-16 (A *Pratihara* grant, dated 836 A.D.) Ghoshal (pp. 51-52) says that many of the religious endowments under the Lichchhavi rulers (5th-7th centuries A.D.) mention only reduced state demand on the agrarian lands of the donees. Apart from this, a land grant of the Calukya dynasty in Gujrat (*Ibid.,* p. 65) mentions the assignment of revenues chargeable from only three cultivators in a village.
16. Fleet 55. (A land grant made by the Vakataka King Pravarasean II in his 18th R.Y. vide Kosambi, *op. cit.,* pp. 296-297).
17. E I. IV, No. 11, 52-53; IA. X/VII, pp. 304ff., 11. 39-46.
18. E I., XXII, No. 17, 11. 34-35.
19. It may be suggested that a detailed description of land grants mentioning the fruit trees, means of irrigation (walls and reservoirs etc.) fertile cultivable lands, infertile and low lands, pasture lands, waste cultivable lands, paths, habitations and their residents etc. was not meant for the purposes of creating the ownership rights of the donee over the soil of the assigned villages and their residents. In fact, it served two-fold purpose. Firstly, it involved cadastral survey of the assigned villages or land which secured a degree of accuracy sufficient for the purposes of demarcation which might as well give some topographical features, such as the homestead, roads, canals and large sheets of water. Secondly, apart from the land revenue, the state always levied cesses on irrigation, fruit free, pasture lands and products of barren lands and small scale industrial products in the villages. When the assignment was made of the total revenues of a village or even when certain items of income had to be reserved, a detailed description of all the sources of income was rather essential. It may be further suggested that even during the 17th and 18th centuries, the sale transactions of the Zamindari villages in Awadh give similar details of the villages under transfer though the alienations were limited to the revenue collection and the enjoyment of the zamindari fiscal rights without involving any ownership claim over the agrarian lands of the peasants. As the zamindar during the Mughal age belonged to a secular intermediary landed class, the analogy may not be very apt. But it is suggestive of the methodology of the description of the village involved in transactions.
20. Fleet 80 vide Kosambi, *op. cit.,* p. 298.
21. *E I,* 15 I ff., 363; JBORS 2. 423, 407, 415 vide Kosambi, p. 298.
22. *E I,* III, 44 (A late 11th or 12th century grant in Orissa vide Ghoshal, pp. 71, 114, f.n. 20).

23. It is possible that a village grant from the private lands of the king may also attach a few mentioned slaves or serfs to the grants. See E I, V, 19 vide Ghoshal, pp. 70, 114 f.n. 20 (An 11th century grant in the region of Assam).
24. *E I,* XXIII, No. 47, 11. 17-24 (A village made by Dharmapala in Nalanda area to a Buddhist religious leader). Also see f.n. 17.
25. *E I,* IX, No. 1, Plate A, I. 19, Also Kosambi, *op. cit.,* p. 300.
26. See land grants vide Ghoshal, pp. 62-75.
27. R.S. Sharma, 'Feudal Elements in Pala and Pratihara Polity (750-1000), *op. cit.,* p. 7.
28. *E I,* IX, 40 (Dated 602-603) vide Ghoshal, pp. 50, 111 f.n. 4.
29. *E I,* V, No. 204, 11. 6-9 (in Jodhpur area, Rajasthan, Also Ghoshal, p. 63.
30. See land grants vide Ghoshal, pp. 51-61, 64-75.
31. *Arthasastra* (tr. S), pp. 194-95. Also see Bose (A. 'Social and Rural Economy of North India', p. 18) who makes a clear distinction between the assigned revenues of the villages without rights of ownership in land and brahmadeya gift entailing rights of land ownership. This practice seems to have continued right till the early medieval age.
32. *E I,* 15. 115-145 (Sixth century Damodarpur grants); I A. 1910, 193-26 (Sixth century Faridpur plates) vide Kosambi, *op. cit.,* p. 297.
33. Also see *Arthasastra* (tr. S), p. 44.
34. Fleet, 55, mentions a village grant given by the Vakataka king Pravavarsena II to a thousand brahmins collectively of whom the names of forty nine (*i.e.,* the heads of families) are named vide Kosambi, *op. cit.,* p. 296.
35. See f.n. 8.
36. Also see Kosambi, *op. cit.,* pp. 291-96.

III

Land Ownership and Land Rights

The problem of land ownership in ancient and early medieval periods under the Hindu rulers has been extremely controversial amongst the historians. Some have asserted the royal ownership while others have contended for the individual ownership of land.[1] These two opposite views are thought to be representing the imperialist and the nationalist school of thought. The protagonists of both of the schools have tried to base their interpretations on the ancient Indian legal texts. While the imperialists comprised most of the British Indian administrator scholars, the nationalists are considered to have overstressed the progressive and democratic features of ancient Indian society with the deliberate purpose of creating impact on nationalist and patriotic feelings of the Indian people in the pre-Independence era. However, leaving the agrarian peculiarities of the society which in the course of the centuries passed through various socio-economic phases of civilization, on a mere theoretical plane the adoption of either of the above mentioned rigid views is rather misleading. A fresh approach based on the socio-economic and political factors operating at different stages of Indian civilization would reveal various rights of the parties connected with land for the enjoyment of its produce or surplus produce.

No documentary evidence is available for the pre-Aryan civilization. Based on archeological and ethnological evidence, a few scholars think that agriculture was known to the pre-Aryan Indian people and that the earliest agricultural communities were founded in Western India.[2] Agriculture was also practised in the Indus Valley civilization on a fairly large scale and its people had developed indigenous means of irrigation dependent upon natural floods of the rivers and construction of the seasonal dams.[3] Apart from this a few ethnologists have asserted that when the Aryans came to India, they found the indigenous peoples living in communities under tribal or local chieftains. The indigenous tribes viz. Kolarians and Dravidians had established permanent villages and possessed community of ownership in land.[4] Modern scholarship is generally agreed that the Aryan invasion occurred in the middle of second millennium B.C.[5] and that the Aryans who entered the Indian plains in successive clannish waves were in a semi-nomadic and pastoral stage. However, with the gradual spread of the Aryan settlements in North India by the sixth century B.C., a settled agricultural economy had replaced the semi-nomadic pastoral life of the Aryans. The Aryans took to agriculture as means of production on a scale unknown to the local people earlier which resulted in the new varieties of production.[6] The local population that survived was enslaved and

III

Land Ownership and Land Rights

The problem of land ownership in ancient and early medieval periods under the Hindu rulers has been extremely controversial amongst the historians. Some have asserted the royal ownership[1] while others have contended for the individual ownership of land.[2] These two opposite views are thought to be representing the imperialist and the nationalist school of thought. The protagonists of both of the schools have tried to base their interpretations on the ancient Indian legal texts. While the imperialists comprised most of the British Indian administrator scholars, the nationalists are considered to have overstressed the progressive and democratic features of ancient Indian society with the deliberate purpose of creating impact on nationalist and patriotic feelings of the Indian people in the pre-Independence era.[3] However, viewing the agrarian problems of the society, which in the course of the centuries passed through various socio-economic phases of civilization, on a mere theoretical plane, the adoption of either of the above mentioned rigid views is rather misleading. A fresh approach based on the socio-economic and political factors operating at different stages of Indian civilization would reveal varying rights of the parties connected with land for the enjoyment of its produce or surplus produce.

No documentary evidence is available for the pre-Aryan civilization. Based on archeological and ethnological evidence, a few scholars think that agriculture was known to the pre-Aryan Indian people and that the earliest agricultural communities were founded in Western India.[4] Agriculture was also practised in the Indus Valley civilization on a fairly large scale and its people had developed indigenous means of irrigation dependent upon natural floods of the rivers and construction of the seasonal dams.[5] Apart from it, a few ethnologists have asserted that when the Aryans came to India, they found the indigenous peoples living in communities under tribal or local chieftains. The indigenous tribes viz. Lolarials and Dravidians had established permanant villages and possessed community of ownership in land.[6] Modern scholarship is generally agreed that the Aryan invasion occurred in the middle of second millennium B.C.[7] and that the Aryans who entered the Indian plains in successive clannish waves were in a semi-nomadic and pastoral stage. However, with the gradual spread of the Aryan settlements in North India by the sixth century B.C., a settled agricultural economy had replaced the semi-nomadic patoral life of the Aryans. The Aryans took to agriculture as means of production on a scale unknown to the local people earlier which resulted in the new varieties of production.[8] The local population that survived was enslaved and incorporated within the Aryan fold for doing labour work and tillage of land.[9] The earliest written reference about the Aryan way of life is known from Rig Veda.[10] The Aryans were divided into tribes viz. *Janas* which equally denoted the tribal territory. A tribe (*Jana*) was the highest level of political organisation and the tribe was further divided into groups called *Visas*. A *grama* or village was at first simply a collection of a related families and served as the basic social-cum-political unit. The family was consangiuineous and patriachal. There was a headman (*gramani*) in most of the villages. In the background of this tribal organisation of the Aryans, it is surmised that in its earliest stages, the concept of ownership of agrarian land was communal and land was regarded as the collective property of the clan. However, the progressively evolutionary stages of the notions governing proprietary rights evolved from the communal ownership of the tribe, further divided into clans to village community ownership, joint family holdings and the individual rights in the course of the centuries.[11] The communal *Vesh, i.e.*, periodical redistribution of land amongst various branches of clan or the practice of redistribution and readjustment of land within a single village or periodical exchange of certain ancestral land within a single family were traced in many a village in North Western portions of North India during the second half of the 19th century.[12] It is not intended to suggest that the same old tribes with their communal order continued to exist in these regions from the ancient times to the 19th century as these regions have passed through various political vicissitudes and many a tribe settled in succession from the ancient times to the middle of the 19th century. However, the ethnological and economic study of these tribes suggests how the individual landed rights have gradually descended from the communal rights of the tribe, village communities and the joint-family proprietary notions. It is quite conceivable that in view of the varying qualities of the soil with different facilities for natural irrigation from the hill streams or through flooding of the rivers in a particular region under the territorial jurisdiction of a clan, the holdings of the families were subjected to periodical exchange and the concept of the communal ownership of the tribe or clan was triumphant.[13] But with the gradual improvement of land in particular villages and holdings of the families, both through human labour and the development of the artificial means of irrigation, the concept of ownership on the part of severalty gradually gained ground.[14] Against this view of communal ownership of land, Sir Henry Maine held[15] that the concept of the joint family property was known to the Aryans from the very first settlements in India. He argued that the social unit, which originally owned the land among the Aryans, was the family community descendant from a common ancestor dwelling in the same house, labouring in common and enjoying in common the produce of agricultural labour. The village community was derived from house community and the latter was the expansion of joint family. Sir Henry Maine also maintained that the institution of the self-existing village communities was known to the Aryans before they came to India and was not a Hindu contribution to ancient India. However, in view of the above explained tribal character and the communal ownership of land in the early stages of Aryan settlements in India, Sir Henry Maine's theory is no longer tenable.[16]

During the Vedic age, the expansion of the warring Aryans demanded organisational efficiency which resulted in the divisions of the society into the four well known castes, viz. the Ksatriyas (warriors) Brahmans (priests), Vaisyas (craftsmen and the husbandmen) and the Sudras (the labour class and the cultivators).[17] Though in the initial stages the Aryans gang-pressed the aboriginal tribes who constituted the Sudras class subjected to the cultivation of land,[18] the expanding nature of the agricultural economy obliged a section of the Vaish class, to take to the tillage of land.[19] It seems that in the Vedic period, in concept, land was still considered the property of the community whereas the joint family had occupied permanent holdings for the purposes of production but without any rights of alienation. The disposal of land was still a social concern. At the same time, it seems that land-owned families developed their own artificial means of irrigation for the improvement of their lands.[20] No land could be donated without the consent of the clan though no instances of donation are known for the Vedic age.[21] In the post-Vedic age, with the gradual absorption of the local peoples within the Aryan fold and the ever growing composite ethnic nature of the agrarian civilization in the expanding villages in various regions, the landed rights of the joint families got more pronounced. Moreover, the development of money economy in the 6th and 5th centuries B.C. and the expansion of trade and commerce with Persia had great impact on the village economy and the territorial polity in North India. An individual family in some regions could sell or mortgage its land but only with the consent of the village council the exact composition of which is not known.[22] This shows that the landed rights of a family were still subordinate and were regulated by the limitation imposed by the concept of the community rights of ownership.

Prompted by military factor for fighting against the hostile tribes and the subsequent Aryan expansionism, the communities of the families and the tribal structure had led to the growth of kingship during the Rig Vedic age. The king claimed a share in the produce of the land (*bali*) as well as certain cesses (*kara*). However, the king could not override the tribal customs and communal rights of the village community and the agrarian families. In the post-Vedic period, *Mimamsa-sutras* (4th-3rd centuries B.C.)

by Jaimini clearly state that the king could not give away the land of his kingdom for the earth was common to all.[24] This shows the communal concept of ownership of land and the existence of the landed rights of the families evolved within the limitations imposed by the village communities which have already been explained. It should also be conceded that the phase of civilization and the agrarian relations underlining the social structure could by no means be uniform throughout North India as there were regions where the hold of the communal orders had relaxed while in others the village communities and even the republican orders of the Government held sway. There were two important factors, social and political, which gradually undermined the communal concept of the ownership over agrarian lands. Socially within the tribal order, the village communities entrenched their rights against the tribal control and in their own turn the households and, wherever possible, the land-owing families did the same thing. Politically speaking, the constant mutual warfare amongst various Aryan tribes, the tribal chiefs representing the regional and communal concept of authority gave place to the growing phenomenon of a strong and absolute monarchy. The growing conflict between the royal claim over lands and the old concept of communal ownership is quite apparent during the period of the Brahamanas. It is evident from the well known story that the king Visvakarman Bhauvana was rebuked by the earth when he treated the land as his private property.[25] Satapatha Brahamana held that the grants of the land made by the king were valid only when given with approval of the people or clan (vis). [26] This statement shows that the king may have disposed off the land arbitrarily but was looked upon with suspicion and the Brahamanas gave verdict that the king's authority to give gifts of land was subject to the consent of the people and that it should be in accordance with the tribal or customary law. This also clearly shows that the assertion of royal claim over land was already making its way even though the Brahmanas texts shelved it of any moral or legal claim. In fact, the king's claim over land ownership could not be separated from his growing political superiority.[27] At the same time, it is extremely doubtful if the Hindu polity developed any concept of state ownership as distinct from the royal ownership of lands. Thus with the concentration of political authority in the hands of monarchy, the natural logical step was to convert the public lands claimed by the tribes into the royal lands claimed by the monarchs.[28] By the middle of the 4th century B.C., with the rise of the Magadh kingdom of Nandas and later on with the establishment of a strong and centralised Mauryan kingdom (late 4th and 3rd centuries B.C.), the concept of agrarian ownership was bound to undergo a change. The monarchy was the true inheritor of the authority of the tribal chiefs and their communal orders. It is no surprise that Magasthense declared that all land was the property of the crown and no private person was permitted to own it.[29] Significantly, the *Arthasastra* is completely silent on the theoretical question of ownership of land. But at the same time, it asserts that the king had the right to evict the defaulting peasants and confiscate the holdings if they were left uncultivated.[30] Even in the earlier stages of Aryan civilization, the communal tribal chiefs had claimed a share in the produce of the land under cultivation and the increase in the agricultural produce had always been valued. It is possible that the evasion of land revenue payment, rendering the cultivated land uncultivated or its desertion would have entitled the tribal chief or the village community to pass it on to another person capable of cultivating it. But now with a centralised state, it was the prerogative of the king to enforce this regulation. Quite distinct from the revenue which the king got from the agricultural lands of the peasant families, he claimed ownership of all unappropriated and jungle lands.[31] The king also had royal villages, *i.e.,* crown lands which were developed by the purely temporary tenants with stipulated share in the produce, hired labour and slaves managed by the agricultural department of the state.[32] These lands were considered as crown property, most likely appropriated for the privy purse of the king. Apart from this, it is very doubtful if the king ever claimed the virtual ownership rights over the self-developed land of the peasant families in the settled villages. The ownership rights of such families inherited from the pre-Mauryan period continued status-quo subject to the payment of revenue and regular tillage.[33] Though in its chapter on the inheritance of private property[34] the *Arthasastra* says nothing about the inheritance of land rights, the occupancy rights of the cultivating families in the settled villages were undeniably recognised. The *Arthasastra* does mention the sale of lands of kinsmen and neighbours and the delimitation of the property in the presence of village elders.[35] It lays down the rules that tax payers and the Brahmana holders of revenue free lands should sell or mortgage only to their respective classes.[36] At the same time, it allows full rights of sale and mortgage to the founders and restorers of irrigation works.[37] But is cannot be stated with certainty if the right of sale or mortgage on the part of tax-payers applied only to urban property, home steads with small fields, and orchards or it equally applied to the possessors of the agrarian property in old settled village. It does seem in the context that the state did permit the ownership of land[38] with rights of sale and mortgage to such families who may have developed their own means of irrigation.[39] It is not clear if it were only the rights of permanent hereditary possession of land and the enjoyment of the produce thereof which were involved in such transactions or whether the proprietary rights over the lands as a saleable commodity were also attached.[40] Whatever be the legal implications, in practice, that would make little difference to the peasant land-owing families. It has been suggested that the Brahmanical law makes distinction between the ownership of land and restricted rights of the state over the enjoyment of the surplus produce of land. For the former, the word *'swam'* (and its derivatives, *svatva svamya* and *svamitva*) is used while for the latter, the word *'bhuj'* (and its derivatives) is used.[41] This implies two-fold aspect of land ownership viz. the lands personally owned by the king who could dispose them as he pleased and secondly, such lands over which the king did not claim any proprietary rights but only enjoyed their revenues as the head of the state.[42] As in the Hindu polity there was hardly any distinction between the position of the king and the state, the king being the head of the state claimed royal ownership over the crown lands from which he derived his personal income. Over the other lands in possession with the peasant families, he claimed only theoretical ownership for the purposes of the imposition of revenue which was meant for the royal exchequer than for his personal income (*i.e.,* privy purse). The Mauryan state, of course, encouraged fresh colonisation of the waste cultivable lands. The families exploiting such lands would be given life-term lease subject to the payment of the land revenue.[43]

Later on, Manu considered the villages as forming territorial units with clear-cut boundary demarcations[44] and the cultivator called 'owner-of-the-field' was required to enclose his land with a hedge of thorny plants.[45] The Brahmanas had subsistence grants (*brahmadeya*) and even the Ksatriya class, not in active service, could also take to cultivation.[46] Manu enunciates the theory of land being the property of the first clearer.[47] With growing population and the need for increase in the state revenues, the extension of the cultivable land through the clearance of jungles and reclamation of waste lands continued throughout the ancient Indian period. This could be undertaken only by families rather than a single individual. Hence, Manu's theory of the ownership of the first clearer vested occupancy rights with the families on a joint family basis rather than with a single individual. Though Manu deals with the sales and pledges of livestock and the acquisition of wealth through inheritance or purchase,[48] he does not mention about the transfer or mortgage of agrarian land. It seems that the right of the king to the revenues and alienation of waste and jungle lands to whomsoever he pleased and the occupancy rights of the cultivating families lay at the basis of the theoretical concept of the ownership of land on the part of the king. For justifying the claim of the king to the levy of one half of the underground hoards and precious minerals, Manu observes that the king was entitled to this share not simply because of his general protection, but also because "he was the lord paramount of the soil".[49] It is also enjoined that a husbandman was liable to penalty if he injured the land or caused a crop failure for late sowing.[50] All this asserts the general claim over the soil of the kingdom with a right to a share in the treasure troves and mines as well as the royal power for the regulation of the agrarian development. It is also quite understandable that a formal permission of the local officials representing the royal power was necessary for the reclamation of jungle or waste land on the part of the pioneer cultivating families who would, in due course, develop occupancy title to land. Unlike the *Arthasastra,* Manu does not talk of any practice of the eviction of the defaulting peasants of desertion of land as in such circumstances the state was bound to make alternative arrangement for the cultivation of land.

The economic historians have mostly missed the impact of the political and socio-economic factors upon each other by which the concept of land ownership was evolved. The centralisation of political authority in the hands of the monarchy during the pre-Mauryan ages had led to the assumption of the hitherto communal ownership rights on the part of the king which lay at the basis of the theory of the royal ownership of land. The royal attack was on the communal estate of landed society rather than the land rights of the families and village communities in the settled villages which, having been freed from the communal hold of the tribal chief, were subjected to the inquisition of the royal laws. Another important phase came with the disintegration of the Mauryan kingdom and emergence of the local chieftains when the land-owing families having been the main beneficiaries consolidated the proprietary rights of land ownership in the course of the centuries. This accounts for the fact that by the Gupta and the post-Gupta ages, the right of the land owning families to partition the agrarian land in accordance with the law of inheritance[51] and the right to sell the land is an accomplished fact.[52] A land owner could equally mortgage his land and may be obliged to sell the agrarian land in order to clear the debts or arrears of land revenue. Such a right would prevail only in such regions where the agrarian land may have acquired saleable value. The right of sale was subject to the consent of the village clansmen and before its transfer to outsiders or persons of other castes, the right of pre-emption lay with the near kinsmen, neighbours and creditors.[53] Such a limitation upon the free transfer of land inherited from the original communal rights of the tribe continued to persist in many a part of North India throughout the medieval age and, in fact, could be traced right till the late 19th century. In the early medieval period, a land owing family could transfer the land to religious institutions.[54] It had also the right of leasing land to the tenants though the responsibility for the land revenue payment lay with land owner.[55]

Notwithstanding the evolution of the above mentioned rights of the land owing families, it is remarkable to note that with the establishment of a strong empire under the Guptas, the royal theory of ownership of land is again asserted. This was not only the verdict of Fahien,[56] the Chinese traveller but also of Katyayana, a late Gupta law giver.[57] The royal claim to land ownership was definitely qualified and limited by the landed rights which the peasant families had acquired in the course of the centuries. It was no longer possible to put the hands of the clock back and efface the impact of the evolution of the civilization upon the agrarian set up. In this context, the concept of royal ownership meant the assertion of ownership over the waste lands, jungles and mines etc., claim over the revenues from the jungles and mines, the right of alienation of jungle and wastelands for reclamation and colonisation, the power of making rent free grants from waste lands for charitable purposes, the right of the collection of land revenue from the peasants along with other customary dues and prerogative for making assignments of revenues of the villages either from military or religious purposes. At the same time, in order to enhance the agricultural purposes. At the same time, in order to enhance the agricultural produce and the revenues, the state claimed full executive jurisdiction over the peasants.[58] It not only helped the peasants with advance money for the purchase of the seeds etc., it would not allow the land to be left uncultivated. It equally regulated the relations between the land owners and their tenants. It could penalise even the tenants either for the non-payment of the landlord's share or having left the rented agricultural fields uncultivated.[59] Katayana equally mentions the land ownership of the families settled on agrarian lands. Thus Katyayana asserts the dual aspect of land ownership, that of the king as the lord of the earth (*bhuswami*) underlying the general authority with entitlement to revenues and the peasant families as the real owners of agrarian land under their possessions. Asahaya, the commentator[60] of Narda, explained the king's right of ownership (*swam*) the same thing as his claim to the royal share of produce.[61]

The unqualified support of Hiuen Tsang for the royal ownership under Harsha's empire[62] could not mean more than the position and rights of the king already explained for the Gupta age. The empire of Harsha based on the concept of combination of subordinate and vassal chiefs was less suited to assert better claim over royal ownership than the early Gupta monarchs with more centralised empire. After the breakup of Harsa's empire and with the establishment of a congeries of Rajput kingdoms in North India, the established land rights of the peasant families were bound to be strengthened. The concept of family ownership of land became strongly entrenched. The later Smritis not only emphasise mere possession of land but accord clear title to undisputed permanent possession constituting ownership in land.[63] Moreover, with the growing use of money in the eleventh and twelfth centuries, the private rights of ownership comprising mortgage could be still more effective. Al-Biruni (11th century A.D.)

justifies the royal share in the produce "in recognition of the protection which he (*i.e.,* king) affords to the subjects, their properties and their families...Further, trading businesses, too, pay a tribute for the same reason".[64] Thus, to Al-Biruni, the peasant's possession of his holding is on the same plane as the merchant's right to merchandise, though both enjoyed proprietary rights over their respective possessions subject to the payment of taxation in lieu of the protection afforded by the state. The emphasis is as much, if not more, on the royal share being the first charge on the land as on the proprietary possession of the peasant on his holding. Al-Biruni's statement was derived either from his study of the Hindu jurisprudence or was based on an eye-witnessed situation of the contemporary agrarian relations. The fact that his analysis was meant for the Muslim world before the establishment of the Turkish rule in North India is all the more significant. The commentaries written by the Hindu theorists during the 11th and 12th centuries propounding the royal ownership of land, based on the interpretation of *Naradiaya Purana* or *Arthasastra,* covered only theoretical aspect and were not even applicable to their own age when the agrarian land rights had undergone considerable change in the course of the centuries. However, the Hindu rulers independent or semi independent, continued to assert royal ownership of land within their territories throughout the medieval age before the Mughal conquest.[65] As explained later, such a general claim was always aimed at the revenues and was qualified by the occupancy rights on the part of the land owing families on their agrarian lands.

What still remains a most intriguing problem is the position of the Sudras as a cultivating class. Even though as cultivators, the Sudras played an important economic role for the purposes of production, modern scholarship, which has looked upon ancient Indian History mostly from the viewpoint of the upper classes and higher castes, has not paid adequate attention to the evolution of the socio-economic position of the Sudras and their role in the agrarian society from the period of Aryan conquest down to the beginning of the medieval ages. Such of the scholars, who have worked on the origin and growth of the caste system, have offered conflicting views and justifications for the social status of the Sudras.[66] The social disabilities of various kinds imposed upon the Sudras have been explained on the basis of the ancient legal texts. But no serious attempt has been made to analyse the role of the *Sudras* as a labouring class and least of all has any enquiry been made into the nature of socio-economic and politico-legal relations of the sudras with other castes (*Varnas*) in the changing pattern of the agrarian set up in the ancient and early medieval ages. Even the nature of extent of slavery on the agrarian land still remains a desideratum.[67] It has been suggested that the *Sudra* helot cold not own land. But no final verdict can be passed on this aspect whether a Sudra simply remained as a slave and chattle or his social status gradually came to be recognised as a free man and as tiller of the soil he worked under the land owing families on sharing basis when the *Arthasastra* suggests the working of the hired labourers on sharing basis on the crown lands[68] as well as on the privately owned lands.[69] The *Sudras* were always placed on different socio-economic footing from the slaves (*Dasas*) who comprised original tribes, *Sudras* or even other castes enslaved in the wars or through debt or mortgage in the ordinary course of life and constituted an altogether a different class in the social structure.[70] With the growing agrarian economy, the paucity of agricultural labour is already evident from the *Arthasastra*.[71] It also states that for the growth of villages, the *Sudra* settlers were immigrated from other places or deported from king's own over-populated villages.[72] The *Arthasastra* also mentions that new villages of between a hundred and five hundred families of *Sudra* cultivators were to be settled who would be sufficiently close to each other for mutual protection. When such lands were leased to revenue payers for life, the self-developed *Sudra* settlements could have easily enjoyed this benefit. Later on while explaining the colonisation of waste lands, the *Arthasastra* does not prefer the settlements on cooperative basis (*serni*) as these may be incapable of standing calamities and prove recalcitrant. At the same time, the settlement of lands by the lowest castes (*i.e., Sudras*) are favoured in preference to the other three *Varnas* as the former would be more serviceable, plentiful and permanent.[73] This shows that as tiller of the soil, the *Sudras* were most sought after as they were easy of economic exploitation. However, it is equally known from Megasthenes that during the Mauryan age, a peasant enjoyed good social and economic status. This accounts for the fact that of all the seven castes (*i.e.,* classes) of the Indian society enumerated by Megasthenes, the peasant occupied the second position.[74] The peasant class also formed the majority of the population of the Indian society. It is reasonable to believe that both the *Sudras* and a portion of the *Vaisya* caste constituted the peasant class.[75] Manu thinks of the *Sudras* as the labourers who would get only food and clothes from those of the three higher classes whom they served.[76] It is quite understandable that the *Vaisya* land owners, the Brahmana revenue free assignees and even *Ksatriyas,* who later on took to agriculture mostly employed *Sudras* when they could not till the entire lands of their own. It is difficult to imagine how despite religious disabilities, the *Sudras* could remain under constant economic exploitation especially when in the face of scarcity of agricultural labour they were in constant demand both with the state and the land owing families. It is also inexplicable why the *Sudras* could not develop occupancy rights in the self-developed villages and colonised lands. There is every probability that they did develop such rights in the course of the centuries. The fact that Hiuen Tsang mentions that despite the social inhibitions and taboos imposed on them, the low born (*i.e.,* Sudras) and the mixed classes indulged in free commercial transactions with the other classes especially due to the paucity of cash economy, shows the important economic role of the lower classes. Hiuen Tsang also says that people were not subjected to forced labour and even that for the construction of the public works, labour was paid for. The cultivators on the royal estates (crown lands) paid only 1/6 part of the produce. In general, the cultivators remained busy in the growth of seasonal crops and enjoyed rest after hard labour. Hiuen Tsang makes no distinction between free cultivators and servile cultivators. He would have mentioned this fact if the *Sudras* constituted a servile class attached simply as labourers either to the crown lands or the land owing families. Similarly, at the beginning of the 11th century A.D., Al-Biruni does not make any distinction between the *Sudra* and the non-*Sudra* cultivators enjoying produce of their crops subject to the payment of land revenue and even claiming rights of ownership over their lands. Though in the medieval age certain restrictions based on tribal and caste character continued to be enforced by the village communities upon the right of the transfer of land on the part of the peasants, it is extremely doubtful if any invidious distinction was ever made between the *Sudra* and the other Hindu castes for the occupancy rights over their respective lands.

References

1. V. S. Smith, *Early History of India,* (Oxford, 1904), p. 123; *Oxford History of India,* p. 90; Keith, *History of Sanskrit Literature,* (London 1940), pp. 259-60; *Note on Manu,* VIII, p. 39; The same view was held by E.W. Hopkins, *India, old and new,* pp. 221 and MacDonell. The latest adherents of this view point is A. L. Basham, *op. cit.,* pp. 109-112.
2. K. P. Jayaswal, *Hindu Polity.* (Calcutta, 1924), 2nd ed., pp. 343-51; P. N. Banerji, *Public Administration in Ancient India.* (London, 1916), p. 179; P. V. Kane, *History of Dharmasastra.* (Poona, 1941), Vol. II, p. 886. Prof. Kane comments that the theory of state ownership was adopted by the British scholars as it was conveniently suited to the British policy and legislation. Also, see views of various authorities in T.E.C. Report (1924-25) , Vol. II, Appendix IV. Also, Shrimati S. Ambiah, 'Ownership of Land in Ancient India', *I.H.C.,* 1952, p. 70-73; *Report of the Land Revenue Commission of Bengal,* Vol. I, pp. 5-9; *Report of the United Provinces Zamindari Abolition Committee,* Allahabad, 1948, Vol. I, pp. 59-69.
3. Basham, *op. cit.,* p. 109.
4. S. Piggott, *Pre-historic India* (*H'worth,* 1950), p. 67.
5. D. H. Godon, D. D. Kosambi, *op. cit.,* pp. 70-72.
6. J. F. Hewitt, *J.R.A.S.,* July, 1897, pp. 610-614, contrary to it, Baden-Powell (vide 'The Origin of Village Land-Tenures of India', *J.R.A.S.,* 1898, pp. 605-616; *The Indian Village Community,* (London, 1876) does not accept this idea. He has argued that the pre-Aryan agricultural tribes had settled villages with a powerful headman each and separate peasant holdings like the modern raiyatwari villages.
7. Gordon, *op. cit.,* p. 158; Charles Drekmeier, *Kingship and Community in Early India,* (Bombay, 1962), p. 17.
8. Kosambi, *op. cit.,* pp. 79-80, 83-84; Drekmeier (*Ibid*), p. 18.
9. *Ibid.,* pp. 87-93; Drekmeier (*Ibid*), pp. 17-19.
10. *Rig Veda,* III, 45, 3; Also, Drekmeier, *Ibid.,* pp. 18-19.
11. For details, see M. de Lavaleya, '*Primitive Property,* (Eng. Tr. by R. R. Marriot), p. 3; C. L. Tupper, *Punjab Customary Law,* 3 vols., Calcutta, 1881, Vol. II, *Statements of Customary Law in Different Districts* (Extracted chiefly from the *Settlement Reports*), Introduction, pp. 1-98.
12. For details, see Mr. Thorburn's *Report on Vesh in Marwat, Bannu District,* Lahore, 1879 and Backett's Paper in Vesh in Swat Vide *Punjab Gazetteer, Supplement,* 27th March 1873 and 27th November 1873 respectively; Also Fryer's *Settlement Report on Dera Ghazi Khan,* 1875, Paragraphs 215-220, pp. 32-34; Major Wace's *Settlement Report on Hazara District,* 1874, Paragraphs no. 60, 64, pp. 109, 111; Bellew's *General Report on the Yusufzais,* 1884, pp. 194-200; Also, C. L. Tupper, *op. cit.,* Vol. II, *District Peshwar,* p. 15; *District Multan,* p. 25; *District Rawal Pindi,* pp. 27-28; *District Sialkot,* p. 32; *District Gurgaon,* A letter from Mr. Silson, Assistant

Settlement Officer, pp. 42-43; Vol. III, *District Rohtak*, p. 138; *District Bannu*, p. 138 based on Thorburn's unpublished Settlement Report, paragraph 136.

13. Fryer's *Settlement Report on District Dera Ghazi Khan*, 1878, paragraphs 219-220; C. L. Tupper, *op. cit.*, Vol. II, p. 15 (*Peshawar Settlement Report*, 1876, para 206, pp. 85-86), Vol. III, pp. 141-42.

14. Fryer's *Settlement Report* (*Ibid*), para 215, pp. 32-34; A letter from Mr. Wilson, Assistant Settlement Officer, dated 16th March, 1880 on District Gurgaon vide C. L. Tupper, *op. cit.*, Vol. II, pp. 42-44.

15. Sir Henry Maine, *Village Communities in the East and West*, (London, 1876), pp. 108-128.

16. Also, see C. L. Tupper, *op. cit.*, Vol. II, pp. 4-12; Charles Drekmeier, *op. cit.* p. 4, on the contrary, Baden-Powell vide The Origin of Village Land-Tenures in India, *J.R.A.S.* 1898, pp. 605-616, supports Sir Henry Maine's theory as he could not trace any communal element in the proprietary notions of the Indian Village and communities which during the course of the 19th century were governed by the *Zamindari, pattidari* and *bhaichara* characteristics. (Also, *Land Systems of British India*, II, pp. 98-156). Baden Powell is quite correct in his assertion that common ownership as implied in *bhaichara* villages is quite distinct from joint ownership or 'Communistic' idea of property. It is also true that the 19th century *bhaichara* and *pattidari* villages did not owe their origin and evolution to the communal concept of property. But where Baden Powell failed to understand was the fact that in the North Western/partition of India, some of the tribes and villages were governed by the communal concept of '*Vesh*' which was rather 'archaic' and could not be aligned with the *Zamindari, pattidari* or *bhaichara* villages which existed in other positions of North India and that the latter owed their origin to the 17th and 18th centuries land tenures. The tribes in the North Western portion of India practising '*Vesh*' may have settled in these regions during the course of the 18th century but the principle underlying '*Vesh*' was '*archaic*'. Baden Powell's criticism of the earliest *Settlement Reports of the North Western Provinces* is completely unjustified.

17. Charles Drekmeier, *op. cit.*, p. 19; Kosambi, *op. cit.*, pp. 94-95.

18. *Ibid.*, pp. 17-19; *Ibid.*, pp. 92, 95, 104.

19. Kosambi, *Ibid.*

20. *Rig Veda*, III, 45, 3; VII, 49, 2; X, 101, 3, 4, 6-7. Though Ghoshal believes in the communal concept of land in the earlier stages of Indian civilisation, he maintains that the private ownership of land was an established institution among the Indo-Aryans in the oldest times to which their history can be traced. According to him, Rig Veda Samhita shows that arable land was held in family ownership whereas communal ownership was confined to grass lands lying on the boundaries of the fields. In fact, it is difficult to say when the communal concept ultimately gave way with self-developed means of irrigation seems to be an established fact during the Vedic age. However, the communal limitation did not permit any transfer of land at this stage.

21. Ghoshal (pp. 86, 118, f.n. 24) quotes Gautama. Also R. S. Sharma, 'Land Rights in Early Medieval India', read at the XXVI *International Congress of Orientalists,* New Delhi, 1964; Charles Drekneier, *op. cit.,* pp. 24-25.
22. *Ibid.,* Kosambi (*op. cit.,* p. 145) denies if any rights of sale of land existed even at this stage though he concedes that land could be transferred for charitable purposes.
23. *Rig Veda,* I, 70, 91, V, 1, 10.
24. Jaimini *Nyayamalavistara,* p. 358; *Dharmakosa* Ed. *Laxanshastri* Joshi, I., p. 793; R. S. Sharma, *op. cit.;* K. P. Jayaswal, *Hindu Polity,* (Calcutta, 1924), 2nd ed., p. 345, thinks that this asserts the individual rights of ownership. But it seems in the context that the contrast is not between the rights of the king versus individuals but that between the king and the existing social structure, which, of course, recognised the landed rights of the joint families subject to the clannish restrictions. Also, see Madhav's commentary (entitled *Nyayamalavistara-14th century A.D.*) on the *Mimamsa-Sutras* (vide Ghoshal, pp. 99-102; 123 f.n. 83) R. K. Mukerji (vide *Reports on the Land Revenue Commission,* Bengal, *op. cit.,* quotes the commentaries of Sabara Svamin (4th century A.D.), Sayana and Vyavahara Mayukha to contradict the royal claim of ownership over land which was confined to a share in the produce by reason of affording protection to his subjects. In fact, the above mentioned commentaries lay emphasis on the contradiction of the royal claim to land ownership and cannot be twisted in favour of individualistic land rights which at this stage were vested with the joint families subject to the communal concept.
25. *Satapatha Brahama,* XIII, 7, I, 15.
26. *Ibid.,* III. 46; Also, Ghoshal, p. 83; Ghoshal further maintains (p. 84) that the concept of ownership both as regards movables and immovable is known to Brahmanical sacred law from early times.
27. Ghoshal, p. 83. Ghoshal (pp. 93-98) further suggests that *Satapatha Brahmana's* hints at the arbitrary disposal of the tribal lands by the king may have converted such lands into private royal farms which find mention in the *Arthasastra* and the later general claim of royal rights over lands. It is difficult to agree with the entire viewpoint of Ghoshal. Though the royal claim over the unappropriated lands viz. jungles and waste lands as well as the revenues of the state etc. were inherited from the original tribal jurisdiction, the royal farms seem to have been developed directly by the state than to have been userped from the private land owners.
28. *Ibid.,* Also, Ghoshal, *The Beginnings of Indian Historiography and Other Essays,* (Calcutta, 1944), Essay VI, pp. 158-66.
29. Merindle, Megasthenes and Arrian, pp. 41-42.
30. *Arthasastra* (tr. S), p. 46.
31. *Ibid.,* pp. 158, 324-26.
32. *Ibid.,* pp. 57-58.

33. Relying on the *Jatakas,* R. Fick, *The Social Organization in North East India in Buddha's Time,* Calcutta, 1920, pp. 253, 305 has considered the possibility of the existence of land owing gentry in the rural life. Similarly, Bose, A. N., *Social and Rural Economy N-E India, 600 B.C.-A.D. 200,* (Calcutta, 1945), p. 38 has expressed the same opinion. But Romila Thaper (*op. cit.,* pp. 63-65) does not agree with this view. She has considered five-fold possibilities of land ownership viz. the king, the state, large scale land owners, communal ownership and the cultivators. She comes to the conclusion that land was owned by the state though it did not exclude individuals from owing small areas of cultivable land, which they could cultivate themselves with a little assistance. It merely means that small scale ownership of land was not the dominant feature. It is difficult to agree with Miss Thapar's conclusion. The *Arthasastra,* in its chapter on colonisation and development of waste lands (tr. S. pp. 325-26), does refer to sale of lands by the king to a coloniser who is supposed to develop with his own men and money. Such a process of colonisation was bound to create land owing gentry. It is thus evident that apart from the crown lands, both the land owing gentry and the small land owners cultivating land of their own and as well as with the assistance of agricultural labour existed under the Mauryas. R. S. Sharma in his latest paper (Land Rights in Early Medieval India Circa A.D. 500-1200 *op. cit.*), contends that for the major portion of Ancient India, the ownership of land was essentially communal in character but from the Gupta period onwards, the land ownership was claimed by the king. Moreover, from the late Gupta age onwards, the Indian polity also developed a feudal character and right till the early medieval age under the Hindu rule, the land ownership continued to be vested with the king. Though Sharma has labouriously referred to numerous legal texts, his interpretation of the texts is not very correct. In fact, the communal character of land ownership had faded long before the Mauryan age though some of the traits of the communal character viz. the hold of the village community for the alienation of land and the right of pre-emption of the clannish kinsmen continued to persist in various portions of North India right till the 19th century (see f.n. 50). As explained further, even from the Gupta age onwards, the theoretical enunciation of the royal ownership of land did not interfere with land rights of the revenue paying peasants who were the owners of their lands. Nor did the Indian society acquire feudal character in the European sense.
34. *Arthasastra* (tr. S) pp. 181-89.
35. *Ibid.,* pp. 191-92.
36. *Ibid.,* pp. 194-95, Ghoshal (p. 87) thinks that the smritis as well as the *Arthasatra* law permits the sale, gift and mortgage of land (with a few restrictions in some cases).
37. *Ibid.,* pp. 192-93.
38. According to Ghoshal (p. 117, f.n. 12), it is rather significant that the *Arthasastra* (III, 8-10) refers to *Grhasvamin* while at the same time applies

the epithets of *Svamin* and *Svamya* not only to immovable property in general but also to the fields (*Ksetra*) irrigation works (*selubandha*) the wells (*Kupa*) and so forth.

39. Timmer (vide *Megasthenes en de Indische Maatschappij*, p. 123) explains that as opposed to the western idea of absolute ownership, the Indian idea of property just meant permanent possession and the enjoyment of its produce. Also see Vinogradoff, *Outlines of Historical Jurisprudence*, Vol. I, pp. 324-25.
40. Ghoshal, p. 84.
41. This is exactly the view of Nilakatha, who in his Vyavaharamayukha (17th century A.D.), comments both on Gautama and Kautilya's *Arthasastra* and concludes that proprietary rights over the villages and fields etc. belonged to their respective possessors (*bhaumika*) and the king was entitled only to take the taxes (vide Ghoshal, pp. 85-86, 102-103, 118, f.n. 22).
42. *Arthasastra,* (tr. S), pp. 45-46.
43. Manu, Chapter VIII, pp. 245-61.
44. *Ibid.*, p. 239.
45. *Ibid.*, p. 237.
46. *Ibid.*, Chapter IX, p. 44.
47. *Ibid.*, Chapter VIII, pp. 143-57; Ghoshal (p. 86) however, thinks that the references made by Gautama and then by Manu to the acquisition of wealth by purchase to cover the agrarian lands as well.
48. *Ibid.*, p. 39.
49. *Ibid.*, p. 243.
50. The *Mitaksara* and the *Madanaparijata* (vide *Dharma Kosa)* I, 1231-1232) permit the partition of agrarian lands amongst the Brahmana families. R. S. Sharma (*op. cit.*) argues that such an interpretation of *Mitaksara* is also supported by Devannabhatta. Thus the legal texts of 11th-13th centuries provide for the break up of landed property owned by the Brahmana families and this may have been equally true of the other non-Brahmana families.
51. *Dharma Kosa,* I, 900-901; Ghoshai (pp. 86, 88), 119 f.n. 42 and 43) quotes the authorities of Brhaspati and Narda on this point.
52. *Ibid.*
53. *Customary Laws (Rivaj-i-Am) of the Districts in the Punjab; District Gujrat,* Vol. IX, p. VI.
54. *Dharma Kosa,* I, pp. 954, 961 (opinions of Brhaspati and Vyasa).
55. Ghoshal, H.R.S., pp. 191-92.
56. P. V. Kane, *'Katyayanasmrti'* tr. verses 16 and 17. Katyayana declares the king as the owner of the earth (*bhusvami*) claiming 1/4th of the produce. Also Ghoshal, pp. 97-98. On the basis of Mitramisra's explanation, Ghoshal puts the king's claim at 1/6th of the produce.
57. See f.n. 55.

58. Also, Ghoshal (p. 88, 120 f.n. 45) who quotes the authorities of Apastamba, Vyasa and Brahspati for the compensation which the landlord could claim from the tenants.
59. This was the view of Mitramisra, the commentator on *Katyayana*. See details Ghoshal, pp. 97-98, 102.
60. *Dharma Kosa,* I, p. 949.
61. Beal I, 215; Also, see Ghoshal's criticism in Hiuen Tsang, *H.R.S.*, pp. 167-70, 191-92, 225-226.
62. Ghoshal (pp. 85, 118, f.n. 15-20) quotes *Yajnavalkya Brhaspati,* Narda, Vyasa and Pitamaha in support.
63. Al-Biruni, tr. Sachau, Vol. II, p. 149.
64. *Narasinha Purana,* quoted by M.A. Buch, *'Economic Life in Ancient India,* (Bombay, 1924), 11, 24, f.n., also Sen, *Hindu Jurisprudence,* p. 52 f; Bhattasvamin's Commentary on *Arthasastra, Pratipada-Pancika by Bhattasvamin* (on Bk II from Sect. 8) ed. K. P. Jayaswal and A. Benerji-Sastri, *JBORS,* XI-XII, (4th Ed. tr., p. 144) respectively.
65. For the views of the various writers on the Caste System in Ancient India, see details, R. S. Sharma, 'Historiography of the Ancient Indian Social Order' in *'Historians of India, Pakistan and Ceylon',* E. C.H. Phillips, 1961, pp. 102-114.
66. D. R. Channana, *Slavery in Ancient India: As Depicted in Pali and Sanskrit Texts,* PPH, 1960.
67. *Arthasastra* (tr. S), pp. 128-131.
68. *Ibid.*, pp. 208-211; 325-26.
69. *Ibid.*, pp. 205-207. Also, Kosambi, *op. cit.*, pp. 92-108; 136-141; also, Charles Drekmeier, *op. cit.*, p. 19.
70. *Ibid.*, p. 128. It clearly states that the fields were left unsown due to the inadequacy of hands (Vapatiriktan).
71. *Ibid.*, p. 45.
72. *Ibid.*, pp. 325-26.
73. Diodorus, II, pp. 40-41.
74. Also, see Kosambi, *op. cit.*, pp. 91-108.
75. Manu, Chapter I, p. 91.
76. Also, see J. N. Helhed, Memoirs on Land Tenure and Principles of Taxation'.

IV

Emergence of Tribal and Clannish Landed Interests

Politically speaking, the institution of monarchy and the concept of the Empire underwent a considerable change from the late Gupta period onwards. In proportion to the extent of the Empire, the directly administered territories were much limited. The later Gupta rules acquiesced to the idea of getting their recognition as the overlords of the vassal states rather than bringing the latter under direct administration. In fact, even the epics and *Smriti* literature had discouraged outright absorption of the conquered kingdom and urged its reduction to a vassal status.[1] Similarly, the *Arthasastra* advises a weak king to render voluntary homage to a powerful neighbour.[2] During the Maurayan times, vassal chiefs existed in more remote regions of the empire.[3] The establishment of centralised kingdom under Magadhan imperialism, the Mauryas or Samudra Gupta were not strictly in accordance with the ancient Indian custom or the sacred law.[4] The assumption of 'Great king of kings' and high sounding epithets of the overlordship (viz. *Paramabhattaraka, Parmesvara* and *Maharajadhiraja*) adopted by the later Gupta ruler and then by the Pala and Pratihara kings do not point towards the centralisation of the authority and uniformity of the empire but merely indicate the assertion and exercise of overlordship over the lords, chiefs and princes owing allegience to them.[5] The vassal chiefs came to be designated by various graded epithets viz. *Mahasamanta, Mahasamntadhipatis, Maharaja, Raja, Rana* and *Rajarjankas,* etc. The transformation of the term *Samanta,* meaning hitherto 'neighbour' or 'neighbouring king' into a vassal chief of the overlord monarch is quite significant. At times, the vassal chiefs had their further vassals in the Rajas or small Chieftains. The exact terms of relationship and the extent to which the overlord monarch could interfere or have any effective control in the internal revenue administration of the vassal chiefs cannot to determined. However, it can be well imagined that these vassals chiefs would have paid tribute to the overlord in proportion either to their revenues or in accordance with the terms of submission. They had also to render military service to the overlord. They may as well have struck coins in the name of the suzerain. In fact, Harsa made a successful bid to create a personally administered centralised empire. He exercised the prerogative of issuing land grants in the territories of the vassal chiefs and such grants issued by him bear directions given to them for the compliance of the royal order.[7] After Harsa, a number of independent and semi-independent states sprang up in different regions of North India. The kingdoms of the Palas and the

Pratihars were comparatively smaller ones but a number of graded vassal chiefs owed allegiance to them. Usually, the latter were vanquished and reinstated local chieftains who undertook to pay fixed tribute and render military service to the overlord. The vassal chiefs had the authority to make religious land grants to the deserving priestly families or institutions.[8] Where the overlord exerted greater control, a vassal chief had to take the approval of the former or the royal officials for making a religious grant in his own territory[9] or else he would make the grant on his own authority. Most likely, the exercise of such power on the part of the vassal chiefs depended either upon personal equation of mutual strength with the overlord or the terms of submission. Very few secular grants for the early medieval period can be traced. For any meritorious services, the overlord could reward the vassal chief with a land grant in the shape of the assignation of the revenues from a certain territory.[10] The vassal chief was fully responsible for the realisation of the revenues and the administration of such an assigned territory.

On the basis of the above mentioned land system and political order prevalent from the Gupta period onwards, some historians are inclined to concede the development of feudal elements in North India.[12] This is a completely erroneous view. In a purely feudal status society in Europe, the land in theory belonged to the king who granted to the feudal lords fiefs on the condition of military service and feudal aids. The feudal lords always held the land of the king. The basic relationship between the king and feudal lords rested on contract and the feudal lord's estate was considered as an 'honor'. The feudal lord not only further alienated the land on military condition but also exercised Jurisdictional rights of administration and justice in his territory. On the economic aspect of feudalism, the manorial lord was the owner of land and he got it cultivated with the help of the serfs. The church organisations also not only held land of the king but exercised jurisdictional powers in their territories.

In ancient and early medieval India, the concept of land ownership originally emanating from the communal tribal idea came to be vested in the king as well as land-owing families. Apart from the royal claim on the crown lands, the waste cultivable lands and jungles, the royal theory of land ownership was nothing more than a theoretical enunciation, which implied the royal claim over the revenues from the agrarian lands in possession and in ownership with the peasant families. The assignment of secular and religious land grants were made over but the revenue of villages and the ownership rights of the peasant families in the settled villages were not disturbed. This has nothing of parallelism with the administrative jurisdictions entrusted to the organised churches in feudalised Europe. Above all in the political aspect, the relationship between the king as the overlord in vassal chiefs never rested on a contract which is the essential criteria of the feudal bond. Nor can it be asserted that the vassal chiefs or the local chieftains ever held their own territories out of the recoveries of the overlord. A vassal chief may be granted a revenue assignment in lieu of his services rendered in any administrative or military capacity in the overlord's state but not a single land grant is traceable in which the personal territory of the vassal chief was conferred by the overlord as the conditional grant in lieu of the military service. On the contrary, the vassal chief or a local chieftain always claimed his own state or territory as a patrimony acquired at any historical stage through the process of conquest. It is only after either forced or voluntary submission to the overlord that a vassal chief would undertake to render military service, pay a fixed tribute, attend the overlord's court occasionally, to mention his name in his own charters and at times to accept his representative at his capital. This relationship between the overlord and the vassal chiefs may bear some rough resemblance with contemporary feudalised Europe but the similarity is rather superficial. The Indian polity and landed interests influenced by the regional socio-economic and ethnic factors ran on their own pattern and cannot be easily aligned either with feudalised Europe or with any other contemporary Eastern Asian civilization.

From the agrarian viewpoint, more important than the polity of kingdoms, which is a history of the hegemonies over the vassal chiefs, were the tribal and the clannish landed interests imposed on the caste ridden settled villages during the early medieval age. The conquering tribes and clans always apportioned territories and villages for the realisation of the revenues. In the wake of the Huns, the Gujars came from Central Asia and settled in various portions of North India. It has been maintained on the basis of the traditional accounts that for the purposes of the revenue realisation and administration, the Gujra-Pratiharas and the vassal chiefs ethnically related to them resorted to the practice of division of the settled villages into units of twelve each or their multiple upto eighty four (chaurasi).[13] Whereas the chief or the Raja of a state was entitled to the revenue, his clansmen were entrusted with the revenue management of the villages with a claim to a share in the revenues as the collection charges and the management of the general administration of law and order.[14] The conquering clans usually dispossessed the erstwhile clans and established their own intermediary rights of collection and a share in the revenues as their emoluments. The intermediary landed classes were named by various local designations from time to time but the basic traits of their relation to the villages comprising peasant families of the suppressed clans and castes remained the same. The members of the suppressed clans were mostly reduced to the status of the cultivators. Some dispossessions of the previous land owing families may as well have taken place but this was rather a rare phenomenon. Many members of the conquering clans did as well take to colonisation or reclamation of the jungle and waste lands attached to the settled villages and became the peasants under the rule of their own clannish authorities. This was rather inevitable with the growth of the clannish population and the pressure on the settled villages. The imposition and reimposition of the intermediary rights of the conquering clans was a recurring phenomenon which persisted throughout the medieval ages. The Rajput clans ruled over the last Hindu states which fell to the Turkish onslaughts. They ruled over North India from the 7th or 8th century to the end of the 12th century before the establishment of the Turkish rule. What specially distinguished the Rajput polity was the imposition of the clan aristocracies and hierarchical order of landed intermediaries between the peasants of the settled villages and the ruler. At the top, the polity was governed by the same old Hindu idea of establishing hegemony over each other through mutual clannish warfare extending the territories of the conquering state at the cost of the vanquished and imposing tribute and military service on the vassal chiefs. Within the state, a ruler usually assigned the revenues of the settled villages to his own kinsmen and clansmen on the condition of rendering military service. He also made grants to his officials in lieu of their salaries. Religious grants were also made to the Brahmanas in shape of assignation of the villages or revenue free grants of lands. The grantee served as the intermediary and below him were Headmen of the villages who may as well belong to the ruling clan and would collect the revenues after having reserved their own collection charges. The Headman was usually a land owner in his village. The grantees or the Headmen had to maintain law and order, possessed a right to alienate waste cultivable land and to introduce new cultivators on behalf of the ruler but could never claim rights of ownership on the agrarian land of the peasant in the settled villages. The Rajput families may own lands in the colonised or old villages and as well may enjoy rent free grants of land out usually they belonged to the intermediary classes and had no clannish or families' ties with the peasants in the settled villages.[15] It is only when some of the Rajput families took to cultivation, either in the settled or in the colonised villages, that a clannish bond can be said to have subsisted between the ruler and cultivating families. The Rajput socio-political structure does bear greater resemblance to a feudalised set up than the preceeding Hindu social orders.[16] But, here again, the resemblance is only superficial.[17] The assignment of the revenues on military condition depended purely on the discretion of the Chiefs and were considered as conditional life grants dependent on service to the state. The assignments of the grantees never constituted as 'fiefs', nor were the grantees regarded as the owners of land. According to an economic interpretation, feudalism may be said to have prevailed in a society where the landed intermediaries lived on the surplus produce of the peasants.[18] It is only in this generic sense that feudalism can be said to have existed in India either under the Rajput polity or throughout the medieval Indian period under the Muslim rulers.

References

1. Basham, *op. cit.*, p. 94.
2. *Arthasastra,* (tr. S), pp. 293, 338, 411.
3. Basham, *op. cit.*, p. 94.
4. *Ibid.*
5. Kosambi, *op. cit.*, pp. 279-291; R. S. Sharma, 'Feudal Elements in Pala and Pratihara Polity, 750-1000 A.D.'
6. For the details of political relationship between the Overlord king and the vassal Chiefs, see Basham, *op. cit.*, pp. 93-96.
7. *E I,* 7, 155-60. (Land Grant of Harsa issued in the 25th R.Y.); Also, Kosambi, *op. cit.*, pp. 298-99.
8. Of the various available land grant plates, only few can be quoted, *E I,* X, No. 1. A, 11. 1-20 (A village grant made in 893 A.D. by Balavarman, a Calukya vassal in Kathiawad); *I A,* XII, p. 195, Plate II, 11. 1-24 (a village grant dated 914 A.D. made by Dharanivaraha a Capa Vassal in Eastern Kathiawad).
9. *E I,* IX, No. 1, B, 11. 32-58. (A village grant dated 898 A.D. made by Avanivarman II, a Calukya, a vassal in Kathiawad with the approval of the royal official Dhiika).
10. *E I,* III, No. 36, 1.4 (This indicates that the district of Vamsapotaka in the Gujjaratrabhumi was conferred on a Gujara vassal of the Pratiharas).
11. *Ibid.*, pp. 266-67.
12. Kosambi, *op. cit.*, pp. 275-317; S.A.Q. Husaini, *The Economic History of India,* Calcutta, 1962, Vol. I, pp. 152-242; R. S. Sharma, vide f.n. 5. Against this view, Basham (*op. cit.*, pp. 93-96) denies if in the technical sense of the word there was any feudalism in ancient India though he thinks that something very like European feudalism did evolve among the Rajputs after the Muslim invasions. However, he puts the ancient Indian polity under Quasi-feudalism.
13. *E I,* IX, No. 1 A, 1. 10 (A 9th century inscription of Calukya vassal of the Pratiharas); Also, see R. S. Sharma, 'Land grants to Vassals and officials in Northern India (1000-1200)', *Journal of Economic and Social History of the Orient,* IV, pp. 88, 90-91, 94. (for Cahamanas, Parmaras and Calukyas). Also see details vide Ghoshal, pp. 66-67 (for the land grants issued by the Calukyas in Gujrat and the Paramaras of Malwa 9th-11th centuries A.D.). Though such an arthimatical aggregation of the villages for the purposes of assignments and administration may have continued in the Rajput kingdoms of the early medieval age, it seems to have fallen in disuse and cannot be traced on epigraphical or archival basis from the 16th century onwards. It left only a tradition or a legend which was maintained by H. M. Elliot. For the Rajput settlements in Awadh from the 15th century onwards, C. A. Elliot, *'Chronicles of Oonao,'* could not trace any existence of the '*Chourassie or tribal estates of eighty four villages*'. The Palas had fiscal units of one and sometimes ten villages put under the charge of state officials (vide *EI,* IV,

No. 34, l. 47). But it seems that the Rajput kingdoms from the 11th and the 12th centuries onwards had larger units of villages depending on the assignment made to the landed intermediaries and were not co-terminous with the *Chaurasie* idea.

14. Also, see Ghoshal (pp. 65-66) who quotes a Calukya land grant in Gujrat which uses a special title of *'talapada'* which implies assessed revenues due to the state. It had to be collected by the assignee and there is every possibility that like the later medieval practice in Gujrat, he was assigned revenues from other villages than the '*talapada*' in lieu of his services to the state, military and administrative for the revenue collection and the maintenance of local law and order. For the later practice of demarcating between the state revenues (talpad), see *Mirat-i-Ahmadi,* I, pp. 21, 173-74; supplement, pp. 228-29.

15. Also see W. C. Bennet's interpretation of socio-economic and political order of the Rajput principalities in the early medieval age in Awadh vide, '*Gazetteer of the Province of Oudh*', Introduction, pp. X/ III-X/ IV.

16. James Tod (vide *Annals and Antiquities of Rajasthan*), edited by William Crooke, Vol. I & II, pp. XXXVIII, 153 and 962 respectively gave currency to the theory of the existence of feudal system in Rajputana. Since then, some scholars have followed it up for the Rajput principalities even in the other regions of North India during the early medieval age. The latest adherent of this school is R. S. Sharma vide his paper, 'Land grants tò Vassals and Officials in Northern India 1000-1200', *op. cit.*, vide f.n. 14.

17. Also, see W. C. Bennet, *op. cit.*, P. X/IV; P. Saran, 'The Feudal System of Rajputana', vide *Studies in Medieval India History,* Delhi, 1952, pp. 1-23.

18. Kosambi, *Studies in the Agrarian History of England.* (Oxford, 1956), p. VI.

Chapter 2

Land Revenue Administration Under the Sultanate Period

The land revenue administration of North India entered a new phase under the Muslim rule. Sindh was occupied by the Arabs in the beginning of the 8th century and it remained attached to the Umayyad and the Abbassid Caliphs of Baghdad. However, with the decline of the Abbasid Caliphate, the kingdoms of Multan and Mansurah lost link with Baghdad and continued to remain independent local states side by side with the other Rajput kingdoms in the North.[1] As a consequence of Mahmud of Ghazni's raids (first quarter of 11th century A.D. 1021-1022 A.D.) Punjab was annexed to the Ghaznvid Empire.[2] Mahmud wrested Multan from Qaramitah muslim rulers of Shia sect and attached to his Panjab Province but his occupation of Sindh remained incomplete. A few years after Mahmud's death, Multan again became independent and occupied even greater part of Upper Sindh.

Local converted tribe of Sumra established its rule in the lower portion of Sindh with capital at Debal. The Ghaznvid Empire was ended by the Seljuqs and the Ghaznvid rulers took refuge in the Panjab which henceforth remained their sole possession. During the 12th century, the south-east frontiers of the Panjab remained quite unstable and the Rajput rulers made steady intrusions. Nothing much is known about the land revenue practices in these north-west portions before the establishment of the Turkish rule towards the close of the century. The fact that Multan and Sindh broke away from the Arab Caliphate of Baghdad and came to be ruled by the local converted Muslim tribes suggests that the indigenous notions of socio-economic order must have continued to predominate.[3] The Ghaznvid occupation of the Panjab was mostly a military occupation.[4] All this points towards the continuance of the early medieval village communities based on clannish order though it can be well imagined that for the purposes of land revenue collection, the Muslim officialdom in line with the Arab and the Turkish institutions of revenue machinery must have been imposed upon the local landed intermediaries in Sindh, Multan and the Panjab. From the close of the 12th and the beginning of the 13th centuries, the major portions of Northern India came under the domination of the Turkish rule of the Delhi Sultanate. From this period onwards right till the submergence of the Delhi Sultanate in the Mughal Empire under Akbar, the evolution of the land revenue system in North India may be considered into two distinct territories viz., the Muslim kingdom and the independent or semi-independent Rajput states.

Before the Turkish conquest of India, the Muslim jurists had developed a well calculated theory of agrarian administration with great ingenuity and minuteness suited to the Muslim countries in Egypt, Middle Eastern and South Asian countries.[5] The Islamic ideas of taxation were originally based on the Byzantine and Persian practices. They were further evolved in line with the practical canons of fiscal administration under the Umayyads, especially under Caliph Omar and the Abbassid Caliphate. The Turkish administration in the Middle East and Afghanistan, originally very much indebted to the Persian ideas and practices, was further developed by the Samanid rulers and the Ghaznvid State.[6] For the fiscal organisation of the state, the early Mamluk rulers of the Delhi Sultanate were obliged to adopt the Turkish ideas of administration,[7] within the limitations imposed by the socio-economic and political structure of pre-Muslim India.

There were four principal schools of law in Islam. The Hanafite, the Malikite, the Shafite and the Hanbalite. But in India, the Hanafite School was adopted by the Muslim Sultans.[8] The Muslim jurists classified the revenues of a Muslim state under two heads: religious and secular. The religious charges leviable on the property and income of the Muslim were known as *zakat* and the secular revenues collected from the non-Muslims consisted principally of *Jizya* (a religious cess), *ghanimat* (spoils of war), *kharaj-i-khums* comprising land revenue and other agrarian and non-agrarian cesses, *khums* on mines and treasure troves, etc. The *zakat* was levied on the Muslims in respect of land produce, grains, fruits, dates and grapes etc., animals of pasture and other quadrupeds, gold, silver and merchandise.[9] The varying details of the minimum possession (*misab*) liable to the payment of *zakat* was laid down in accordance with the law (*Shara*). Of the *zakat* levied on the produce of land, varying rates of assessment were applied viz., 1/10th (10%) of the produce in respect of land dependent on overflow of rivers and periodical rainfall, 1/20th (5%) on the land watered by wells, tanks, canals as well as watered by means of buckets. The minimum produce (*nisab*) subject to *zakat* should exceed five ass-loads of weight (*kharwars*). In contrast to the *zakat*, which was a charge on the produce, the *kharaj* denoted a tax on the productive land in the shape of share in the produce of land. Whereas *zakat* was leviable only upon the Muslims, '*kharaj* could be charged both from the Muslims and non-Muslims'. The Muslim jurists give further details of the *ushri* lands owned by the Muslims and the *kharaji* lands owned both by the Muslims and non-Muslims in the conquered territories. There were certain lands categorised as *Sulli, Bani Nafran* and *Bani Taghlab* which could be owned both by Muslims and non-Muslims but were regarded as *ushri* lands.[10] The reclaimed lands by the Muslims were also subject to *ushr.* The lands which were irrigated from sources constructed from public revenues were essentially regarded as *kharaji.*[11] Thus the nature of land in the possession of the peasants was determined both by their religion and the means of irrigation. The non-Muslims of the conquered territories were subjected to the payment of land revenue leviable on the *kharaji* lands. The incidence of the state share in the produce of land also depended upon the method of assessment of land revenue. The different methods of assessment were *kharji muqsamah, kharj-i muazzafah* or *kharaj-i wazifah, kharaj-i matuf* and *kharaj-i muqatih.*[12] *Kharaj-i- muqsamah* was based on the division of the produce and the state share could be fixed at 1/5th, 1/4th and 1/2 of the gross produce. *Kharaj-i- muazzafah* or *wazifah* was a periodically fixed assessment in kind or cash per unit area according to the species of the crops grown and could also be fixed per fruit tree. It was collected from the cultivators whether he cultivated the land or not. *Kharaj-i-muqatiah* was a fixed charge on land in kind or cash fixed for a fixed term of years, though subject to revision. As against this, there was no provision for the revision of the assessment involved in *kharaj-i-wazifah.* All this system represents the Muslim theoretical concept of agrarian administration. It is difficult to believe that the Muslim theoretical concept of agrarian administration could be entirely enforced in India—a primarily agricultural country which already possessed an equally advanced agrarian administration based on ancient practices evolved in accordance with the regional geographical features and the tribal customs of the peoples settled in different parts of the country. Moreover, it may be equally borne in mind that in India, unlike the other countries of the Middle East and South Asia conquered by Islam, the local chieftainships and the village communities based on landed and clannish order never lost their identity.

The problem of land revenue administration in India under the Sultans of Delhi has already been studied by many scholars but there has been either more of emphasis on the theoretical concept of the Islamic theories of administration or on the administrative policies of the Sultans from time to time. The account of the land revenue practices is too hazy, confused and inconclusive. This is partly due to the paucity of contemporary source-material available on the subject and the lack of proper interpretation of the few technical and obscure passages known from the Persian chronicles.

The Delhi Sultanate was quite meticulous in organising its machinery for the collection of the revenues from the suppressed chiefs and zamindars as well as keeping a proper financial control over its own provincial administrators and assignees.

In accordance with Turkish practice, the revenues of the Sultanate were divided into two main categories, the *khalisa* and the *iqatat* (plural of *iqta*)'. The revenues of the *khalisa* territories were earmarked for the state exchequer whereas *iqtas* were assigned to the administrative and military personnel (*amirs, maliks* and soldiers). The general administration and the revenue collection of the directly administered territories were put under the charge of *muktas.*[13] A *Mukta* (or Wali) held the administrative charge of particularly specified territory (in the 13th century also known as an administrative *iqta* on Turkish lines but usually known as a *Wilayat,* a province or a still smaller territory) and had under him various *amils, karkuns* and *mustasarrafs* who were responsible for the collection of the *khalisa* revenues and maintenance of accounts.[14] A *Muqta* could be removed or transferred by the Sultan from one place to another and his territorial jurisdiction could be reduced or extended in extent. A *muqta* also raised and equipped troops. Though the strength and salaries of the troops was fixed by the Sultan, the *muqta* was responsible for the payment of their salaries from within the *khalisa* revenues realised by him. The *muqta* himself may be paid either in cash or assigned in *iqta* in lieu of his personal salary. After defraying the expenses of the administration and the salaries of the troops, he had to remit the balance to the Central Government. *Diwan-i-Wizarat*). A *Muqta* had also to realise tribute from the vassal chiefs.

Quite distinct from the *khalisa* administration, a revenue assignee of an *iqta* was designated as *muqti* or *Iqtadar.*[15] An *iqta* was not a uniform territorial unit but was defined only for the purposes of revenue assignment in lieu of the salary of an *Iqtadar.* An *iqta* assignment to a military officer was conditional on military service and *Iqtadar* had to meet his personal and the full expenditure of his military establishment from within the assigned revenues. An *iqta* grant to a single soldier was equally conditional on military service. An *iqtadar* was responsible for the collection of both *kharaj* and *jizya* but the income of the *jizya* was not assignable and had to be despatched to the Central Government. Moreover, during the Sultanate period, the assignments were not done on the basis of exact valuation of the villages in an *iqta* and the revenues realised in excess of the entitled assignment (*fawazil*) had to be remitted by the *Iqtadar* to the Central exchequer. His accounts were regularly audited by the *Diwan-i Wizarat.* An *iqta* assignment was always non-hereditary and a conditional grant, and the grantee was assigned only usufruct rights rather than any proprietary claim over the agrarian lands of the peasants. An *Iqtadar* could be dismissed by the Sultan and was liable to be transferred from one *iqta* to another. The khalisa administration under a *Muqta* and the *iqtadari* system were not based on a feudal concept.[16] The *Muqtas* and the *Iqtadars* (or *muqtis*) constituted a bureaucratic class rather than a landed feudal aristocracy of the Sultanate. As explained further, in the background of the vested interests of the local landed intermediaries and the fissiparous tendencies on the part of the Hindu Chiefs, the Delhi Sultanate could not organise machinery covering all the aspects of land revenue administration in its vast territories and was compelled to adopt the well-known Turkish method of collection of revenues through the *Muqtas* and the *Iqtadars.*

In accordance with the Muslim practice, the Sultanate also made religious grants to the deserving individuals or the institutions like the madrasas, mosques and works of public utility. They were known as *inam, i.e.,* gift of land free of rent; *milk*, giving the grantee a permanent proprietary right in land and *waqf,* as an endowment of the revenues from particular villages and lands.[17] Most of such rent-free grants were made from the waste cultivable lands and the beneficiaries were only the Muslims. Unlike the *iqta* grants, the rent-free charitable grants to the individuals were not conditional on the rendering of any services but may be in lieu of either the past services or good act on the part of the assignee. An *inam* grant would be made either for specified assessed revenues or for specified measured units of waste culturable lands. Usually, such grants were hereditary in nature but the state could always claim right of resumption.

Iltutmish, the founder of the Delhi Sultanate, apportioned the revenues of the various portions of the centrally administered territories as *iqtas* amongst his Amirs, Maliks and soldiers.[18] *Muqtas* were appointed in the provinces. Nothing else is known about the fiscal administration of Iltutmish. It seems that after the latter's death, there was considerable laxity and misuse of the state revenues especially in the assigned territories of the *iqtadars.* Balban tightened the machinery for the administration of the *iqtas* and formulated new rules for their grants.[19] The *iqtas* of such families which were no longer in active service, were resumed to the *khalisa* and the families were pensioned off. The *iqtas* of the persons capable of active service were clearly stipulated and the surplus revenue from their *iqtas* were to be taken over by the Revenue Department of the state. Balban's regulations definitely rejected the principle of hereditary *iqta* and *khwajas* were appointed by the Central Government for keeping a watch on the financial activities of the *Muqtas* and the *Iqtadars.* A *khwaja* was a civil official and kept regular records and accounts of the revenues.[20] For the purposes of revenue collection, the provincial territories (*Wilayat*) were further subdivided into *khittas* and *qasbas.* The revenue officials like *Mutsarraf* and *Karkun* were appointed who collected revenues through the landed intermediaries viz., the petty zamindar, chaudharies and the *muqaddams* of the villages.[21]

Under Alauddin Khaliji, the *iqta* system was not abolished but its role was limited and it would not be granted in certain reserved territories (*Sharaf Qai*).[22] Realising the fact that the religious rent free grants constituted a big drain on the royal exchequer, Alauddin resumed the grants like *milk, inam, idarat* (pensions) and *waqf,* etc.[23] Alauddin also exercised a tight control on the state revenue officers like the *Muqtas, Mutasarrafs* and *Karkuns.*[24] But this rigid policy of Alauddin died with him. After him, Ghiyas-ul-Din Tughluk adopted a moderate and conciliatory policy towards the state revenue officers. The religious rent free grants were renewed as before and *iqta* system was equally practiced on an extensive scale.[25] Under Muhammad Tughluk, the troops were mostly paid in cash and the *iqta* system was not very much favoured.[26] But the revenue assignments to the military commanders and troops assumed great dimensions under Firoz Shah.[27] It seems that under the Sultanate, the strong rulers like Alauddin Khalji, Muhammad Tughluk and Sher Shah laid emphasis on the extension of the *khalisa* territories and to pay the standing army as far as possible from the *khalisa* revenue.[28] On the other hand, the Muslim military class always preferred *iqtas* which they could manage of their own.

The system of revenue collection with a clear cut demarcation of the *khalisa* territories under the *Muqtas* and the military assignments to the *Iqtadars* practically broke down after the Tughluks and became quite blurred.[29] The *Muqtas* of provinces became semi-independent tributaries with their own private armies, and the audit of the revenue accounts became extremely rare. In the Afghan period prior to the Mughal conquest, the *iqta* assignments were made on a fairly large scale even on tribal and clannish basis. The military assignees of the *iqtas* became more or less defacto rulers of their territories and even aspired for the throne of Delhi.[30] The revenue farming of the villages and much larger territories became quite common under the Tughluks and thereafter. Even under Muhammad Tughluk, the revenue-farming was prevalent and sometimes even the entire revenues of a province were farmed out.[31] Firoz Tughluk further extended the scope of the farming and the revenues of the provinces were farmed out to the Government officials themselves.[32] Firoz also made lavish *iqta* grants and the assignees even sold the right on the revenues to bankers against advance of loans.[33] The assignees shifted their own responsibility for the revenue collection and the bankers played the role of the revenue farmers and made considerable profits in such transactions. The extension of the system of farming to the Government officers and the further alienation of the assigned revenues to the bankers on the part of the *Iqtadars* shows laxity of the state revenue machinery. It is doubtful if the Delhi Sultanate imposed any restrictions upon the revenue-farmers so as not to coerce the local landed intermediaries and the village communities for the realisation of the state revenues. Firoz Tughluk also estimated the total income (*jama*) of his state which amounted to six crores and seventy five lakhs of tankas.[34] This estimate was based on approximation (*mushahida*) of the revenues of different territories of the state. This was perhaps intended to facilitate the role of assignments and revenue-farming of different regions of the state. Moreover, for strengthening its hold for the revenue collection, the Tughluks appointed military-cum-revenue officials in the sub-divisions of the provinces. Evidence about regular sub-divisions as administrative units within a provice (*iqta* or *wilayat*) is rather scanty but it is clear that under the Tughlaks, *Shiqdars* and above them *Faujdars* were appointed with jurisdiction specified parganas on 'ad-hoc' basis.[35] The parganas were not defined administrative units with uniform territorial jurisdictions over the villages. In fact, a pargana usually represented the territorial jurisdiction of a suppressed Hindu Chief though it is possible that the state of an erstwhile Hindu Chief might comprise a few parganas and in such a case, a pargana might represent the territory of a vassal chief owing allegience to a bigger Rajput Raja.[36] The headquarters of a pargana was known as *qasba.*[37] Ibn Battuta's description of a *Sadi* t o have been a territorial unit comprising a hundred villages,[38] has no historical foundation and is not corroborated by any other contemporary evidence. During the 14th century, in general usage, a *shiq* represented a sub-province[39] or a smaller province. The concept persisted throughout the 15th century though with the disintegration of the Delhi Sultanate, the territorial jurisdiction of a province of *Shiq* in line with political situation was bound to be much smaller than in the past.[40] In the 16th century, this further degenerated into a Sarkar and was adopted as such by Sher Shah and was placed under the military command of a *Shiqdar-i-shiqdaran.* A pargana was put under the executive charge of a *Shiqdar.*

This it is clear that the Delhi Sultanate laid considerable emphasis on the organisation of the military-cum-revenue machinery for the collection of the land revenue from the conquered territories in North India. Apart from this it very doubtful if the Sultanate rule (excepting Sher Shah's reign) brought about any fundamental changes in the existing pre-Muslim revenue practices and the Hindu principles of agrarian administration either with regard to the incidence of state demand (excepting Alauddin Khalji's reign) or methods of assessment prevailing in different regions of North India.

As already explained, a detailed Muslim theory of taxation had been worked out even before the Turkish conquest of North India. But it may be wondered if all these Muslim fiscal ideas relating to state demand and methods of assessment were really enforced in actual practice even in such regions of North India which were under the direct control of the Sultanate. It has been suggested that the Muslim ideas of the agrarian administration were identical with the local existing Hindu revenue practices and, as such, the latter could be easily continued though the Islamic revenue terminology with Persian and Turkish connotations was adopted.[41] Undeniably, some broad similarity and parallelism could be drawn between the Islamic and the Hindu theories of agrarian administration in respect of the state claim over the revenues, the measurement process and certain modes of assessment of land revenue. The identity of the fiscal ideas was not a matter of simple fortuitous coincidence and could be explained both on historical and geographical factors in the process of agrarian civilisation in the South Asian countries. Apart from this, there still remained various aspects of land administration in which the Muslim fiscal ideas would not fall in exact line with the Hindu notions of revenue administration. Unlike the Hindu theory, the Hanafite School of the Islamic law did not make any theoretical claim over the ownership of the agrarian lands. Even in the non-Islamic conquered territories, the Muslim theory recognised the ownership of land on the part of the peasants subject to the payment of *kharaj* and *jizya.*[42] Moreover, the administrative concept evolved by the Turkish elite in South Asian Muslim countries had left a large measure of autonomy in law and custom to the economically productive sections of the population.[43] The Muslim emigrees to India largely belonged to the professional classes and did not involve any economic and social displacement of the agrarian population. The landed intermediaries intervening between the state and the cultivators did not find any place in the Islamic theory but this situation had to be conceded in India in the context of the socio-economic and political situation in the country. As the Muslim state in India was an alien one, the ancient practice of two-fold aspects of land ownership, viz. state-owned lands or personally owned by the king and the agrarian lands of the peasants could not work any longer. The main division of lands under the Muslim state, as already explained, was on the basis of the utilisation of the revenues which were either reserved for the state exchequer (*khalisa*) or assigned to the administrative and military officials (*iqtas*). There is every probability that the personal lands of the suppressed chiefs remained their personal property and their families and future descendants in the course of the centuries claimed them as exclusively privately owned *zamindari* villages which stood quite distinct from such villages in their zamindari jurisdiction wherein the agrarian lands were owned by the peasant families and the zamindars claimed only zamindari perquisites (*haquq*) for the collection of the revenues on behalf of the Muslim state.[44] In line with the Hindu practice, the Muslim state also made assignation of the revenues and land grants (*milk, inam, waqf,* etc.) to the religious assignees but their resumption under Alauddin Khalji casts doubt if they carried with them the same name of proprietary rights which the Hindu theory and practice had emphasised.

As regards the state demand, both the Muslim and the Hindu theories accepted the differential scale of assessment governed by the nature of the soil, means of irrigation and the labour necessary for cultivation. Whatever be the theoretical concept, the Hindu states had claimed between 1/6th and 1/3rd of the gross in accordance with the above explained principles. The Muslim theory demanded between 1/5th to 1/2 of the gross produce on the *kharaji* lands and between 1/5th and 1/10th on the *ushri* lands.[45] But in actual practice, the Turkish government in Persia had even demanded the differential scale of land revenue at the rate of 1/3rd of the gross produce as the normal demand.[46] Apart from it, both the Hindu and the Muslim states levied various types of cesses on the agriculturists. It also seems that on the eve of the Muslim conquest, the concept of social relationship between the racially and politically dominant classes with the tax paying and productive classes in the Turkish-administered South Asian countries was not very much different from the Hindu society in India.[47] During the Sultanate period, it is possible that in accordance with the Shariat principles, a distinction was made between the incidence of state demand levied on the Hindu and the Muslim agricultural communities[48] but for want of evidence, no definite opinion can be expressed on this aspect. The earliest statement made by Fakhruddin Mubarak Shah that Qutbuddin ordered the abolition of all taxes except the Shari at ones which in some cases were fixed at 1/10th and in others at 1/20th,[49] most likely refers to the *zakat* on the produce of the lands owned by the Muslims in the Punjab.[50] This equally shows that in the Panjab, which had been under the Ghaznvid rule, the Muslims had been subjected to taxation policy which was not entirely in accordance with the Shariat principles. The reference made in the statement about the fixation of *kharaj* at 1/5th is only a theoretical enunciation of the Shariat and does not indicate that it was enforced by the Sultan. Moreover, Qutbuddin's period is too early to assert any taxation policy for other portions of North India which had not been even fully conquered so far. Except for Barani's statement of raising of the state demand to 1/2 of the gross produce by Alauddin Khalji[51] under abnormal circumstances, there is no other unambiguous statement in any of the Persian chronicles which would throw light on the normal state share during the Sultanate period. It is also not clear if 1/2 of produce under Alauddin Khalji was demanded only on the grain produce or on all types of crops. It goes without saying that this maximum state demand was in consonance with the Shariat principle rather than with the past Hindu practice. Howsoever, warranted by the need of the state exchequer in the fact of the Mongol invasions and internal difficulties, it must have been extremely harsh on the peasants. This was surrendered after Alauddin's death and the normal state share was once again practiced. The statement of Barani about Ghyasuddin Tughluk simply suggests that the rate of revenue was raised by 1/10th or 1/11th (9% to 10%) on the existing state demand[52] but there is nothing to ascertain as to what the latter demand was. Similarly, Barani's statement on Muhammad Tughluk's increase of taxation in the Doab is quite obscure. Most likely, it suggests an increase of 5% to 10% on the existing state share.[53] From all these statements, it is difficult to determine the normal state share under the Sultanate.

There is no justification in maintaining that the Sultans of Delhi claimed 1/5th of produce as the normal state share in accordance with the Islamic principles.[54] A 16th century evidence shows that in the territory of Multan, the normal state share was 1/4th of the produce. As it was based on long standing practice, status-quo was maintained by Sher Shah even after the incorporation of Multan in his Empire. Before the Turkish conquest, Multan was a Muslim state. In fact, there is every justification to suggest that by and large, the pre-Turkish notions of state demand prevalent in the other portions of North India continued to persist during the Sultanate period.

It may be asserted with still greater vehemence that for the assessment of land revenue, the Muslim revenue officers and assignees in the Sultanate period simply followed the principles and practices of the pre-Muslim period. The Hindu methods of assessment viz., the sharing of the produce (*batai*), appraisement (*kankut*), a standard rate of demand per unit area based on actual measurement according to the crop sown, fixation of demand based on measurement even on certain cultivable fields left uncultivated by the peasants and assessment on the agrarian land based on rough and ready method of measured lands in accordance with the cultivable capacity of the plough-oxen (*hala*) continued to prevail in different regions of North India throughout the Sultanate period and with some modifications were adopted under Sher Shah and Akbar. Though these methods of assessment continued to be known in the local terminology and dialect, the Persian Chronicles designate the *batai* as *hukm-i-hasil*.[55] Appraisement as *hukm-i-mushahada*[56] and assessment according to measurement of the area and fixation of demand per unit area regardless of the fact whether crops were grown or not as *hukam-i- misahat*.[57] The lump sum assessment of the villages, also traceable during the Hindu period, was known as *muqtai.* The assessment on the lands according to the cultivable capacity of the plough-oxen or the seed capacity do not find any mention in the Chronicles but their continued existence throughout the medieval age is confirmed by the *Ain-i-Akbari* and other Mughal sources. In fact, it is only in the sharing method that a true parallel could be found in the *kharaj-i-muqasimah* of the Islamic theory. The other Islamic methods, *i.e.,* the *kharaji-muzzafah* or *wazifah* and *kharaj-i-mutatah,* despite apparent similarities, differed from the above mentioned Hindu methods of assessment in matters of technical detail. In actual practice, the Turkish kingdom in South Asian countries, especially in Persia and Afghanistan, had mostly known two methods of assessment *i.e., muqasamat* and *misahat.*[58] The *muqasamat* involved sharing method assessable only on the cultivated crops. In contrast to it, the *misahat* was based on the measurement of land and would involve assessment on all cultivable lands on record whether the peasants cultivated or not.[59] In major portions of Persia, the method fo *misahat* was applied and in Shiraz, which was a highly irrigated region, separate rates per area unit (*harb* based on *jarib* and *gaz*) were applied to irrigated and unirrigated tracts yielding cash crops like melons and other horticultural fruits.[60]

As explained above, the Hindu states had known both the above mentioned methods of assessment. In the early medieval age, the Hindu theory had stressed the imposition of revenue on such cultivable fields, which a landlord or his tenants left fallow out of negligence.[61] The process of measurement and an assessment based on differential scale of rates of assessment had been known ever since the time of the *Jatakas* and the Mauryan age and had been practiced in various regions throughout ancient and early medieval times under the Hindu rule. Being alien to the agrarian situation of India and with the instability of the political situation, it is very doubtful if the early Muslim Sultans tried to supplant their own Islamic ideas on the Indian pattern of agrarian administration. Throughout the 13th century, 'status quo' was maintained. However, in the early 14th century, in order to augment his financial resources, Alauddin Khalji stressed the adoption of measurement of land and the imposition of revenue on all cultivable lands in possession with the landowning families regardless of the fact whether such lands were cultivated or not. (*Ba hukam-i-misahat wa wafa-i-biswa*).[62]

Though Barani has also used technical Turkish terms, the adoption of measurement of land and the *mishat* method for the assessment of the revenue did not preclude from its process the margin to be given for such cultivated areas and crops, which may have either fully or partially failed to mature due to any calamity. However, in actual practice under dishonest revenue officials or any weak Government, this rebate for the immaturity of the sown crops could be denied to the peasants. This accounts for the fact that the peasants always preferred the sharing method based on actual yield to the measurement method and throughout the medieval age whenever the latter method was enforced under any strong ruler, it usually lapsed after him and there was reversion to sharing or other methods of assessment usually prevalent in a region.

Ghyasuddin Tughluk reverted to the sharing method based on actual turn over of the crops and ordered that full margin of the immature crops and natural calamities should be afforded to the peasants.[63] In fact, Alauddin Khaliji was the first Muslim ruler who laid an emphasis on the system of measurement though it seems that like his other revenue measures, this was enforced only in the limited territories of the Sultanate. Later on, Muhammad Tughluk too favoured measurement and enforced it in the Doab region.[64] The practice of simple land measurement for the purposes of assessment of revenues continued in some regions with a limited scope. However, its continuance under the Lodhis is confirmed by the fact that Sikander Lodhi adopted a uniform yard of forty-one digits as a standard unit of measurement. Before Sher Shah's reign, the practice of land measurement was not very common either. The *Ain's* statement about the suppression of the lumpsum assessement of the villages (*muqtai*) by Sher Shah shows that this may have been quite in vogue before his reign. There is every probability that along with the practice of farming out larger territories either by the Government itself or by the *iqtadas,* the process of assessing the revenues of the villages in a lumpsum manner (*muqtai*) without involving either the measurement of land or taking into consideration the individual holdings of the cultivators and further farming them to the *Muqaddams* or any other local landed intermediary gained sufficient currency from Firoz Tughluk's reign and persisted throughout the 15th and first few decades of the 16th centuries.

As regards the mode of payment of land revenue, *Barni's* version of Alauddin's market control system in Delhi and the enforcement of payment in kind rather than in cash in the *Khalisa* territories, Doab[65] and Delhi clearly shows that cash nexus was quite well known in the rural areas in the 13th century. In fact, the numismatic evidence shows a considerable use of coins and the development of money economy and rural trade in the 11-12th centuries[66] which continued throughout the 13th century. Alauddin's insistence on the payment of revenues in kind, even though impelled by his dire necessity of providing grain stocks in the Delhi market, was more of a retrogressive step for the growth of money economy in the agrarian life of North India. The practice of making the revenue payment both in kind and cash depending on the regional economic progress and the use of money economy persisted throughout the Sultanate period.

In line with Alauddin Khalji's policy, Ibrahim Lodhi stressed for the payment of revenue by the peasants in kind rather than in cash which resulted in the cheap prices of the grains.[67] This was perhaps necessitated by the shortage of currency, especially silver in the market. Ibrahim Lodhi's measure is quite suggestive of the fact that hither to cash nexus for revenue payment in the 15th and early 16th centuries may have been quite in use in some territories of North India, but it is difficult to determine its extent. In the interregnum of the Mughal age preceding Sher Shah's reign, it seems that in the major portions, the general practice was to make payment in kind rather than in cash. It was only Sher Shah and later on Akbar who introduced important currency reforms and officially encouraged the greater use of cash nexus in the agrarian economy.

The Islamic concept and the ideal of kingship on the part of Sultanate rulers stood for the welfare of the peasantry. While describing the revenue policy of the Sultans of Delhi, Barni repeatedly mentions the fact that the cultivators should be left with sufficient means of subsistence not too small as to make them desparate and quit cultivation and nor so large as to provide him with means for recalcitrance and rebellion.[68] Though Barani praises Balban's honest disposition towards the welfare of the rural classes,[69] he is highly critical of Alauddin Khilji's[70] policy. Looked at from the viewpoint of the State, Alauddin's attack on the Hindu landed intermediaries, who exempted their own agrarian lands from revenues and defined the revenue regulations,[71] can be well appreciated. But the heavy incidence of state demand and the additional cesses must have been extremely harsh on the peasantry. Barani's criticism against Alauddin's revenue policy is not without foundation.

For the increase of the state revenues, the Tughluks emphasised the increase of the agricultural lands and produce. Ghyasuddin Tughluk gave remissions of land revenue on account of natural calamities.[72] He was also the first Muslim Sultan to provide irrigation facilities through the opening of canals on a small scale.[73] Mohammad Tughluk initiated the famine relief policy by advancing *taqavi* loans for the sinking of the wells and providing the peasantry with elementary means of production.[74] He also opened a new branch in the revenue department (*Diwan-i Kohi*) for the reclamation of waste lands and colonisation as a state enterprise under the direct administration of the Central government.[75] Later on, the canal work was extended by Firoz Tughluk in the East Panjab and two canals—Rajiva and Alaghkhani—were opened up.[76] This was an important step in the agrarian policy of the Sultanate. It led to the extension of the agricultural lands in the *Parganas* of Hissar and Firuzabad and also led to the growth of the superior crops like wheat, sugarcane, lentils and the growth of superior quality of orchards.[77] Firuz charged water tax (*haw-i-shirb*) over and above the land revenue from the canal irrigated areas.[78] All these measues undertaken by the Tughluks are reminiscent of the ancient Indian practices. Firuz is also credited for having abolished numerous cesses which were contrary to the Shariat.[79]

Notwithstanding all this benevolence and ideal concept of the Delhi Sultans, it may be well realised that taking a rounded picture of the entire Sultanate period from the beginning of the 13th century to the first quarter of the 17th century, effective agrarian steps were taken only in the 14th century under the rule of the Khaljis and the Tughluks. Though Alauddin's Imperial Policy was successful in suppressing the Hindu Chiefs and weaning them around the Delhi Court,[80] his agrarian policy proved completely ephemeral in nature. Some of the agrarian measures undertaken by the Tughluks were of constructive nature but their military inability, administrative limitations and the extension of the farming system led to the disintegration of the Sultanate. Taking the entire Sultanate period in the round, the 13th Century represents the Sultanate in the making, the 14th Century covers some agrarian experimentation but from the closing year of the 14th Century down to its submergence in the Mughal Empire, the Sultanate is characterised only by more or less sterile agrarian policy. This is not to belittle the administrative achievements of the Delhi Sultanate but the agrarian set up of North India in the pre-Akbar medieval age has to be viewed in the socio-economic background and the nature of the political hold that the Muslim rulers were from time to time able to exert on the local Hindu Chiefs and the petty landed intermediaries (all designated as Zamindars) who formed the backbone of the agrarian society throughout the medieval age. Throughout the Sultanate period, the prevailing Hindu revenue practices and the socio-economic structure based on landed intermediaries played a dominant role. In general, this is true not only of the Delhi Sultanate but also of the contemporary Muslim sultanate in Kashmir (1343 to 1586-7 A.D.) and other independent Muslim states like Gujrat, Malwa, Jaunpur and Bengal which sprang up from the late 14th century onwards, on the disintegration of the territories of the Delhi Sultanate. In fact, from the viewpoint of agrarian administration, the hitherto accepted version of the division of North India into the territories under the direct central of the Delhi Sultanate and its further administrative divisions into provinces (*Wilayats*) and the regions under the domination of the independent or semi-independent tribute paying Hindu Rajas[81] does not portray the correct picture of rural India. Quite distinct from the independent or semi-Independent Hindu states, the so-called directly administered territories comprised regions of the erstwhile Rajput ruling Chiefs and the latter's vassal Chiefs, both Rajput and non-Rajput. On conquest, some of the families of the Rajput ruling Chiefs fled to far places in the sub-Himalayan ranges,[82] Rajasthan[83] and well protected regions in Awadh.[84] A few families may have been even completely exterminated. But usually on submission, whether forced or voluntary, the families of the ruling chiefs were allowed to maintain their territories on the condition of the payment of the revenue to the Delhi Sultanate. The landed intermediaries in the territories of the suppressed chiefs were also permitted 'status-quo' on similar condition. For want of any archival evidence, it is not possible to suggest if the families of the suppressed chiefs were granted any revenue free villages for their maintenance or they were required to pay tribute (in general term) which approximated to the revenues of their territories after having left them their maintenance allowance and the perquisites of their further landed intermediaries.[85] It seems that the complete suppression of the ruling chiefs worked to a much greater degree in the North Western portion of India, *i.e.*, Sindh, Multan and the plains of the Panjab where Muslims had ruled even before the Turkish occupation as well as in the territories of Delhi and Doab where the Turkish rule was enforced quite rigorously during the 13th and 14th centuries. Even in such territories where the rule of the former Rajput Chiefs became extinct the landed intermediaries like the petty chiefs (*Khuts*), Chaudharies and Muqaddams continued with status-quo. Besides this, there were also village communities based on tribal and clannish character and in certain portions of North-West of India still governed by the communal concept of agrarian possessions and paying revenues to the state through their tribal chiefs who enjoyed the perquisites in lieu of collection of the revenues.[86] In other territories of the Sultanate, the erstwhile rulers were mostly accepted as suppressed Chiefs (*Zamindars*). Thus the concept of agrarian administration and the collection of the state revenues of the centrally administered provinces (*Wilayats*) basically rested on the local agency of the suppressed Hindu Rajas, petty chiefs, the Chaudharies, *muqaddams* (all designated as Zamindars in general language) as well as the tribal chiefs of the village communities. Both the *Khalisa* revenue collectors and the *Iqtadars,* even though with their separate territorial jurisdictions, had to collect revenues from the above mentioned intermediaries. Throughout the 13th century, the Turkish revenue machinery in the directly administered territories remained par excellence an agency of the revenue collection from the suppressed or half recalcitrant Hindu Rajas, Rais and petty Zamindars. The ease and rapidity with which the Turks occupied North India due to the internecine warfare and lack of military strategy on the part of the Rajput Chiefs by no means put the Turkish government in saddle for the consolidation of the agrarian administration. Of course, in the conquered territories under direct administration, it gave a fatal blow to the authority of the Hindu Rajas to claim any suzerainty over the vassal chiefs for the role of sovereign power was in fact claimed by the Muslim Sultans themselves. Many of the lower-caste chiefs (in certain regions named as Ranas and Thakurs) who had been suppressed to submission by the Rajput Rajas now owed direct allegience to the Sultanate as its Zamindars. The Turkish government had its establishment of military and civil administration in the important cities of the provinces and exerted consistent military pressure on the local chiefs and the petty zamindars for the exaction of the revenues. There were regions in which the Hindu chiefs were completely suppressed while in others the recalcitrant Rajput chiefs, if unable to fight a pitched battle against the Turkish army, would flee and come back to mobilise their resources in the rural areas and put up a defiant attitude for the payment of the revenues. In such regions which were away from the main Turkish military centres, the Rajput clans remained not only politically active but also ran their own administration based on established Hindu notions prevalent in these regions.[87] The picture known from the rhetoric statements of the Persian chronicles for the imposition of the Turkish rule and the conquest of Islam in North India[88] is rather too general, if not superficial. It may be that the Turkish Sultans and the Hindu Chiefs were both animated by the religious fervour for aggression or defence, but there were more important issues at stake, which were essentially political and economic in character. The recalcitrance or open rebellion on the part of the Hindu Chief was mostly actuated by his interests to continue with his political hold in his territory as well as to enjoy the surplus produce of the peasants through the local intermediaries. At times, he still wanted to continue his political and economic hold ever the suppressed lower caste Chiefs who owed him allegience before the Turkish domination. In his recalcitrance against the Muslim state, he was mostly supported by the Brahminical order which enjoyed the surplus produce through the religious revenue assignations and rent free grants of land and at the same time exercised considerable influence on the local landed intermediaries and the general Hindu population. Not only the Hindu Chiefs, at times even the tribal chiefs and zamindars of the converted Muslim communities, evaded payment of land revenue and offered persisting resistance to the Sultanate. There were various lower caste Hindu tribes who had been traditionally recalcitrant against any established authority and even when converted, the Islam continued in their habitual attitude of defiance for the payment of revenues.[89] Thus forced by the political situation in the 13th century and its own administrative expediency, the Turkish government was constrained to continue status-quo in the land revenue practices in the rural territories and to confine its role as the collector of the revenues through the *muqtas* and his subordinates as well as the *Iqtadars*. It is only in the early 14th century during the reign of Alauddin Khalji that the policy of imperialism was aimed not only at an expansion without even consolidation of the rule within the centrally administered territories. For the first time in the history of the Sultanate, the government machinery came in intimate contact with rural areas. The recalcitrant Hindu Chiefs were reduced to submission. The Hindu intermediary zamindars, viz. the *khuta* (petty chiefs) Chaudharies and *Muqaddams* were not only completely subordinated for the payment of the state revenues but even shelved of their usual perquisites (*haquq*) for the revenue collection.[90] They were required to pay revenues on their personal lands which hitherto they had evaded and in the assessment of revenue had unduly imposed heavier demand on the poor cultivators.

In matters of assessment and payment of revenues, as a stern administrator, Alauddin did not permit the slightest distinction to be made between a village *Muqaddam* and a poor ordinary cultivator (metapharically put by Barani as *bilahir, i.e.,* an ordinary peasant or a poor man of the village).[91] It seems from Barani that Alauddin's revenue measures were not extended to all the centrally administered empire but were confined to limited territories.[92] It can be well imagined that the recalcitrant Hindu chiefs and the petty zamindar were reduced to revenue paying classes but it is difficult to understand as to how long could the iron hand of administration deny the legitimate perquisites (*haquq*) of the intermediary zamindars who were responsible for revenue collection. In the medieval agrarian society, a strong government might keep this agency under proper control for the payment of revenues on their own lands and those collected from the peasants but could never run a normal peaceful revenue administration by denying them their usual collection charges and perquisites. Perhaps Barani has given an ever drawn picture about such an administrative measure of Alauddin Khalji. Alauddin Khalji also crushed the tribal converted communities in Mewat (the Meos, popularly known as *Mewatis*)[93] but after him, their submission remained of imperfect nature right till the end of the Delhi Sultanate.[94] Alauddin's measures proved too harsh and short-lived so as to leave any permanent imprint on the agrarian administration. However, according to Barani, this rigid policy was surrendered by Ghyasuddin Tughluk who once again exempted the *khuts* and *Muqaddams* from payment of land revenue on their own cultivated lands and cesses on the grazing lands and allowed them all their legitimate dues provided they collected only legal revenues from the riaya.[95] The Tughluks also made a strong attempt to keep the Hindu Chiefs and the petty Zamindars under control and to maintain contact with the rural areas. It is difficult to say as to what extent they were successful though it seems that they could operate well only within limited territories of the Sultanate.

After the death of Firoz Tughluq, the process of disintegration had already started. Timur's invasion in 1398 A.D. gave a further edge to the political anarchy and in the early 15th century, the independent kingdoms of Malwa, Gujrat, Jaunpur and Khandesh were established. Not only did the Rajasthan chiefs assume complete independence but the Rajput Chiefs within the Delhi kingdom became equally recalcitrant. The active role of the Rajput Chiefs during the 15th century is reminiscent of their attitude throughout the Sultanate period except under Alauddin Khalji. During the rule of the Sayyids and the Lodhis, the Rajput Chiefs of Katehar, Etawa, Chandwar, Bayana and Gwalior remained constantly defiant as regards the acknowledgement of suzerainty and the payment of the revenues or tribute to the Delhi state.[96] This state of affairs continued right up to Mughal occupation of North India. Thus it may be argued that right from the beginning of the 13th century till the end of the Delhi kingdom, the Rajput Chiefs and the petty zamindars in the rural territories of the Sultanate, even when forced to submission, were never reduced to unarmed impotance either by the Turks (excepting the short period of Alauddin Khalji) or the Afghans.[97]

The problem of agrarian administration did not rest simply upon the direct relationship between the Delhi kingdom on the one hand and the Rajput Chiefs and the petty zamindars on the other. A microscopic study of some of the rural regions of North India would show that by and large, the Delhi Sultanate was ineffective in stopping private clannish warfare amongst the Rajput clans themselves, between the Rajput and lower caste Hindu agrarian tribes and above all, Rajputs and Muslim tribal communities who had settled around their territories.[98] The main issues in such conflicts were the disputed villages and parganas settlement, acquisition of agrarian lands or imposition of the zamindari rights on the suppressed clans. At times, a stronger Rajput clan would push out another weaker Rajput clan from certain villages or might drive out a lower caste Hindu tribe or a Muslim tribe from a certain region. It would also forcibly impose its zamindari or Chaudhari rights ever other Hindu or Muslim clans in the settled villages. At times, a powerful Muslim clan overpowered a Rajput clan and acquired a few villages or the zamindari of a disputed pargana. The leit-motif of social action and regional conflict was not essentially religion. Bloody feuds based on clannish rivalry might continue for generations and the disputed villages and the zamindari rights of dominant clan might also change hands after the victory of one clan over another. The revenue collectors of the Sultanate, posted in the provinces, had no options but to accept the regional reshufflings in the agrarian possessions and the zamindari rights provided the state revenues were paid by the zamindars with established authority.

In the independent and semi-Independent states of North India, the traditional Hindu land revenue practices continued. As such, the sub-Himalayan states in the Panjab, Kumaon, Tehri and the Eastern Himalayan ranges and Assam, Rajasthan and some portions of Gujrat and Orissa remained completely uninfluenced by the Muslim concept of administration. Even though some of these regions were invaded by the Muslim armies at some intervals for getting the recognition of the suzerainty of the Sultanate, the local socio-economic and political order remained unchanged. The epigraphic and literary evidence available for the Panjab hill states, and more especially for Rajasthan, throws considerable light on the contemporary Hindu system of land revenue administration during the medieval age before the Mughal occupation of these territories. In both these regions, not only the old Hindu states continued but many a Rajput family fleeing from the plains after the Turkish invasions settled and carved out new states by suppressing the local non-Rajput chiefs and indigenous tribes.[99] They were considerably helped by the geographical features of those regions to withstand the Muslim penetration and were able to continue their independence till Akbar's age. In line with the past Hindu tradition, the Raja asserted a theoretical claim over the land ownership (known as *Prathvipal, Bhupal, Adeshatu*)[100] though in practice, the hereditary and transferable rights of the peasants were fully recognised.[101]

The agrarian lands were possessed and cultivated by the joint families.[102] The Raja claimed complete ownership over the waste lands and jungles and could alienate them as he pleased. The Raja also made both secular and religious assignations of revenues as well as rent free grants of land. In Rajasthan, a sovereign Raja claimed military service and tribute from the vassal chiefs.[103] The process of the establishment of the new Rajput states,[104] subduing the weaker rulers of the Rajput clans as vassal chiefs through mutual warfare,[105] at times fighting the Muslim states of Malwa, Gujrat and Delhi Sultanate,[106] the suppression of the lower caste Hindu chiefs as well Muslim tribal chiefs[107] and communities on the part of the Rajput Rajas for the extension of their own states continued throughout the medieval age till the merger of these territories in the Mughal Empire under Akbar. Within the state, the revenue-free grants (*sasan*) of the villages were made to the Brahmans, the Bhats, the temples and their attendants (*charnas*).[108] The revenue-free grants of the waste cultivable lands were also made to the above mentioned beneficiaries. In line with the old Hindu tradition, these grants were regarded as hereditary and perpetual in nature. The donees possessed the further right of alienation. The assignments of land were made in terms of measured units of land against the cultivable capacity of plough-oxen (*hala*).[109]

On the secular side, small scale grants of villages in *bhum* were made to the *Bhumias* who paid small quit-rent (*bhum barar*) and rendered local service of watch and ward of the villages and other miscellaneous services to the state. Based on the caste system, the caste groups played important role in the socio-economic life of the village communities (*Gosthi, Shersthi, Sangh*) based on clannish character and casteism was well organised.[110] The main agricultural classes were Gujars, Jats and Patels. At times, even Vaishyas and Brahmans[111] cultivated lands. The village headman (*Mandapika*) functioned on behalf of the ruler for the fixation of land revenue assessment and collection of revenues.[112] The village headman worked under other revenue officials of the state.[113] The government always gave due consideration to the elders of the village community and the revenue assignments revenue free grants of waste cultivable land were made in the presence of few village elders.[114] The assessment on the joint family holdings was based on sharing and appraisement (*lata*) methods.[115] The land was often measured through the *hala* method. The exact incidence of state demand for this period cannot be traced but it is clear from the epigraphic sources that a differential scale of state share was based on a detailed classification of the agrarian lands in accordance with the means of irrigation.[116] Besides the land revenue, the state claimed various cesses on the agriculturists. On the whole, the growth of the agricultural produce and the life of the peasantry is stated to have been in a good condition.

References

1. For details of the Arab rule in Sindh, see P. K. Hitti's *History of the Arabs,* (London, 1940). Also A.B.M . Hibibullah; *The Foundation of Muslim Rule in India,* pp. 32-37.

2. For details of the Ghaznwid raids on India and occupation of Panjab, see Muhammad Nazim, *The Life and Times of Sultan Mahmud of Ghazna,* (Cambridge, 1931); Mohammad Habib, Makmud of Ghazna, (Aligarh, 1951), Habibullah, *Ibid.*, P. Hardy, *Mahmud of Ghazna and the Historians* (Historical Research Institute Panjab University, Lahore), 1963, pp. 1-36.

3. At the time of Arab occupation of Sindh (711 A.D.) by Muhammad bin Qasim, Islam was not an orthodox religion and the Arabs were quite receptive to adopt the local ideas and traditions. Also see P. Hardy, *Islamic Sources of Indian Tradition,* ed. S.W. Theodore de Bary. (New York, 1958), pp. 377-78.

4. Of all the historians discussed by P. Hardy vide 'Mahmud of Ghazna and the Historians' no historian refers to the establishment of any regular machinery for the civil administration or any revenue machinery on Turkish lines in the Panjab. On Muhmud's concept of Civil administration, vide P. Hardy (*Ibid.*) pp. 15-16. The Ghaznwids could have, of course, appointed Turkish officers for the collection of tribute or revenues from the local petty chiefs and landed intermediaries.

5. For the evolution of the Muslim theory of taxation, see details vide J. Sachacht, *Origins of Muhammadan Jurisprudence* (Oxford 1950); P. N. Aghnides, Mohammadan Theories of Finance; R.P. Tripathi, *Some Aspects of Muslim Administration,* (Allahabad, 1959), Appendix A, pp. 338-348; K.A. Nizami, *Some Aspects of Religion and Politics in India during the 13th Century,* (Aligarh, 1961), pp. 15-40; I.H. Qureshi, *The Administration of Delhi Sultanate,* (1942), pp. 92-103; *Encyclopaedia of Islam,* (London, 1924), Vol. I.

6. See details vide Nizami, *Ibid.*, pp. 21-33.

7. *Ibid.*, pp. 23, 24; P. Hardy vide 'Delhi Sultanate; in The *Encyclopaedia of Islam,* Vol. II, (London, 1965), p. 272.

8. See details, Colonel Galloway, *Observations on the Law and Constitution of India,* (1825), Vol. II, pp. 26-141 vide I.T.E.C.R. (1925-26) Vol. II, pp. 42-43; P. Hardy, 'Sources of Indian Tradition', pp. 379-80; Tripathi, p. 338.

9. See details vide Aghnides, pp. 203-204, 271, 289, 297, 290, Tripathi, pp. 344-348.

10. *Ain-i-Akbari,* Br. M. Add 7652, fols. 146 b-147 a; tr. Jarrett, Vol. II, pp. 61-62.

11. For the details of Kharaji and Ushri lands, see *Ain* (*Ibid.*). Also, Sir J. N. Sarkar's 'Note on Islamic Land Tax?' tr. Jarret, Vol. II, pp. 60-61; Aghnides, pp. 292, 377; Qureshi, pp. 97-101.

12. For the detailed description of these methods of assessment, see Ain, *Ibid.;* Aghnides, pp. 268, 378; Qureshi, pp. 100-103. Also, compare with

Aurangzeb's *Farman* to Muhammad Hashim vide *Mirat-i-Alumgiri* compiled by Sheik Nizam and others in Arabic, Vol. IV, pp. 371-73.

13. For details, see Sheikh Abdur Rashid, 'Land Revenue Administration During the Sultanate Period'; P. Hardy, 'Delhi Sultanate', *op. cit.*, pp. 266-74. For *Muqta,* p. 272. In place of *muqta,* some scholars have designated the governors or general administrators as *muqti.* See Hibibullah, pp. 252-59; Qureshi, pp. 186-87; Moreland W.H., *Agrarian System of Moslem India,* Appendix B. (Cambridge, 1920), pp. 216-23. As explained later, the term *muqti* was associated with the *iqtadars* and not with the general administrators. The details of the functions given by Habibullah and Qureshi stand for the *muqta* and not *muqti.*
14. P. Hardy (*Ibid.*) for the administrative, military and salary *iqta* etc.; For details of local administration, see Qureshi, pp. 193-97.
15. For the *Iqta* system, see details vide Sheikh Abdur Rashid; O. Hardy and Habibullah quoted in f.n. 13; Nizami, pp. 128-31. Nizami holds the *iqtadar* and the *muqti* as synonymous. It seems that in line with the Persian tradition, the term *muqti* and the *iqtadar* were synonymous (vide A.K.S. Lambton, *Land Lord and Peasants in Persia.* (Oxford, 1953)), pp. 61-64 whereas *muqta* was associated with the governor and an administrator.
16. See Moreland, 'Feudalism? in the Moslem Kingdom of Delhi' *J.I.H.,* Vol. VII, part I, April 1928, Serial 109; pp, 1-8. Also, Moreland *'Agrarian System'* Appendix B, pp. 216-23; Sheikh Abdur Rashid, Habibullah vide f.n. 13 and Nizami vide f.n. 15.
17. See details, Sheikh Abdur Rashid, vide f.n. 13, Tripathi, pp. 251-52.
18. Barni, pp. 61-63.
19. *Ibid.;* also Tripathi, pp. 249-53; Sheikh Abdur Rashid vide f.n. 13; Nizami, pp. 130-131.
20. *Ibid.*, p. 36; Tripathi, p. 251.
21. *Ibid.*, p. 106; *Ibid.*, p. 252.
22. Also see P. Hardy, Delhi Sultanate, *'Encyclopaedia of Islam'*, p. 272; Tripathi, pp. 259, 263.
23. Barani, pp. 283-84; Tripathi, pp. 255-56; Sheikh Abdur Rashid, vide f.n. 13.
24. *Ibid.*, pp. 287, 289, 292, 296; *Ibid.*, pp. 262-63.
25. *Ibid.*, p. 428; *Ibid.*, pp. 268-69.
26. Otte Spies, 'Masalikal absar fi mamalik al amsar' of *Shihabnd Din al Umari,* tr. *M.U. Journal,* Aligarh, March, 1943, pp. 28-29; P. Hardy (vide Delhi Sultanate, *op. cit.*, p. 272) accepts this view. However, may examples of *iqta* grants can also be found in Muhammad Tughluk's reign. See *Barni*, pp. 487-88.
27. Afif (Shams-e-Siraj Afif, *Tarikh-i-Firuz Shahi,* Pers. text. Bibl. Indica), pp. 296-97; P. Hardy (*Ibid.*); Tripathi, p. 290.
28. P. Hardy, 'Delhi Sultanate', *op. cit.*, p. 272.

29. *Ibid.*

30. *Ibid.*, pp. 270-272; Also A. Rahim, The position of the Afghan Chiefs, *Journal of Pakistan Historical Studies,* IV, 2, (April 1956), pp. 116-32; S.M. Imamuddin, The nature of Afghan monarchy in India, *I.C.*, XXXII, 4th Oct., 1958, pp. 268-75; Tripathi, pp. 78-93, 292-93.

31. Barni, pp. 487-88; Tripathi, p. 281.

32. Afif, pp. 500-501; Tripathi, pp. 289-90.

33. Barni, pp. 558-61; Afif, pp. 296-96; Tripathi, pp. 283, 290.

34. Afif, p. 94; Tripathi, pp. 284-85.

35. Barni, pp. 479; P. Hardy, Delhi Sultanate, *op. cit.*, pp. 272-73; Tripathi, pp. 280-81.

36. It is difficult to say as to when the term *Pargana* appeared for the first time though the Persian chronicles mention its existence as an administrative and fiscal territorial unit in the 14th century, (Ibn Battutah, III, pp. 388-89). It seems that the term 'Pargana' may have been vague in some regions even in the pre-Muslim era. However, in the pre-Muslim age, a *Pargana* (or its equivalent in local dialect varying in different regions) denoted the territorial unit of a local chieftainship based on clannish concept. Though etymologically, a Pargana may be associated with the ancient 'gana' (vide Prannath 'Economic History of Ancient India', *J.R.A.S.*, 1929, pp. 53-56), in concept it was not essentially a unit of military establishment of an ancient Hindu state as considered by Prannath (*Ibid.*). A *Pargana* or its preceding equivalent in a local dialect stood for the house (roughly a manner) with this territorial jurisdiction comprising numerous villages under the rule of particular dominant clan and a chief. Similarly, a clannish chief with smaller jurisdiction may rule only a *tappa* comprising a few villages and a tappa was always a smaller until than a *Pargana*. A minute regional study of a particular territory would show that in many cases, the names of the *Parganas* bear the original names of the dominant clans who may have been the pioneer settlers or the conquering clans to impose their names on the conquered house with a territorial jurisdiction. From the 8th to the 12th century A.D., as a consequence of the wars and conquests amongst the non-Rajput and Rajput clans themselves, the suppressed chiefs of the chieftainships usually continued as petty vassal chiefs (designated with various local epithets) along with their houses denoted by the *Parganas*. This process may work on a very large scale where a Hindu kingdom may be generally known to consist of vast territories comprising numerous *Parganas* but underlying such a state should be the *Parganas* representing the suppressed clannish chiefs. This may be well illustrated by the History of the Western sub-Himalayan Hindu states (right from Kashmir to the Panjab Hills states) as well as Rajasthan states. Both these regions remained immune from the Muslim influence before the Mughal age and for both these regions, ample of inscriptional, epigraphic and literary sources for the medieval age are available. For the Western Himalayan States, see Cunningham, *A.G.I.*, Vol. I; *Rajatarangini,* tr. Stein; Antiquities of Chamba State, pp. 120-136; *Chambe Gazetteer,* pp. 171, 280;

Barnes, *Kangra Gazetteer,* 1901 A.D., p. 25; J.B. Lyall, *Kangra Settlement Report,* p. 74. The territorial chieftainships of the suppressed chiefs were usually associated with *tappas* and *kothis.* (Lyall, *Ibid.*). When the Chamba state expanded in the 11th and 12th centuries, the *Kothis (i.e.,* houses) of the suppressed chiefs came to form the headquarters of a *Pargana,* vide *Chamba Gazetteer,* p. 261. The fact that a *Pargana* denoted the house of suppressed clannish chief is equally borne out by *Ain-i-Akbari.* For example, compare the *Ain's Pargana* of some of the West Himalayan states viz Pathan, Dhameri Shahpur, Goler, Kangra, Mau (Sarkar Bari Doab, *Subah* Lahore vide *Ain,* tr. J. II, pp. 322-23), Jammu, Jasotra, Chari Chamba Mankot (Sarkar Rechnan Doab, *Ibid.,* p. 324) with the history of these chieftainship known from the above mentioned sources. Also see J. Hutchison and Vogel, *History of the Panjab Hill States.* (Lahore, 1933), Vol. I, pp. 1-98.

In Rajasthan, Rana Kumba (1433-1468 A.D.) of Guhilet clan conquered Bundi, Chatsu, Malpura, Amber, Narwar, Nariana, Dungarpur, Sohbhar, Didwana, Mandor, Nagor, Ranthambhor, Sirohi, Gagron, Abu, Mandalgarh, Ajmer and Toda. Kirtisthambha inscription dated V.S. 1517/1460 A.D. vide Cunningham, *R.A.I.,* Vol. 23, Plates, 20 and 21; Kumbalgarh Inscription dated V.S. 1517/1460 A.D. vide *J.A.S.B.,* Vol. 55, Part I, pp. 71-72; Rampur Inscription dated v.s. 1496/1439 A.D. vide R.A.S.I. 1907-8, pp. 214-216). Many of these chieftainships changed hands in the later 15th and 16th centuries. Similarly, Jodha of the Rathor clan (1438-88 A.D.) conquered many chieftainships and his son Bika (1472-1504 A.D.) subdued the Pathans, Bhuts and other local chieftainships and founded the principality of Bikaner. (See f.n. 110).

He extended his territories to the southern borders of the Panjab afer having subdued the chiefs of Sirsa, Ladnu, Bhatnar, Bhatinda, Singhana, Rinim Nehar and Pungal. A close comparison of the chieftainships subdued by the Guhilots and Rathors with the list of *Parganas* given in the *Ain* for Ajmer (tr. J. II, pp. 278-82) and sarkars of Hisar Firozah, Sirhind, *Subah* Delhi (*Ibid.,* pp. 298-301) would show that by the Mughal age, they are all shown as the *Parganas.* Based on a thorough study of the medieval history of the clans of Awadh, E.A. Elliot and W.C. Bennet (vide Elliot, *Chronicles of Oonao,* p. 149, n.; Bennet, *A Report on the Family History of the Chief Clans of Roy Barreilly District,* 1870, p. 59; also Bennet; *Gazetteer of the Province of Oudh,* 1877, Vol. I, p. XI, Vol. III, p. 250) arrived at a similar conclusion. They have also shown how the process of conquest by the dominant clans led to reshuffling in some of the *Parganas* wherein at times more than one clan might claim zamindari rights—a *tappa* or a few *tappas* with one clan and the remaining portion of *pargana* within another clan (Elliot, *Ibid.,* pp. 52-55, 65).

37. Also see Moreland, *Agrarian System,* pp. 18-19. The *qasba* is an Arabic word. During the Mughal age, the headquarters of a *Pargana* was known as *qasba.*

38. Ibn Battuta, III, pp. 388-89; Qureshi, pp. 191-92.

39. Barni (p. 501) mentions the division of Deccan in four *Shiqs* under Muhammad Tughluk. Afif (p. 128) refers to the *Shiq* of Hansi which was as large as a province.
40. Also see Qureshi, pp. 190-91; P. Hardy, *'Delhi Sultanate', op. cit.*, p. 273.
41. Moreland, *Agrarian System*, pp. 17-20; Qureshi, pp. 100-103, 106-110.
42. Col. Galloway, *Observations on the Law and Constitution of India*, 1825, Vol. II, p. 26-141. See the detailed discussion on the Shariat, the position of the *zammis* in conquered Muslim countries of Suwas of Iraq, Syria and Egypt as well the land rights of the Hindus during the Muslim rule. Also see Fakhr-i-Mudabbir, *'Abab-u'l-Harb Wa'* Shah Shuja a h', Br. M. Add. 1853, fols. 155 b-158 b vide Nizami, pp. 313-314; also *Kibal Kheraj* by Imam Abu Yusuf (Cairo Edition), pp. 35-39; *Ahkam-us Sultaniya* tr. Urdu (Hyderabad) vide Sheikh Abdur Rashid f.n. 13. The Muslim theory concedes the right of sale, mortgage and bequeathing on the part of the *Zimmis*. For the Sultanate, *Futuhat-i-Firoz Shahi* (Aligarh Edition, p. 20) statement that the owner of the *kharaji* land on conversion to Islam should be subjected to *ushr* payment shows the proprietary rights of both the Hindus and the Muslims on their agrarian lands.
43. P. Hardy, *Delhi Sultanate*, *op. cit.*, pp. 271-272.
44. See my papers 'Nature of Land-Rights in Mughal India', *The Economic and Social History Review*, Vol. I, No. 1, July-Sept. 1963, Delhi, pp. 10-11; Also Nature of Dehat-i-Taaluqa (zamindar village) and the evolution of the Talluqdari System during the Mughal age, *Ibid.*, April-June, 1964.
45. See f.n. 5, 11, 44.
46. Ms. Orient. fol. 3177, Berlin, fols. 44 a-b. This is a transcribed copy of an original Ms. Written in A.H. 380/963 A.D. during the Samanid period. It gives details of the geography, revenue taxation, the methods of assessment and the land rights of the peasants.
47. Also see P. Hardy, 'Mahmud of Ghazna and the Historians', pp. 35-36.
48. The only general statements available on this point are by *Tarikh-i-Fakhr-u'd-din Mubarak Shah* (tr. & edited by E.D. Ross), pp. 33-34; *Futuhat-e-Firoz Shahi*, p. 20 (vide f.n. 44). Also Qureshi, pp. 99, 110, 111, 113, Appendix E, p. 221.
49. *Ibid.*
50. Also Tripathi, p. 287.
51. Barani, p. 287.
52. *Ibid.*, pp. 429-30. The text runs that Ghiyasuddin directed the officers of the Diwan not to make an increase of more than 1/10 or 1/11th on *iqtas* and *wilayats* on surmise or work on the report of spies or enhancement mongers, and that efforts should be made every year and that the revenue be enhanced very gradually. Also Qureshi, pp. 111-112.
53. *Ibid.*, p. 473. *Tarikh-i Mubarak Shahi*, (Bib. Indica), pp. 113-115. tr. P. Hardy vide, Historians of Medieval India, pp. 61-62; Also Tripathi, p. 276. This

has been variously interpreted the by the scholars. Qureshi (p. 112) has considered various possibilities of interpreting it and he finally agrees with Firishtah and Jaji-ud-dabir who hold that the demand was increased by three fold or four fold. In the face of the Barani's text, this view cannot be accepted.

54. On the basis of general statements of *Tarikh-i- Fakhr-ud-din Mubarak Shah* and *Futuhat-i- Firoz Shahi* (vide f.n. 51), enunciating the theoretical Shariat principles, Qureshi's view (pp. 110, 111, 113) cannot be accepted. Also see Sheikh Abdur Rashid, *op. cit.*
55. Barani, p. 429.
56. Afif, p. 94. Afif uses the term bar *hukam-e mushada* for the approximation of the valuation done under Firoz Shah. But the same term was applied to the method assessment based on appraisement. Also see P. Hardy, 'Delhi Sultanate', *op. cit.*, p. 273.
57. Barani, p. 287. Also see P. Hardy, 'Delhi Sultanate', *op. cit.*, p. 273.
58. Ms. Orient. fol. 3177, Berlin, fols. 44 a-b. Also see f.n. 49.
59. *Ibid.*, The text is very clear about the explanation of the *mishat* method of assessment.
60. *Ibid.*
61. See the views of Yajnaval Iya, Brahspati and Vyasa (5th Century A.D.) vide *Dharmakosa,* I, pp. 943, 954, 961.
62. Barani, p. 287, (i) The terms (*Bahukam-i- mishat wa Wafai Biswa*) simply mean that Alauddin resorted to (the method of assessment of) *hukam-i-misahat* and measurement of land (*wafa-i biswa*). That *hukam-i mishat* was a particular method of assessment in contrast to *muqasamat* (sharing method) is clear from the Ms. Orient, fol. 3177 Berlin (vide f. nos. 49 and 64). Here, Barani uses this Turkish term for the first time. The other words '*wa wafai biswa*' simply mean that the assessment on the crops was fixed on the basis of an area unit of a biswa (1/20th of bigha). The method of *hukam-i- misahat* assessment 'ipse facto' involved the measurement process and there was no need to duplicate his language by adding the words *'wa wafai biswa'* as is often thought. If Barani were to imply by these words simply process of measurement they would be rather redundant. But Barani is particular to mention the area-unit (*biswa*) which formed the basis of measurement and assessment for otherwise the procedure of measurement and the concept of indigenous area unit which could have formed the basis of the assessment of the crops may have varied in different regions in which *hukam-i misahat* was enforced. Thus the emphasis by Barani is on the adoption of the process of measurement with biswa (1/20th of a bigha) as the uniform area-unit in the regions in which *hukam-i- mishat* was enforced and the latter involved assessment on all the cultivable lands per unit area (here *biswa*) in the possession of a peasant whether he cultivated the entire holding or left any field uncultivated due to any reason. This would naturally lead to the increase in the State revenues, which was equally to main aim of Alauddin for the introduction of the agrarian measures. Thus Barani's idea is also to show a contrast between the measurement process and *hukam-i mishat* adopted by

Alauddin as against the pre-Alauddin's methods of assessment like the sharing and the Appraisement wherein measurement was not necessary and assessment had to be made only on the cultivated fields.

(ii) Prof. Sheikh Abdur Rashid suggests that '*misahat*' stands for simple process of measurement and '*was fai biswa*' emphasises assessment on individual holdings of the peasants and the share of revenue to be borne by an individual holder in the total demand assessable on the entire village was henceforth to be levied in proportion to his holding. This reforms of Alauddin stood in contrast to the summery assessment of villages in vogue prior to his reign which had resulted in the disproportionate distribution of the revenues on the holdings of the cultivators by the headmen. (Sheikh Abdur Rashid, *op. cit.)* This may be considered as an alternative interpretation. But on the basis of the positive evidence that *hukam-i-mishat* was a Turkish technical term standing for a particular mode of assessment (also p. 273) and also the fact that the methods of assessment prior to Alauddin's reign may have been even sharing and appraisement and not essentially summary assessment of the villages, the first interpretation seems more plausible. (Here I beg to differ with the learned scholar).

(iii) Thirdly, considering '*wa fai biswa*' standing metaphorically for the actual assessment based on individual holdings and '*hukam-i mishat*' as a method of assessement the sentence may also mean that Alauddin resorted to the assessment of '*hukam-i-nishat*' and the assessment was levied in proportion to the actual measured holding in possession with a peasant which avoided all possibilities of exploitation at the hands of the *muqaddams* and the chaudharies. Of all these interpretations the first one seems most feasible. Moreland and Tripathi (*Agrarian System,* Appendix C, pp. 224, 226; Appendix B, pp. 349-50) think that both '*Ba hukam-i mishat*' and *wa wafai-biswa*' stand for the measurement method of assessment and involve duplication of each other. Moreland gives up the interpretation in despair and Tripathi, too, is unable to arrive at any conclusion. Qureshi's (pp. 103-104) interpretation that henceforth the rule of measurement and the yield of the *biswah* were to be adopted does not convey any conviction.

63. Barani, p. 429. Here, Barani uses the term *hukm-i hasli* for the sharing method. Also see P. Hardy, Delhi Sultanate, *op. cit.*, p. 273; Moreland, Appendix C, pp. 224-26; Qureshi, p. 104; Sh. Abdur Rashid, *op. cit.*

64. Tripathi, p. 281.

65. Barni, pp. 305-306. The rest of the state share of the grain produce was to be accepted in kind in the *khalisa qasbas* (parganas) of the Doab and the territories intervening Doab and *Shahr-i Nau* (*i.e.*, Delhi). The state share at half of the grain produce was to be stocked in different places and *qasbas* in the state granaries and was to be transported to the *Shahr* (*i.e.*, Delhi). This shows that the state demand at 1/2 of the produce was enforced only on the grain crops and not on the other crops (like vegetables, sugar cane, betel, melons etc. which were regarded as *jins-i kamil* or cash crops). For varying versions of the above text, see Moreland, pp. 36-38; Tripathi, p. 263; Qureshi, pp. 107-108; Major Fuller, JASB, 1870, p. 26.

66. R.S. Sharma, 'Land Rights in Early Medieval India (800-1200 A.D.), *I.C.O.*, New Delhi, January, 1964.

67. *Tarikh-i Daudi,* Pers. text., Aligarh; Also Tripathi, p. 294.

68. Barani (p. 100), in his didactic approach to have an impact on the state policy of the Sultans, is quite conscious of the role of the peasantry and the landed intermediaries. He comments, "While he (*i.e.*, a petty landed intermediary and peasant) should not be allowed to develop into a rich potential rebel, ruinous exaction on him would cause a falling in agriculture and the consequent impoverishment of the state." Barani (p. 429); he puts it more bluntly in connection with the agrarian reforms of Ghiyasuddin Tughluk who instructed the Diwan's office to see that the Hindu cultivators were not taxed so much that they should be forced to leave their lands and cultivation. Also see Barani's *'Fatawa-i Jahandari'* (tr. Afsar Begum under the title *Political Theory of the Delhi Sultanate,* Kitab Mahal, pp. 26-27; also tr. P. Hardy, *Sources of Indian Tradition,* p. 501-502). This partly accounts for his praise of Balban, Ghiyasuddin Tughluk and Firuz Shah as well the domination of the policies of Alauddin Khalji and Muhammad Tughluk. See details of Barani's account vide P. Hardy, *Historian of Medieval India,* pp. 28-39.

69. *Ibid.*, pp. 40-41. In other respects, he is quite critical of some of Balban's un-Islamic actions. See details vide P. Hardy (*Ibid.*, pp. 30-31).

70. *Ibid.*, pp. 288-289.

71. *Ibid.*, pp. 288-289.

72. *Ibid.*, pp. 429-30. As already explained (vide f.n. 70) that the ***hukam-i hasil*** stands for the introduction of the Sharing method which replaced Alauddin's measurement method. Barani further clarifies the position that in the procedure of assessment of the crops (under the sharing method) due consideration and relief was given in lieu of the natural calamities (*muhadsat*) and the partial failures of the crops (*Bud-e-nabud*). This does not mean that consideration for the partial failure of crops was not given in the measurement method (*hukam-i misahat*). Rather, it was inherent in the latter method. But in actual practice, the revenue officials were not considerable to the peasants on this point. (Also see *Ain-i Bitikchi,* vide *Ain,* Br. M. Add. 7652, fol. 144 a: Kh. S. N.A. 1, pp. 23-24. Thus Barani asserts that with the adoption of the sharing methods, the peasants (*riayas*) were naturally relieved of the uncertainties of the documentation or ascertainment (*quomat*) usually inherent in the measurement method for the new method based upon actual division of the produce would 'ipse facto' take into consideration the partially failed crops due to any calamity. For various other views on the sentences, see Moreland, *Agrarian System,* Appendix C, pp. 227-30; Qureshi, p. 105, Sh. Abdur Rashid, *op. cit.*

73. *Ibid.*, p. 442; Tripathi, p. 286.

74. *Ibid.*, pp. 482-83; Afif, p. 92; Tripathi, pp. 277-78.

75. *Ibid.*, pp. 498-99; Tripathi, pp. 278-79; Qureshi, pp. 122-23. This is reminiscent of the Hindu practice of reclamation and colonisation as a state

enterprise. Compare with *Arthasastra*, tr. R. Shamasastri, (Mysore, 1909), pp. 45-46, 324-27.

76. *Ibid.*, pp. 567-71; Afif, p. 127. Also see details, A.K. Bhattacharya, 'Some Agricultural and Irrigational Activities of the Muslim Rulers in Medieval India', *Indo-Iranica,* IX, 3, 1956, pp. 69-71; also Tripathi, pp. 286-88; Qureshi, pp. 121-23; also my paper on 'Classification of Agrarian Land under Akbar, *I.H.C.*, 1960, part I, pp. 201, 206, f. nos. 52-55.

77. *Ibid.*

78. Afif, pp. 129-31; Also Qureshi, pp. 121-22, Appendix G, pp. 225-27.

79. Qureshi, Appendix H, pp. 228-31.

80. P. Hardy, 'Delhi Sultanate', *op. cit.*, p. 269.

81. Habibullah, *op. cit.*, pp. 250-59; Tripathi, pp. 246-47; Moreland '*Agrarian System*', pp. 71-72; Qureshi (pp. 114-116) does mention the two distinct categories of the Hindu chiefs, those old Hindu chiefs with long tradition of authority in their territories and who remained semi-independent subject to the payment affixed tribute to the Sultanate and those who were reduced to headmen acting as middle men for the realisation of the revenues. Qureshi is not correct in his statement that the latter were reduced to the position of mere headmen and he has failed to realise the scope of role played by these Hindu chiefs in the set up of the Delhi Sultanate and the agrarian economy. Many of these were as old and with long tradition of authority as the independent or semi-independent Hindu chiefs.

82. See details vide Hutchison and Vogal, *History of Panjab Hill States,* vol. I, pp. 1-98.

83. See f.n. 110.

84. C.A. Elliot, *Chronicles of Oonao,* pp. 29-65; W.C. Bennet, *A Report on the Family History of the Chief Clans of Roy Bareilly District,* pp. 1-27.

85. Both faithful and recalcitrant Hindu chiefs find mention in the chronicles. For example, the Chief of Bhatti who helped Firuz Tughluk in escaping from the trap of Khudawan dzadah's house was a suppressed but faithful chief. (Afif, p. 103). The picture becomes still clearer from the chronicles of the 15th and early 16th centuries. Also see P. Hardy, 'Delhi Sultanate', *op. cit.*, p. 271.

86. For example, the Mewatis of Mewat who were suppressed by Alauddin Khalji (vide f. n. 104); For the tribes and clans of Sehwan and Bhakkar in Sindh. see *Mazhar-i Shah Jahani* (17th century work). For want of any direct evidence, it is not possible to have an exact picture of the internal organisation of these clans. It cam be surmised that these clans may have led communal feud and paid revenues to the state through the tribal chiefs.

87. Based on epigraphic evidence, see H.C. Ray, *The Dynastic History of North India,* Vol. I, pp. 544-47, 565; Vol. II, pp. 729-35, 908, 1096-1103, 1132-34. Also P. Hardy, 'Delhi Sultanate', *op. cit.*, p. 271. Based on family documents and the local traditions, see W.C. Bannet, *Gazetteer of Province of Oudh,* Introduction, pp. XXVII-XI, XI iii-XI iv; vol. III, pp. 225-229; *A*

Report on the Family History of the Chief Clans of Roy Bareilly District, pp. 1-27; Also C.A. Elliot, *Chronicles of Oonao*, pp. 29-65.

87. For a brilliant commentary on the medieval historiography, see P. Hardy, *Historians of Medieval India*, Also 'Some Studies in Pre-Mughal Muslim Historiography' vide '*Historians of India, Pakistan and Ceylon*', ed. C.H. Phillips, pp. 115-127.

88. Also see W.C. Bennet's Introduction to *Gazetteer of Province of Oudh*, (vide f. n. 97). It is not possible to accept the thesis of Prof. M. Habib and Nizami that the caste ridden Hindu society, Rajput aristocratic order and the Brahmanical tyranny over the lower castes and the general apathy, if not alienation, of the masses led to the downfall of the Rajput kingdoms against the Turks (Prof. M. Habib's Introduction to Elliot and Dowson's '*History of India as told by its Own Historians*', Aligarh edition, 1952, Nizami, *op. cit.*, pp. 75-88). It is difficult to believe that the Rajput clannish hold and the Brahmanical influence were lost on the general Hindu population of their territories. In fact, despite all social evils of the caste system, the political hold of the Hindu chief and the religious hold of the Brahmanical orders mostly persisted throughout the medieval age. For some reflections and queries on the Turkish and the Hindu society, see P. Hardy, Mohamud of Ghazna and the Historians, *op. cit.*, pp. 35-36.

89. See f. nos. 93-94.

90. Barani, pp. 287-91, gives details of Alauddin's revenue regulations. The term *khot* means a petty chief or a zamindar. (Also Moreland, *Agrarian System*, Appendix C, pp. 225-26). The etymology of *khot* cannot be determined, Tripathi's (p. 256) association of the term with a revenue farmer and with a marathi origin is based on inconclusive evidence. Qureshi (Appendix K, p. 236) considers him to be a village official.

91. Like the *khot*, Barani uses another obscure word in *bilahir* the etymology of which is extremely uncertain. The contrast shown in the *muqaddam* and a *bilahi* points towards the two extreme positions—a muqaddam being a privileged landlord and *bilahir* as an ordinary peasant both being subjected to the state revenue regulations by Alauddin. Also M. Habib vide Introduction to K.A. Nizami, *op. cit.*, p. XX. Moreland considers him a low-caste menial in a village (*Agrarian System*, Appendix C, p. 225). Tripathi, p. 258 takes *balhar* to be a washerman and Elliot and Dowson (vol. III, pp. 179-83) associate *balhar* with a scavenger of a village.

92. Barani (p. 288) states that these regulations were extended to all the villages around the capital, the towns and districts in the Doab from Biyana to Jhayin, from Palam to Deopalpur and Lahore. This shows that the regulations were not enforced in the West Panjab, Sindh, Gujrat, lower Doab, Gorakhpur, Awadh, Bihar and Bengal. Also see details vide Tripathi, p. 265.

93. *Ibid.*

94. *Babur Nama*, tr. Beveridge, II, p. 577.

95. Barani, pp. 429-30.

96. Also see. Hardy, 'Delhi Sultanate', *op. cit.*, p. 270.

97. *Ibid.*, pp. 271-72.

98. For details, see C.A. Elliot, *op. cit.*, pp. 29-72; W.C. Bannet, *Gazetteer of the Province of Oudh*, Introduction, pp. XXXV-XXXIII; *'A Report on the Chief Clans of Roy Bareilly District'*, pp. 1-27, 51-53.

99. For Panjab Hill States, See Hutchison and Vogel, *op. cit.*, vol. I & II especially Introduction and Historical Survey, vol. I, pp. 1-98. In Rajasthan, the Guhilots of Mewar, the Kachwahas of Amber and the Bhatti's of Jaisalmer had pre-Muslim states. But the Rathor state of Marwar was established near about the middle of the 13th century and Bikaner was established by a descendant of the Marwar family towards the seventh decade of the 15th century. For the details of the establishment of the Marwar state and Bikaner by the Rathors, see Tod. I, pp. 153-169; Ohja, Jodhpur, vol. I, pp. 146-155.

100. For Panjab Hill States, Hutchison and Vogel, *op. cit.*, Vol. I, pp. 10, 21, 28-29, 62-72, 269-77, 283 based on archeological and epigraphic sources vide Cunningham, *R.A.S.I.;* A.G.I. Antiquities of Chamba state and District Gazetteers. A revenue free village assignment was known as *Sasan.* For Rajasthan, *I.A.*, Ingoda inscription 1-2, (Sanskrit) dated, V.S. 1190 (1133 A.D.), vol. VI, pp. 55-56; Cunningham, *R.A.S.I.* Chitor Vijayastamba, commonly known as kirtistambha inscription (Sanskrit) dated 5th Margashirsha (dark half) V.S. 1517/3rd December, 1460 A.D., vol. 23, Plates 20-21; O.D.R. Udaipur, copper plates no 1725 and 866 (Sanskrit) dated V.S. 1589/1532 A.D.and V.S. 1593/1536 A.D. respectively.

101. *Ibid.*, The owners of land other than the religious grantees had also the right of mortgage and transfer.

102. *Ibid.*

103. Ohja, *Udaipur,* II, pp. 869-991; *Jodhpur* II, pp. 834, 847-48; *Bikarner,* II, pp. 615-751.

104. For example see the *History of Rathors of Jodhpur and Bikaner* (vide f.n. 99), *Udaipur Rajya ka Itihas.* (Ajmer, 1925), *Jodhpur Rajya ka Itihas.* (Ajmer, 1941), *Bikaner Rajya ka Itihas.* (Ajmer, 1940).

105. See inscriptional evidence vide f. n. 36; The History of Rajasthan states are full of such instances (vide Ohja's *Udaipur, Jodhpur* and *Bikaner;* Vir Vinod and Tod).

106. Vir Vinod, Vol. I, pp. 338-42; Ohja, *Udaipur,* I, pp. 327-30, Tod I, pp. 171-175.

107. The suppression of the Meena race by the Kachhwahas of Amber persisted throughout the medieval age. For the suppression of Bhils by the Mewar chiefs, (*Ibid.*, pp. 180-181); the suppression of the local chiefs of Sirsa, Ladnu, Bhatner, Bhatinda, Singhana, Rini, Nohar and Pungal (all towards Southern Panjab) by the Rathors of Bikaner. (vide Ohja, *Bikaner,* I, p. 96); the expansion of Bhatti's of Jaisalmer towards Multan and Sindh vide Amarkot inscription (Sanskrit) dated 3rd Vaishakha (bright half) V.S. 1561, 16th May 1504 A.D., *Jain Inscriptions,* III, no. 2487, p. 119; Tod II, p. 180.

108. Ajmer Museum, copper plate dated 15th Asadha (dark half) V.S. 1494/31st August 1437 A.D. makes a revenue free grant (Sanskrit). A rent free grant of land was known as dolika (vide *E.I.*, Bijoliyan inscription dated 3rd of Phalgun, dark half, V.S. 1226/5th February, 1170 A.D., vol. XXVI, pp. 90-106.

109. O.D.R. Udaipur, Thakrada plate (Sanskrit) dated V.S. 1212/1155 A.D. (unpublished); plate no. 1725 (Sanskrit) dated V.S. 1589/1532 A.D.

110. Jain Inscriptions, Osia Inscription dated 5th Phalguna (bright half) V.S. 1245/4th Febuary, 1188 A.D. vide vol. I, no. 807, p. 198; Parashwanath temple inscription Jaisalmer dated V.S. 1415.1358 A.D. vide vol. II, pp. 18-23; Also Bhandarkar Report, 1904-5 and 1905-6 A.D. no. 49, p. 93.

111. E.I., Kumbhalgarh inscription dated V.S. 1517-1460 A.D., vol. XXI, 1931-32; Slabs 4-5, p. 217; O.D.R. Udaipur copper plate no. 285 dated V.S. 1494/1437 A.D.

112. Jain Inscription, I, no. 389, p. 207. Nodol copper plate dated V.S. 1218/1161 A.D.

113. E.I, Vol. XXVI, p. 112. Bijoliyan rock inscription dated V.S. 1226/1169 A.D. puts the name of the revenue official as *Pratigrahi.*

114. O.D.R. Udaipur, copper plate no. 285, dated 11th Magh (bright half) V.S. 1494-1437 A.D. A grant of ten *halas* of land by Maharana Kumbha in village Kheroda in the presence of Purohit Bhokha and Shah Shahana, the two elders of the village.

115. O.D.R. Udaipur, no. 866, Bokhrahedi grant dated 15th Sravana (Dark half) V.S. 1593/1536 A.D., no. 193 (3) dated V.S. 1785/1728 A.D., Tod I, p. 48.

116. Ajmer Museum, Annual Report, 1914, Pratapgarh inscription (sanskrit) dated V.S. 1003/946 A.D. mentions irrigation of water by leather bucket (*koshvakaka*); Jain inscription vol. I, no. 959, pp. 266-67, Vaghina inscription dated 10th Vaishakha (bright halg) V.S. 1359/8th April, 1302 calls the well irrigated land *dimdu.*

Chapter 3

Farid as a Jagirdar or the Shiqdar of his Father's Jagir—Some Important Extracts from Original Sources

Farid asked his father to give him full powers in the management of the jagir as he might treat the workers harshly if they did not obey him and most of the workers were his father's friends. (*Tarikh Sher Shah,* p. 20).

He gave his views also that he would encourage cultivation and prosperity as both could depend on justice. He would follow a state policy which will bring density of population and prosperity to the jagir. He would ask the workers to leave oppression, if they did not, he would take them to task to give a lesson to others (*T.S.S.*, p. 23), as oppression and cruelty to the subjects forces them to leave the place and these things lower the revenue and empty the state treasure (*T.S.S.*, p. 25).

As he came to the Parganas, he gathered all the Mukadams, argiculturists, Patwaris and the soldiers and gave a speech; "Mian Hussain has assigned the management of the parganas to me. I shall try to increase the produce and the revenue and it will profit you and bring credit to me. (*T.S.S. MS. S,* p. 26). You are to recover the land revenue from the agriculturist whatever settled with them at the time of harvest and not to go back on your promise and forbid your Amils and soldiers from oppression upon the cultivators. They should not be greedy to their produce as it brings desolateness to the parganas and a bad name to the ruler (*T.S.S. MS. S,* p. 28) and the revenue of the next year will also lower down. If from this onwards, I come to know that somebody has even taken a straw of grass from the agriculturist by oppression or aggression, I shall take him to task. I shall not discriminate between my near ones and others and will be harsher to near ones than others". He then told the agriculturists to increase the produce and revenue and that he would not take any thing from the soldiers. (*T.S.S. MS. S.*, p. 29).

He then turned to the subjects and said, 'I give the choice in your hands to accept any one of the two ways of assessment—fixation by way of jarib or on past records.

Prof. P. Saran criticises Mr. Moreland for his views that Sher Khan gave the choice of assessment to the agriculturist and says it is wrong and that Moreland's reading of Abbas Sarwani's text is wrong.

He, on page 141 of the journal, says:—

"It is really incomprehensible how Mr. Moreland could discover in an option for the mode of assessment instead of the mode of payment".

Prof. Saran says, I hold that Sher Shah from the very first, even in his administration of the jagir of his father adopted the system of measurement in assessment of land revenue and secondly that he offered to the peasants option in the mode of payment and not in the mode of assessment.

The words of the *Makhzan-i-Afghana manuscript* clearly show that the choice was for assessment and not for payment and perhaps Dr. Saran is wrong to assume the choice of payment.

S.C. Misra, in his article in the Indian history Congress, 15th Session 1952, also says, "Though Sher Shah might have had a decided preference for the system of measurement, he did not press his choice except in areas where the system could be worked without handicapping the cultivator. The peasant enjoyed the freedom of choosing any of the prevalent methods of assessment though his rights over his land were clarified and the field mapped. He was freed from the vexatious extortions of the Muqaddams and other petty functionaries, the Amin contacting him directly to assess his revenue according to the system he preferred."

According to the words of the manuscript, he gave the choice of assessment to the agriculturist and gave them the deed paper in which was written the state due and fixed the *Muhasalana* and *Greebana* fees also there and then and gave orders that he would himself investigate into everything.

He ordered the functionaries not to leave dues pending which will create enmity between the subjects and the ruler and that they should be lenient in assessment but strict at the time of payment. *(Naimat Ullah's Makhzan-i-Afghana* MSS, p. 207). After this, he turned towards the rebellious Zamindars who did not present themselves. He sent orders to the Amils of his father to prepare two hundred horses. He investigated the number of young men in the two parganas from the Afghans who had no jagir and then said to them, I shall give you pay and robes according to the rules of Mian Hasan and whatever you give, provisions, clothes or money from the rebellious zamindars, will be yours. I shall have nothing. He who shows valour will be rewarded by Mian Hussan, jagir and horse through my efforts, (*T.S.S.*, p. 33). Thus he reised a considerable force. He got horses from the public on loan with the promise of returning back after the action (*T.S.S.*, p. 34).

He then attacked the rebellious zamindars. He took their horses, men, women, money and belongings into possession. He gave money and cattle to the soldiers and imprisoned their women and children. He sent orders to the Muqaddams to give the dues or their ladies and children will be sold and won't allow them settling again. When the Muqaddams heard these words, they asked his forgiveness and promised not to do so again (*T.S.S.*, p. 36). Sher Khan asked them to pay their dues and present those who will stand a surety for them. Thus he got the dues and released them on bail. He then turned to the Zamindars who had taken to robbery, theft and lawlessness. He ordered the people to ride a horse if they had any and to come on foot if do not have any horse. Half of the men should remain engaged in cultivation and half should come to him.

When the soldiers and the subjects presented themselves, he marched towards the villages of the rebels. He erected a *kacha* fort at a distance of one *Kroh* from the village and ordered his men to clear off the forest. The riders were ordered to surround the villages, kill the men, capture their ladies and children, bring their cattle, not to allow them cultivate their land, to waste their crops and not to let any help come from any side and anything go out of the village and to watch day and night. The footmen were ordered to clear off the forest. When the forest was cleared, he marched from one village to the other. The rebels were forced to ask forgiveness through their vakil. Sher sent words, "I do not accept your appeal. There is war between you and us and one of us will be victorious. The rebels entreated much and presented much money but Sher Khan did not accept and said to himself: "These rebels have the principle. First they show resistance to the ruler. If they find the ruler weak, they do not leave rebellious attitude and if they find him strong, they ask forgiveness and whenever they find a chance they again take to evil deeds. I shall uproot them fully and will settle others in their homes." (*T.S.S.*, p. 39).

He, therefore, killed them all, took possession of their belongings and sold their ladies and children. When other rebels heard of this action; they took a vow not to rebel or take to robbery. All praised Sher Khan except his step mother. (*T.S.S.*, p. 45).

Other Reforms

He ordered the village authorities to keep the welfare of the subjects in view and to prefer it to all other things.

He abolished different kinds of taxes upon the agriculturists and thus relieved them from the heavy burdens under which they were collapsing day by day.

They were to pay nothing over and above the land revenue.

He appointed a public relation officer in every village whose duty was to look after the welfare of the villages. He was to provide full facilities to the villagers and to show full justice in their cause. (*Daulati-i-Sher Shah* by Hasan Ali Khan, M.I.Q. Journal of Aligarh University, 1950).

Result of His Reforms

India was passing through a great revolution at the time. The life and security of the people was in peril. The Afghan Government was collapsing and the Mughals were forcing their way into this big country. The news of Sher Khan's administration reached far and wide. Finding peace and tranquility, one thousand villagers came from other parts of the country and settled on his lands. They took to cultivation and thus land revenue was increased much. (*Daulat-i-Sher Shahi* by Hasan Ali Khan).

Chapter 4

Land Revenue Administration Under Sher Shah

No other phase of Sher Shah's career has attracted so much attention as his land revenue administration and yet none other is as controversial. In fact, his land revenue system is a continuation of the system as he had found it. His reign does not represent any administrative haitus. There was no basic break with the past, nor was anything new introduced except that he picked and chose all that was of permanent value in the system. He was, as Dr. Tripathi aptly remarks, more of a reformer and less of an innovator. Nevertheless as any stern rule naturally would, his reign witnessed radical modification in several aspects of that system resulting in the improvement of the condition of the *Raiyats,* the efficiency of the administration and betterment of the financial conditions of the state.

Sher Shah, in fact, was a born administrator. In the Indo-Muslim history, very few rulers had such comprehensive understanding of the land revenue affairs as he had. As *Shiqdar* of the Jagir of his father in Sahasram[1] and Khawaspur Tanda;[2] he got experience and training, which he improved upon later. The direct and intimate contact with the cultivators as well as the officials of the Paraganas had afforded abundant personal knowledge and experience of the technical details of the land revenue administration. Though the Afghan sources, make a pointed reference to Sher Shah's (Farid's) land revenue reforms as the administrator of his father's Jagir, they are not as explicit about the system as it finally evolved. His earlier experiments, therefore, are the basis of his system, which he established later and a careful analysis of the same gives us an insight into his ideals and achievement in this field. Hence, any careful study of the final development must determine and incorporate the two-fold sources, namely, as the *Shiqdar* and as the *Sultan.*

In regard to Sher Shah's land revenue system, various points of controversy are raised by Moreland, Qanungo, Saran and Quershi who defend or contradict each other mostly on the basis of their interpretation of passages in *'Tarikh-i- Sher Shahi'* of Abbas Sarwani, *'Makhzan-i-Afghana'* of *Niamat Ullah* and *Ain-i-Akbari'* of Abul Fazl. There is no contemporary Afghan authority giving details of administration excepting some fragments of a manuscript of *'Tawarikh-E-Daulat-E-Sher Shahi'* by Hasan Ali Khan. In spite of this general paucity, an accurate interpretation of the technical terms employed either in the Afghan references or the *Ain* enable us to understand afresh and correctly the whole pattern of land revenue system and assess his own distinctive contribution.

The system needs to be discussed under the following outlines.

I. Methods of assessment with the improvements effected by Sher Shah therein and in the modes of survey

II. The Demand as the share of the State under him

III. The object of Sher Shah's revenue administration and the measures initiated by him to realise the same

IV. The agency for revenue collection

V. (a) The continuation of Sher Shah's administration upto Akbar's reign

(b) The extent of the indebtedness of Todar Mal and Akbar to Sher Shah's system

VI. Modification or improvement of the system by his successors

The Methods of Assessment

According to the evidence available, two methods of assessment—the *Gallabakshi* and the *Jarib*— appear to have been in use in the time of Sher Shah.

I. Gallabakshi

This was based on the division of the gross produce of the crop (when ripe) between the cultivator and the State according to the stipulated share of the latter.[3] This method had been in existence since the Hindu times and there is conclusive evidence to show that it was one of the systems in vogue when Farid was appointed the *Shiqdar* of the Jagir at Sahasram and Khawaspur Tanda. Both Niam Ullah[4] and Abbas Sarwari[5] quote at length Farid's words on his taking over the administration of the said Pargana and when he addressed the soldiers, the *Ryots,* the *Muqqadams* and other officials. He enjoined the soldiers not to oppress the *ryots* and to recover the land revenue from the agriculturist on the basis of the terms settled with them at the time of harvest. Then turning towards the *Raiyats* he said, "Today the choice rests with you. If you like, I will have the cultivated lands measured and the land revenue assessed on the basis of measurement, or if you prefer, I will fix the demand against you on the basis of the cultivated land (with due regard) to the condition of the crops. Some of the *ryots* agreed to the method of *Jarib* and others undertook to pay the *Kharaj* and (both the groups) gave their written deeds of acceptance".[6] Thus Farid gave the option to the peasantry to either accept the assessment on the basis of measurement or to agree to the method of sharing based upon the division of the produce.

The latter option is the same as *Gallabakshi* or division of produce, which implies fluctuating assessment contingent upon inspection of crops and the actual division in proportion to the shares of the State and the cultivator.

(a) This method would take into consideration the success or the failure of crops,[7] the land revenue being levied with due regard to the condition of the crops.

(b) In this system, there is no need of measuring the cultivated fields.

(c) This is based upon assessment either by apprisement or by *Batai.*

(d) The term *'Kharaj'* stands for the revenue in kind.

That Farid offered the choice to the agriculturists between the above two methods of assessment is an interpretation not acceptable either to Saran[8] or Qanungo[9] though Moreland fully accepts it.[10] The first two writers hold that the choice offered was not between the methods of assessment but the mode of payment of land revenue by the *Ryots* who could either pay in cash or kind. Saran holds this view on the basis of Abbas Sarwari, arguing that Moreland's reading not of Abbas Sarwari's text is not correct. It is really incomprehensible how Moreland could discover in them an option as to the method of assessment, instead of mode of payment.[11] Dr. Saran concludes that "Sher Shah, in his administration of the Jagir of his father, adopted the system of measurement in assessment of land revenue, and secondly, that he offered to the peasants option in the mode of payment and not in the method of assessment.[12]

But these foregoing scholars have relied only on a single text of Abbas Sarwari though differing in its interpretation. Both Moreland and Saran have quoted only part of the statement. Farid is reported to have made without taking into consideration the entire text of the offer made by him. Abbas gives a very detailed account of what Farid said on this occasion.[13] On reaching the Pargana, Farid sent for all the *Muqqadams,* the peasants, the *Patwaris* and the soldiers.[14] He first addressed the soldiers thus: "Mian Hassan has assigned the management of the Pargana to me.[15] I shall try (a) to increase the produce and the revenue and it will profit you and bring credit to me.[16] You are to give up oppressing the *ryots* and (b) you should recover the land revenue from the peasants on the basis of whatever is settled with them at the time of the harvest and forbid your *Amils* and soldiers, from oppressing the cultivators.[17] For if the ruler himself, alongwith the *Amils* and the soldiers becomes greedy at the time of the collection of the land revenue, it brings desolation to the *Pargana*, a bad name to the ruler and the revenue of the ensuing year would dwindle.[18] It from this time onwards, I come to know that somebody has taken a straw of grass from the agriculturists by oppression or aggression, I shall take him to task.[19] The *Ryots* should take to the enhancement of the agriculture and that I would not accept anything from the soldiers.[20] After he was free from the talk to the soldiers, he turned to the *Ryots* and said, "Today I leave the choice to you", whereupon some of the *Ryots* accepted the *Jarib* measurement as the basis of assessment while others undertook to pay in kind (division of the produce).[21] Having accepted their consent, he got written agreement from the *ryots.* He also fixed the *Jaribana* and the *Mahaslana* and the rate of rations payable to the collectors. Then he addressed the *Muqqadams,* "I would, of course, come to know of those among you who would opress the *ryots.* I have fixed the *Jaribana* and *Mahaslana* and the rations for the collection. If you take from the *ryots* more than this, I would not give you your complete emoluments at the time of the settlement with you; and you should also realise that if you remain honest and keep the proper accounts, I would even allow you the actual expenditure incurred (for collection) to be realised from the *ryots.* You should deposit the amounts (collected) in the treasury—the realisations of the *Kharif* and the *Rabi* within the respective seasons for the arrears of the treasury would not only lead to the desolation of the *Pargana* but would also cause enmity between the *Raiyat* and the *Amils.* The officer (here the *Muqqadam* and the *Amils* etc.) should also be lenient at the time of measurement (if assessment is by measurement) and considerate and careful at the time of the inspection of the crops (if the assessment is based on the division of the produce of the crop) but should not at all be indulgent towards the *ryots* at the time of collection. He should realise all the revenue and if he thinks that the *ryots* are reluctant to pay, he should give them an exemplary punishment so that others also should know it and that they should not repeat the same.[22]

The option by Farid was accepted by the *Raiyat.*[23] Some accepted the *Jarib* which was based on the measurement of the cultivable land; fixation of the demand on the basis of measurement per bigha of land; and payment either in cash or in kind at a fixed rate per bigha. Others preferred to pay in kind, *i.e.,* by the division of the produce of the crop, *i.e.,* through the system of *Batai* or by appraisement.

It is evident that choice in regard to the mode of payment is not offered here but a discretion is given to the cultivator to accept assessment on the basis of measurement of the area in cash or in kind or (ii) assessment by the actual division of the produce of land, implying, of course, payment in kind. Hence, the choice offered was in regard to the two modes of assessment.

All the same, the option is for the acceptance of either of the modes of assessment and not for the payment either in cash or kind.

The system of the division of the produce, as explained above, is the same as described by *Makhzan-i-Afghana* as one based on the inspection of the crops and division thereafter. Though the words and the technical terms used by the writers of *Tufa-i-Akbari Shai* and *Makhzan-i-Afghana* are different, the meaning is the same. They do not contradict each other.

Moreover, in the foregoing passage, Farid directs his officials to recover the revenue from the agriculturists on the basis of whatever is settled with them at the time of the harvest. This settlement at the time of the harvest is possible only in the method of division of the produce, *i.e., Batai.* Such settlement at the time of harvest is not possible in the *Jarib* system where the assessment is fixed on the sown areas long before the crops are ripe. If, as according to Saran, only one method of assessment, *i.e., Jarib* was enforced by Farid, this passage of Abbas is rendered inexplicable. All this, on the other hand, rather confirms the prevalence of *Gallabakshi* as alternative to the *Jarib* method in Farid's Jagir.

In fact, Elliot's translation of Abbas, as adopted even by Qanungo, has caused much controversy. It runs thus: "Turning to the peasantry, he said: 'This day I give you your choice as to the mode of payment. Do whatever is most advantageous to you in every possible way. Some of the headmen asked for written agreements for a fixed money rent (*Jarib*) while others preferred payment in kind (*Kismat-i-Ghalla*).[23] Accordingly, he gave out leases and took agreements from the peasants. Elliot's Manuscript may have contained the words 'Mode of Payment' but they cannot be traced in any other available manuscript.[25] Moreover, the translation of *'Jarib'* as 'fixed money rent' is absolutely incorrect for in the method of *Jarib, i.e.,* assessment based on measurement, the land revenue could be fixed both in cash and in kind. The payment in cash was just one of the modes of payment, the other being payment in kind. Hence, Elliot's version of the passage and consequently his interpretation cannot be accepted. Qanungo's acceptance of this translation is unacceptable for the same reason.

Saran translated the passage of Abbas as "Some of the cultivators agreed to *'Zaribs'* (*i.e.,* fixing of rent by measuring the area under cultivation. This would mean a money commutation, others agreed to an actual division of the crops. Farid took written *Qabuliyats* signed by the *Ryots*[26] ..,......Saran interprets the same passage at another place as "this day I give you the choice: Some peasants chose *Zabt,* while others preferred sharing".[27] Not only Saran's translation of *Jarib* (or *Zarib* as he used it) is incorrect, he is even contradictory in his interpretation.[28] His definition of *Jarib* so far as fixing of rent by measuring the area under cultivation is correct and also his statement that here money commutation is meant is true only to the extent that commutation was at the market rate if the revenue was to be realised in cash. Saran has even identified the method of *Jarib* of Farid's Jagir with the *Zabt* based on the fixed payment in cash. Saran's arguments are weak and unconvincing. He presumes that Sher Shah was the best judge of what was good for the peasants as far as the methods of assessment were concerned and made the choice on their behalf. He left to the peasants only the choice as to the mode of payment. This is a weak but noble attempt to give credit to Sher Shah for what he did not deserve.

All this belaboured psychological study of Farid's mind and the various arguments advanced by Saran are hypothetical. No single system of assessment, however good and beneficial, was ever forced upon the peasantry by any Government against their wishes in medieval times and even Sher Shah later had to accept the force of custom. Even in Akbar's reign, when *Zabti* was so much favoured, in a *Zabti* province, it was the discretion of the cultivator to ask for the system of *Ghallabakshi* if he disliked the *Zabti* method.[29]

Apart from these controversies and conclusions based upon the version of Abbas Sarwari, the version of *Makhzan-i Afghana,* as already examined, is very definite. What Sher Shah offered to the peasants was the choice as to the method of assessment and not as to the mode of payment.

II. The Measurement System

The second method of assessment in Sher Shah's time was that of assessment based on the measurement of the land. This system was known in the ancient Hindu times and later the Muslims. It had been in force in the time of Ala-ud-Din Khilji but appears to have fallen into disuse. All the Afghan sources and most of the later chronicles credit Sher Shah for introducing the practice of measurement of land, though in fact it was only the revival of Ala-ud-Din's system.[30]

Abbas Sarwari says that Sher Shah ordered that land be measured every year and land revenue be assessed on that basis so that the *Muqqadams* and *Amils* should not be in a position to oppress the *Ryots* and that before Sher Shah's time, yearly measurement (of the land) was not in vogue whereas a *Qanungo* in every *Pargana* used to estimate the (total) assessment on the average of past and present yields.[31]

Hasan bears testimony to the fact that all lands of the dominion, cultivated and uncultivated, were measured.[32] This task was accomplished by Ahmad Khan Tangi with the help of the expert Hindu staff of the Brahmans. Regular registers (*Khata*) were prepared which contained the names and the titles of the owners (the occupants) and in which was recorded the measurement of all arable and other pieces of land. This was one of Sher Shah's unique achievements that regular records (*Jama bandies; Khata Khatauni* and *Khasaras*) were prepared for all kinds of land, barren or arable, and under actual cultivation together with the names of the occupants of the various holdings of all the *Parganas* of the Empire. This stupendous task was accomplished by Ahmad Khan Tangi with the help of the Hindu revenue experts as most of the records at that time were kept in Hindi.[33] The measurement of the arable land was an essential feature of the *Jarib* system and necessary for the classification of the land as arable land may not be fit for tillage continuously. Such measurement of the arable land under actual cultivation would be of great help in fair assessment of revenue in regions where *Ghallabakhsi* or *Kankut* were the prevalent systems.[34]

Sher Shah had introduced measurement of the land even in his father's Jagir as is clear from the option that he extended to the cultivators for assessment either by measurement or by sharing.[35] But when he became the Sultan, the measurement of the land of the whole Empire became more or less a general practice and only in exceptional cases did he exempt a territory from measurement, e.g., in Multan, where Haibat Khan on suppressing the rising of the Biluches received instructions from Sher Shah to observe the custom of the *Langhas,* and not to measure that land but to take a share of the produce.[36] The assignment of the Jagirs and religious grants was done strictly on the basis of measurement, particularly as certain cases came to the Sultan's notice that *Inamdars* and religious persons had got more land than they were entitled to hold by bribing the *Amils* since the time of Sultan Ibrahim.[37] Sher Shah henceforth issued the *Farmans* directly to the *Shiqdar* of the *Pargana* who determined the area of the assignment after measurement and demarcation, (*i.e.,* the *Chakbandi*).[38] Whenever any cultivator had to be compensated for the damage to the crops through the movement of the army, the compensation would be assessed by the *Amin* on the basis of the measurement of the area of the damaged crops.[39]

Abul Fazl, while describing the *Illahi Gaz* incidently, refers to the introduction of the method of *Zabt, i.e.,* based on the measurement of the land with the help of *Gaz* more or less as a general practice.[40] All chroniclers, Afghan and others, have highly praised Sher Shah for the general measurement of land for determining accurately the state demand and protecting the cultivators against fraudulent practices on the part of the revenue officials.

The method of *Jarib* was not rigidly and uniformly applied by Sher Shah throughout his territories though Moreland is inclined to believe this on the basis of the testimony of Abul Fazl who speaks of the substitution of the methods of (a) *Ghallabakshi* and (b) *Muqtei* by (c) *Zabat* in the time of Sher Shah.[41] In fact, to interpret it as Moreland does, that Hindustan passed completely from the system of *Ghallabakshi* and *Muqtei* to that of *Zabt* (or *Zabti*) is not correct. Abul Fazl does not imply that the *Ghallabakshi* and the *Muqtei* were completely abolished but that the system of measurement of land was mostly preferred and generally prevailed. Moreover, there is no reference in any of the chronicles that Sher Shah completely abolished the system of *Ghallabakshi* and *Muqtei*. Apart from Sher Shah's instructions to Haibat Khan, Governor of Multan, other references can also be found to the effect that *Ghallabakshi* was in practice in Sher Shah's time.[42] Moreover, the *Ain* in the instructions to the *Amal Guzar,* clearly mentions the existence of systems other than that of measurement *i.e.,* the *Kankut* and the *Ghallabakshi* and Abul Fazl has explained these at length.[43] Abul Fazl does not mention anywhere that these were reintroduced in the time of Akbar. On the other hand, while describing the history of the Provinces, he clearly states the prevalence of (a) the *Ghallabakshi* or (b) the *Kankut* or (c) *Nasq* in some of the provinces since old times as customary.[44] It is doubtful if Sher Shah had any intention of uprooting such entrenched systems. It was not possible either to do so in the course of five years, *i.e.,* to substitute the prevailing system by that of measurement in toto.

The Nature of the Measurement System

As to the nature of the measurement system introduced by Sher Shah, certain writers are inclined to the view that in order to assure accuracy of the respective shares of the State and the cultivator, the cultivated land would be measured after the crops were sown and the apportionment between the State and the cultivator fixed.[45] This is simply *Batai* method.[46]

Though measurement was adopted for this aspect of the sharing, it worked out to a more developed stage with Sher Shah. It involved (a) measurement of the cultivated land, (b) fixation of land revenue upon the cultivated areas, regardless of the kind of crops grown, and whether the crops were grown or not and whether they matured or failed. This implies the fixed assessment, (c) fixation of the land revenue per bigha as the assessment was based upon measurement and fixation of the rate of the entire field thereupon, (d) It necessarily follows that the fixation per bigha would, in turn, be based upon the average yield of the various crops over a number of previous years. Ordinarily, it would be done on the basis of the past few years' records, but if no records were available, it would be made after making enquiries from the *Qanungo* or other officials of the villages.[47] (e) The fixation would imply assessment in kind per bigha or in cash after commutation in accordance with prevailing market rates. Such fixed nature of the *Jarib* system is evident from the option given by Sher Shah (Farid) in his father's Jagir because the system of inspection and the division of the crops with regard to *Bud-o-Nabud,* which is in fact a fluctuating assessment, is evidently in contrast to the fixed system of the *Jarib.*[48]

Elliot has interpreted the assessment on the basis of *Jarib* as 'the fixed money rent' in contradistinction to the payment in kind.[49] But his interpretation is not free from objection as the fixation could be both in cash and kind whereas the former was just one of the two modes of payment. The term 'fixed rent' would convey the correct meaning as the fixation of assessment per bigha would primarily be in kind unless some schedule of cash assessment rates (*Dasturulamal Naqdi*)[50] were framed on the basis of the past rates to which there is no reference relating to Sher Shah's time. Of course, the fixation per bigha in kind could be commuted into cash on the basis of the current rates every year and rent could be fixed for the whole holding upon this basis.

That payment in the *Jarib* method was in cash has been inferred from the oft-repeated sentence of Abbas that the revenue (*Zar*)[51] was taken on the basis of the yearly measurement. In fact, Abbas has used the word *'Zar'* not in a literal sense but in a general sense meaning revenue. Even if interpreted literally, it would be true as Sher Shah usually preferred payment in cash rather than in kind. If Elliot's version of Abbas about the share of the State, one share of the *Muqqadam* and two for the *Ryots* was accepted,[52] Abbas's statements are rendered contradictory as this division would be possible only in the sharing system and payment in kind. Even in the *Jarib* method, the assessment primarily was in kind and is as well clear from the example of the fixation of Sher Shah's *Ray* quoted by Abul Fazl in the *Ain.*[53] Moreover, much evidence exists to prove that in the earlier years of Akbar, the demand was fixed in kind and that much of Akbar's experimentation till the 24th year of his reign was for the commutation of the kind to cash on a rational and scientific basis.

Classification of the Land

When Sher Shah became the Sultan of Hindustan, the system of assessment on the basis of *Jarib* developed further. Not only were the lands measured but the yearly assessment on the cultivated areas was fixed after the classification of the land as a whole. Hasan is clear on the point that the land was divided into several classes and the rate of assessment determined on that basis.[54] He, however, has not explained the way in which the land was classified. Evidently, the classification was done according to the fertility of the soil and the means of irrigation. The actual division of the land into three classes, good, middling and bad did exist in Sher Shah's time whereupon he fixed the *Ray*. This is clear from the *Ain.*[55] The classification would naturally have involved consideration of other factors, in addition to the fertility of the soil determined by the yield per bigha of good, middling and bad; such as the capacity of the soil for continuous or intermittent cultivation; and for providing one, two, or three crops (*i.e., Yak Fasli; Do Fasli, Seh Fasli*) in a year,[56] and the capability of producing multiple crops in the same harvest.

Even though no evidence for the existence of such technical terminology of classification, e.g., *Polaj, Parauti, Chachar* and *Banjar* in Sher Shah's time can be traced, it seems probable that Sher Shah's classification was more or less on the same lines as of Akbar, for, according to Hasan, separate rate for each class was classified. Hasan's language is expressive of elaborate method of classification though the process of its details are not mentioned and no comparison with that of Akbar can be determined with precision.

The Fixation of *'Ray'*

Sher Shah's reign witnessed further evolution in the *Jarib* system *i.e.,* the fixation of the *Ray.*[57] This implied the cropwise assessment rates computed according to the average of the mean produce (of various classes of land) per bigha in kind.[58] Various versions of *Ray* have been given by the scholars but none appears to be clear and precise. In the *Ain,* Jarrett has translated it differently at different places, as produce,[59] gross produce,[60] and revenue.[61] Produce and gross produce do not fit in the context but revenue conveys a correct meaning though not from the technical viewpoint as the revenue could be taken according to any method of assessment. Gladwin explains *Ray* as 'harvest'[62] which is apparently wrong though its interpretation as what was exalted may like revenue be acceptable. Qureshi criticises Jarrett for his translation of *'Ray'* as revenue which he thinks to be incorrect.[63] He has interpreted it as the medium or produce of a homogeneous area calculated by adding its best, middling and poor yields and dividing the total by three and that the technical term for the medium produce is *'Masul'* which is another form of *'Hasil'* meaning the yield.[64] Qureshi's process of finding a medium produce of the yield of the three classes of land per bigha is correct, but his version of the medium produce as *'Ray'* itself is not acceptable. For the medium produce, Abul Fazl, as Qureshi himself suggests, uses the technical term *'Mahsul'* and it was surprising that Abul Fazl did not use the latter in these instances. That *'Mahsul'* and *'Ray'* are not synonymous is clear from *Akbarnama* when

Abul Fazl describes the Revenue Settlement of the province of Kashmire where *'Ray'* is fixed per crop and per *patta* (Two and a half *Pattas* and a fraction of Kashmire measurement make one Standard Akbar's bigha) in kind for both the Rabi and the Kharif crops.[65] The entire *Jama*[66] of the province for the whole year is fixed on the basis of the *'Ray'* of *Rabi* and the *Kharif* crops and this could not have been fixed by totalling the mean produce of the *Rabi* and te *Kharif* as Qureshi would suggest. The description of the fixation of *'Ray'* in the Kashmir Settlement clearly brings out its meaning.

Moreover, Qureshi's explanation of *'Ray'* as 'mean produce' renders the meaning of the entire sentence inexplicable. It is incredible that the mean-produce per bigha of Sher Shah should have been the lowest in any of the provinces of Akbar's time unless it were to represent the years of the drought of which there is no evidence during the five years of Sher Shah's rule.[67]

Moreland's rendering of *Ray* as 'Schedule of Assessment rates'[68] is quite correct if it were more explicit that the schedule of rates are not in terms of cash but in kind and represent each crop per bigha based on the average of the mean produce of different classes of land. Moreland has correctly suggested that *'Ray'* and *'Dastur'* containing schedule of rates are two alternatives.[69] Abul Fazl is explicit on this point as the term used by him for cash assessment rates is *Dasturul-Amal-Naqdi.*[70] Certain crops like musk melons, ajwain (*lingustiam ajowan*), onions, and other greens' are not assessed on the basis of *Ray* but according to the rules and regulations of cash payment. Similarly indigo, poppy, *pan,* turmeric, water chestnut (trapa bispinsosa), hemp, *kachalu* (arum colocasia), pumpkin, hinna (*lawsonia inermis*), cucumbers, *leadrang* (a species of cucumber), the egg plant (*solanum melongolia*), raddishes, carrots, *karela* (*momordica charantia*), *Kakura,* (*momordica muriata*) *tendas,* and musk melons are assessed not according to the Ray but *Dastur-ul-Amal-Naqdi.*[71]

The payment in cash would imply commutation of *Ray* into *Dastur-ul-Amal-Naqdi,* which only can form the basis of the price schedules of the various crops—a process which was definitely evolved in Akbar's time.

Abul Fazl in the *Ain,* while giving illustration of the fixation of the state demand on the classification of land[72] into good, middling and bad[73] within the homogenous blocks, brings out threefold characteristics of the fixation of *Ray:*

(a) Mean produce per bigha per crop of the three classes of land

(b) One third of the mean produce as the State demand or the *Ray*

(c) Fixation of the state demand in kind per bigha per crop

This procedure of the fixation of *Ray* was the work of Sher Shah and continued to be in operation in Akbar's reign. This was the logical development of the *Jarib* method based on the classification of the land. It was a scientific method of fixation of the State demand, which would obviate the possibility of any loss either to the state or to the cultivators.

The Jarib System and the Zabti

Moreland[74] and Saran[75] considered the *Jarib* method of Sher Shah the same as *Zabti* (Regulation System of Assessment), which was later on adopted and developed by Akbar. Their conclusion is mainly based upon the classical instance in the *Ain,* where Abul Fazl, while describing the *Illahi Gaz* and its length, incidently remarks, "In the time of Sher Khan and Salim Khan, when in Hindustan, the methods of assessments passed from *Ghallabakshi* and *Muqtei* to one based on the measurement of land, the same *Gaz* was used.[76]

The whole controversy hinges on the word *'Ba-Zabt Amad'* (باضبط آمد) which is used by Abul Fazl meaning that the system of measurement of land was introduced and not that the *Zabti* system was introduced. It signifies that the system of the measurement of the land as a means of assessment was introduced.

Moreland's translation of the passage "Hindustan passed from *Ghallabakshi,* or crop division, and *muqtai,* to *Zabt,* or Regulation System of Assessment"[77] is not misleading. Moreland has taken *'Ba-Zabt'* (باضبط) as synonimous with *'Ba Zabti'* (باضبطی) which signifies the 'Regulation System' as defined by Abul Fazl in the *Ain* and which came into operation after the 24th year of Akbar's reign.[78]

Abul Fazl uses the word *Zabti* in a technical sense signifying a particular method of assessment in operation after the enforcement of the 'Ten Year Settlement' (*Ain-Dah-Sala*) and *Zabt* simply means the measurement of land and the method of assessment based on it.

All contemporary *Dastur-ul-amals* of the Mughal age, while describing the *Zabti* method, have clearly used the word *Zabti* and have nowhere substituted the word *'Zabt'* for *'Zabti'*.

Jarrett translates the passage thus: "Sher Khan and Salim Khan under whom Hindustan was released from the custom of dividing the grain and its apportionment, in measuring the land used this *Gaz"*.[79] This is not correct so far as he thinks that India was absolutely released from the *Ghallabakshi* method and also that *Muqtei* is taken to qualify the system of *Ghallabakshi* as apportionment, *i.e.,* the division of produce in the *Ghallabakshi.* This is a wrong interpretation as *'Ghallabakshi'* and *'Muqtei'* were two distinct methods of assessment. But in the later portion of the translation, Jarrett has correctly stated that *Zabt* as 'the measurement of the land'—which implies the simple measurement with the *Gaz* rather than the initiation of the *Zabti* system involving the use of *Gaz.* Jarrett is clear on the point of the introduction of some system based on measurement in place of *Ghallabakshi.*

Saran is inconsistent and contradictory in his statements. On the other hand, he correctly recognises that it was only in Akbar's time, that *'Jarib'* came to be used in a technical sense.[80] On the other hand, he accepts the introduction of *Zabti* both in the Jagir and later in the Empire of Sher Shah.[81] Saran, like Moreland, commits the same mistake of identifying *Zabt* with *Zabti*[82] as signifying the regulation method though he acknowledges that it could not have been enforced by Sher Shah throughout his empire.[83]

It is very doubtful if Sher Shah had any intention of changing the system so radically from *Ghallabakshi* and *Muqtei* to *Zabti.* It was not possible for him to abolish the prevailing systems of *Ghallabakshi* and *Muqtei* completely and to have replaced the same by *Zabti* in the short time when Akbar's ministers took about twenty four years after repeated experimentation to evolve this system.

Thus in Sher Shah's time, both the *'Ghallabakshi'* and the *'Jarib'* method were in operation side by side. Both were in the nature of the *Ryotwari* system[84] as neither the *Muqaddams* nor the Jagirdars were intermediaries as the former were simply village officials for the collection of the land revenue and the latter entitled only in the State's share in their respective Jagirs in lieu of their emoluments.

Hasan mentions that there were three ways of revenue administration prevalent in the country but he gives account of only one.[85] According to this, one person from a village named *'Malguzar'* was made responsible for the collection of the land revenue from the various occupants and to pay a fixed sum to the state. Safeguards were provided against the oppression and over-exacting by the *'Malguzar'* as the state officials (*i.e.,* the *Amils*) were specially instructed to keep in mind the protection and security of the people. Misra has interpreted this *Malguzar* system as analogous to the *Zamindari*[86] and that in such a system, *Jarib* or measurement was not enforced as the revenue was not realised from the individual cultivators by the state.

This system if *Malguzari* was not at all based upon the *Zamindari* principles; rather it was one of the aspects of the *Ryotwari* system itself. In this system, the sum for the village—which the *Malguzar* was bound to pay—was fixed keeping in view all the factors and the principles of the measurement and the fixation of rates on different classes of the land as already described by Hasan. The assessment on the individuals and for the whole village was made by the State and not by the *Malguzar.* He was responsible simply for the collection of the land revenue as by the state officials who were to see that there was no over-exaction and that the *Ryots'* interests were safeguarded. If the assessment had not been made by the Government officers, they could not interfere in the distribution of the assessment over the Ryots by the *Malguzar* but on the contrary, as is clear from Hasan, they were strictly enjoined to look to the interests of the *Ryots.*[87] In fact, the *Malguzar* may be termed as the village official rather than as an intermediary. He was responsible for the collection of the revenue of the entire village and after keeping a margin of percentage as his remuneration or personally having been exempted from the payment of the land revenue, would transmit the fixed amount to the state. The *Malguzar* had thus the duties of the *Muqaddam* (or the *Lambardar* or the *Patel*) of the village for the collection of its land revenue and it seems that the office of the *Malguzar* and the *Muqaddam* was the same.

Hasan speaks of three methods of assessment but is silent about the other two. It may be presumed on the strength of the *Ain* that the other two were the *Ghallabakshi* and the *Kankut* which prevailed in most of the provinces.[88]

The State Demand

The determination of the share of the State is one of the most controversial topics of Sher Shah's land revenue administration. Qanungo[89] and Qureshi[90] have reached the conclusion that he took from the cultivators one-fourth of the produce as the state's share whereas Moreland[91] and Saran[92] have put it at one-third. Misra[93] agrees with the latter view. It would serve no purpose in repeating all their arguments but certain points do need clarification.

Hasan does not mention the precise share of the State but he merely enunciates a general principle for fixing the state's demand. "The principle is that the Government demand should be less than the income accuring from that land, so that every land holder may have interest in cultivation, and so that they might not be afraid of the Government demand and tax if there were scarcity of water or insufficiency of rains.[94] Hasan emphasises the moderate nature of the demand so as to leave sufficient to the cultivator for his subsistence both in normal times and in times of drought. He nowhere mentions that the proportion of the State's demand was in any way curtailed in Sher Shah's time in terms of the above principle.

Besides Hasan's general testimony, there are three other sources, namely, *Ain,* 'Elliot's version of Abbas's *Tarikh-i-Sher Shahi* and *Makhzan-*

i-Afghana of Niamat Ullah which afford some direct clues to the subject of the demand.

The statement of the *Ain* about the fixation of *'Ray'* by Sher Shah determined the State's demand in his time.[95] The *'Ray',* in fact, stood for the state's demand as explained by Abul Fazl.[96] The procedure in the fixation of *Ray* of finding the mean produce in kind per bigha of every crop for the three different categories of land and dividing the total by three shows the State's demand. The procedure of its fixation, which was inherited from Sher Shah for which Abul Fazl has shown indebtedness, clearly proves his share was one-third which continued to prevail in most of the provinces of Akbar as the lowest demand.[97]

In fact, there is an implied admission on Abul Fazl's part of Sher Shah's demand at one third and its continuation in Akbar's reign, as well representating the lowest rates in most of the provinces—a very unusual compliment and recognition of Sher Shah's moderate fixation of the State demand.[98]

The second direct inference can be drawn from Elliot's version of Abbas stating that Sher Shah ordered his Governors to measure the land every harvest, to collect the revenue according to measurement, and in proportion to the produce, giving one share to the cultivator, and half a share to the *Muqaddam.*[99] Besides reference to the method of assessment by measurement, the demand of the State on the above statement can be clearly fixed at 2:1—two shares for the cultivator and one for the *Muqaddam* for collecting the revenue. Thus, even in the measurement method, the State demand remains at one third. It is true as Qureshi says, that this version of Abbas is not traceable in any of the available copies of *Tarikh-i-Sher Shahi*[100] but the categorical statement in Elliot's version cannot be ignored on this account particularly when it is in complete accord with Sher Shah's produce of fixation of assessment rates as quoted in the '*Ain*'.

The third direct reference on which both Qanungo and Qureshi have mostly relied is Niamat Ullah's statement in the *Makhzan-i-Afghana* that Sher Shah "enempted Multan from all public charges, except a fourth of the produce which was to be levied".[101] So Sher Shah abolished all extra cesses in the newly conquered province of Multan while assessing the land revenue at one fourth of the produce. Both Qanungo[102] and Qureshi[103] maintain that this State's share as demanded from Multan was uniformly applicable to his entire dominion and was in no way an exceptional levy. Abbas does not mention the State's share settled in Multan but clearly states the context in which Sher Shah issued orders to Haibat Khan on his conquest of Multan for fixing a moderate assessment based upon measurement—"Sher Shah was exceedingly rejoined and made him (Haibat Khan) *Masnad-i-Ali* and bestowed upon him the title of *Azam-Hamayun.*

He offered him the red robes and with regard to the rehabilitation of the people of Multan, he wrote that a moderate assessment be levied upon the *Langha* people and not to assess the land revenue upon measurement rather to accept the share of the produce (*i.e., Batai*).[104] This clearly shows that this settlement in the province of Multan (*i.e.,* 1/4th of the produce as clear from *Makhzan-i-Afghana*) was an exceptional concession, which means that the normal demand of the state in the other provinces must have been higher than this. Admittedly, the normal demand of 1/3rd of the produce was not applied to the province of Multan where the exceptional demand of 1/4th was fixed as a concession to the people of Multan for reasons of expediency.

Besides, Qureshi's genesis of the evolution of the State demand "that the rate of assessment was a fifth, except in Alauddin Khilji's reign when it was raised to a half, it was later reduced to fifth by Ghiyas-ud-Din Tughlaq; Muhammad Bin Tughluq raised it to a fourth which seems to have remained the prevalent proportion until the death of Sher Shah; Akbar raised it to a third,"[105] is based on hypothetical interpretation. The precise share of the State in the time of Muhammad Bin Tughluq is a matter of doubt and it also is a controversial fact that it was reduced by Feroze Tughluq.[106] The demand under the Lodhis was altered by Babar who fixed according to the Mughal practice.[107]

Further, Qureshi's argument that Timur demanded a third in some of his dominions, that Babar demanded a hundred and thirty instead of a hundred and and that Sher Shah's demand was not exceptional,[108] is not convincing. Babar's demand was continued by Hamayun but there is no evidence to show that Sher Shah reduced it. Had Sher Shah done so, Abbas and other Afghan sources would have certainly mentioned it while bestowing a lot of praise while describing Sher Shah's other philanthropic deeds in such laudatory terms. Hasan would have made it emphatically clear especially when he states that the demand was moderate and also when he could be so minute as to mention the extra assessment of 2½% for the draught period and advance of loans by the State.[109] On the other hand, Abbas affirms that Sher Shah considered the financial source of the land revenue as the most profitable and stable as compared to other sources of income.[110]There is no reference to any reduction of the demand in the Jagir of his father in otherwise the most detailed picture of his revenue reforms which Abbas and other writers have given. On the contrary, there are clear references to the increase in the revenue of the Jagir, which would not have been possible by cutting down the demand. Sher Shah, rather, raised the revenues of the Jagir to the maximum. As Sultan also, it is doubtful, if with all his military expenditure he could cut at the very root of the income of the State consistently with his ideas of trying to be as just to the *Ryots* in realising the revenue as in increasing the finances of the State through accuracy of the measurement and eradication of corruption. Moreover, there is no clear reference in the *Ain* supporting the contention that Akbar raised the existing demand of the State to one third.[111]

Apart from settling the land revenue at one-third of the produce, Sher Shah showed full consideration in the abolition of the other cesses. Hasan states that as the administrator of his father's Jagir, he abolished the practice of forced labour which had prevailed in India since the time of Sultan Ghori. He exempted the cultivators from all miscellaneous payments (cesses) also and realised from them nothing but the land revenue.[112] But Abbas[113] and Niamat Ullah[114] confirm the realisation only *'Jaribana'* and *'Mahslana'* in addition to the land revenue. The *Muqaddams* were strictly instructed not to realise anything besides these two cesses and if they did, the extra realisation was to be deducted from their emoluments at the time of the settlement of the accounts.[115]

It is reasonable to assume that Sher Shah even as the Sultan remitted all cesses in his Empire (excepting the *Jaribana* and *Mahslana*) though there is no contemporary evidence to prove this categorically beyond the fact that at the time of conquest of Multan, he exempted it from all cesses whatsoever while fixing one fourth as the State demand.[116] That later on Akbar abolished various cesses shows only the recurrence of such taxes after the death of Islam Shah. Besides the land revenue, Sher Shah levied 2½% for the public treasury so that it might be spent in case of accidents or heavenly misfortunes.[117] Besides, in cases of damage to crops due to any natural calamity, the poor cultivations were given grants from the State treasury,[118] advanced *Taqqavi* loans and allowed remissions of the land revenue.

Sher Shah's Idea and Purpose of Administration

The principles, which underlie the entire land revenue administration of Sher Shah mark an absolutely new orientation of the outlook on the part of the Sultan with regard to the agrarian problems. Sher Shah emphasised in equal degree the concept of the welfare of the *Ryots* and the financial interests of the State. Sher Shah's (as Farid) address to the officials of his father's Jagir shows his anxiety to safeguard the interest of the *Ryots* contribute to their well-being and increased agricultural output as they formed the backbone of the entire agricultural economy.[119] The *Ryots'* welfare was essentially interlinked with the increase in the State's revenues.[120]

The protection of the standing crops against any damage through movement of troops or other wayfarers was emphasised. If the soldiers' tents came to be pitched near the corn fields, the soldiers had to keep a watch so that the crops would not be harmed, and those injurying them were made to suffer.[121] He would not even harm the crops of the adversary observing that the farmers were innocent and would submit to any Government in power.[122] Abbas says that while on march, Sher Shah himself looked in all directions and that if any one harmed the crops during the movements of the troops, he promptly cut off his ears and hanging the trampled corn around neck, paraded the culprit in the camp. If the damage to crops could not be avoided owing to the narrowness of the passage, the cultivator was compensated for the loss.[123]

Sher Shah stamped out corruption and took stringent measures against officials who exercised extortion against the cultivators. In his address to the officials of the *Pargana* in his father's Jagir, he strictly forbade them the acceptance of even grass from the peasantry.[124] With his keen sense of minute administration, he stretched his attention far and wide even to the extent sometimes of checking the private ledgers of the cultivators for detecting cases of official corruption. He believed that "Wise and experienced men having given the advice,— that a Governor, suspecting any of his functionaries of depredation, ought to suspend him and proceed to a minute investigation of his conduct, by enquiring of every subject and inspecting the account books of the tenants, in which no extortion on the side of the collectors would be passed over unnoticed. For it was customary with most of the Indians, he continued, to keep the accounts a secret, lest the depredations of the prefects might be detected; which proceeding, in their opinion, was even attended by something meritorious and praiseworthy".[125]

Efficiency of the administration was as good for the financial position of the State as it was for the good of the peasantry.[126] Sher Shah usually changed the revenue officials after short periods of a year or two by means of transfers. He observed that experience showed that no department of Government could be so lucrative financially as revenue from land and hence he would appoint experienced persons as its officials and would replace them by another team of equally experienced men after every couple of years or so in order to benefit all people equally from his rule.[127] Thus

Sher Shah re-organised the revenue department as a well-knit one with the State as a whole and thereby created strong financial position for himself.

References

1. Sahasram in Sarkar of Rohtas. *Ain-i-Akbari,* edited by Blochmann, Vol. I. p. 117.
2. Khawaspur Tanda, "A Pargana of Sarkar of Jaunpur." *Ain-i-Akbari.* Persian text, edited by Blochmann, p. 119.

   Abbas Sarwani describes them as situated near Benares. Nizamudin and Badayuni mention them as dependencies of Rohtas while Farishta does not mention any location. Erskine locates them as dependent in Rohtas. Qanungo says that the Jagir was situated in the present district of Shahabad while in Rennel map, both the districts fall with the district of Rohtas which concides with Abul Fazl' Sarkar of Rohtas. It comprised roughly the *Barang, Tilothee* and *Sahsram* thanas of Shahbad District. Dr. Qanungo's determination of this location is not exact as he has omitted from other Pargana of Khawaspur Tanda which has been mentioned as the Pargana of Sarkar of Jaunpur in the 'Ain'. At present, it forms a part of the Tanda Pargana Fyzabad District.
3. This system is explained at length in *Ain-i-Akbari.* Persian text edited by Blochmann, Vol. I, pp. 286-290. Translation of *Ain-i-Akbari* by Jarrett, Vol. II, p. 47.
4. *Makhzan-i-Afghana* by Niamat Ullah Ms. No. 379, State Library Rampur; pp. 206-207.
5. *Tufa-Akbar Shahi* by Abbas Sarwani, pp. 26-44; Ms. No. 80402, Delhi University, (Copy of Br. Museum Ms).
6. *Makhzan-i-Afghana,* p. 207, Ms. no. 379. State Library Rampur, Persian text.

   رو بجانب رعایا کردہ گفت کہ امروز اختیار بدست شما است و اگر گویند اراضی مزروعہ را جریب
   کردہ موافق آن جمع مقرر نمایم و اگر خواہند ملاحظہ بود و نابود مزروعاتِ فرمودہ مطالق آن
   گفتن برشمایاں مقرر سازم۔ بعض بجریب و بعض بخراج رضا دادہ خطِ قبولیت نوشتہ دادند و
   ہمدرانِ مجلس خرچ جریبانہ و محصلانہ مقرر نمودہ "با مقدماں و کلانزاں شرکیاں قرار داد کہ من
   اورا آخر فصیل خورد ونزار عاسی در حضور خود طلبیدہ جمع و خرچ فرد فرد را تحقیق خواہم فرمود۔

   This portion of Persian text is to be found only in this Ms. This cannot be traced in the two Mss no. of M.U. Aligarh or in the translation by Dorn in the *'History of the Afghans'* or in Elliot's translation.
7. This is the system known as ہوی بہوی existing today in the Panjab.
8. Dr. Saran; *Journal of Behar and Orissa Research Society,* 1931, pp. 140-145; *Studies in Medieval Indian History,* pp. 74-79.

9. Dr. Qanungo; *Sher Shah*, p. 18.
10. Moreland, *The Agrarian System of Moslem India*, p. 171.
11. Dr. Saran, *Journal of Behar and Orissa Research Society*, Vol. XVII, 1931, p. 141, *Studies in Medieval Indian History*, p. 75.
12. Dr. Saran, *Journal of the Behar and Orissa Research Society*, 1931, p. 144, *Studies in Medieval Indian History*, p. 79. *Ibid.*, pp. 144 and 79 respectively.
13. *Tufha-i-Akbar Shahi*, by Abbas Sarwari Ms. no. 40402, University of Delhi, pp. 26-44. (This is copy of the Ms. of British Museum).
14. *T.A.S.* by Abbas, p. 27.
15. *T.A.S.* by Abbas Ms, p. 27.
16. *T.A.S.* by Abbas Ms, p. 27.
17. *T.A.S.* by Abbas Ms, p. 27, 28.
18. *T.A.S.* by Abbas Ms, p. 28.
19. *T.A.S.* by Abbas Ms, p. 29.
20. *T.A.S.* by Abbas Ms, p. 29.
21. *T.A.S.* by Abbas, p. 30.
22. *T.A.S.* Ms, p. 30-32; Original Persian Text quoted in Appendix A, p. 27; B, p. 27; C, p. 29; D, p. 30, E, p. 31.
23. *T.A.S.* by Abbas, p. 29.
24. Elliot, Vol. IV, p. 313. Elliot's Ms. contains the words *Kismat-i-Ghalla* (قسمتِ غلہ) instead of (غلہ داون). In fact, both bear the same meaning and imply the division of the produce of the crops.
25. Elliot used the India Office Ms. Dr. Saran used the British Museum Ms. which does not contain this word. He also, on comparison, failed to find it in India Office Ms. either. I have used the British Museum Ms. as copied by the University of Delhi as well examined the Ms. of Dr. Saran which incorporates differences between the India Office. Ms. I have also gone through the Rampur and the Aligarh Mss but none of them contain the word 'Mode of Payment'.
26. Dr. Saran, *The Journal of the Behar and Orissa Research Society*, Vol. XVII, 1931, p. 140, Studies in *Medieval India History*, p. 74.
27. Dr. Saran, *Studies in Medieval Indian History*, p. 88.
28. Dr. Saran's Ms. bears 'Zarib' and not Jarib. Elliot consulted two copies containing Jarib. In fact, the correct word is Jarib which is borne out by all the Mss I have consulted and the use of the word in *Ain* and the later Chroniclers of the Moghal times.
29. *Ain-i-Akbari*, Persian text edited by Blochmann, Vol. I, p. 285.
30. Abul Fazl contemptuously remarks about the reforms of Sher Shah as copied from Alaud Din's measures described by Zia-ud-Din Barani in *'Tarikh-i-Feroze Shahi'*. (*Akbarnama* Persian text of Royal Asiatic Society of Bengal, Vol. I, p. 98). *Khulasut-Tawarikh;* Shujan Rai Bhandari, p. 72.

31. *T.A.S.* Abbas Sarwani, Persian Text Ms., University of Delhi, p. 305 (Copy of British Museum Ms.); Ms. India Office F. 106 a; Ms. M.U. Aligarh, p. 247; Elliot's translation, Vol. IV, pp. 413-14, Persian text as follows.

وقانونِ تحصیلِ زداز رعیت وآبادانی مملکت چناں قرار یافتہ بود کہ در ہر پرگنہ یک شقدار و یک
وحکم چناں فرمودہ بود کہ سال بسال جریب وکند واز روی جریب زر دیگر یند تا مقدم وعمال
بریزہ رعیت کہ مدار آبادنی ایشاں اند ظلم وتعدی نکند۔ قبل او جریب سال بسال بنود ودر ہر
پرگنہ قانون گوہ نگاہ داشتہ بود کہ حلِ ماضی واستقبال پرگنہ از روی برسید۔

Waqiat-i-Mushtaqi by Rizqullah (Rotograph No. 3, Copy of Br. Museum Ms.) has the same wording in Persian as T.A.S. of Abbas), p. 213.

32. *Tawarikh-e-Daulat-E-Sher Shahi* by Hasan Ali Khan. Translated by Dr. R.P. Tripathi, *Medieval India Quarterly,* Vol. I, July 1950, M.U. Aligarh, Farman Tenth, p. 62.

33. The translation of the Hindi Revenue terminology into Persian was started in the reign of Sakinder Lodhi and ultimately accomplished by Todar Mal when the Revenue Records in Persian were maintained. This is clear from *'Haqiqat Hai Hindustan'* by Lachmi Narain; and *Khalaq-ns-Sayyaq,* F 3a, Ms. No. 114. M.U. Aligarh.

34. *Ain-i-Akbari,* Persian Text, edited by Blochman, Vol. I, p. 286.

35. *Makhzan-i-Afghna* Ms. No. 379. State Library Rampur, p. 207.

36. T.S.S. Elliot and Dowson, Vol. IV, p. 399, *Ibid.*

37. India Office Ms. F. 113a; M.U. Ms. No. 1.33

38. T.S.S. in Elliot, Vol. IX, p. 423 (India Office Ms. F 113a; Ms. M.U. Aligarh, No. 133; p. 263).

39. *Ibid.*, p. 422 (India Office Ms. F. 112b).

40. *Ain-i-Akbari,* Persian text by Blochmann, Vol. I, p. 286

درزمانِ شبیر خان وسلیم خان کہ ہندوستان از غلا بخشی ومقطعی بضبط آمد بہمیں گز پیمودند۔

41. *Ain-i-Akbari,* Persian text, Blochmann, Vol. II, p. 296.

42. T.S.S., Elliot and Dowson, Vol. IV, p. 379.

43. *Ain-i-Akbari,* Persian text, Blochmann, Vol. I, pp. 285-86.

44. *Ain,* Persian text, Blochmann, vol. I, p. 270.

45. Dorn's translation of the *Makhzan-i-Afghana* in the *'History of the Afghans,* Vol. I, p. 82.

46. *Ain-i-Akbari,* Persian text, Blochman, Vol. I, p. 286.

47. The practice of making enquiries from the Qanungo about the fields of the harvests in the Pargana already in vogue even before Sher Shah's time. T.S.S. Persian text Ms. University of Delhi, p. 305 (Copy of Br. Museum Ms.).

48. *Makhzan-i-Afghana,* Ms. No. 377. State Library, Rampur, p. 207.
49. T.S.S. by Abbas Elliot and Dowson, Vol. IV, p. 313.
50. *Ain-i-Akbari,* Persian text, Blochmann, Vol. I, p. 298; pp. 304-347.
51. T.A.S., Persian text Ms. No. 40402—Delhi University, (Copy of British Museum Ms.), p. 304, 308, 309.
52. T.S.S. by Abbas Elliot and Dowson, Vol. IV, pp. 413-414.
53. *Ain-i-Akbari,* Persian text, Blochmann, Vol. I, p. 297.
54. *Tawarikh-E-Daulat-Sher Shahi* by Hasan Ali Khan, translation by Dr. R.P. Tripathi in *Medieval India Quarterly,* Vol. I, July 1950, No. 1, p. 62.
55. *Ain-i-Akbari,* Persian text, Blochmann, Vol. I, p. 297.
56. Such classification was done in the Moughal times as is clear from the *'Ain'* Persian text, Blochmann, pp. 297-303 and the *Farman* of Aurangzeb Persian text, p. 242. *Journal and Proceeding of the Asiatic Society of Bengal,* Vol. II, 1906. As Hasan's language shows comprehensive classification of land, such classification as of the Moughal times may be presumed is Sher Shah's reign as well.
57. *Ain-i-Akbari,* Persian text, Blochmann, Vol. I, pp. 297-301.
58. *Ibid.,* p. 298.
59. *Ain-i-Akbari,* translated into English by Jarrett and corrected and annotated by Sir J.N. Sarkar, Vol. II, p. 170.
60. *Ain-i-Akbari,* translated by Jarrett and Sarkar, Vol. II, p. 172.
61. *Ibid.,* Vol. II, p. 68.
62. *Ain-i-Akbari,* translated by Gladwin, Vol. I, p. 260.
63. Dr. Qureshi, 'Akbar's land revenue reforms', *Journal of Pakistan Historical Society,* 1954, pp. 207-08; *The Administration of Delhi Sultanate,* p. 72.
64. *Ibid.,* p. 198 and 181 respectively.
65. *Akbarnama,* Persian text, edited by Maulvi Abdur Rahim, Royal Asiatic Society of Bengal, Vol. III, pp. 997-98.
66. *Ibid.,* p. 998.
67. Rather on the contrary, it is asserted that there was prosperity and famines were averted in his reign. T.A.S. Persian text.
68. Moreland, 'Sher Shah Revenue System', *The Journal of Asiatic Society of Great Britain and Ireland,* 1926, p. 456.
69. Moreland, *Ibid.,* p. 456.
70. *Ain-i-Akbari,* Persian text, Blochmann, Vol. I, p. 298.
71. *Ibid.,* Vol. I, p. 298.
72. *Ibid.,* Vol. I, p. 300.
73. *Ibid.,* Vol. I, pp. 297-303.
74. Moreland, Akbar's Land Revenue System as described in the *Ain-i-Akbari, Journal of Royal Asiatic Society of Great Britain and Ireland,* 1918, p. 9.

75. Dr. Saran, *"The Revenue System of Sher Shah." The Journal of the Behar and Orissa Research Society,* Vol. XVII, 1931, p. 144; also *Studies in Medieval Indian History,* p. 80.
76. *Ain-i-Akbari,* Persian text, Blochmann, Vol. I, p. 296.

در زمانِ شبیر خان و سلیم خان کہ ہندوستان از غلا بخشی و مقطعی بضبط آمد بہمیں گز پیمودند۔

77. Moreland and Ali, 'Akbar's land revenue system as described in the *'Ain-i-Akbari'. Journal of Royal Asiatic Society of Great Britain and Ireland,* 1919 c.
78. *Ain-i-Akbari,* Persian text, Blochmann, Vol. I.
79. *Ain-i-Akbari,* English translation Jarrett and Sarkar, Vol. II, p. 66.
80. Dr. Saran, *'Revenue System of Sher Shah.' The Journal of Behar and Orissa Research Society,* Vol. XVII, 1931, p. 141; Also *Studies in Medieval Indian History,* p. 75.
81. *Ibid.*, p. 144; Studies, p. 75.
82. *Ibid.*, p. 144; Studies, p. 80.
83. *Ibid.*, p. 144; Studies, p. 80.
84. Dr. Saran also agrees with this version, 'Revenue System of Sher Shah', *Studies in Medieval Indian History,* p. 80, *Journal of Behar and Orissa Research Society,* p. 144.
85. *Tawarikh-E-Daulat-Sher-Shahi,* by Hasan Ali Khan, Translation by Dr. R.P. Tripathi in *Medieval Indian Quarterly,* Vol. I, July, 1950, p. 62.
86. Dr. Misra, 'Revenue System of Sher Shah.' *Indian History Congress,* Proceedings of the 15th Session, 1952.
87. Hasan, *Tawarikh-E-Daulat-o-Sher Shahi,* Translation by Dr. Tripathi, *Indian Medieval Quarterly,* Aligarh.
88. *Ain-i-Akbari,* Persian text, Blochmann, Vol. I, p. 287.
89. Dr. Qanugo, *Sher Shah,* p. 72.
90. Dr. Qureshi, *The Administration of Delhi Sultanate,* p. 89; 'Akbar's Land Revenue Reforms' *Journal of Pakistan Historical Society,* p. 216, Jan. 1954.
91. Moreland, 'Sher Shah's Revenue System,' *The Journal of Asiatic Society of Great Britain and Ireland,* 1926, p. 453.
92. Dr. Saran, 'Sher Shah's Revenue Systems.' *Journal of Behar and Orissa Research Society,* Vol. XVII, p. 147; *Studies in Medieval Indian History,* p. 84.
93. Dr. Misra, 'Revenue System of Sher Shah,' *Indian History Congress,* Proceedings of the Fifteenth Session, Gwalior, 1952, p. 238.
94. *Tawarikh-E-Daulat-E-Sher Shahi* by Hasan Ali Khan. Farmans translated by Dr. R.P. Tripathi, *Medieval India Quarterly,* Vol. I, July, 1950, No. 1, M.U. Aligarh, p. 62.
95. *Ain-i-Akbari,* Persian text, Blochmann, Vol. I, p. 296.

96. *Ibid.*, pp. 298-300.

97. *Ain-i-Akbari,* Persian text, Blochmann, p. 297.

98. *Ain-i-Akbari,* Persian text, Blochmann, Vol. I, p. 297, Usually Abul Fazl is very contemptous about the Reforms of Sher Shah, *Akbar Nama,* Vol. I, Persian text, edited by Maulvi Abdur Rahim.

99. T.S.S., Elliot, Vol. IV, pp. 413-414.

100. Dr. Qureshi, *The Administration of Delhi Sultanate,* p. 81.

101. *Makhzan-i-Afghana* by Niamat Ullah, translated by Dorm as *The History of the Afghans,* Part I, p. 135; *Makhzan-i-Afghana,* No. 60. Morley Catalogue, R.A.S. of Bengal.

102. Dr. Qanungo, *Sher Shah,* p. 72.

103. Dr. Qureshi, *The Administration of Delhi Sultanate,* p. 89.

104. *T.A.S.* by Abbas, Persian text, Ms. no. M.U. Aligarh, p. 218 (Copy of Br. Museum Ms.) Elliot's translation of T.S.S. of this passage is defective. Sher Shah was exceedingly rejoined and made him *Masnad-i-Ali* and gave him the title of Azam Hamayuṇ. He also gave him a red tent and wrote to him *to repeople Multan, and to observe the customs of the Langahs, and not to measure the land, but to take a share of the produce.* Elliot & Dowson, Vol. IV, p. 399. Elliot has translated *Amil-i-Mahmuli* (عملِ معمولی) as the customs, which is entirely wrong.

Persian text as follows:

ملتان را کہ بلوچاں ویران کردہ بود آباد ساخت شبیر خان بسیار خوشحال شد و ہیبت خان را و
سر پردہ شرف عنایت فرمودہ او در باب آباداں شدن ملتان نوشت کہ عملِ معمولی بہ نگاہ
نگاہدارد و جریب نکند بلکہ حصہ از غلہ بیگرد۔

105. Dr. Qureshi, 'Akbar's Land Revenue Reforms,' *Journal of Pakistan Historical Society,* Jan, 1954, p. 216.

106. *Tarikh-i-Feroze Shai* by Ziauddin Barni; Persian text, p. 171.

107. *Tuzuk-i-Babri;* Mrs. Beveridge, p. 180.

108. Dr. Qureshi, *The Administration of the Sultanate of Delhi,* p. 98.

109. *Twarikh-E-Daulat-E-Sher Shahi* by Hasan Ali Khan. Farmans translated by Dr. R.P. Tripathi, *Medieval Indian Quarterly,* Vol. I, July, 1950, M.U. Aligarh, p. 62.

110. *T.A.S.,* by Abbas, Persian text, p. 306.

111. Dr. Qanungo's reading of the *'Ain'* is incorrect. *Sher Shah,* p. 98.

112. *Twarikh-Daulat-E-Sher Shahi* by Hasan Ali Khan. Persian text Ms. no. M.U. Aligarh, Persian text published in *Medieval Indian Quarterly,* Vol. I, July, 1950, M.U., Aligarh, p. 3.

113. *T.A.S.* by Abbas, Persian text, p. 30.

114. *Makhzan-i-Afghana* by Niamat Ullah, Persian text, Ms. No. State Library, Rampur, p. 207.
115. *T.A.S.* by Abbas, Persian text, p. 31.
116. *Makhzan-i-Afghana* by Niamat Ullah translated by Dorn '*The History of the Afghans*', Part I, p. 135.
117. *Tawarikh-i-Daulat-E-Sher Shahi* by Hasan Ali Khan. Farman translated by Dr. R.P. Tripathi, *Medieval India Quarterly,* 1950, p. 62.
118. *Ibid.*, p. 62.
119. *T.A.S.* by Abbas, Persian text, pp. 27-37.
120. *Ibid.*, pp. 29, 31, 36.
121. *T.A.S.* by Abbas, Ms. M.U. Aligarh, p. 260, Ms. 1.0. F. 113, *A-Waqiat-i-Mushtaqi,* f. 52a; *Tarikh-i-Dandi,* Persian text, Ms. M.U. Aligarh, p. 128. Both *Waqiat-i-Mustàqi* and *Tarikh-i-Daudi* relate a story that when Sher Shah marched towards Malwa, he saw a camel driver eating green grams. He at once came upon him and asked when he has issued orders that no passer-by should lay his hands in the agriculture, why he had disobeyed. The driver's nose was hored, his hands and feet tied and he was hung by the nose in the camel's neck and was kept in this position throughout the way. (*Waqiat-i-Mushtaqi;* f. 52A) (*Tarikh-i-Daudi,* p. 128).
122. *T.A.S.* by Abbas, Persian text, p. 322; *Waqiat-i-Mushtaqi,* p. 220 and *Tarik-i-Daudi.*
123. *T.A.S.* by Abbas, Persian text, p. 321; *Waqiat-i-Mushtaqi,* p. 220.
124. *T.A.S.* by Abbas, Persian text, p. 321.
125. *Makhzan-i-Afghana* by Niamat Ullah, translation by Dorn, '*History of the Afghans*', Part I, p. 86.
126. *T.A.S.* by Abbas, Persian text, p. 305.
127. *Ibid.*, p. 305; *Waqiat-i-Mushtaqi,* pp. 213-214.

Chapter 5

Machinery of Collection of Land Revenue Under Sher Shah

The working of the land revenue system depends on the various officials and the machinery of collection which was well organised under Sher Shah and which was more or less a continuation of the administration of Delhi Sultanate. Dr. Qureshi[1] has given a fairly correct analysis of the functions of the officials connected with the land revenue administration, but he has not laid emphasis on certain aspects of administration nor even clarified certain important points connected with it.

The most important unit was the village administration upon which rested the entire operation of the land revenue system and Hasan has attached considerable significance to it.[2]

The head of the village administration was the *Muqqadam*[3] (*Mukhia*[4] or *Malguzar*)[5] who, besides his duties of preservation of law and order, was responsible for the collection of land revenue in the village.[6] He was, since the ancient Hindu times, more of a representative of the people of the village as *Mukhia,* than a Government official and the office was usually hereditary. It is clear from Farid's (Sher Shah's) address to the *Muqqadams* in his father's Jagir that much of the prosperity of the peasantry and of the agriculture depended upon the sense of integrity and honesty on the part of the *Muqaddams* for the discharge of their duties.[7] The *Muqqadam* was to collect the land revenue from the various occupants in accordance with the assessment made by the Pargana *Amin* upon various holdings, and to take from them the *'Qabuliyat',* i.e., the documents of acceptance for the same.[8] He would deposit the amount or the entire collection in kind in the Pargana treasury. Farid strictly enjoined the *Muqaddams* to collect the land revenue every harvest, *rabi* and *kharif,* and to deposit in the State treasury regularly and not to allow it to fall in arrears as the arrears of the Government dues led to the desolation of the Pargana and enmity between the Government officials and the *Raiyat.*[9] He had to be considerate with the *Raiyat* at the time of the collection of the land revenue and he was to use coercion only with the refractory *Raiyat* unwilling to pay the Government share.[10]

The work of the *Muqaddam* was inspected by the Pargana officials who would safeguard the interests of the *Raiyat* against any high handed men or over-exaction on the part of the *Muqaddam.*[11] The *Muqaddam* was in no case to oppress the *Raiyat.*

The *Muqaddam* was entitled to emoluments, usually some percentage on the total amount collected in cash or a fixed share in kind of the total land revenue collected. He would get *'Mahaslana'* and the rations for *'Mahaslana'* as Farid assured the *Muqaddams* that if he could not get it, he would help them in realising from the *Raiyat.*[12] On the other hand, they were strictly instructed to do collection of the cesses, in accordance with the rate fixed, failing which the surplus collected by them would be deducted from their emoluments at the time of the accounts settlement.[13] As a safeguard against corruption, all the documents of income and expenditure were to be verified from the cultivators of the village themselves.[14]

The *Muqaddam* was assisted in his functions by two persons who were either appointed by the *Mukhia* himself or by the Supreme Government where the management was directly in the hands of the Government officials.[15] They were to be paid by the people of the village. It was the duty of the *Muqaddam* and his assistants to keep the central authority in touch not only with the disturbance of peace, and the ingress and egress of the travellers but also of the rain fall and of the conditions of the drought and famine as well.[16]

Another important village official was the *Patwari*— a very ancient office in India. He is mentioned by Abbas as one of addressees in the assemblage when Farid issued comprehensive instructions for land revenue collection in his father's Jagir.[17] He was a village accountant. Hasan mentions his important duties. Every village has a writer, the discharge of whose duties is like the discharge of Keepers' duties. Among his (their) duties is the entering of the rights of ownership, the boundaries of land, and the amounts of tax in his (their) diary. Means should be found to despatch all sums of money to the centre.[18] Thus the *Patwari* had the full records of the village comprising the various holdings along with the names of the occupants, the village boundary and the boundaries of the various holdings; the assessment levied from crop to crop and year to year upon the various holdings; the amount due and realised from the occupants, the issue of demand for payment and the receipt for the same to the cultivators and thereby the entire accounts of the village. Such records were indispensable for the assessment of the land revenue based on measurement.

Every village had *'Gumashtas'* and *'Karkun'*[19] who helped the *Muqaddam* and the *Patwari* in the discharge of their functions. In case a village was assigned in Jagir, soldiers were maintained by the Jagirdar who were to help the *Muqaddam* in the collection of the land revenue from the cultivators. The soldiers, who too were invited by Farid in his father's Jagir in the gathering, were the first to be addressed by him and were strictly instructed to give up oppression upon the *Raiyat* and to collect the same amount of land revenue from them at the time of realisation, which was settled at the fixation of assessment of the crops, as any greediness on their part would lead to the destruction of the *Raiyat*, bad name to the *Jagirdar* and the dwindling of the land revenue.[20] The soldiers were to encourage the cultivation and to increase the realisation of the revenue and thereby to benefit their *Jagirdar*.[21] As they were the agents of the *Jagirdar* for the collection of the land revenue, they were paid and maintained by the *Jagirdar* as his personal staff in the Jagir.

A few villages made up one *'Qasba'* or a centre, which was the next higher administrative unit with supervisory powers for administration over the entire circle of the villages. Hasan states, "the truth of the matter is that a place is named as the central market, and the management of every surrounding village, on its north, south, east and west situated within five *Kos* of it, is placed under it".[22]

The *Qasba* comprising the jurisdiction of five *kos* was as much of a centre for civil administration as for the land revenue collection under the control of a *Nazim*. Hasan says, 'Every centre has a *Nazim* who is called the *Muhasil* of that place. On him depends the control and administration (of that place). He keeps the administration going'.[23] The *Muhasil* was responsible for the entire land revenue collection and administration and kept a strict supervisory control over the land revenue administration of the villages. He was the link between the village and the Pargana administration and responsible to the *Shiqdar* of the Pargana.

In fact, the popular name of the *Muhasil* was the *Amil*—a designation usually used by the other Afghan sources. Dr. Qureshi has not enumerated this office in the Pargana organisation of Sher Shah[24] but it can be asserted with certainty that the office, though an old one, was in existence in the administrative set up of Sher Shah. None of the Afghan sources in the respective lists given mention him to be a full-fledged Pargana Officer but he has been frequently mentioned in connection with administrative measures of Sher Shah though his exact jurisdiction is not clearly mentioned. Abbas mentions him in connection with the regulations of Sher Shah for the preservation of law and order.[25] Thus the *Amil* had both the executive and the judicial powers and was the direct Officer-in-Charge of the *Muqaddams* and supervised strictly their police duties.

The *Amil* had equally important duties connected with the land revenue collection and its administration. This is clear from the statements of Abbas. It became known to him (Sher Shah) that the Imams and religious persons had, since the time of Sultan Abrahim, by bribing the *Amils*, got into their possession more land than they were entitled to hold; he, therefore, resumed their holdings, and investigating the cases himself, gave to each his right, and did not entirely deprive any man of his possessions'.[26] The existence of the *Amil's* office is as well proved by the description of the administrative set up given by Abbas. 'In every Sarkar, he (Sher Shah) appointed a Chief *Shiqdar* and a chief *Munsif* that they might watch the conduct of both the Amils and the people, or embazzle the king's affairs'.[27] Clearly, the *Amil* in his area was responsible for putting into execution the *Farmans* of the grants of lands, for making the entries of the various holdings of the Khalsa, the Jagir and the *'Madad-i-Maash'* lands. He had also to demarcate the boundaries of the various holdings and of the Parganas themselves and to keep up the proper records for the same. He was as well responsible for the supervision of the work of the treasury.

The rank of the *Amil* was definitely lower than that of the *Shiqdar* to whom, in fact, he was responsible for the discharge of his functions. That Sher Shah stopped the practice of handing over the *Farmans* of the grants of land to the assignees for giving to the *Amil* concerned and sent them directly to the *Shiqdar* of the Pargana for the proper enforcement of the entries of the grants of the land, shows that the *Amil* was under the *Shiqdar* who was the superior most officer of the Pargana. As he is not mentioned as the Pargana officer itself under the *Shiqdar*, his jurisdiction was clearly less than the entire Pargana and worked under the *Shiqdar* of the Pargana.

In fact, for the land revenue collection he was the chief officer concerned with the *Raiyat* directly in his circle. Sher Shah realised the importance of this office and made it a rule to transfer the *Amils* every second year so that they may neither oppress the *Raiyat* nor incur any loss to the State in the revenue collection by any dishonest means.[28]

No other Afghan source has mentioned this territorial administrative division but the division of the *'Qasba'* was an old one and its existence can be traced even after the Sur regime.

Besides the *Muhasil*, the other officials of the *Qasba* were the *Qanungo* and the *Chaudhari*.[29] The *Qanungo* had more or less the same duties on a large scale as the *Patwari* in the village. He was responsible for the maintenance of full revenue records for his entire circle with full supervisory control over the *Patwaries* in his jurisdiction. He was also responsible for the inspection of the crops at the time of assessment and would help the *Amil* of the Pargana in the fixation of the assessment of the villages under him. He could be trusted to possess the knowledge of the assessment of the various villages from year to year.[30] He was responsible to the Pargana *Amil* for his functions. He was most likely paid a monthly salary by the State and was considered to be one of the important officials in the Pargana.

The Chaudhari was the head of the *Muqaddams* of the various villages in his circle.[31] He was, likewise, responsible for the peace and order and the collection of the land revenue in the villages under his jurisdiction. He supervised the work of the *Muqaddams* under him and assisted them in the discharge of their duties.

Next higher administrative unit was the Pargana, which too was a continuation of the Sultanate administration. There were one hundred thousand and thirty (100030) Parganas in the whole of the Empire.[32]

Abbas, Rizqullah and Abdullah, have all given a list of the officers connected with the Pargana administration. The head of the Pargana administration was the *Shiqdar*. In him were combined the military, civil and the revenue powers. Besides his functions of preservation of law and order, he was responsible for the realisation of the entire revenue in the Pargana and especially to suppress the refractory elements who refused payment of the revenue.[33] Sher Shah entrusted the *Shiqdar* with duties of the land revenue, administration, which were formerly performed by the *Amil* of the Pargana.[34] Sher Shah would send the *Farmans* of assignments and religious grants directly to the *Shiqdar* of the Pargana concerned, who, was enjoined upon to allot the grant after proper measurement and demarcation.[35] All the revenue officials of the village, *Qasba* and the Pargana worked under his strict supervision and would bank upon him in the difficulties that befell the realisation of the land revenue. The *Shiqdar* had equally to safeguard the interests of the *Raiyat*.[36]

The *Amil*[37] was the assessment officer of the Pargana. He was responsible for the assessment of the land revenue upon the holdings of the cultivators in accordance with the methods of assessment in operation in a particular area. His duties of assessment were all the more important after the introduction of the measurement method, wherein sown field had to be surveyed and assessment to be levied upon. He would naturally be responsible for the maintenance of the full records which were prepared by the *Patwaries* in the villages. In his duties, he was assisted by the *Qanungos*, *Patwaries* and *Muqaddams* who acted in their respective circles on behalf of the *Amil*. Whenever any crop was damaged due to the march of the forces, the assessment of the compensation was determined by the *Amil* of the Pargana.[38] The *Amil* had to be very vigilent as Sher Shah was very particular about the proper assessment for the realisation of the land revenue. Abbas mentions special interest taken by Sher Shah in the appointment of honest and competent persons appointed as the *Amil* of the Pargana.[39]

The *Fotehdar*[40] or the *Khazanchi*[41] was the Pargana treasurer. He was responsible for the receipt of the land revenue received from the *Muqaddams* of the villages or the *Muhasils* of the *Qasbas* (centres). He had to keep regular accounts of the total land revenue received in the Pargana and safeguarding the *Khazana* itself.

Two clerks (*Karkun*), one dealing with the papers and records in Hindi and the other in Persian were attached to the main Pargana Office.[42] They assisted the *Amil* and the *Shiqdar* in the correspondence and preserved the records in Hindi and Persian respectively. All revenue records concerning various villages and the *Qasbas* in the Pargana were maintained in the *Muhafizkhana* under their supervision.

Above the Pargana, the largest unit known to exist in the days of Sher Shah was the Sarkar which comprised of numerous Paraganas under its jurisdiction.[43] There were in all forty seven Sarkars in the empire.[44] The head of the Sarkar administration was *Shiqdar-i-Shiqdaran*.[45] He too, like the *Shiqdar* of the Pargana under him, comprised military, civil and the revenue powers. He was specially enjoined to look to the interests of the *Raiyat* so that nobody should oppress them.[46] He had also as well to safeguard the finances and the treasuries of the State in the Sarkar against any misappropriation on the part of any official. If any of the *Raiyat* rebelled or caused disturbance in the realisation of the land revenue, he was to inflict upon them deterrent punishement.[47]

The Chief Officer to assist the *Shiqdar-i-Shiqdaran* in the discharge of his civil and revenue duties was *Munsif-i-Munsifan*.[48] The Chief *Munsif* was to supervise the finances, treasuries, and the entire land revenue administration in the Sarkar. He had to inspect the work of all the land revenue officials of the Sarkar so that none of them oppressed the *Raiyat*. He would once checkmate any high-handedness on the part of the revenue officers and safeguard the interests of the *Raiyat*. He would adjudicate all land revenue disputed cases and the dispute of the boundaries of the Pargana.[49]

No *Subhas* are known to exist in the reign of Sher Shah as the Empire was divided into the *Sarkars*. But there are certain references to the territorial portions of the empire like Bengal and Multan where the *'Hakims'* were appointed. It seems that the military and the civil powers as well for the collection of the revenue were entrusted to them. In Bengal, *Qazi Faziliat* was appointed as the Governor of Bengal.[50] As the *Amin* of Bengal, he was naturally the head of the land revenue administration as well of the entire province. In Multan, Haibat Khan Naizi, who supported the Biluchis, was entrusted with all powers of land revenue administration.[51] In both the cases of these provinces, the *Hakims* were entrusted with the financial and the revenue affairs as well and no separate officers for these functions can be traced. Beside these two provinces, no other units larger than the Sarkar can be traced from any of the sources.

At the centre, the minister incharge of the revenue and finances was *Diwan-i-Wazarat.* He supervised the entire finances and the revenue collection of the whole of the empire. He combined in him the powers of the financial Secretary, audit and accounts and the revenue ministry. Above him was the Sultan himself who devoted himself to the interests of the peasantry and regularly checked the accounts of the empire.

References

1. Dr. Qureshi, *The administration of the Sultanate of Delhi,* p. 98; The Pargana officials under Akbar.
2. *Tawarikhi-i-Daulat-E-Sher Shahi* by Hasan Ali Khan. Farmans translated by Dr. K.P. Tripathi, *Medieval India Quarterly,* Vol. I, 1950, M.U. Aligarh, p. 63.
3. *Tarikh-i-Shah Shahi* by Abbas Sarwani, Persian text, p. 30.
4. *Tawarikhi-i-Daulat-E-Sher Shahi* by Hasan Ali Khan; *Medieval India Quarterly,* M.U. Aligarh, p. 63.
5. *Ibid.,* p. 62.
6. *Tarikh-i-Shah Shahi* by Abbas, Persian text, p. 31.
7. *Ibid.,* p. 31.
8. *Ibid.,* p. 30; *Makhzan-i-Afghana* by Niamat Ullah, Pers. text; Ms. 379 State Library Rampur, p. 207; Dorn's *History of the Afghans,* Part I, p. 82.
9. *Ibid.,* p. 31.
10. *Ibid.,* p. 31.
11. *Tawarikhi-i-Daulat-E-Sher Shahi* by Hasan Ali Khan. *Medieval India Quarterly,* 1950, M.U. Aligarh, p. 62.
12. *Tarikh-i-Shah Shahi* by Abbas, Persian text, p. 31.
13. *Ibid.,* pp. 30-31.
14. *Makhzan-i-Afghana,* Persian text, Ms. no. 379, State Library Rampur, p. 207.
15. *Tawarikh-i-Daulat-E-Sher Shahi* by Hasan Ali Khan. *Medieval India Quarterly,* M.U. Aligarh, p. 63.
16. *Ibid.,* p. 63.
17. *Tarikh-i-Shah Shahi* by Abbas, Persian text, p. 27.
18. *Tawarikhi-i-Daulat-E-Sher Shahi* by Hasan Ali Khan *Medieval India Quarterly,* M.U. Aligarh, p. 63.

19. *Tarikh-i-Shah Shahi* by Abbas, Persian text, p. 304.
20. *Tarikh-i-Shah Shahi* by Abbas, Persian text, p. 27.
21. *Ibid.*, p. 29.
22. *Tawarikh-i-Daulat-E-Sher Shahi* by Hasan Ali Khan, *Medieval India Quarterly,* M.U. Aligarh, p. 63.
23. *Ibid.*, p. 63.
24. *The Administration of the Delhi Sultanate,* Dr. Qureshi has identified the office of the *Muhasil* with the *Khazanadar* or the *Fotadar*—an officer who received payments of revenue. 'The Pargana officials under Akbar, *Islamic Culture*, Jan. 1942, p. 88. But this view is contradicted by the description of Hasan who calls him *Nazim* responsible for the general administration of the centre. In fact, the term *Muhasil* underwent a change from the time of Ziaud Din Barani to Sher Shah. The office of the *Amil* as well underwent a change from the full fledged revenue officer incharge of the Pargana to an officer of the circle of a Pargana.
25. *Tarikh-i-Shah Shahi* by Abbas, Persian text. p. 260; Elliot, Vol.IV. p. 420.
26. *Tarikh-i-Shah Shahi* by Abbas. Persian text. M.U.Aligarh, p. 263; Ms.1.0. F113a; Elliot, Vol.IV, p. 423.
27. *Tarikh-i-Shah Shahi* by Abbas. Persian text, p. 305.
28. *Tarikh-i-Shah Shahi* by Abbas. Persian text. p. 306. *Waqiat-i-Mushtaqi*. Rotograph. M.U.Aligarh, p. 213.
29. *Tarikh-i-Daudi*. Persian text. Ms.no. M.U.Aligarh, p. 179.
30. *Tarikh-i-Shah Shahi* by Abbas. Persian text, p. 305; *Waqiat-i-Mushtaqi* Rotograph. Persian text. M.U.Aligarh, p. 213.
31. This practice continued in the Mughal times. Various letters in *Daftar-i-Dewani-wa-Hazuri*, Jaipur.
32. *Tarikh-i-Shah Shahi* by Abbas; Persian text, p. 264. M.U. Aligarh; *Tarikh-i-Shah Shahi* by Abbas, Delhi, Ms., p. 326; I.O. Ms. F 113b; *Tarikh-i-Daudi*; printed by M.U.Aligarh, p. 130.
33. *Tarikh-i-Shah Shahi* by Abbas. Persian text. p. 304; The Pargana staff has been mentioned especially for the collection of the land revenue. So, the *Shiqdar* was naturally the head of the land revenue administration as well.

    وقانون تحصیل زراز رعیت وآبادانی مملکت چنان قرار یافتہ بود کہ درمہر پرگنہ یک شقدار و یک

    آمین و یک فوجدار و یک کارکن فارسی تعین نمودہ بود۔

    Tarikh-i-Shah Shahi Persian text, p. 304; Waqiat Mushtaqi. Persian text, p. 213, *Tarikh-i-Daudi*. Persian text, Ms.no. M.U. Aligarh, p. 117.
34. From the description of Barni, it appears that the *Amil* was the head of the land revenue administration of the Pargana. *Tarikh Feroze Shai*. p. 36, 'The Pargana officials under Akbar' by Dr. Qureshi. p. 72; Now the position of the *Amil* was submerged to the revenue officer of the Circle under the Pargana.

35. *Tarikh-i-Shah Shahi* by Abbas. Persian text. Ms. M.U.Aligarh, p. 263; Ms. I.O. F113a; Elliot, Vol.IV. p. 423; *Waqiat-i-Mushtaqi*. Rotograph. Persian text, M.U.Aligarh. p. 221.
36. *Tarikh-i-Shah Shahi* by Abbas. Persian text. p. 304.
37. *Ibid.*, p. 304; *Waqiat-i-Mushtaqi*. Rotograph. M.U.Aligarh, p. 213.
38. *Tarikh-i-Shah Shahi* by Abbas. Persian text, p. 259, Ms. M.U.Aligarh, Ms. 1.0.F111b-112a; Elliot Vol.IV. p. *Waqiat-i-Mushtaqi*. Rotograph. M.U.Aligarh, p. 220.
39. *Tarikh-i-Shah Shahi* by Abbas. Persian text.
40. *Ibid.*, p. 304; *Waqiat-i-Mushtaqi*. Rotograph Br.Museum. M.U.Aligarh, p. 213.
41. *Tarikh-i-Daudi*. Persián text. Ms. M.U.Aligarh, p. 117.
42. *Tarikh-i-Shah Shahi* by Abbas. Persian text, p. 304; *Waqiat-i-Mushtaqi*. Rotograph. Persian text. M.U.Aligarh. *Tarikh-i-Daudi*. Persian text, Ms. M.U.Aligarh, p. 117.
43. *Tarikh-i-Shah Shahi* by Abbas. Persian text. p. 305; *Waqiat-i-Mushtaqi*. Rotograph. Persian text. M.U.Aligarh, p. 213.
44. *Tarikh-i-Shah Shahi* by Abbas; *Waqiat-i-Mushtaqi*. Persian text. ; *Tarikh-i-Dilkhusha* by Innayat Ullah f, 47A.
45. *Tarikh-i-Shah Shahi* by Abbas. Persian text, p. 305; *Waqiat-i-Mushtaqi*, p. 213.
46. *Ibid.*
47. *Ibid.*
48. *Ibid.*
49. *Tarikh-i-Shah Shahi* Persian text by Abbas, p. 305; *Waqiat-i-Mushtaqi* Persian text, p. 213. The text of Abbas for the duties of the *Shiqdar-i-Shiqdaran* and *Munsif-i-Munsifan* is joint and have described their functions in a combined manner but their respective spheres can be worked out.
50. *Tarikh-i-Shah Shahi* Persian text, p. 311; *Waqiat-i-Mushtaqi*. Rotograph. Persian text. M.U.Aligarh, p. 216.
51. *Tarikh-i-Shah Shahi* by Abbas. Ms. M.U.Aligarh. pp. 217-18.

Chapter 6

Land Revenue System During the Early Period of Akbar's Reign (First Ten Years)

The first ten years of Akbar's reign is a preparatory period and hence of transitionary stage in the evolution of the Indian Land Revenue System. The methods of assessment and collection of the period of Sher Shah and Islam Shah and, in fact, the whole administrative machinery continued during the brief interregnum of Hamayun's rule after his return from Persia. The only change effected by Hamayun was the replacement of the Afghan service personnel with the loyal Mughal servants down to the *Qasba* organisation where too a Mughal Chaudhary and a Qanungo were appointed.[1] The village administration, which had more or less hereditary officials, continued to run as before but under the supervision of the Mughal officials. After his installation at Delhi, Hamayun made vigorous efforts for full six months for the management and financial organization of the Parganas, as of the assignments of the territories he occupied.[2]

Though, inevitably, there was political disorder and financial collapse at Islam Shah's death, there was no breakdown in the administration and operations of the methods of land revenue as had been worked out by the Sur rulers. Nevertheless, Hamayun's sudden demise left the whole task to be completed during the early years of Akbar's reign. Some writers unduly stress the dislocation of operations after the death of Islam Shah[3] as if these meant a complete cessation or a relapse to the method of assessment of the pre-Sher Shah days.[4] The fact, however, is that Akbar's early years do not indicate any fundamental breach with the Sur regime. Hence, Akbar's ministers did not have to start 'de novo' from the pre-Sher Shah phase of land administration and to re-incorporate the notions and patterns of Sher Shah. Rather, the revenue system presents an unbroken continuity. That the traits and benefits of the Sur administration were not lost to Akbar's inheritance has an explicit recognition from Abul Fazl himself.[5] The old principles and canons continued in operation and even further developed according to the ideas of the experts of Akbar's reign.

One outstanding feature of Akbar's early regime is that some of the officials who had served the Surs were picked to run his administration. Khwaja Bahlol Malik Khwaja Sara had served Salim Shah, son of Sher Shah with distriction and integrity and had been awarded the title of Mohammed Khan.[6] He was an expert in revenue matters[7] and had risen to eminence through sheer merit.[8] He was promoted to the office of *Wazarat* with the title of Itimad Khan in the 7th *Ilahi* era (1563)[9] and was assigned the administration of the crown lands, collection of the revenues, the treasury and the *Bayutat.*[10] And, of course, the celebrated Todar Mal had gained first-rate experience under Sher Shah. The re-employment of such men by Akbar was a very sagacious move as it provided the incipient Empire much technical knowledge of revenue matters of the earlier period in the absence of which the entire working of the administrative machine would have been woefully retarded.

Thus the first five years witness the re-arrangements of the finances, revenue and assignments of the jagirs under Bairm Khan's tutelage, while the Emperor himself was being nurtured behind the veil. In the very first *Ilahi* year (1556), most of the districts which came to be occupied were distributed as Jagirs and left to the Jagirdar's management.[11] Ali Quli Khan Shaibani was assigned the Sarkar of Sambhal and the Parganas of the Doab and was raised to the title of Khan Zaman.[12] Abdullah Khan was appointed to the Sarkar of Kalpi and received the title of Shuja-at Khan.[13] *Qiya Khan* was entrusted the charge of the Agra regime.[14] Iskander Khan with title of Khan Alam and Maulana Pir Mohammed Shirwani, being attached to the royal person were stationed at the Centre in charge of political and financial matters.[15] In the third year (1559), Khan-i-Khanan Bairam Khan renewed his efforts to strengthen civil matters further. Regular biweekly meetings of important officials were held in the Diwan Khanna by the Khan-i-Khanan for closely deliberating political and financial matters, and the decisions thereof were forwarded for royal signature.[16] Despite Bairam Khan's displeasure, Mulla Pir Muhammed remained the finance minister till the end of 1560.[17] After Bairam Khan's dismissal, the political and the financial affairs of the State were run by Satan Khan-i-Azam Shamsud Din Mohammed quite efficiently with strict impartiality.[18] At the same time, Udham Khan (son of Maham Anga) was promoted to the office of Diwani-Ala.[19] Later, in the same year, Shihabu-d-din Ahmad Khan was entrusted with the political and the financial affairs.[20] Khwaja Abdul Majid earned the title of Asaf Khan and was appointed as the Diwan-i-Sarkar Ala (Chief Diwan). As such, he was to look after the governance of Delhi, forming part of the office of *Vizier.*[21] The administration under these men showed marked progress. Abul Fazl remarks, 'The market of administration became brisk'.[22] In the same year, on Abul Majid Asaf Khan going off towards Pannah against Raja Ram Chand, Shamsud Din Muhammad Khan took control of political and financial affairs and acquitted himself well with his sound judgment.[23]

Likewise, the newly conquered territories were brought under the same principles of financial and revenue management with the interests of the peasantry being always kept in view. The conquest of Malwa and the revenue reforms made there in 1563 form a marked stage in the early administration. Khwaja Muin-d-din Ahmad Farankhudi, with the fresh rank of Khan, was placed in charge of the revenue affairs of the Province and had especially to look after the Jagirdars and to define the exchequer lands.[24] Abdulla Khan Uzbeg, who had conquered the province, was appointed as Governor and under him Muin Khan for revenue matters. The latter gave an excellent account of his knowledge. He remedied the absenteeism, which had occurred on account of the marches and counter-marches of the troops.[25] He encouraged the peasantry and the farmers for increasing cultivation. He allotted the fiefs to various dignitaries in accordance with the rulers.[26]

In the 7th *Ilahi* era (1563), Itimad Khan was called upon to set in order the financial conditions of the state which had deteriorated in the sense that though the territorial expansion had brought in considerable addition to the revenues, the *mutsaddis* had shown great negligence and incapacity to manage the Khalsa lands and the revenues.[27] Further, they had been fraudulent in collecting treasures for themselves while neglecting collections from the Khalsa lands.[28] The royal household officers had suffered great losses and hardships on this account.[29] At this critical juncture, Itimad Khan presented his views and plans for augmenting revenues, which met with the Emperor's approval.[30] The latter put him in control of all the royal revenues, which hitherto were being embezzled.[31] Itimad Khan introduced new regulations for accountancy and treasury management as well as for realising the land revenue.[32] He started the work in the middle of the year and made a clean sweep of corrupt and dishonest persons and replaced them by honest and efficient personnel. Within a short period, Itimad Khan increased the yield from the Khalsa lands and thereby added very largely to the royal treasure.[33] The entire revenue and the treasury departments were given a new lease of life[34] and the finances of the State were made sound and stable for running the Civil government of the State efficiently.[35] In fact, Itimad Khan's measures stopped the doom of the State and saved it from bankruptcy.

Thereafter, the State did prosper greatly for in the 8th year of the *Illahi* era, with the ever-expanding domain and the cultivation, the revenues increased and multiplied and the lowering of the prices manifested itself year by year, month by month, and day by day.[36] In the very same year, a royal *Farman* was issued in the interests of the Ryots against any oppression. It said that from that day onwards throughout the Empire no revenue official, while realising the land revenue, should exercise any coercion or oppression upon the Ryots and full treasury became the settled policy of the State for its expansion.[37] In the same year, Muzaffar Khan Tarbati was appointed as the Diwan for this purpose.[38] Muzaffar was a capable revenue administrator. He had been the Collector of the Pargana Parasarur, and as a result of his success was made Diwan-Biyutat.[39] Thereafter, because of his competence and keen sense of integrity, he was promoted to the office of the Diwan with the title of Muzaffar Khan.[40] He implemented treasury operations in an admirable manner and his efforts led to improvements among the peasantry. For his good work in the *Wazarat*, he was further raised to the rank of an Amir.[42]

The method of assessment in the first ten years of Akbar's reign, so far as the measurement system went, was the adaptation of the procedure of the fixation of '*Ray*' of Sher Shah to the new method of the fixation of the prices thereupon. It is evident from the nineteen years' table of rates in the *Ain*,[43] and Abul Fazl's own statement that the most preferred method of assessment was that of measurement and the fixation of '*Ray*' thereupon—a system which had been devised by Sher Shah and which had continued till the early years of Akbar.[44] The main problem faced by Akbar's revenue experts was the procedure of the fixation of the prices of various crops to the '*Ray*' of a particular territory. It seems that in Sher Shah's time the commutation of '*Ray*' of a locality was done by the revenue officials themselves in the Pargana itself in accordance with the current prices of the various crops of the season (*Rabi* and *Kharif*) of the years. But this procedure of commutation of the prices underwent a change. In Akbar's early years, every season of the year (*i.e., Rabi* and *Kharif*) the revenue officials would pass on the '*Ray*' and the current rates of respective crops of every locality to the Central Government which fixed the rates of the various crops in accordance with the averaging process of the available '*Ray*' and price rates in different provinces.[45]

Moreland credits himself for discovering the fact that the tables of the '*Ray*' described in *Ain*,[46] were worked out in Sher Shah's time and adopted as such by Abul Fazl in the '*Ain*'.[47] As such, these historians have thought that these were adopted by the early Government of Akbar which had only to commute both the *Rabi* and the *Kharif* crops into cash rates in accordance with its own method of commutation of rates though Moreland has interpreted '*Ray*' rightly, he, too, has committed various errors in the details.[48]

Sharma has based his interpretation of all the land revenue measures and methods of Akbar on the fact of commutation of the *'Ray', i.e.,* the very schedule of the kind rates of Sher Shah into cash rates and that the 'Ray' of Sher Shah formed the basis of the Zabti System in the 25th year and thereafter as well for all assessments.[49]

Similarly, Misra holds that these tables are apparently those of Sher Shah and continued to be used for conversion into cash rates till the so-called 19th year settlement.[50] Moreland also thinks that the adoption of this 'Ray' figures forms the first phase of Akbar's administration until the 15th year when they were replaced by new Schedule-rates by Muzzaffar Khan and Todar Mal.[51] That Akbar began by enforcing a schedule of crop rates which had been made by Sher Shah and that it broke down in practice (and the failure was, of course, inevitable), for even the small area which he then ruled was too diverse in point of productivity for a single schedule to work for long.[52] Qureshi[53] and Saran,[54] though agreeing with Moreland about the retention of Sher Shah's '*Ray*' figures by Akbar, have not stated the period of their adoption in the latter's reign.

The thesis of Moreland and the concurrence with it of the other writers are not tenable on various grounds:

1. It is very doubtful that the *'Ray'* tables under question pertained to the original schedules of Sher Shah's time rather than of Akbar's reign.

(a) All the above writers have read into the particular sentence of the prevalence of the '*Ray*' in Sher Shah's period and its acceptance in Akbar's reign[55] in an isolated manner. In fact, the passages of the *'Ain'* describing the notions of the *'Ray'* and various cesses in different countries,[56] the determination of the same in Akbar's reign based upon the fixation of the Illahi *Gaz,*[57] the *Tanab,*[58] the *Bigha,*[59] the classification of the land and its details,[60] the fixation of the *'Ray'* thereupon[61] and the conversion of the same into cash rates through various experiments,[62] Nineteen Years' Rates,[63] the Ten Year Settlement (*Zabti*)[64] and the details of its application in different provinces[65] should be studied in continuation as one forms the basis of another and explains the evolution of the entire system or land revenue assessment in cash rates.[66] After explaining the method of measurement of the land with the *Ilahi Gaz, Tanab,* and the fixation of the *Bigha* as the unit of measurement of the land, Abul Fazl explains the classification of the land in accordance with the productivity of the soil. The *'Ray'* for the *Polaj* and the *Paurti* lands was fixed. This is quite evident from the example of the *Rabi* and *Kharif* crops quoted by Abul Fazl.[67] That the process of the fixation of *'Ray'* thus described was worked out by

Sher Shah and it continued in the reign of Akbar is absolutely clear. But this should not imply that the very quotations of different crops for the *Rabi 'Ray'* and the *'Kharif 'Ray'* were those of Sher Shah. These are simply examplary or illustrative quotations—either hypothetical or actual—prevailing in one of the *'Dasturs'* of Akbar's dominions at the time of compiling the *'Ain'* and quoted by Abul Fazl for explaining the method of fixation of *'Ray'* which is just one of the stages in the entire process of the evolution of the Zabti System. Moreland, at another place in conjunction with Ali, admits that these tables may be an 'example of the table of a particular *Dastur* and it may be generalisation from the *Dastur* figures.[68] Moreland and Ali have rightly hit in their imagination about the probability of the above mentioned *'Ray'* tables to be examplary quotation or generalisation but the joint writers are unable to come to any definite conclusion. If Moreland believes over here in the probability of the Ray quotations being examplary, all his previous convictions about the figures being of Sher Shah's *'Ray'* render him self-contradictory and even his open mind on the point render his main arguments and those of his followers rather dubious or questionable.

(b) Abul Fazl has not given any introduction before the quotation of the rates. If the schedule rates were the exact rates of the time of Sher Shah, Abul Fazl would have stated the name of the Pargana or the Sarkar of which the rates were. Such an omission and vagueness are in marked contrast to the entire exactitude of the tables elsewhere in the *Ain*.

(c) Abul Fazl does not give the Schedule rates for the *Prauti* lands but just observes that the process of the fixation of the *'Ray'* for the *Prauti* lands is the same as of *Polaj*.[69] Sher Shah, as already stated, had some classification of the land, but it is certain that his classification was not in the nature of *Polaj, Prauti, Chachar* and *Banjar*, which was definitely of Akbar's creation. This fact is admitted even by Qureshi.[70] It is, therefore, incredible that the schedule rates of the *Polaj* and the *Prauti* lands should be that of Sher Shah when such classification did not even exist. Saran also recognises that howsoever comprehensive Sher Shah's classification of land might have been, Akbar's was not a copy of his.[71] On the same plea, Saran himself has expressed doubts on the applicability of Sher Shah's schedule of Rates in Akbar's time.[72] Clearly, either Saran contradicts himself or at least leaves the matter inconclusive.

(d) In fact, these schedule rates of the various crops (*Ray*) do not represent the early phase of Akbar's administration either. Nor, as Moreland would imagine, are they quoted in the *Ain* as a document of merely historical interest when they had become obsolete after the changes in the *bigha* in Akbar's reign. The truth of the natter is that Abul Fazl's main idea is to explain with examples the process by which the State demand (in kind per *bigha*) came to be fixed, based on the average of the different categories of the soil—a method known to Sher Shah and which had continued in Akbar's reign as well.

(2) (a) Moreland's contention that these tables of Sher Shah's *'Ray'* were applied to all the portions of the Empire till the 15th year,[74] resulting inevitably in the failure of the experiment, is a mis-calculation of the process by which cash schedule rates were evolved. The mistake committed by the early revenue experts of Akbar was not the uniform applicability of a single *'Ray'* to the entire Empire but of averaging approximately the local Cash-Schedules rates already applied to the respective *'Rays'* into uniform Cash Schedule rates for the whole Empire or lesser territory thereof.

(b) Moreland believes that this Single *'Ray'* may have been applicable as a general schedule for the entire kingdom of Sher Shah and may have lasted for five years without breaking down.[75] But in reality, this mistake of the uniform application of one set of Schedule rates *'Ray'* was neither committed by Sher Shah nor by Akbar.

(c) The versions of Misra that Sher Shah's Schedule rates in kind continued to be the basis of the State demand in Akbar's time right till the so called 'Nineteen Year Settlement' and Sharma that it not only continued till the 25th year and formed the very basis of the *Zabti* system and got perpetuated thereafter are merely imaginative interpretations of the whole process of development of Akbar's assessment methods. Right from the beginning of his reign, the Schedule rates in kind (*Ray*) of all crops were prepared afresh every year according to the season—*Rabi* and *Kharif*—and prices of the crops were applied thereupon.[76] The question of the continuation of the same Schedule rates in kind (*Ray*) does not arise when yearly Schedule rates in kind were prepared. One set of rates for every year would be different from another set, as either the total produce for any kind of land per bigha or the mean produce or the '*Ray*' fixed thereupon would naturally differ from one year to another. It is untenable to think that one set of rates continued for so long. There was no 'Nineteen Year Settlement' in the reign of Akbar,[77] nor could the same '*Ray*' year after year form the basis of price commutation recorded in the 'Nineteen Years Rates'. Least of all, the same so-called Schedule rates (*Ray*) of Sher Shah could form the basis of the fixation of the *Zabti* Method of the 25th year. Both Misra and Sharma have completely misunderstood the implication of the use of '*Ray*' in the assessment policy in Akbar's revenue reforms.

The process by which the State demand in terms of the prices for the various crops was fixed and the determination of the total valuation of the whole Empire was known as *'Raqmi'*. According to Abul Fazl, in the times of Bairam Khan[78] and Khwaja Abdul Majid Khan,[79] the '*Jama*' of the Empire was *'Raqmi Qalmi'* (رقمی قلمی) [80] which continued in operation till the 11th year (1567) when it was replaced by another system by Muzaffar Khan.[81] This is one of the most perplexing passage in the *Akbar Nama.*

The passage contains the two-fold system of the fixation of the *'Jama'* which stands both for the fixation of the State demand and the total valuation of the revenues of the whole Empire.[82] On the basis of the prices of various crops and the *'Mahsul'* (average mean of different classes of the land per bigha each crop) received from the various parts of the Empire, the price for the bigha for each crop was somehow worked out. Thereafter, an approximate average mean of the price of the produce of the bigha for each crop of the different territories of the whole Empire or of the whole Province or still of a lesser territory depending on the policy and prices of the year was determined. One third of the price of the total produce of the bigha per crop was levied as the State demand which was 'fixed' and made 'uniform' for the entire circle. It is evident from the 'Nineteen Years Rates' that the demand for the same crop per bigha in the 6th and the 7th year was more or less uniform in the whole of the Province itself and in all the provinces of the Empire, excepting Malwa which has its own quotations.[83]

Wheat: 90 Dams in Agra, Allahabad, Oudh, Delhi and Lahore.

Common Rice: 70 Dams in Agra, Allahabad, Oudh, and Delhi. In Lahore 80 Dam.

Common Sugar Cane: 180 Dams in Agra, Allahabad, Oudh Delhi and Lahore.

Bareley: 80 Dams in Agra, Oudh and Delhi. 70 Dams in Allahabad and Lahore.

Indian Vetches: 80 Dams in Agra, Allahabad, Oudh and Lahore. 70 Dams in Delhi.

Ajwain: 80 Dams in Agra, Allahabad, Oudh, Delhi and Lahore.

Cotton: 120 Dams in Agra, Allahabad, Oudh, Delhi and Lahore.

Mash: 48 Dams in Agra, Allahabad, Oudh, Delhi and Lahore.

In the 8th year, for most of the crops the rates are uniform in the whole of the Province, though for some, the rates start varying within the same Province. Still in the case of many crops, the rates are uniform in all Provinces and in others, the rates are common in some Provinces only.[84]

Wheat

90 Dams in Allahabad and Oudh

80-90 Dams in Agra

84-90 Dams in Delhi

80 Dams in Lahore

Common Rice

70 Dams in Agra, Allahabad, Oudh, Delhi and Lahore.

Barley

80 Dams in Allahabad

70 Dams in Oudh in Lahore

60-70 Dams in Delhi

60-76 Dams in Agra

Indian Vetches

80 Dams in Allahabad and Oudh

70-86 Dams in Delhi

70-80 Dams in Agra

70 Dams in Lahore

In the 9th year as well, the uniformity of the demand for many crops is maintained in the Province itself and also for many, the uniformity in all the Provinces is maintained, as for example:[85]

Wheat 90

Dams in Agra, Allahabad, Oudh, Delhi and Lahore

Common Rice

70 Dams in Agra, Allahabd, Oudh, Delhi and Lahore

Common Sugar Cane

180 Dams in Agra, Allahabad, Oudh, Delhi and Lahore

Barley

80 Dams in Allahabad;

60 Dams in Agra, Oudh, Delhi and Lahore

Indian Vetches

80 Dams in Agra, Allahabad, Oudh, Delhi and Lahore

Similarly, the rates for cotton and Mash are common in Agra, Allahabad, Oudh, Delhi and Lahore

In the 10th year, uniformity for demand of a crop in the whole province and with certain variations for crops is kept up. Only in a few crops, the uniformity for the whole Empire is continued.[86]

Wheat

50-60 Dams Agra

60-64 Dams	Allahabad
52-60 Dams	Oudh
44-60 Dams	Delhi
50 Dams	Lahore

Common Rice

60 Dams in Agra, Allahabad, Oudh and Lahore.

70 Dams in Delhi

Barley

38-50 Dams in Agra

80-120 Dams in Allahabad

42-50 Dams in Oudh

32-50 Dams in Delhi

40 Dams in Lahore

Indian Vetches

44-56 Dams in Agra

56-64 Dams in Allahabad

40-56 Dams in Oudh

44-56 Dams in Delhi

48 Dams in Lahore

Ajwain

80 Dams in Agra, Allahabad, Oudh and Lahore

70-80 Dams in Delhi

Cotton

110 Dams in Agra, Allahabad, Oudh, Delhi and Lahore

Mash

44 Dams in Allahabad, Oudh and Lahore

36-44 Dams in Agra and Delhi

Of course, from the 11th year onwards, there is no uniformity for the demand for the whole Empire and the demand for most of the crops even within one Province varies excepting Lahore and Malwa where uniformity of rates for the crops continued till the 14th year.[87]

11th Year

Wheat

56-60 Dams in Agra

80-100 Dams in Allahabad

52-80 Dams in Oudh

48-56 Dams in Delhi

56 Dams in Lahore

Common Rice

52-60 Dams in Agra

80-90 Dams in Allahabad

60-80 Dams in Oudh

52-60 Dams in Delhi

60 Dams in Lahore

Barley

38-50 Dams in Agra

80 Dams in Allahabad

42-60 Dams in Oudh

32-40 Dams in Delhi

40 Dams in Lahore

Mash

44 Dams in Agra

54-70 Dams in Allahabad

44-54 Dams in Oudh

40 Dams in Delhi

44 Dams in Lahore

Cotton

110 Dams in Agra, Delhi and Lahore

120 Dams in Allahabad

110-130 Dams in Oudh

Thus, the demand for a crop per bigha was fixed (*Raqmi*) either in the whole Empire or in the Province or in a lesser territory depending upon the princes of the year.

Moreland asserts that for the 6th to 9th years when a single set of commutation rates was adopted for the five Provinces, the uniform grain demand was commuted by a single price-list, probably based on the rates prevailing in the Imperial Camp and that this is especially true of the pulses.[88] This view cannot be accepted as it is in direct contradiction to the average process of *'Raqmi'* price fixation as explained before. Moreland has drawn the inference from some of the examples quoted by him. This involves much of generalization, which is not at all borne out by the

'Nineteen Year Rates'. No distinction was made in the procedure of the fixation of the price list for the grain crops and the other ones. Usually, the prices are comparatively higher in the above three years as much for other crops as for grain. As for example, the price of cotton in Delhi is 12 Dams for the 6th to 9th year, 110 Dams from 10th to 12th year and 90 Dams in the 13th year.[89] In Agra, its price is 120 Dams from the 6th to 8th year, 130 in 9th year, 110 from the 10th to 11th year, 70-92 Dams in the 12th year.[90]

Apart from this, there are grain crops whose princes remain the same even after the 9th year and some which would even show rise and some fall in the prices thereafter.

Province	Crop	Price Years
Allahabad[91]	Common Rice	70 Dam from 6th to 9th year
		60 Dams in the 10th year
		80-90 Dams in the 11th and 12th year
	Barley	70 Dams in the 6th and 7th year
		80 Dams in the 9th year
		80-120 Dams in the 10th year
		80 Dams in the 11th and 12th year
		70-76 Dams in the 13th year
		50-106 Dams in the 14th year
		50-100 Dams in the 15th year
Allahabad[92]	Kodram	44 Dams in the 6th to 10th year
		44-64 Dams in the 11th year
		54-64 Dams in 12th and 13th year
		36 Dams in the 14th year
		21-60 Dams in the 15th year
Oudh[93]	Kodram	44 Dams in 6th to 8th year
		44-50 Dams in the 9th year
		44 Dams in the 10th year
		44-54 Dams in the 11th and 12th year
		50-54 Dams in the 12th year
Delhi[94]	Kur Rice	60 Dams in the 6th to 9th years
		40-60 Dams in the 10th year
		60 Dams in the 11th year
		40-54 Dams in the 12th year

30-70 Dams in the 24th year

Moreland's generalisation is not true even for the pulses as some of them retain the same price level even after the 9th year and would even show progressive rise in the prices thereafter.

Province	Crop	Price	Years
Agra[95]	Mung	48	6th to 9th years
		44	10th to 13th years
		22-65½	21st year
		22-50	22nd year
		27-44	23rd year
		32-50	24th year
Allahabad[96]	Mustard	80 Dams	6th/9th years
		70-80	10th year
		80	11th to 13th years
	Moth	48	6th to 8th year
		54	9th year
		44	10th year
		54-70	11th year
		50	12th and 13th years
		36	14th year
		22-60	15th year
	Mash	48 Dams	6th to 8th years
		54 Dams	9th year
		44 Dams	10th year
		54-70	11th year
		50	12th year
Oudh[97]	Mash	48	6th to 8th years
		54	9th year
		44	10th year
		44-54	11th year
		44-50	12th year
		50-54	13th year

All these examples go contrary to Moreland's grain-price-theory from the 6th to 9th years. It seems from the 'Nineteen Years Rates' that on the whole for most of the crops—whether grains or others—the prices are usually higher as compared to the later years.[98] This was most likely due to the prevalence of the genuine higher prices in the market. The fact that the circle of uniformity of the prices was much wider in the earlier years in itself usually gave higher price in average approximation. The process of the 'fixation' and of 'uniformity' based on the mean averaging process was naturally very complicated and tedious.[99] From the official viewpoint, it was an extremely laborious task and even from the viewpoint of the cultivators' interests, it might do injustice to the peasants of any region or Province where the current prices for the crops happened to be depressed or it might benefit a section of the peasantry where the prices happened to be high, because the Empire as a whole or even one whole Province was too large an area for the uniformity of the prices. This, therefore, was definitely a retrogressive step as compared to the Sur regime during which the demand was fixed on the current prices in the locality itself.

The 'fixed' nature of the term '*Raqm*' is also borne out by the practice of the fixed demand with the same term even in the 19th century in the district of Dhawar, Bombay State.[100] Sir Richard Burn adopts the same interpretation of the term with uniform cash rate fixed on a given area in the whole of the Province or the Empire.[101] He has rightly hit on the significance of the term but he has not been able to elucidate it in terms of Akbar's System where the uniformity of the cash demand was per bigha per crop in his whole Empire or the Province, whereas in the 19th century, the uniformity of the demand rates in cash quoted by Captain Wingate[102]or in the *Dharwar District Gazetter*[103] are for the standard unit of an area regardless of the crop sown. Moreover, Burn is not correct in thinking that the practice of averaging process of the demand land (good, middelling, bad) of Sher Shah had relapsed.[104] In fact, the process, *i.e., 'Mahsul'* of each territory was the basis for working out the uniformity of the demand. His assertion that the cash demand had no relation to the productivity of the soil is too much of a generalisation as the demand was fixed on the average mean of the *'Mahsul'* (average produce per bigha) and the prices of the crops of the various territories. There is no denying that at places, the application of the uniform prices would prove harsh for the peasants in unit so large as the whole Empire or the whole Province.

The second stage in the *'Jama Qalmi Raqmi'* was the total valuation of the State demand thus fixed. Normally, the summing up of the State demand in various regions and the Provinces should make up the entire valuation of the Revenues of the Empire. But during this phase of Akbar's regime, the territories of the Empire were not so extensive,[105] and with much less income in proportion to the large and ever-expanding personnel of the state servants with rapid promotions[106] and entitled to Jagirs in lieu of their salaries.[107] This need of larger income for assignment of Jagirs was met by the artificial inflation in the total valuation, which was taken for granted by the high State authorities.[108] In other words, the total valuation of the Revenues was based not on the actual return figures from various portions but rather on the approximate conjectural returns and assumed valuation of the various portions of the Empire.[109] It seems even the inflation was arbitrary and approximate, and not based on any exact ratio for artificial enhancement of the valuation. Consequently, the valuation of the Jagirs assigned was done by the authorities at their discretion with (artifically) enhanced amounts.[110] Much favouritism and corruption prevailed for making assignments even with more or less artificial enhancement.[111] This state of things prevailed until the system of total fixation of valuation (*Jama*) was replaced by Muzaffar Khan by one based on actual return in the 11th year.[112]

Other writers have offered different versions on the subject. Beveridge thinks, "most probably the word *'Raqmi'* refers to the assessment being made according to the kind of produce".[113] This over-simplified and superficial view cannot be accepted as various other systems like *'Ray'* and *'Zabti'* too were based on the kind of produce but none was termed *'Raqmi'* by Abul Fazl. Beveridge's other conjecture that the "assessment which was expressed in *Raqam* or *Sayak* characters, *i.e.,* contractions of Arabic words instead of Hindi figures"[114] seems plausible to Moreland and Ali who also imagine it as an "affair of figures" or "a Paper affair".[115] In reality, this is too much of a literal translation of a term, which Abul Fazl used in a purely technical sense. That Hindi terminology of revenue terms was translated into Persian in Akbar's reign by Todar Mal is undobtedly true, but that was done at a later stage.[116] When Arabic *Sayaq* (*Raqmi*) for the Revenue terminology once came to be adopted, these could not be found unsuitable and abandoned in the 11th year. Indeed, it is clear that they continued to exist throughout the Mughal reign.[117] What was dropped was the *'Raqmi Qalmi'* System. Mutamad Khan has explained the procedure of the fixation of *'Jama'* based on approximation and conjecture in a clear language,[118] which is entirely contrary to the version of Beveridge. Abul Fazl himself describes, in simple unambiguous language,[119] the setting aside of *'Raqmi'* fixation of *'Jama'* and its substitution by another in the 11th year by Muzaffar Khan. This clearly would throw out any likelihood of the *Sayyaq* figures for the *'Jama'* in either methods of *'Jama'*.

Moreland and Ali emphasised the divergence between the *'Jama'* assessed and the actual yields of the crop[120] rather than the difference between the actual and the inflated valuations—a point which they failed to understand. Later on, Moreland gave it the meaning as 'arbitrary'[121] in relation to the valuation of the Empire.

Moreland agrees that *'Jama'* could be defined in both ways, *i.e.,* as the State demand and the 'Valuation', but in the context of this passage, he argues it could stand only for the latter sense.[122] Qureshi's criticism of Moreland is irrelevant as both explain the passage in terms of valuation.

Qureshi based his arguments on (i) *Raqmi'* simply means written;[123] (ii) the word *'Jama'* has nowhere been used for State demand;[124] (iii) The purpose for this was the artificial increase in the salaries of the high officials which was paid by assignment and an inflated demand would not have required inflation in the value of the assignments,[125] and (iv) That the inflation in valuation was the cause of corruption and that the peasant would not be in a position to offer bribes to the officials of the Ministry and, therefore, corruption could increase and decrease only the valuation of the assignment.[126] (v) Finally, Qureshi accepts Moreland's conjectural arguments against *Raqmi's* relation to State demand—that the figures in *Ain-i-Nuzdah Sala* would become meaningless and fictitious,[127] and this would further imply a lumpsum assessment, which is opposed to the entire spirit of Akbar's measures from the beginning.[128]

The views of either of them, Moreland and Qureshi, cannot be accepted. Qureshi's analysis is not only insufficient but based on the wrong reading of the *Ain.* In regard to point (i) of his arguments, it is admitted that *'Raqmi'* literally does mean "written" and yet to Abul Fazl it was a technical revenue term signifying a method of assessment, and valuation. The use of the term *'Jama-i-Raqmi-Qalmi'* in *Akbar Nama*[129] does not in any way help its definition excepting to state clearly that the *'Jama'* which was *'Raqmi'* was recorded (put down). *'Qalmi'* simply means 'recorded' or 'taken down'. This is also confirmed by the explanation of procedure of fixation of the *'Jama'* given by Mutamad Khan in simple language as a substitute for *'Raqmi'.*[130]

As regards Qureshi's point (ii), in order to appreciate the two-fold significance of the term *'Jama',* both as State demand and valuation, Qureshi has only to refer to some of the *Dasturulamls* and chronicles.

As regards point (iii), the passage not only conveys the means of payment of the assignees by inflated valuation but it also implies the method of assessment which was the basic thing. The reference of the *'Jama'* to both the State demand and the Valuation would not necessarily imply the inflation in the former as well. In fact, these are two distinct things conveyed in the passage, the method of assessment which was *'Raqmi'* and the inflation in the valuation to meet the needs of the assignees.

As to Qureshi's point (iv), his reading that the corruption was the cause of inflation is not correct because inflation and artificially raised valuation were the outcome of deliberate official policy which was intended to meet the ever-growing demands of the assignees against the shortage of land. This is clear from *Akbar Nama* as well as from Mutamad Khan. No uniform inflation in accordance with any ration, however, was adopted[131] and the fact that artificial valuation depended on the wisdom or discretion of the State officials at times resulted in corruption. In other words, corruption might have been the outcome of arbitrary inflation but it was not its cause and in the context, inflation and corruption related to assignees of Jagirs, as far as the attitude of the State was concerned, and not to the cultivators.

As to Qureshi's point (v), both Moreland and Qureshi have failed to appreciate that the figures in the 'Nineteen Years Rates' confirm the *'Raqmi'* fixation of the assessment rather than contradict it. They are by no means rendered fictitious and meaningless. They were intended for application as there was no difference in the demand levied and demand assessed. The inflation was effected on the total *'Jama'* rather on the demand itself. Moreland's arguments against the 'arbitrary' fixation of the State demand are quite weighty[132] and Qureshi's assertion against the inflation of the assessment demand on the peasants is equally justified as in that case Abul Fazl and Mutamad Khan would have mentioned the hardship of the cultivators rather than the Jagirdars[133] who actually suffered in the inflated valuation. But the entire difficulty both with Moreland and Qureshi is that they have missed the significance of the *'Raqmi'* procedure of assessment and have rendered *'Raqmi'* and inflation as synonymous. In fact, Abul Fazl has describe these two distinct developments, 'fixed' assessment and inflation of the total valuation jointly in a technical and terse language.

'Raqmi' assessment would not in any case and actually did not, lead to the lumpsum assessment. That the assessment was based on the actual *'Mahsul'* and the prices applied thereupon is stated by Abul Fazl himself.[134] This would be levied on the individual holders according to the 'fixed' rates in the Empire of the province as is evident from '19 Years Rates.' This procedure of assessment on the individual holdings is just the antithesis of the lumpsum assessment.

Besides this, when the *'Raqmi'* method was discarded in the 11th year, both Abul Fazl and Mutamad Khan emphasise the change in the procedure of the assessment and the total valuation based on actual returns.[135] It is not consonance with the changes effected by Muzaffar Khan that the *'Raqmi'* should have concerned only with the total valuation. Qureshi following the *Ain* blindly has omitted reference to the 11th year's reform and believes that the defect of inflation was removed in the 15th year.[136]

Even the latter reform, as explained further, was directed both at the re-adjustment of Schedule rates and the new valuation. Moreland believes that the *'Raqmi'* was set aside in the 11th year.[147] Though he surprisingly considers the 11th and the 15th years reforms as a part and parcel of the same scheme,[138] still he thinks that the former attempt was aimed only at re-evaluation and the latter both at the re-fixation of the assessment demand and new valuation.

Abul Fazl in the passage of *'Jama-Deh-Sala'* starts with the difficulty of the fixation of the procedure of State demand and thereafter mentions the method adopted for the fixation of the State demand and the nature of the total valuation determined in the abnormal situation of the shortage of the land. Then he proceeds to the modifications effected later on in the State demand and total valuation ultimately resulting in the fixation of the Zabti System of State demand[139] (which must have resulted in the total valuation as well though not stated by Abul Fazl in the same passage). From the beginning of the text to the end, the *'Jama'* as State demand and as 'total valuation' are linked up—a fact which is ignored by the above writers. Clearly, *'Jama'* in the text of *'Jama Qalmi Raqmi'* refers to both the State demand and the valuation.

The second phase of Akbar's Revenue Administration begins with the promotion of Muzaffar Khan to the rank of Finance Minister in the 11th year of the reign.[140] The territorial expansion of the Empire had necessitated a change in the fixation of the revenues of the Empire[141] and the task was assigned to Muzaffar Khan. Muzaffar set aside the previous practice of the *'Raqmi'* fixation of the *'Jama'* which had existed so long from the time of Bairam Khan[142] and Khwaja Abdul Majid Khan.[143] Qanungos and Chaudharies from the various parts of the Empire were summoned for production of the correct revenue documents along with the current prices of the various crops of their respective territories. Having ascertained the *'Hasli'* (the produce and the land revenue to be assessed thereupon),[144] the Qanungos and the revenue experts at the Centre assessed the *'Hasli'* (State demand) of the year on actual fact[145] for the different territories according to their best judgment and also fixed the total *'Jama'* for the whole Empire. Thus Muzaffar Khan's reforms implied two-fold changes in the revenue administration. Firstly, on the basis of these returns, the revenue experts at the Centre would fix the demand of the State of the basis of the *'Ray'* and the application of the current prices for every area thereupon. It is clear from the 'Nineteen Years Rates' that from the 11th year onwards, the rates of the same crop show much variation within the same Province and are marked by the maximum and minimum.[146] This shows that the area where the same prices per crop applicable to the *'Ray'* prevailed was much smaller than the whole of the Province and the uniformity of rates existed only in the areas with more or less akin prices. This was a complete negation of the method of the 'fixed' and the uniform rates in the *'Raqmi'* System.

The second aspect of the reform was that the fixation of the total *'Jama'* (revenues) of the entire state was factual and based on the exact returns of the revenues from different territories. The previous practice of the artificial inflation of the total valuation was done away with, as with territorial expansion, the revenues of the State were abundant and did not need inflating any longer. Moreover, artificial inflation had caused much administrative and financial confusion which had to be ended and it fell on Muzaffar Khan to achieve this task.

Despite much improvement, the new method of the State demand was by no means perfect. Abul Fazl remarks, "Although in reality the assessment thus levied for the actual demand to be realised was not exact, it could be termed so when compared to the previous *'Jama'*[147] (the State demand). In fact, despite best efforts, the collection of the exact current rates for all the territories of so vast an empire was by no means an easy task as these would fluctuate from one area to another even within one Pargana. Hence, return were flexible than absolutely correct and the assessment based thereupon was only approximately correct than rigidly exact.

None of the method of assessment introduced by Akbar is free from objection and criticism by the scholars, and much would depend upon the fact as to how it worked. However, of all the methods of land revenue assessment, 'Nasq' is the most perplexing and has resulted in conflicting views in regard to its nature expressed by various scholars. Moreland and Ali in their commentary on the 'Ain' were the first to read correctly the term 'Nasq' as a particular mode of assessment[148] as distinct from its literal meaning of 'fixation or arrangement'.[149] Abul Fazl has used the term both in the technical and literal sense,[150] to be interpreted according to the context. The technical meaning is also borne out by revenue literature of the 17th and 18th centuries.[151]

The *'Ain'* puts the 'Nasq' as an alternative method of assessment to '*Paimaish*[152] (yearly assessment). Later, the revenue collector is enjoined not to make 'Nasq' with village headmen as this leads to inefficiency and 'strengthens the hands of the oppressors'. He should rather approach the individual cultivators and enter into mutual agreement with them on behalf of the government.[153]

'Nasq' was definitely an easier and cheaper method than the 'Yearly Zabt' which implies annual measurement rather than 'Zabti' system.[154]

The adoption of 'Nasq' as an alternative to one based on 'annual measurement' did not by any means surrender the process of measurement from its procedure. In 'Nasq', the land instead of being subjected to 'annual measurement', the previous measurement on record entered against individual cultivator after personal survey of the increase or decrease in the cultivation or condition of the land was accepted for that year. The application of this procedure is confirmed by Todar Mal's reforms in the 27th year when, as a remedy against the diminishing of the area of the cultivated land in the Khalisa Parganas, the revenue officers were enjoined to measure the cultivated land and then should enhance it from year to year, corresponding to the ability of the peasants, and then strike 'Nasq'.[155]

'Nasq' could be adopted both in the 'Zabti' and the 'non-Zabti' areas. The evidence deduced from the '*Ain*' and '*Akbar Nama*' shows its application in the 'Zabti' provinces, of which it was an occasional appendage. Moreover, as 'Nasq' was quite old and a common practice[156] and the references having already been made in the Instructions to the Amal Guzar[157] and *Akbar Nama*, Abul Fazl omitted its specific mention as an appendage in the 'Zabti' provinces. Thus the scope of the 'Nasq' was by no means confined only to the Provinces mentioned to be under it.

As to its independent working in a non-Zabti province, the '*Ain*' refers to the practice of 'Nasq' in the three provinces of Bengal, Gujrat, Berar and the Sarkar of Kashmir (Subah Kabul). The '*Ain*' describes the entire land of Kashmir as under 'Nasq'—where 'Ghallabakshi, (annual) measurement (based on regular annual revenues) and the practice of payment (of land revenue) in cash does not prevail.[159] Moreland has summarily dismissed the system of Kashmir as 'indigenous' without any bearing on the land revenue system in other parts of India.[160]

'Nasq' could as well be assessed on the basis of the individual holdings of the cultivators without the measurement operations. *Ain's* statement that measurement was not often repeated does not deny the basic measurement but rather conforms to the idea of 'Nasq' which avoided repeated or annual measurement.

Though the distinct features of 'Nasq' both in the 'Zabti' and 'non-Zabti' areas for the reign of Akbar are clear enough, its other aspects cannot be fully appreciated without the 17th century sources. The *Farang-i-Kardani*, while explaining various methods of assessment, defined Nasq thus: "Firstly, the 'Nasq'. The Amin makes the Jamabandi (assessment) either after examining the *muwazna* (comparative figures) of the (last) ten years and the preceding and adjoining year or by averaging the *'Jama'* of the (last) ten or twelve years".[161] Thus, according to this, 'Nasq' could be introduced in two-fold manner. Firstly, it was a method of assessment in which the *'Jama'* (demand) was determined on the basis of the ten-year-muwazna (comparative demand figures) and area under cultivation.[162]

The *Muwazna* could be prepared village as well as pargana wise. The *Muwazna* would denote 'Jama' as well as details of the area.[163] According to this method, assessment would be made by the Amin taking into consideration the *'Jama'* and the details of the area under cultivation for the last ten to eleven years, noting any trend of increase or decrease, as well as looking into the state of the land under cultivation.

The second form of 'Nasq', as noted in the 'Farhang-i-Kardani', could be done by fixing the average *'Jama'* (revenue demand) of the past ten or twelve years.[164] The procedure is confirmed by 'Nigar-Nama-Munshi', which directs in an assignment, *Sanad*, a jagirdar to resort to 'Sarsari' method for fixing the 'Jama' in his jagir.[165]

'Nasq' could be practised inside and outside the 'Zabti' areas as much before as during and after Akbar's reign. Moreover, 'Nasq' had the potentialities of developing into 'Group Assessment' in case the demand was fixed for the entire village or the pargana simply on the basis of the past records showing the 'Jama' and the cultivated area figures of the past few years and ultimately the 'Jama' to be distributed over the individual peasants by the village headmen or the pargana officials, as the case many be, at their discretion.[166]

The 'Nasq' System did not continue for long and was replaced by another one in the 15th year again by Muzaffar Khan in conjunction with Raja Todar Mal.[167] It seems that they were enamoured of the 'yearly measurement' which seemed to them more justifiable. 'They received the *'Taqsimat-i-Mulk'* from the Qanungos and having determined the *'Mahsul'* on speculation and approximation, fixed a new *Jama'* upon it.[168] Ten Qanungos were appointed who would gather the documents (concerning revenue assessment) from various Qanungos[169] (of the Empire) and submit it to the Ministry (for refixation of the *'Masul'* and the *'Jama'*).[170]

The new method of assessment and the fixation of the State demand was based on the comprehensive information received in the *'Taqsimat-i-Mulk'* from the Qanungos of the various localities. *'Taqsimat'* is plural of *'Taqsim'* which is purely a technical term for a document comprising the details of *'Arazi'*—culturable and non-culturable and also showing the *'Jama'* (land revenue) of the last few years.[171] Some of the 17th century *'Dasturulamls'* put *'Taqsim'* and *'Muawaza'* as interchangeable terms.[172] In this context, *'Taqsimat-i-Mulk'* would show relative *'Arazi'* produce figures of the various parts of the Empire. Thus a regular Central administrative machinery with ten Chief Qanungos was set up to collect and supervise all such land revenue documents received through the channel of the Qanungos of the different *Parganas* of the Empire. Accordingly, with the help of the Chief Qanungos, the Revenue officials of the Central Ministry would fix *'Mahsul'* (mean yield per bigha), of different parts of the Empire, prepare *'Ray'* for the same, apply local price-rates of different crops and fix State demand of different areas and thereupon the total valuation of the Empire.[173] The assessment thus made was based on more uniform local productivity and prices—a fact borne out by the 'Nineteen Years Rates', which show still more divergence in the maximum and minimum rates per crop in various Provinces and also add a few more crops to their tables.[174]

Historians have indulged in much speculation about the *'Taqsimat-i-Mulk'*. Sharma's view that full particulars of the areas under cultivation were despatched to the Ministry is quite acceptable but his assertion that no crop records were maintained during the *'Nasq'* System which necessitated the preparation of new records is not correct.[175] Nor were the returns despatched to be simply converted into cash rates[176]—as the Ministry had, as well, to fix the *'Mahsul'* and the *'Ray'* for the respective areas before conversion to cash rates.

Moreland very wrongly explains *'Nuskha'* as 'Schedule'[177] and *'Taqsimat-i-Mulk'* as 'the office name for the Schedules'[178] for various Parganas, which showed the demand in terms of produce.[179] As such, to Moreland's mind, the Schedules were prepared locally by the Qanungos and the Central Government only applied the price-rates to them.[180] This procedure is absolutely contrary to the one adopted wherein, as noted, the *'Taqsim'* papers of the Parganas were prepared and forwarded by the Qanungos and the Schedules of demand both in kind and cash were fixed by the Central Ministry. Qureshi has also committed various errors in the interpretation of this System. His idea that *'Taqsimat-i-Mulk'* is the same thing as *'Qismat-i-Bud-o-Nabud'* described by Barani[181] is baseless. Whereas *'Taqsimat-i-Mulk'* pertain to documents of details of *'Arazi'* and produce of the different parts of the Empire, upon which the assessment was levied according to the 'Measurement System', *Bud-o-Nabud* by itself is a system of assessment based on the inspection and the division of the crops. Qureshi believes that the *'New Jama'* involved a change only in the method of the total valuation of the Empire rather than in the assessment method.[182] The basic mistake committed by Qureshi is that he had relied only upon *Ain* and believes that the 15th Year reform replaced the *'Raqmi'* System.[183] Though the *Ain* puts the *'Taqsimat-i-Mulk'* in the 15th Year after description of the *'Raqmi'*, there had been two more changes in the method of assessment in the intervening period which Abul Fazl has described in the *Akbar Nama.*[184] *'Nasq'*, which immediately preceded the

'Taqsimat-i-Mulk', was definitely a method of assessment of the State demand. The replacement of the above by another method of the 'Measurement' could not be confined to the change only in the method of valuation. The basic change was in the method of the fixation of the State demand. It is quite clear form the *Ain* itself that the *'Mahsul'* would be fixed by the Central Ministry—and *'Mahsul'* is an aspect of the fixation of the *'Ray'*—a method of assessment rather than the total valuation of the Empire. The valuation as well would naturally be prepared on the basis of the State demand for different parts thus fixed. Of course, the fixation of the State demand on a new method and the valuation are essentially interlinked. Qureshi feels that Abul Fazl leaves the problem of the *'Jama'* in its aspect of the total valuation and jumps over to the *'Jama'* in the method of assessment for the fixation of the *'Zabti',* the fate of the former to be filled in by Akbar Nama.[185] This is by no means a happy position that Abul Fazl should fill up the lacuna of his thoughts in a preceeding volume. Qureshi has put a glass on the meaning of the *'Jama'* in which Abul Fazl is very clear and himself mentions the shortcomings of this assessment, because of which it was replaced by the 'Zabti' in the 25th year.

Moreover, despite the elaborate methods of the fixation of the new *'Jama'* , it was by no means a scientific one for determining the actual *'Hasil'* to be realised from the peasantry. Though the figures of the new assessment showed some decline in returns[186] as compared to the previous *'Jama'* based on *'Nasq'* and tended towards the accuracy of the demand, the new demand was by no means exact and was far more excessive than the actual 'Hasil.'[187]This naturally implied injustice to the cultivators, which was later remedied in the *Zabti* System.[188] Here, too, Qureshi continues to think in terms of the difference in the new valuation and the old one. It cannot be imagined that the new valuation rather than new assessment should affect the position of the peasantry. Another difficulty with Qureshi has been that he takes the *'Mahsul'* (average-produce) and the *'Hasil'* as synonymous interchangeable terms.[189] Nowhere has Abul Fazl used these terms bearing the above meaning nor do they occur as such in the entire range of the Mughal Literature which rather confirms the synonymous use only in the sense of the State demand.[190] Clearly, whereas *'Mahsul'* (mean produce per bigha) is referred in the former sentence for the process of the fixation of assessment of measurement system, *'Hasil'* stands for the exact cash share of the State in the produce. The comparison asserted and the difference pointed out by Abul Fazl is between the new demand fixed (New *Jama*) and the actual *'Hasil',* (obviously to be realised through a scientific system) and not between the total valuation and the *'Hasil'* (as was the case in the so-called medium produce). The latter version of Qureshi is rendered negatory when the valuation in this very system was based on the actual *'Mahsul'* and his demand fixed thereupon and as such the question of the comparison betwen the valuation (so-called New *Jama*) and the *'Mahsul'* or *'Hasil'* does not arise.

Even this was by no means a fool-proof system. It involved a very lengthy procedure and a stupendous task for the Revenue Ministry to fix the State demand after the scrutiny of the multitude of papers of areas and yield of the crops and the rates in different parts of the Empire. Though it safeguarded against the dishonesty of the local revenue officials, it aimed at too much centralisation. This would naturally result in delay for the fixation of the State demand for various areas and consequently in the revenue collections themselves causing vexation and inconvenience both to the officials and the peasantry.[191]

It may be observed that the early phase of Akbar's land revenue system showed a pattern of unbroken continuity with the past, which was not accidental but duly recognized by Abul Fazl. Some of the officials who had served the *Surs* were also picked up in order to ensure that there was no break from the past and the interest of the peasantry was duly kept in view. Despite the fact that the procedure of commutation underwent a change, the method of assessment during this period, as far as the measurement system was concerned, was an adaptation of Sher Shah's method. Moreover, in order to understand and appreciate the exact nature of the evolution of conversion into the cash rates, the details of application in different provinces have to be studied in continuation as one forms the basis of another. The study also indicates that the demand on a particular crop (per bigha) was fixed either in the whole empire or in a particular area depending upon the prices of the year. It seems different experiments were made with the sole objective of arriving at a perfect method of State demand. In order to achieve the purpose, the old principles and canons continued in operation and even developed further according to the idea of the experts of Akbar's reign.

References

1. *Tarikh-i-Daudi,* B.M.O.R., 197.
2. *Nafais-ul-Maasar,* Ms. Cod. Pers. 3 Munich fol. 305a-306b; Ms. 94 Rampur fol. 185 b.
3. I.H. Qureshi, 'Akbar's Revenue Reforms', *P.H.J.*, p. 206.
4. Burn, 'Raqami', *J.R.A.S.,* 1943, p. 261.
5. *Ain-i-Akbari (Ain),* B.M. Add 7652 fol. 148a, fol. 149 a, Blochmann, p. 296-97; *A.N.,* Printed text, p. 281.
6. *Akbar Nama (A.N.),* B.M. Add, O.R. 27, 247 fol. 173 a; *Ain,* Ms. Minntoli 215 Berlin fol. 170 b; Ms. F. 2076, Rampur, p. 273.

7. *Ain., Ibid., A.N., Ibid.*
8. *A.N., Ibid., Ain., Ibid.*
9. *Ibid.*
10. *Ain., Ibid.*
11. *A.N.*, Printed text tr. Beveridge, pp. 350-359.
12. *Ibid.*, p. 356.
13. *Ibid.*, p. 360.
14. *Ibid.*, p. 368.
15. *Ibid.*, p. 377.
16. *Ibid.*, p. 279.
17. *Ibid.*, p. 440.
18. *Nafais-nl-Massan,* Ms. Code Pers. 3 Munich, fol. 314 b; Ms. 94, Rampur, fol. 190 a.
19. *Ibid.*
20. *A.N.*, Printed text, tr. Beveridge, p. 449.
21. *Ain,* Ms. Rampur, p. 237.
22. *A.N.*, Printed text tr. Beveridge, p. 450.
23. *Ibid.*, p. 451.
24. *A.N.*, tr. Beveridge, p. 467; *Ain,* Ms. Minntoli 215 Berlin, fol. 167b.
25. *Ibid.*, p. 467; *Ibid.*, fol. 167b.
26. *Ibid.*, pp. 467-468.
27. *A.N.*, B.M. Add., O.R., 27, 247, fol. 173a;
    Ain, Ms. Minntoli 215 Berlin, fol. 170b; Ms. Rampur, p. 273.
28. *Ibid.*
29. *A.N., Ibid.*
30. *Ibid.*
31. *Ibid.*
32. *A.N., Ibid.*
33. *A.N.*, B.M. Add. O.R. 27, 247, fol. 173a, tr. Beveridge, p. 477.
34. *Ain,* Ms. Minntoli 215 Berlin fol. 170b; Ms. Rampur, p. 273.
35. *A.N.*, Add. O.R. 27, 247, fol. 173a. tr. Beveridge, pp. 478-480.
36. *Ibid.*
37. *Ibid.*
38. *Ibid.*
39. *A.N.*, Printed text, tr. Beveridge, p. 487.
40. *Ibid.*
41. *Ibid.*

42. *Ibid.*

43. *Ain*, B.M. Add. 7652, fols. 151b-160a; Blochmann, Vol. I, pp. 304-348.

44. *Ibid.*, fol. 149a; *Ibid.*, p. 297.

45. *Ain, Ibid.*, fol. 160b; *Ibid.*, p. 347. Also see, pp. 350-359.

46. *Ain, Ibid.*, fol. 149a-151b.; *Ibid.*, pp. 297-303.

47. Moreland, *'Agrarian System'*, p. 76.' The new fact that I have to bring forward is that a Schedule of Sher Shah's assessment-rates is preserved in the *'Ain'*, where it has always been a stumbling block to those students who took it as a part of the work of Todar Mal. Its recognition as Sher Shah's tell us the amount of produce which he claimed, as well as the method by which his claim was calculated; and at the same time removes the outstanding difficulty in interpreting this portion of the *'Ain......'* (Moreland, 'Revenue System of Sher Shah', *J.R.A.S.*, 1926, p. 454).

48. Moreland's suggestion of change in Blochmann's text from *'Ray'* to 'Re-Re-ain' (Revenue System of Sher Shah, p. 454) cannot be borne out by any of the texts of the *Ain* consulted in the Indian and European Libraries. Nor is *'Ray'* a short vowel of 'Re-Re-ain' as the former by itself is a technical land revenue term defined by the *Ain* itself. (Hamilton I, Berlin, fol. 125 b, Blochmann, Vol. II, p. 294). Even though 'Re-Re-iyan be accepted as a better version, 'Raiyan' meaning the first or the best part of anything (Steingass, pp. 603-4) would qualify here the first two classes of land, *Prauti* and *Polaj*, already described in the *Ain* in the classification of the land as the fixation of *'Ray'* is only for the first two classes of land.

49. Sharma states, 'The *Ain* has preserved statistics proving thereby that Akbar took these rates for granted and concerned himself with the task of translating grain rates into cash rates....' and that 'all experimenting on the part of Akbar concerned the commutation of rates in kind of Sher Shah's period into rates in cash'. (Assessment and collection of the Land Revenue under Akbar; *I.H.Q.*, Dec., 1938, pp. 706, 708).

50. Misra remarks, "Abul Fazl goes on to give tables which were apparently those of Sher Shah. They were generally accepted as the basis of the Land Revenue before the 19th year Settlement. Until then, Akbar's only modification was to demand cash instead of kind. The full and the fresh evolution resulted in the 19th year Settlement and for which Abul Fazl gives figures, changed this state of affairs". *P.I.H.C.*, 1952, p. 238.

51. Moreland, *Agrarian System*, p. 87. Moreland recognises only three stages of assessment rates, "Sher Shah", "the Qanungo", and "The Ten Year" in the evolution of measurement method of assessment in Akbar's reign (Agrarian System, p. 82).

52. *Ibid.*, p. 87.

53. Qureshi, I.H., *The Administration of the Sultanate of Delhi*, Lahore, 1944, p. 105.

54. Saran P., 'Revenue System of Sher Shah', *J.O.B.O.R.S.*, Vol. XVII, Part I, p. 148.

55. *Ain,* B.M. Add. 7652, fol. 149a; Blochmann, Vol. I, p. 297.
56. *Ibid.,* fol. 146b-147a; *Ibid.,* pp. 292-94.
57. *Ibid.,* fol. 147b-148a; *Ibid.,* pp. 294-96.
58. *Ibid.,* fol. 148a; *Ibid.,* p. 296.
59. *Ibid.,* fol. 148b; *Ibid.,* pp. 296-97.
60. *Ibid.,* fol. 148b, 150b-152a; *Ibid.,* pp. 297, 301-303.
61. *Ibid.,* fol. 149a-150a; *Ibid.,* pp. 297-300.
62. Various measures were adopted in Akbar's reign before the enforcement of the Zabti System for the conversion of the yearly *'Ray'* into cash payment (See Raqami, 11th, 13th and 15th years reforms respectively).
63. *Ain, Ibid.,* fols. 152a-160a; *Ibid.,* pp. 303-347.
64. *Ibid.,* p. 286.
65. *Ibid.,* pp. 347-48.
66. Abul Fazl has not stated these measures in the chronological order but in the sequence of the final development of the land revenue system.
67. *Ain, Ibid.,* 149a-150a, *Ibid.,* pp. 297-300.
68. Moreland and Ali, 'Akbar's Land Revenue System', *J.R.A.S.,* 1918, p. 16.
69. *Ain, Ibid.,* fol. 150a; *Ibid.,* p. 300.
70. Qureshi, 'Akbar's Land Revenue Reforms', *P.H.J.,* 1952, p. 207.
71. Saran, 'Revenue System of Sher Shah', *J.O.B.O.R.S.,* Vol. XVII, Part I, p. 148.
72. *Ibid.,* p. 148.
73. Moreland, *Agrarian System,* p. 76.
74. Moreland, 'Revenue System of Sher Shah', *J.R.A.S.,* p. 457.
75. Moreland, *'Agrarian System',* p. 77.
76. *Ain,* B.M. Add. 7652, fol. 160b.
77. Misra very strangely calls the process of collection of 'Nineteen Years Rates' as the 19 Year Settlement.
78. *A.N.,* B.M. Add. O.R. 27, 247, fol. 202 a, Printed text, p. 463.
79. *Ain,* B.M. Add. 7652, fol. 160b; Blochmann, Vol. I, p. 286.
80. A.N. Printed text, p. 378. Contrary to the other available versions, Ms. B.M. Add. O.R. 27, 247, fol. 202a bear the wording *'Raqam Raqami'* (رقم رقمی) , which does not seem to be correct. The *Ain* and *Darj ul Nafais* put it only *'Raqami'.* (Ms. B.M. Add. 7652, fol. 160b, Ms. Rampur, p. 283 respectively).
81. *A.N.,* B.M. Add. O.R. 27, 247 fol. 202a, Printed text, p. 287.
82. *Jama* denotes both the assessment and the valuation. Abul Fazl and other 16th century writers have used in both the senses and at times simultaneously for double connotation and it has to be interpreted only in its context. 17th

century Mss. with very rare exception put *'Jamabandi'* for valuation. Mss. Fraser 86 Bod, Oxford, fols. 1b-5b; *Intkhab-i-Dastur-ul-amli Padshai,* Edinburgh, fols. 1b-10b put *'Jama'* denoting the total valuation of the Empire and 'Jamadami' for the detailed valuation of the Subahs, Sarkars and the Parganas. *Farhang-i-Kardani* (Ms. Aligarh, fol. 19a-20b; Ms. Edinburgh, fols. 15b-17a) puts *'Jamadami'* for the detailed valuation. *Khulasut-s Sayaq* (Ms. Aligarh, fols. 29a-37a, Ms. N.A. New Delhi, pp. 119-131) put *'Dami'* for the total valuation of the Empire and *'Jama'* for the detailed valuation of the Subahs and Sarkars. *Tarikh-i-Shah Jahani* by Mohammed Sadiq (Ms. B.M. O.R., 174 fols. 151a-151b) puts *'Jamadami'* for the total valuation and *'Jama'* for the detailed valuation.

On the other hand, *'Jama'* usually signifies the demand assessed. The Jaipur Archives (uncatalogued) put under the *'Jama'* of a Pargana (Sugher Sarkar Rabi crop 1069 H) land revenue of various villages in accordance with various methods of assessment. *Deh Badehi Subahjat-i-Deccan* (*Dehi Jara*) Ms. 1184 *Daftar-i-Diwani* Hydrabad, fol. 18b-523 a giving detailed list of the Parganas and their villages shows *'Jama'* comprising the actual land revenue assessed on the village. This is confirmed by its interchange with *'Hasil'* (fol. 55a-65a) denoting the land revenue assessed and realised.

Sayaq Nama No. 858 D.D. Hydrabad fols. 25a-25b and *Dasturulaml* No. 748 D.D. Hydrabad, p. 23 describe bonds by the *Tahalkdar* dated 1104 Year Fasli and by the Muqaddams of the village dated 1025 H respectively for the assessment of *'Jama'* in the village and its payment in installments in the treasury.

Baharistan Suppl. Pers. 252 N.B. Paris fols. 61b, 284b, 311b; *Makhzan-i-Ihitsab* Ms. Orient, fol. 217, Berlin, fol. 5 a; *Farhang-i-Kardani,* Ms. Aligarh, fols. 29a, 34b, 'Aurangzeb's *Farman* to Rasik Dass Karori' (Ms. Orient, Quart 259 Berlin fol. 59b; *Nigar Nama Munshi,* Ms. Pers. e I fol. 100a) puts Jama and *'Tashkhish Jama'* for the land revenue to be assessed. 18th century Mss. continue with the same notion of the term. Ms. B.M. 7721 fol. 12b—a land revenue dictionary—defines 'Jama' as the actual land revenue realised by the Amil in cash or kind. Another dictionary B.M. Add. 6603 fol. 57b defines *'Jama Tashkhish'* as the land revenue assessed.

83. *Ain,* Ms. Hamilton I Berlin, Blochmann, Vol. II, pp. 76-93.
84. *Ibid.,* pp. 98-99.
85. *Ibid.,* pp. 105-108.
86. *Ibid.,* pp. 110-111.
87. *Ibid.,* pp. 114-122.
88. Moreland, *Agrarian System,* p. 63.
89. *Ain,* Ms. Hamilton I Berlin, Blochmann, Vol. I, p. 100.
90. *Ibid.,* pp. 105-108.
91. *Ibid.,* pp. 79-81.
92. *Ain, Ibid.,* fols. 98-99.

93. *Ibid.*, pp. 82-84.

94. *Ibid.*, pp. 85-86.

95. *Ibid.*, p. 78.

96. *Ain, Ibid.*, pp.79-80.

97. *Ibid.*, p. 83.

98. *Ibid.*, pp. 76-92.

99. *Ain, Ibid.*, fol. 160b, *Ibid.*, p. 347.

100. (a) *Dharwar District Gazetteer* (1884), pp. 440-3; 447, traces the genesis of the 'Rukhumi' or the 'fixed' or 'settled' since the time of Raja Krishna Devaya of Vijayanagar (1508-42) where it was known as the 'mar' *or unit of area, was based on* 'Raya', *i.e.*, measurement of the 'Rekha', *i.e.*, line or area. When the district of Dhawar was passed on to the Bijapur kingdom in 1573 after the dissolution of the Vijaya Nagar Empire, the term *'Raqmi'* was applied to the standard or uniform cash rate on a given area.

    (b) *Blue Book on Revenue Survey, and Assessment* (India), No. 999, 20th August, 1853, p. 387. Captain Wingate wrote with regard to Bankapur Taluq in Dharwar, ".....Generally, however, the 'Rukhum' or the rate of assessment per *mar*, was uniform throughout each district, and the adjustment of this to the various qualities of soil effected by an alteration in the size of the *mar*......Thus in the Seegaon Mahal of Bunkapoer tallook, there is said to have been three sizes of the *mar*, all assessed, at the same unvarying 'Rukhum'......".

101. Burn, 'Raqami', *J.R.A.S.*, Part III and IV, 1943, p. 261.

102. *Blue Book on Revenue Survey and Assessment*, No. 999, 1853, p. 387.

103. *Dharwar District Gazetteer* (1884), pp. 440-3, 447.

104. Burn, 'Raqami' *J.R.A.S.*, 1943, p. 261.

105. *Ain*, B.M. Add. 7652, fol. 160b; Blochmann, Vol. I, p. 347; *A.N.*, Add. O.R. 27, 247, fol. 202 a.

106. *Ain, Ibid., A.N., Ibid.; I.N.*, Ms. Minntoli 215 Berlin, fol. 204 b.

107. *Ain, Ibid.*

108. *A.N.*, Add. O.R. 27, 247, fol. 202 a.

109. *Ibid.; Ain*, Ms. Minntoli 215. Berlin fol. 204 b.

    (Here *'Hasli'* stands for actual revenue returns.)

110. *Ain*, B.M. Add. 7652, fol. 160 b.; Blochmann, Vol. I, p. 347.

    This aspect of the inflation of valuation is also correctly analysed by Moreland. (*Agrarian System*, p. 241-42).

111. *Ibid.*

112. *A.N.*, B.M. Add. O.R. 27, 247, fol. 202a.

    The *Ain* attributes this change to Muzaffar Khan and Todar Mal in the 15th year.

113. *Ibid.*, Beveridge's tr. (B.I.), Vol. II, p. 402.

114. *Ibid.*

115. Moreland and Ali, 'Akbar's Land Revenue System', *J.R.A.S.*, 1918, p. 17.

116. *Khulasutu-s Sayaq,* Ms. Orient. Quart 243, fol. 139 a; Ms. N.A. New Delhi, p. 5.

117. *Ibid.* This is also clear from various other *Dasturulamls* of the later half of the 17th century.

118. *I.N.*, Ms. Minntoli 215 Berlin, fol. 204b, Ms. Rampur, p. 333.

119. *A.N.*, B.M. Add. O.R. 27, 247. fol. 202a, Printed text, p. 381.

120. Moreland and Ali, 'Akbar's Land Revenue System', *J.R.A.S.*, 1918, p. 17.

121. Moreland, *Agrarian System,* pp. 240-41.

122. Moreland, *Agrarian System,* pp. 212, 214, 240-41.

123. Qureshi, 'Akbar's Revenue Reforms', p. 211.

124. *Ibid.*, p. 211.

125. *Ibid.*, p. 211.

126. *Ibid.*, p. 211-12.

127. *Ibid.*, p. 211. Also see Moreland's Agrarian System, p. 153.

128. *Ibid.*, p. 211; *Ibid.*, p. 171.

129. *A.N.*, Printed text, p. 270.

130. *I.N.*, Ms. Minntoli 215 Berlin fol. 204 b. Ms. Rampur, p. 333.

131. Qureshi admits that the inflation was not uniform but he contrarily thinks that because of corruption, there was no uniformity in inflation. He says, "A uniform inflation of valuation can give the government some insight into the real state of affairs, but because of corruption, the inflation had not been uniform, and, therefore, the entire record of the State, so far as the yield and valuation was concerned, had been thrown into confusion". *P.H.J.*, 1952, p. 212.

132. Moreland, *Agrarian System,* pp. 242-43.

133. *I.N.*, Ms. Minntoli 215 Berlin, fol. 204b. Ms. Rampur, p. 333.

134. *Ain,* B.M. Add. 7652, fol. 160 b.; Blochmann, Vol. II, p. 347.

135. *A.N.*, B.M. Add. 27, 247, fol. 202 a.

136. Qureshi, 'Akbar's Revenue Reforms', pp. 212-14.

137. Moreland, '*Agrarian System*', p. 243.

138. *Ibid.*, pp. 246-47.

139. *Ain,* B.M. Add. 7652, fol. 160 b.; Blochmann, Vol. II, p. 347.

140. *A.N.*, B.M. Add. 27, 247, fol. 202 a; Darajul Nafis Ms. Rampur, p. 283; I.N. Minntoli Berlin, fol. 204b.

141. *A.N., Ibid.*

142. *I.N., Ibid.*

143. *A.N.*, B.M. Add. 7652 fol 160b.

144. *'Hal-i-Hasil'* is a technical term and means net land revenue assessed and demanded after making all deductions. A land revenue document—a *'Yadasht'* of Jaipur Archives (uncatalogued) concerning Kharif *'Mujmil Jama'* (a record of detailed *Jama*) of a Pargana dated 1070 Fashi, gives the total amount under 'Jamabandi', total number of villages in the Pargana, the number of villages fallen desolate, the balance of the villages, the number of the villages assigned to the Jagirdars, given in Inam and the ultimate balance of the villages with its actual amount of the land revenue realised under the heading *'Muqarara-Hal-i-Hasil'*.

 Syaq Nama, No. 858, D.D. Hydrabad, fol. 14b uses the term *'Jama Hal-i-Hasil'* showing actual land revenue returns based on the 'Tumar' and other documents.

 Another 17th century *Dasturulaml* Ms. Orient. Fol. 313 Berlin, fols. 121 b-122 b while giving the detailed revenues of the Subbas of the reign of Aurangzeb describes every Subah with its total number of Sarkars, Mahals; its amount of *'Jamadami'* and finally the amount against *'Hal-i-Hasil'*. Here, the latter term and *Hasil* are put synonymous. *Dasturulaml Alamgiri* B.M. Add. 6598 fols. 131a-132b, makes similar distinction between *Jamadami* and the *Hasil.*

 Both Abul Fazl and Mutamad Khan definitely use the term in a strict technical sense connoting the State Demand—actual land revenue assessed and realised. (*A.N.*, Add. O.R. 27247, fol. 202a; *I.N.*, Minntoli Berlin, fol. 204b). Moreland's understanding of the term as 'an actual-yield' (*Agrarian System,* p. 244) is nearly correct though put in a misconstrued context of the entire passage. Qureshi very wrongly over here puts *'Hasil'* as synonymous with *'Mahsul'* in terms of medium produce. (Revenue Reforms of Akbar, *P.H.J.*, 1952, pp. 207-208).

 It seems that the meaning of the term underwent a change in the course of the 18th century. B.M. Add. 6603 fol. 59b—puts *'Hal-i-Hasil'* as technical term and defines it as 'total produce of the current year' and also as synonymous with *'Hast-o-Bud'*, which is also explained on fol. 84a as 'agricultural produce'. Similarly, C.T. Metcalfe in his correspondence defines it as 'actual produce by measurement or 'Survey'. (Records Delhi Residency, Vol. I, p. 13). But this notion is not borne by the 16th and 17th century revenue literature.

145. *I.N.*, Ms. Minntoli 215, Berlin, fol. 204b. Ms. Rampur, p. 333.

146. *Ain,* B.N. Add. 7652 fols.; Blochmann, Vol. II, pp.

 Provinces of Lahore and Malwa are exception as they do not show any variation till the 15th year.

147. *A.N.*, Ms. Orient, fol. 182, fol. 576b.

148. Moreland and Ali, *J.R.A.S. of Great Britain and Ireland,* 1918, p. 28.

149. Steingass, p. 1400.

150. The *'Ain'* in the 'Instructions to *'Amil Guzar'* uses the term three times, twice in the technical and one in the general sense. (B.M. Add. 7652, fol.

142a-142b). In the account of the Subahs, it used thrice in the technical sense. 'Akbar Nama' uses it in both senses. *Tabqat-i-Akbari* and the chronicles refer to *'Nuskha-i-Nasq, i.e.,* in the general sense various times. Moreland later on confirmed the use in the technical sense in *The Agrarian System.*

151. *Farhang-i-Kardani,* Ms. Aligarh, f. 32b; *Khullasut Syaq* Ms. Orient 243 Berlin. fol. 159b; Ms. O.R. 2026 B.M. fol. 34b, Ms. N.A.I., New Delhi, p. 32.
152. *Ain,* B.M. Add. 7652, fol. 142a-142b, Blochman, text, vol. I, p. 285. "In his measurements, he should possess foresightedness and sense of justice.....if some desire measurement, and others accept *'Nasq',* he should forward the bonds promptly (to the central government). Jarrett's translation of *'Nasq'* as 'appraisement' (Vol. II, p. 47) is entirely wrong, p. 234.
153. *Ibid.,* fol. 142 b, Blochmann, p. 286.
154. Moreland (*Agrarian System,* p. 235) has wrongly thought of 'Zabt-i-Har-Sala' as *'Zabti',* which as a method was not even in existence in the 13th year of Akbar's reign. The term *'Zabt'* denoting a draft comprising simple measurement along with the name of cultivator and the areas under cultivations is borne by various *Dastur-ul-Amals* of the 17th century, (*Khullasut Syaq* Ms. Aligarh, fol. 12b; Ms. O.R. fol. 33b, Sayaq Nama, Hyderabad, fol. 25a-27a).
155. *Akbar Nama,* B.M. Add. O.R. 26, 207 B.M. fol. 161b; A.S.B. Vol. III, p. 281, Ms. O.R. 27, 247 B.M., fol. 331b gives a different text but without making any difference in substance.
156. The *'Ain'* refers to the existence of the practice of *'Nasq'* in Berar since long ago. B.M. Add. 7652 fol. 226a; R.A.S., Text, Vol. I, p. 478.
157. *'Ain'* B.M. Add. 7652, fol. 142a-142b; Blochmann Text, Vol. I, p. 285-86.
158. *A.N.,* B.M. Add. O.R. 26, 207 B.M. fol. 161b; ASB, Vol. III, p. 381.
159. *'Ain'* Add 7652 B. M. fol. 279; Blochmann Pers. Text, Vol. I, p. 570. In contradiction to this, Sujan Rai Bhandari (in *Muntkhibul Tawarikh* printed text, p. 83) puts the entire land of Kashmir under *Ghallabakshi* and Bhandari relied upon his account of the Subhas mostly on the *'Ain'.* It is not possible that the method of assessment changed so radically in the course of a century as such it seems Bhandari relied on a defective version of the *'Ain'.*
160. Moreland, *Agrarian System,* p. 122.
161. *Farhang-i-Kardani,* 1679 A.D. Ms. M.U. Aligarh, fol. 32b.
162. Ms. Add. 7721 B.M., fol. 14a defines *Muwazna* as comparative average mean.
163. Technically speaking, *Mawzna* would denote *'Jama'* and *'taqsim'* for the 'area figures', Ms. Or. Quart. 259 Berlin fol. 89b quotes both *Mawzna Deh Sala-i-Pargnat* and *Taqsim Deh Sala-i-Parganat* as separate

documents in the custody of the 'Moharar'. The same Ms. fol. 91b puts *Muwazna Deh Sala* and *Taqsim Deh Sal wa Hal* as two distinct documents in the office of the Diwan.

164. *Farhang-i-Kardani,* M.U. Aligarh, fol. 32b; B.M. Add. 6603 B.M. fol. 57a defines 'Jama Sarsari' as the average mean.

165. *NigarNama Munshi* Ms. Pers. El Bodlein Oxford, Ms. Aligarh, fol. 148b.

166. But such a practice was open to misuse and oppression over the peasants and, as such, was forbidden by Akbar.

167. *Ain,* B.M., Add. 7652, fol. 160b.; Blochmann, Vol. I, p. 347.

Strangely, this stage of reform in the 15th year has not been described by Abul Fazl in Akbar Nama nor is it traceable in any of the other chronicles of the Mughal age as they usually followed the chronological description of *Akbar Nama.* Its significance has to be interpreted only upon the passage of the *Ain.*

168. *Ibid.*

169. *Ibid.*

170. *Ibid.*

171. Ms. Or. Fol. 217, Berlin, fol. 24 b.

172. *'Sayaq Nama'* Ms. 858 Daftar-I-Diwani Hyd. fol. 25b; Dasturul Amal-i-Alamgiri B.M. Add. 6598 fol. 36b; Khulasut-s Sayaq N.A., p. 21.

173. Moreland agrees that this reform attempted the refixation of both the State demand and new valuation. (*Agrarian System,* pp. 244-45). But in this context, he has wrongly taken the *'Mahsul'* for demand and, as such, his analysis of fixation of assessment by the local Qanungos is not acceptable.

174. *Ain,* Ms. Hamilton I, fols.; Blochmann, Vol. II, pp. 76-93.

From this year onwards, even the Provinces of Lahore and Malwa show marked divergence in rates.

175. Sharma, 'Assessment and Collection of the Land Revenue under Akbar', *I.H.Q.,* 1938, p. 708.

This is returned by the 'Nineteen Years Rates' for the 13th and the 14th years.

176. Strangely enough, Sharma still continues to think in terms of conversion of so-called Sher Shah's *'Ray'* into cash rates.

177. Moreland, *Agrarian System,* p. 244. ('*Nuskha*' simple means a document.)

178. *Ibid.,* p. 244. *'Taqsimat-i-Mulk* was the office name for the Schedules......each Schedule would be headed "Apportionment (*taqsim*) of Parganas so and so", and the whole file would be called 'The apportionments of the Empire'. This meaning is incorrect. 'Taqsim' and Dasturulamls (Schedule) are mentioned as two distinct documents with the Qanungo in a 17th century Ms. Or. Fol. 217 Berlin, fol. 51.

179. *Ibid.,* p. 245.

180. *Ibid.*

181. Qureshi, 'Akbar's Land Revenue Reforms', *P.H.J.,* 1952, p. 212.

182. Qureshi, 'Akbar's Land Revenue Reforms', *P.H.J.,* p. 212.

183. *Ibid.*, p. 212.

184. *A.N.* B.M. Add. O.R. 27, 247, fols. 202a; 220b.

The *Ain* omits reference to the stages of reform in the 11th year (1567) by Muzaffar Khan and the 13th year (1569), *'Nasq'* System. In fact, Abul Fazl is very brief in this passage and makes a general survey from the beginning. Moreover, he had already discussed the details in the *Akbar Nama* and did not deem it necessary to refer to them. He is mostly concerned with describing the method of the conversion of *'Ray'* into cash rate and thereby omitted the *'Nasq'* for reference. As he had touched the second and the more important reform measure of Muzaffar Khan in the 15th year, he as well dropped reference to the earlier measure of Muzaffar in the 11th year which had set aside the 'Raqmi' method. Qureshi being unware of this has followed the *Ain* blindly and has commented that 'Raqmi' was replaced by 'Taqsimat-i-Mulk' in the 15th year (1571). Moreland's belief that the 11th and the 15th year modifications from a part and parcel of a single reform concluded after three years of enquiries and calculations is not tenable. Moreland agrees that *Akbar Nama* being in strict chronological order could not be wrong. Though in the Ain, there is a possibility of confusion between 'Pandzda' (پانزده) and 'Yazda' (یازده) because of the addition of a dot below the first syllable (making from 'Y' to 'P' a common mistake committed by the scribes—in the light of the texts examined, he does not consider the change in the text advisable. (Agrarian System, pp. 246-47). A further scrutiny of the texts of *Ain* both in the Indian and the European libraries not included in Moreland's list (quoted in the Bibliography) confirm that the *Ain* too is not likely to be in error and a change in the text is not at all warranted. Evidently, there were two distinct reforms carried out in the 11th and 15th years respectively and it is impossible to agree with Moreland when a very important experiment of *'Nasq'* introduced in the 13th year intervenes the 11th and the 15th years reforms.

185. Qureshi, 'Akbar's Land Revenue Reforms', *P.H.J.,* 1952, p. 212.

186. *Ain,* B.M. Add. 7652, fol. 160b.

187. *Ibid.*

188. *Ibid.*

189. Qureshi, 'Akbar's Land Revenue Reforms', *P.H.J.,* 1952, p. 207.

190. 'Mahsul' and *'Hasil'* in the sense of State demand are synonymous terms. *Tuzk-i-Jahangiri,* p. 252, and *Nigar Nama Munshi,* N.A., New Delhi, fol. 62b, mention them as interchangeable terms in the same passage. The use of *'Hasil'* as 'average-produce' is unknown in the Mughal revenue terminology.

191. *Ain,* Add. 7652, fol. 160 b.

Chapter 7

Methods of Assessment of Land Revenue Demand in the Mughal Period

To W.H. Moreland belongs the credit of a pioneer, for his was the first attempt to give a methodical presentation of the Land Revenue System of Mughal India. His chief contributions on this subject were an article on the System under Akbar in the I.R.A.S, 1918, written in cooperation with Yusuf Ali and his later independent work, "*The Agrarian System of India.*" It is perhaps a reflection on the one-sided nature of the Indian historiography that Moreland should have had so few successes in this field. Dr. Saran alone in his "*Provincial Government of the Mughals*" has made attempt whatsoever to offer at least a partial re-interpretation.

It is not as if Moreland, extensive as was his reading, has exhausted our sources. He missed a large number of the important chronicles and did not utilise any of the administrative manuals and collections of letters belonging to the 17th century.[1] Had he studied their evidence, he would have found many of his conjectures brilliantly confirmed. On the other hand, one feels sure he would have himself revised a few of his views. Moreover, though Moreland had a much sounder knowledge of Persiàn than many who in his day had chosen to write on the period with much greater assurance, yet he was not uniformly successful in his understanding of the texts and accepted the existing translations for some awkward, but crucial phrases, where there is really much room for doubt as to their accuracy.

Thus, from the point of view of method only, Moreland's conclusions need to be checked both with the evidence he himself has used and with the fresh material that can be brought to bear on the subject. This paper is concerned with the study of the methods of assessment on the peasant and not with the general or collective assessments, to which Moreland gave, a little inaccurately, the name of Valuation. This should not imply lack of appreciation of the value of Moreland's contributions, but indeed, quite the contrary, this is acknowledgement of the debt owed to the scholar.

Zabt

The first, and possibly the most important method of Land Revenue Assessment in the Mughal Period was the *Zabt*, with which every text book links the names of Akbar and Todar Mal. Moreland has painstakingly unraveled the details of the evolution of this system in the 16th Century and several of his conclusions seem to be definitive. The following paragraph gives a summary description of the development of the *Zabt* System, based generally on his interpretation.

Abul Fazl pays one of his very few compliments to the Surs when he says that it was during this time of Sher Shah and Islam Shah that "Hindustan passed from Ghalla Bakshi (crop-sharing) and *Muqt'i* (probably, farming) to *Zabt.*" Moreland shows that *Zabt*, in the beginning, meant measurement (*Paimash*) of land followed by the application of a standard crop-rate (*Rai*), to the measured area, in order to obtain the amount of revenue demand. The *Rai*, instituted by Sher Shah, has been preserved in the *Ain*. It sets the demand at 1/3rd of the produce under each crop per bigha averaged from arbitrarily estimated outputs of good, middling and bad lands. The standard rate applies to *Polaj* and *Parauti*, (representatively lands under constant and rarely interrupted cultivation); for *Chachar* (lands uncultivated for 3-4years) and *Banjar* (uncultivated for 5 years or more). Annually increasing proportions of the standard rate were fixed, (in the case of *Banjar*, for each crop separately) to reach the full amount of revenue in five years. As the *Ain* tells us, Sher Shah's *Rai* "obtained Akbar's acceptance"; it is stated further on that the rates had to be converted into cash rates at annually fixed price rates (*nirkhnama*) approved at the headquarters.[2] The scales of *Dasturulamls*, so obtained, follow at length separately for each province for 19 years from the regnal year 6-7 to 24. The scales would have only applied to the *Zabti* area and the provinces for which such scales are given, have, without exception, areas of measured land (*Arazi*) entered in their statistical tables further down in the *Ain*. Moreland argues that from the 6th - 7th to the 9th year, there was not only a single standard *Rai* or crop rate, but also one single, annual, but territorially universal, price scale, as this alone can explain the identity or near identity of the figures for these years in all the provinces. [3] With the 10th year, the figures begin to vary sharply, and for each two figures- maximum and minimum- become common. In the 15th year, figures appear for several new crops and the divergence in the figures becomes generally still more marked. It becomes obvious that the practice of promulgating single price-scales every year has been abandoned in favour of regional ones, while it is likely that the standard *Rai* for all provinces has been replaced by provincial *Rai's*. [4]

At this point, however, a reservation must be made in regard to Moreland's theorisation about *Qanungo* rates. Both the *Akbar Nama* and the *Ain* speak of the preparation of a *Jama* (general assessment) of the Empire by Muzzafar Khan with the assistance of the *Qanungos*. The former authority which, in the arrangement of the contents, follows a strict chronological order, places it among the events of the 11th year; the latter says it took place in the 15th year. The *Ain* text is the more likely to be in error, as Moreland himself acknowledges, confusion between *Panzada* (15) and *Yazda* (11), owing to the misplacing or omission of dots, is most common in Persian manuscripts. Inspite of this, however, he links up the general recasting of the figures of the 19-year scales, under the 15 year with the aforesaid event, and renders the relevant passage in the *Ain* in such a way as to suggest that the *Qanungos* had also been asked to prepare the local crop rates. Thus the *Taqsimat-i-Mulk*, which the *Qanungos* are said to have provided for the Ministry, is taken by him to mean, "office name for schedules". Again, he uses the word "schedules" for *Nushkha* in the original, in the sentence where it is stated, that this was collected from their local colleagues by ten *Qanungos* appointed for this purpose. In both cases, he is inaccurate. *Taqsim* is expressly defined in two 17th century manuals as a synonym for *Muwazana,* or the record of area under cultivation[5] and *Nushkha* simply means record or document; for schedule in the translation, we should have expected *Rai* or *Dastur* in the text. It is obvious that the collection of area statistics would have been of the greatest use in the preparation of the *Jama'* and it was by no means a simple task that the whole machinery of the *Qanungos* was mobilised. We have no evidence that this particular measure had anything to do with the preparation of regional *Rai's.*

The 19th year scales close with the 24th year and give way to permanent or fixed *Dastur-l-amals.* Running in *Blochmann's* text of the *Ain,* from pages 348 to 385 in a tabulated form, they are preceded by a chapter entitled, *"Ain-i-Deh-Sala",* in which Abul Fazl refers both to the distress caused from the practice of annual price fixing by the headquarters and to the difference between the real revenue (*Hasil*) and the general assessment (*Jama*). The solution to the second difficulty was finally provided by the *Jama'i-Deh-Sala,* obtained, as is explicitly stated, by averaging the revenue (*Mahsul*) between the years 15th and 24th (both inclusive) for each *Pargana.* The first was sought to be overcome by the preparation of the permanent *Dastur-ul-amals* for groups of *Parganas* in place of annual *Dasturs.* This is implicit rather than explicit in the *Ain.* The tables of the final *Dasturs* are, in fact, introduced by the last three sentences of the chapter, *Ain-Deh-Sala,* yet since Moreland has other ideas as to their interpretation, we forbear for the moment discussing their meaning, and follow his own explanation of how these *Dastur-ul-amals* came to be prepared.

To cite Moreland's own words: "The account of their calculation is obscure but my reading of the authorities is that the rates adopted were the average of those which had been fixed for the previous ten years, the periods during which the *Qanungo* rates had been in force. The view that the new rates were averaged from 10 years' experience cannot be checked arithmetically," owing to the previous rates being given in the form of provincial scales with the maximum and the minimum figures representing only the total extent of regional variations. "My viewpoint," Moreland concludes, "is merely that the 10-year rates, as we have them, stand somewhere about the same level which would be reached by an average of ten years' actual charges adjusted for the increase in the size of the bigha." This latter increase, owing to the introduction of the *Illahi Gaz* in the 31st year, he estimates at about 20% of the size of the earlier *bigha.*

Before concerning ourselves with the tables themselves to *see if Moreland's* theory can be checked or sustained by them, it is necessary to stress that his allowance of a 20% increase in the size of the *bigha* is purely arbitrary. He bases his calculations on the separate statements of Abul Fazl that the *Sikandari Gaz* contained 32 *angushts* (finger-breadths) and the Illahi 41 (*angushts*), which, however, means an increase of 28 percent, not 20 percent. In any case, Moreland is not justified in considering the (*angusht*) to be a uniform measure and taking it as the gauge to fix the ratio between the two *gaz*-length, more so, since in another passage, Abul Fazl expressly describes the change in the size of the *bigha,* following the introduction of the new *Gaz*. First, he says, with the introduction of the bamboo measuring rod in place of the *hempen* rope-an event of the 19th year. *Ain,* the bigha increased in size by 15%, for though theoretically, the length of the *Gaz* remained the same, the hempen rope used to contract by 4 *Gaz* in every 60. The *Illahi Gaz,* when introduced, meant an increase of 10.1 percent, the total increase being now 26 percent over the rope-measured *Sikandari bigha.*[6] Now, the fact that the *Illahi Gaz* was only about 10 percent longer than the *Sikandari,* as is here assumed, obtains confirmation from a careful English traveller of the 17th century, who puts the *Sikandari Gaz* at 27 7/8 inches and the Akbari at 31 1/8, the latter thus being 111.6 percent of the former.[7] To dispose of a further complication, it may seem that since the use of the bamboo—*tanab*—enlarged the size of the *bigha,* we should contemplate readjusting the previous figures to the 20th year (the year next to the introduction of the new *tanab*) in accordance with the change of the unit of area for which they are given. However, we should also remember that the change in the measuring instrument meant an alteration in the size of the *bigha* in the realm of practice only and not in its standard size. Had it been otherwise, we should have had a substantial increase in the figures of the scales under the 20th year. Such is obviously not the case: crops, like thick (*paunda*) *sugar* cane and the water nut (*singhara*), show no alteration in their uniform rates under this year or the 19th. The only increase in the size of the *bigha,* for which we have to adjust the figures is, then, that consequent upon the introduction of the *Illahi Gaz,* and this, too, he put at no more than 10 percent or 11 percent of the previous size.

As we have seen, Moreland considers that this theory cannot be arithmetically checked by reference to the tables. This is, without doubt, in part true for the 15-24 year figures, which are supposed to have been averaged, might in the case of the *Dasturs* of a particular area, have stood anywhere between the maximum and the minimum figures given for the *Subah* as a whole under each of the years. However, there still seem to be two ways in which the hypothesis of averaged rates can be tested. In the first place, where we have only a single series of figures in the 19-year scales for a particular group during the years 15-24, we should, under this hypothesis, expect the average thereof, multiplied by 10/100 or 11/100 to be the single unvaried figure for the crop in all the permanent *Dasturs* of the province. Secondly, we should expect the maximum figure in the final *dasturs* of the province never to exceed the highest possible average of the 15-14 year scales of the province, multiplied by the same fraction and the minimum never to fall below the lowest average similarly multiplied.[8]

The most unvarying rates in the 19-years scales (these for *Malwa* excluded) are for *Singhara* (water nut) and *Zardchoba* (turmeric). The figure for both of them is almost throughout 100 *Dams.* In permanent *dasturs,* with only some exceptions, the figure for these two crops is one which can be read variously as 115 dams 20 *jitals,* 115 dams 8 *jitals,* 111 dams 20 *jitals,* 111 dams 8 *jitals,* owing to the confusion between *Panzdah* (15) and *Yazda* (11), and bist (20) and *hasht* (8) in Persian writing. All the above readings appear differently in different manuscripts and often the scribes have not put any dots at all, thus leaving the door open to any of the four figures acceptable to the reader. If we accept either of the latter readings, we may have here a simple case of the earlier scale raised in proportion to the increase in the size of the *bigha.* This proves little, however, both the crops are by nature such as to preclude any methodical process for determining their scales; since any scale promulgaed for them had to be arbitrary, the old one might merely have been continued without implying any acceptance of the principle of averages. Thus, matters do not seem so simple when we come to *Paunda* or *Siyah* or thick sugar-cane. This crop has a uniform, unvaried rate of 200 dams for the years 15-

24 in the provinces of Awadh,[9] Lahore and Multan, and one should, with the previous example of *Singhara* and turmeric in mind, expect a figure around 220 and 224 dams in the final *dasturs* of these provinces. The figures in the latter, however, range from 230 dams 8 *jitals* and 240 dams 9 *jitals* in Awadh and from 180 dams 12½ *jitals* (in one *dastur*) to 240 dams 12 *jitals* (in six, including one giving 240 dams 12 *jitals*). Again, in Illahabad and Awadh, beetel leaf (*Pan*) has single annual figures only, averaging respectively 194 dams and 208 dams. Yet, in the permanent *dasturs* of Illahabad, its rates vary from 210 dams to above 268 dams in 5 *dasturs.* In Awadh, too, the *dasturs* range from 223 dams 15 *jitals* to 260 dams 3 *jitals.* Finally, the annual rates for indigo in Lahore are all in single figures except for the 20th and 21st years; the divergence between the maximum and minimum figures under the excepted years is so slight that the highest possible average of the annual rates amounts to 131.8 dams and the lowest to just 131-0 dams. Similarly, in Multan, we have single annual figures for this crop except under the 20th year, the possible averages ranging from 131.4 to 131.8 dams. But when we turn to permanent *dasturs,* we find that in the case of Lahore, the indigo rates vary from 134 dams 14 *jitals* to 158 dams 19 *jitals* and in that of Multan from 154 dams 9 *jitals* to 159 dams 22 *jitals,* leaving in neither any discernible link with the averaged rates.

Now, though the figures presented above prove conclusively that at least in these cases, the averages of the rates of the years 15-24 were not accepted for the final *dasturs,* it would be fair to concede that the crop to which these figures apply, belong (with the exception of thick sugar-cane) to one class only, namely, of those in respect of which the *Ain,* I, 300, states that no *Rai's* had been instituted for them and their revenue scales were fixed directly in terms in cash. It may, therefore, be argued that since the annual rates for them had been rather arbitrarily fixed, the method of averaging these rates was not extended to these crops. However, the crops to which both regional *Rais'* as well as price rates applied, cannot be expected to, and in fact do not, have single annual figures, in the 19 year scales, in any abundance. For these, we can turn to the second method of verification suggested above, *i.e.,* comparing the maximum and the minimum figures in the permanent *dasturs* with the highest and the lowest possible averages of the annual scales. The results of some of my calculations on these lines are tabulated below. For them, I have purposely excluded all crops which are listed in the *Ain* as being from the beginning outside the *Rai'*. On the other hand, of the seven crops appearing in the following table, all but two,[10] are entered in the *Rai* of Sher Shah.

I

Suba	Crop	A (Average of maximum Rate: Years 15-24	B a x 10/100	C (Maximum Rate in the Pemanent *Dastur*)	D C=A %
Illahabad	Kabuli gram.	56.40*d*	62.04*d*	71*d* 14 J (5 *Dasturs*)	12.6%
do	Safflower	70*d*	77*d*	83*d* 21 J (4 *Dasturs*)	119.6%
do	Rape Seed	47.0*d*	51.7*d*	101*d* (1 *Dastur*)	215%
Awadh	Lentils ('adas-*Masur*)	22.70*d*	24.97*d*	35*d* 20 J (1 *Dastur*)	156%
do	Peas (*matar*)	27.35*d*	30.09*d*	38*d* (1 *Dastur*)	135%
Delhi	*Ajwain* (luigristi cum ajovan')	71.20*d*	78.32*d*	89*d* 15 J (1 *Dastur*) 89*d* 12 J (1 *Dastur*)	122%

II

Suba	Crop	A	B	C
Illahabad	Chena (arzan) Rabi harvest	15.20*d*	16.72*d*	15*d* 19 J (1 *Dastur*)
Awadh	do	15.10*d*	16.61*d*	7*d* 22 J (1 *Dastur*) 15*d* 3 J (1 *Dastur*)

The evidence of these figures seems to be decisive, and the supposition that the permanent *Dasturs* of any category of crops were obtained from the average of the previous ten years is unsustainable. It is worth noticing in this connection that the *Akbar Nama* hints at prices being reported dishonestly during the years preceding the 24.[11]

In fact, this same passage speaks of an entirely new effort to obtain the data required. "The essence of this innovation (*i.e.,* the *Jama Deh Sala*) was that having discovered the state or revenue for ten years (*hal-i-dah Sala*) of every *Pargana* from the categories of cultivation and the levels of prices, he fixed the tenth part (of the total revenue of the ten years) as the annual revenue (*mal-i-har Sala*)[11a]. Now we know that his preparation of the *Jama-i-deh Sala* and that of the permanent *Dasturs* were simultaneous processes. If for the purpose of the former, the productivity and the prices during the previous ten years in each *Pargana* had to be re-investigated, it stands to reason that the information so collected was more likely, than the old annual rates, to have been used for preparing the new *Dasturs*.

The principle on which these *Dasturs* were actually worked on from the fresh data is, I believe, indicated in the last three sentences of the chapter entitled, *Ain-i-Deh Sala* in the *Ain*, I, 348. I transliterate their text below:

("wa *nez mal-i*[12] har Sal Jins (-I) *kamil a'itbar namud. Sal ki afzun bud bar-girift aud chunnchi an ra bar-guzard)*

Since Moreland has given an elaborate interpretation of these sentences, it is, perhaps, best to begin with his translation and explanation. He renders the text thus: "And also taking into account the (figures known as) *mal-i-Jins-i-Kamil,* they took the year which was greatest as the table shows".[13]

Moreland thinks that what is described is but a part of the preparation of the *Jama-i-Deh Sala* and has nothing to do with that of the *Dasturs.* It seems, in his view, that an exception was made in the general procedure of averaging of ten years' revenue in case of land under high-grade crops (*Jins-i Kamil*). The area of such land was continually increasing and it was, in view of this thought, prejudicial to imperial interests merely to strike an average where the prospects were of constant enhancement. In the closing words of the passage, which on the fact of them, have reference solely to the tables of the permanent *Dastur ul Amals* that follow, Moreland attributes to faulty revision. At one time, he thinks, the tables of the *Jama-i-Deh Sala* were placed immediately below this passage, but because of their length as well as redundancy owing to the up-to-date *Jama* figures being including in the provincial statistics, these were deleted. When this deletion took place, however, the introductory sentence in the preceding chapter escaped notice and was allowed to stand as it was.

It would perhaps not be considered unfair to say that most of Moreland's argument consists of sheer speculation. No reader of the *Ain* can really leave the book without feeling that, whatever be its other merits or demerits, it is a very carefully arranged and edited work. It was finished much earlier than the *Akbar Nama*—as Moreland himself argues elsewhere—and there is, therefore, all the less reason for us to assume that it was subjected to a hurried revision. And even if we suppose that the *Jama'i Deh Sala* tables had been there and subsequently removed, we should still expect from introductory remarks preceding the permanent *Dastur ul amals.* Moreover, from the context also, it would appear surprising if there were no reference to them in the *Ain-i Deh Sala.* This chapter tells us in so many words that the revenue administration in the earlier part of Akbar's reign was beset by two main difficulties, viz. (1) the uncertainty and delay of annual revenue scales based on fluctuating prices, and (2) the unrealistic nature of the general assessment. Now the *Jama Deh Sala* was the final attempt to solve the second difficulty and is, as such, described in the chapter. But under Moreland's interpretation, the solution to the first difficulty, which is mentioned twice, would be left unstated for no comprehensible reason. This apparent deficiency could be obviated only if we consider the last three sentences to be concerned with precisely such a solution.

There is also in Moreland's translation of the first of the three sentences a slip, which, though it seems at first sight to affect the meaning only a little, does in fact alter the whole sense. Following Jarrett, he renders the expression "*a' itabar namud*" as "taking into account". There can be no doubt that this is an incorrect rendering. No dictionary gives the meaning of account or any similar sense to the word: *a'itabar.*[14] Even had it borne such a meaning, the translation would have been wrong unless we had *namudand* or *namudah* in the original instead of *namud.* As the text stands, the subject clearly is the *Mal-i-Jins* or *Mal-i-Jins-i-Kamil,* depending on how we put the *Izafat.*

The translation, then, that I would offer for these sentences is as follows:

"And further, the revenue for the crops *mal-i-Jins* exhibited complete reliability (*Kamil a'itbar*). They took the year, which was greater (or, more abundant-*afzun*) (than others) (in revenue). Accordingly, that is presented by the table".

If we accept *mal-i-Jins-i-Kamil* as the subject in the first sentence, it should be rendered thus: "And further, the revenue for the high-priced crops (Jins-i-Kamil)[15] exhibited reliability".[16]

The best way to understand the meaning of this short passage would surely be to see it first in its context. It is preceded by a short description of how *Jama'-i-Deh Sala* was prepared.

We are told that the annual *mahsul* (revenue) of the ten years, from the 15th to the 24th year, was averaged to yield the annual general assessment (*har Sal*). "But", the text continues, "(the particular of) the 20th to the 24th year they obtained by way of actual knowledge (*az rah-i-tahqiq*) and (of) the previous five from the report of the truthful". Surely, this investigation is the same as that concerning "the categories of cultivation and the levels of prices" referred to in the *Akbar Nama.* In the 19th year in the *Zabti* provinces, the *Jagirs* had been resumed, the whole land made *Khalsa* and put under *Zabt.* For the 20th and following years, the Revenue Ministry had presumably all the necessary data on its records. For the previous five years alone, it had to go to the evidence and records from quarters outside its sphere. In any case, the information thus secured removed most of the obscurity, which had till then shrouded the local productivity rates and price fluctuations. The meaning of the first of our these three sentences, which follows immediately upon the sentence of the *Ain* quoted above, now becomes clear. The scales of land revenue (*Mal-i-Jins*) being now based on relatively true and accurate knowledge of the localities, could be considered to possess "complete reliability" in contrast to the old annual rates, determined by more general *Rai's* and prices reported (not always honestly or accurately in the official view) from provincial or lower administrative centres. The second alternative translation would modify the meaning only to the extent that the high priced crops would be singled out for having reliable revenue rates. This, in itself, would not be implausible, for according to an earlier passage in the *Ain,* I, 300, such crops as indigo, betel leaf and hemp, among others, had no *Rai's,* their revenue being directly fixed in cash. Abul Fazl may be only emphasizing that the change in respect of them, following local investigation, was even greater than in that of ordinary crops and they also obtained completely realistic scales.[17]

The other two sentences are crucial in that they show how the *Dasturs* were finally determined. I would paraphrase them like this: This year in which the revenue (presumably) was the greatest was found out for each group of *Parganas.* Then on the basis of local information obtained by the Revenue Ministry, the scales of that year were worked out. These became the permanent *dastur-l'amals* for their respective circles and, as such, are given in the tables that follow. At first sight, this may appear to put to much meaning in two brief sentences, but once we accept the fact that the reference in the last sentence is to the tables of the *Dasturs,* the interpretation that I have given seems to me to be the only possible one, according to both the language and the context.

My view, therefore, is that for each circle or group of *Parganas* of more or less uniform productivity, its *Dastur* represented the revenue scales worked out afresh for the year of the highest revenue. Such a year came to be known as the *Sal-i-Hasil-i-Kamil* or simply, *Sal-i-Kamil.* This term appears frequently in the administrative literature of the 17th century but so far as I am aware, it occurs first of all in the text of the recommendations made in the 30th regnal year of Akbar by Mir Fathullah Shirazi.[17a] Generally speaking, the rates in the *Sal-i-Kamil* would have been neither the highest nor the lowest. If prices increased in any year owing to the loss of crop in one part of the locality, the rates for the unaffected parts would rise, but, on the other hand, the total revenue might diminish in proportion to the extent of the crop failure. Similarly, an abundant harvest (in case there was no fixed *Rai* might mean an increase in the revenue *in kind,* but this would be greatly counter balanced by a fall in the prices—*Arzani* (cheapness, abundance) was often considered as a scrounge for the peasantry. Thus, on the whole, it must have required a moderate harvest with stable prices to yield the maximum revenue total for the area. Moreover, we must remember that the difficulties of transport and general constancy in the proportion of areas under the different crops made for much more uniform trend in the price variations of the crops of the same regions.

Only in exceptional cases, in respect, for example, of crops like indigo and betel leaf, would the price of a particular crop be too far out of step with the general price-level. It can be conjectured that in such cases occurring in the *Sal-i-Kamil,* some corrections or adjustments were made, but admittedly we have no explicit evidence on this point.

It seems tó me that in the method outlined above of determining the final *Dasturs* lies the explanations of why these *Dasturs* appear generally to be pitched higher than the average of the 15-24 year rates, even after allowing for the increase of the *Bigha.* Thus, Moreland had the impression that the permanent *Dasturs* stood at almost 20% above the average of the annual scales, while this increase in the *Bigha* was only of the order of 10 or 11%. It is interesting to note that, in effect, the new scales marked a further divergence from the principle of apportioning to the State but one third of the producc. Thc standard *Rai'* of Sher Shah was prepared on that principle, but its very generality and the eccentric machinery of price fixing in the early years of Akbar inflated the annual revenue scales to almost impracticable proportions. There appears to be a gradual fall to more realistic figures during the years 15-24. But now that these are followed by permanent *Dasturs* representing theoretically 1/3rd of the produce in the best year, and thus not 1/3rd of just the average produce, the theoretical share loses all practical significance. It is no wonder, therefore, that the concept of 1/3rd as the State's portion quietly drops out of officials dicta and three scores of years later, we begin to hear of the one-half being the rightful share of the magnanimous government.[18]

Moreland does not seem to have come across any direct reference to the term *Zabt* after the time of Akbar in the materials studied by him. He, therefore, thought this method, apart from some shrunken survivals, died a natural death during the earlier part of the 17th century. This is not, however, the picture which the administrative manuals of the 17th century present to us and it will be seen that Moreland's ideas here stand in need of, at the least, pretty drastic modification.

Thus, we have in the *Farhang-i-Kardani,* written in 1090 A.H./1679 AD by Jagat Rai Shuj' Kasyasth, a definition of *Zabt,* which accords in all essential particulars with our conception of it as derived from the authorities of Akbar's reign.

"The second (method of assessment)", it says "is the procedure of *Zabt Amal-i Zabt, i.e.,* having measured the cultivated lands village by village (*dahedahi*) he (the *Amin*) prepares the (document called) *Khasra*[19] and in accordance with the *Khasra* whatever quantity of cultivated land is shown in the total, he makes the assessment thereof according to the *Dastur* (revenue scales) of *Mahal* (*Pargana*)".[20]

This work itself gives the draft of a *Khasra,* but a more detailed one is preserved in a still later work, the *Khulasatu-s-Siyaq,* written in 1115 A.H./ 1703-4 AD.[21] The document is called "*Khasra-i-Zabt*" in the latter and is dated the Rabi, Harvest, the 41st regnal year of Aurangzeb. The village assessed is named Munawarpur in the *Pargana* of Kirtarpur, which *Pargana* is elsewhere stated to belong to the province of Punjab. At the head of the document are places for the signatures of the *Munsif* (*Amin*), *Karkun, Qanungo* and his surveyors (Jarib Kashan). Underneath are six columns, (1) the first headed *isami,* giving the names of the peasants together with the crops sown by them (2) the *'arz* (breadth) and (3) *tul* (length) of the fields; these multified give (4) the *arazi* or the area or the fields in terms of *bighas* and *biswas* (5) The fifth column is headed *nabud,* giving the area of the land affected by crop failure (6) The last column gives the *baqi* or the balance of the land revenue under cultivation (arazi minus *nabud*). Below this table, we have another summarizing the figures for each crop separately under the three columns of *arazi, nabud* and *baqi.* The crops which are assessed in the present document are wheat, gram and barley.

The *khasra* provided particulars only to the crops and the cultivated area. The assessment in cash is worked out from these figures in another document entitled *Jama'bandi.* Here, the area given under the *baqi* column of the previous document is, for each crop, multiplied with the respective *Dastur.* The *Dasturs* used in this assessment stand at Rs. 5/- per bigha for wheat, Rs. 4/- for gram and Rs. 3/- for barley.[22] The *Dastur* rates are considerably higher than those in the *Ain* for the *Suba* of Lahore,[23] but much cannot be built upon it in view of the uncertainty of the extent of the fall in value of the Rupee during the intervening 100 years.

However it be, we have a complete and detailed instance of the working of the *Zabt* system in its "classic form", the form in which we meet in the *Ain.* On the other hand, in an earlier manual we come across the *Zabt* in a constricted, though, perhaps, also its oldest as well as last form. The manual is the *Dastur-ul Amal-Navisindagi,* which from its contents can be assigned to the later years of Shahjahan.[24] It *Zabt* and *Jam'bandi* tables follow the same pattern as those of *Khulasatu-a-Siyaq,* but with this difference that the *Zabt* is applied only to what in modern terminology are called "cash crops", while the other crops are assessed by *Kankut* or come under sharing (*Bhaoli*). The crops assessed by *Zabt* are tobacco, brinjal and sugar cane.

The *Pargana* and the province are not named and the rates are so low as to rule out all pretensions to anything beyond a hypothetical existence.[25] The fact of the cash crops being singled out for *Zabt* is very interesting in view of Abul Fazl's statement that a number of such crops, e.g., brinjal, betel leaf and indigo were not assessed by the *Rai'* of Sher Shah but had directly fixed cash rates. Down to recent times, the word *Zabt* has stuck to cash rents paid on particular crops at customary rates to the Zamindars in western Uttar Pradesh.[26]

The conclusion, then is that the *Zabt* continued to be used for assessing holdings in particular villages as well as other certain crops throughout the 17th century. It also co-existed with other methods of assessment, but it is another matter to determine, even in relative terms, the area of the land covered by each system. Moreland takes Aurangzeb's *Farman* to *Rasikdas Krori,* in which the prevailing method is described as summary assessment, checked in cases of complaint by measurement (*'amal-i-Jarib*) or *Kankut,* as the case may be, to signify that Akbar's regulation system had become a dead letter. This, of course, implies that in Akbar's reign, things had altogether been different and that in the *Zabti* provinces, at least, annual assessment had been the universal rule. The question whether we should be justified in making such an assumption is inextricably bound up with what our conception is about *Nasq*, the method which appears in Abul Fazl, coupled with and also as revival of the *Zabt.*

Nasq

Moreland and Yusuf Ali, in their article contributed to the J.R.A.S., 1918, were the first to recognise in the word *Nasq,* a technical term for a particular mode of assessment.[27] From the fact that it was used in Bengal and Gujarat and Berar (which in particular was "*Nasaqi* long ago", they deduced that it was a system already established before Akbar's great administrative measures. As to its nature, they admitted they could not determine the essential features with any confidence but hazarded the view that it was possibly an assessment by agreement and also that it was ordinarily a *Zimmidari* rather than a *Ryotwari* arrangement". Moreland, in his *Agrarian System,* presented this concept in rather more refined form and thought '*Nasq*' to mean "group assessment". Mr. S.R. Sharma, in *Indian Culture,* Volume III, 543-5, questioned this view and on the bases of a 17th century manual of administration, preserved in the Rampur State Library, argued that the *Nasq* was an arrangement in which the revenue demand was summarily determined by averaging the revenue of the previous ten to twelve years. Dr. P. Saran, however, sought to dismiss it as a later and modified, if not distorted, form of the system under Akbar, which he believed to have been the same as *Kankut.*[27a]

Since Dr. Saran has refused to consider any later evidence, it is perhaps judicious to examine the above theories, except, of course, that of Mr. S.R. Sharma, on the sole basis, in the first instance, of the 16th century authorities. It seems to me that on this question neither Moreland nor Saran can really command our confidence once we make an independent examination of the *Ain.* Thus the *Ain* (I, 286) enjoins the Revenue Collector (*Amal Guzar*) that "he should not make *Nasq* with the village headmen from indulgence and ignorance arisen there from and it gives scope to the strong of oppressive best". Moreland argues that it proves that *"Nasq"* would be made with the headmen; but unless it can be shown that here not a particular kind of *Nasq,* but *Nasq* in general is prohibited, it would also mean that it could be imposed directly upon the peasants. That there was far from being such a general prohibition is made clear earlier in the same chapter when the "*Amal Guzar*" is told that "if some desire measurement and others accept *Nasq*, he should keep sending the bonds (*qararnama*) promptly". Similarly, the expression, "he should not make *Nasq"* with the headman" ill accords with Dr. Saran's equation of *Nasq* with *Kankut,* which could not have been made with anybody. It is no wonder, therefore, that he challenges the rendering given of it by Moreland and Yusuf Ali (which is particularly the same as ours), but in so doing he does less than justice, both to the Persian and to the two writers, in a case where there cannot be the slightest doubt as to the meaning of the text.[28] Dr. Saran is as little justified in citing the passage that lists the various modes of assessment, in the same chapter, in support of his theory. It begins with the sentence largely quoted, where measurement and *Nasq* are put as alternatives. It goes on to say that the *Amal Guzar* should not make it an invariable practice to realize revenue in cash and should also take it in kind. In case of the latter, there are two accepted methods to be followed: *Kankut* and sharing in its various forms. Clearly, therefore, *Nasq* and *Kankut,* far from being identical, belonged to different categories altogether: one was a method of assessment in terms of cash, the other in terms of kind.[29]

Enough has been said to show the questionable basis on which both Moreland and Saran have erected their theories, and it is, perhaps, time to see what a fresh start one can make of the relevant evidence of the *Ain* and *Akbarnama.* The first reference to *Nasq* occurs in the *Akbarnama* under the regnal year 13, when Shahabuddin Khan was given the charge of the Khalisa lands. "And, since the Khalisa lands are extensive, and honest minded men, controlled without reins, appropriating little, are scarce, he (Shahabuddin Khan), having set aside in the *Zabt-Har Sala* (annual *Zabt*), which necessitated great expenditure and caused misappropriation by men, established a *Nasq* and going into every detail, swept the domineering off their feet". *Nasaq* was thus an easier and cheaper method than *Zabt.*

Nevertheless, since the annual rates continued to be promulgated during the 13th and the following years as shown by the 19 year scales, we must also suppose that it was consistent with the application of these rates. Now besides the application of rates, *Zabt* had only one other aspect, viz. measurement, and therefore, by the *Zabt-Har Sala,* which the *Nasq* is stated to have replaced, we must understand only annual measurement. This could not mean the abandonment of all records of measurement, since in that case the rates could not possibly have been used. We may conjecture, therefore, that the *Nasq* (or "a *nasaq*" to be literal) in this case meant merely that instead of the land being subjected to annual measurement, the previous measurements were standardized in some way and one constant figure accepted for the area under cultivation from year to year. Admittedly, we could only have given this interpretation with the greatest difference had it not been confirmed, almost to a letter, by the Recommendations of Todar Mal, submitted and approved in the 27th year. "It is known", he says "that in the parganas of the *Khalisa,* the area of cultivated land (*arzi*) diminishes every year. Therefore if once the cultivated land is measured, they (the revenue officers) should, enhancing it from year to year, corresponding to the ability of the peasants, established a *"nasaq"* of the part (*Nasaq-i-Juzv*), and making the peasants stand surety for each other, they should obtain papers (*nawishta* of acceptance) and in realizing the demand (*Baz khwast*) tread the path of virtue". It will be noticed that in the *Nasq* recommended here, the last measurement was to be accepted as the minimum constant figure, raised annually not by actual measurement, but simply by an estimate of the peasants capacity to cultivate more: it therefore remains ultimately based upon measurement. The final position under Akbar is, I believe, presented in the following passage in the *Ain's* chapter in Amal Guzar. "In measurement, he should keep farsightedness and justice before him. He should increase the capacity (*niru*) of the cultivator year by year, and being bound by the *Qarar-dad* (bond, agreement, settlement), should not take anything from the excess cultivation (*fuzun kashta*). If some desire measurement (*paimash*) and others accept *Nasq,* he should keep sending the *Qarar-nama* promptly". By asking the *'Amal Guzar'* to increase the capacity of the cultivator, Abul Fazl doubtless implies that he should do so in terms of an increase in the area of revenue-bearing land, which he is to fix every year in a *Qarar-dad.* If the peasants cultivate more than he has bound them to do under it, the gain ought to be entirely theirs. In view of the two *Akbarnama* passages, we are entitled to consider this procedure as that of *Nasq* and once we do, the meaning of the last sentence of the above passage becomes clear. If the peasants accept "the *Nasq* or the constant figure of the cultivated area, raised by estimate, well and good; if not, and they "desire" actual measurement owing to the reduction of the area or some other reason, this should be conceded an area determined afresh. In neither case, the *Qararnama* or the obligation accepted by the peasants is to cultivate a certain area of revenue-paying land, whether fixed by *Nasq* or by actual measurement. The concept of *Nasq* as implying a constant acceptance of the previous measurement of land and thus being ultimately based on the figures of the cultivable area is, I think, proven beyond doubt by a subsequent statement in the same chapter. "If", we are told "after the dispatch of the record of *Nasq* (*naskha-i-nasaq*) to the court, a calamity strikes the crops, he (the *Amal Guzar*) should at once, having obtained correct information, make an estimate (*andaza*) of the area affected (*nabud*) and, having put it into writing, forward it without delay so that it may either be accepted or an *Amin* (assessor) be sent". Here, *Nuskha-i- nasq* can only mean an area record, however computed. On the other hand, the *Nasq*, as we have been unraveling its details, seems to have had another feature, viz. all enhancements in the area-figures above the constant area, determined by the last measurement, are based on estimate. This has the potentiality in it of degenerating into a mere bargain with the village headman over the figure of the cultivable area, which should go on record in the name of their villages. It is thus probable that Abul Fazl has such arrangements in mind when he says that the *Amal Guzar* ought not to "make *Nasaq* with the village headmen."[29a]

We may, perhaps, be entitled to say that under the interpretation we00 have developed form our evidence in the foregoing paragraph, all the pieces of the jigsaw puzzle seem to fall into their natural places. At the same time, it is fair to concede that the evidence so far used refers, in general, to the *Nasaq* worked in the *Zabti* provinces. This is, of course, obvious in the two passages of the *Akbarnama* but it is also clear that though the chapter on the *Amal Guzar,* from which the rest of the evidence comes, does describe other methods of assessment, it deals with his duties largely as if he were working in a *Zabti* area. From this chapter onwards, we do not meet *Nasaq,* till we come to account of the Subas. Here, Abul Fazl is, as a rule, silent about the method or methods of assessment prevalent in provinces of which he had already given the *Dasturs.* Presumably, he considered any such description in the provincial accounts as either superfluous or mere repetition. In the case of Bihar above, which does not appear in the earlier *dastur* tables, it is specially said that it is largely under *Zabt.*[29b] This being so, it cannot be assumed that the *Nasq* prevailed only in these provinces which are definitely stated to have possessed it; on the contrary, *Nasq* used in the *Zabti* areas is most likely to have escaped description along with the *Zabt* with which it co-existed, or indeed, of which it was merely an appendage. Thus, in fact, none of the three provinces in which the *Nasaq* is definitely said to have prevailed—Bengal, Berar and Gujarat—was in the proper sense of the word, under *Zabt.* Precisely because of this, however, it would be interesting to see what form the *Nasaq* assumed when placed outside a *Zabti* environment.

Of the three *Nasaqi* provinces, our information is greatest about Gujarat. (Thanks for the well-known Provincial History, *Mirat-i-Ahmadi*) (C. 1750). The *Ain's* words (I, 485) are, "(it is) mostly (*beshtar*) *Nasaqi* and measurement (*Paimaish*) is little implied (*kam rarad*)".[30] The latter clause is a little vague and if we take it to mean that except for a few areas the land was not measured, it would be contradicted at once by the statistical tables of the province which give area totals (*arazi*), (*mahalwise*), for all the *Sarkars* except Sorath. The *Miriat-i-Ahmadi* (I, 25) also speaks of the comprehensive measurement of the province undertaken by Todar Mal in a period of six months. If the figures of the area attributed by the *Mirat* to this measurement are less than those given in the *Ain,* this might be due to another measurement carried out in the intervening period by Shahabuddin Khan, some time between 985 and 991 A.H./1577 and 1585 AD. Upon the complaint of the peasantry of the *Parganas* of the *Haveli* of Ahmedabad and some other *Parganas,* it is stated (*Mirat,* I, 141), he made them populous by a second measurement of the area of the cultivated land. Now, I believe, this evidence, which rules out one possible interpretation of the Ain's sentence, also, at the same time, suggests another. If after Todar Mal's measurement, there had been established any machinery for recurring measurement at the desire of the peasants, as in the *Zabt* provinces, the necessity for a fresh large-scale measurement like that of Shibaduddin Khan's would not have arisen. What Abul Fazl, then, means is that in Gujarat, the method of measurement in the ordinary course is only rarely met with, the assessment being rigidly based on the standard measurement once made. We have here, a *Nasaq* essentially similar but much fuller in form than the *Nasaq* practiced in the *Zabti* areas.[31]

Concerning the province of Bengal, the *Ain* (I, 389) says, "The peasantry is submissive and revenue paying. Every year, the demand being for eight months, they pay in installments. They themselves take the rupees and *mohurs* for the fixed place (for receiving them). The custom of crop sharing (*Ghalla-bakshi*) is not followed. There is always cheapness (or, abundance-*arzani*). About the (practice of) measurement in (lit of) it, they do not (give any) report,[32] and the land revenue demand (*khwahishgari-i-mal*) is based upon *Nasaq.* The Lord of the World (Akbar) out of kind heartedness, kept that rule in force". The statement made about measurement here, coupled with the absence of area figures in the *Ain's* statistics for this province, proves that this practice was, at best a rare occurrence in Bengal. It is true, as Dr. T. Rai Chaudri points out, that Mukundarama (late 16th century) gives in his *Chandimangala* "the woeful tale of the oppressive

Shiqdar, who measured 15 *cottahs* to a *bigha"* and that there is a reference in the *Baharistan-i-Ghaibi* (tr. II 741-2) of early 17th century, to a survey carried out in some villages.[33] Still measurement must have the exception rather than the rule[34] and *Nasaq* in Bengal must have meant a system radically different from that bearing the same name and prevalent in the *Zabti* provinces. If we look again at the *Ain* passage, we still find that it also eliminates some other possibilities. Since the peasants themselves paid to revenue directly, it seems unlikely that "group assessment" was the regular procedure. And despite what Dr. Saran has to say on this point, *Kankut* is out of the question for both its necessary components, measurement and assessment in kind, are specifically stated to be absent from the Bengal system. Finally, crop sharing is expressly ruled out by the text. It seems to me, therefore, that we have only got one possible method left, a method, moreover, which would bear some resemblance to the *Nasq* under *Zabt.* That is to say, we could conceive *Nasaq* in Bengal as a form of constant assessment of revenue fixed in cash by custom or experience over a long period of time, it would then have had two features common with *Nasq* elsewhere, viz. (1) it was a constant assessment, and (2) a cash system. Such a method might have well suited a province where the wonderful fertility of the soil precluded rapid shifts in land under the plough and there was an unvarying low level of prices (*arzani*) which is noticed by Abul Fazl himself: here the need for *arazi* records and *Dastur* did not arise. All this is little more than hypothetical, but it is a hypothesis which, at least, is consistent with all the evidence we possess.

Finally, Berar is said to have been *"Nasaqi* since long ago".[34b] The *arazi* figures are missing from the Berar statistics and one may accordingly visualize the form of *Nasaq* prevalent in it to have been more akin to the *Nasaq* in Bengal than to that in the *Zabti* areas but paucity of evidence leaves little scope from drawing any further inference.

From the foregoing, it is possible, perhaps, to hazard this definition of *Nasaq:* that it was a system of constant assessment of revenue, primarily in terms of cash but in the provinces under *Zabt,* it was based on measurements made from time to time whatever and whereever desired by the peasants, but in Gujarat only one standard, large scale measurements; and that in Bengal and possibly Berar, it seems to have been determined largely by the custom and experience without any reference to the measured area.

This definition is entirely derived from the evidence of Akbar's reign but it will be seen that the working of *Nasaq* in *Zabt* areas, as above outlined, was in all respects similar to the system described by *Aurangzeb's Farman to Rasikdas Karori.* The preamble of the *Farman* recites that in its day, "the *Amins* of the *Parganas* of the Empire, keeping in view of revenue (*hasil*) of the *Sal-i-Kamil* and the previous (lit. adjacent) year and the area of cultivable land and the state of capacity of the peasantry and other particularities, assess the demand (*Jama'*) of most of the *Parganas* at the beginning of the year. And if the peasantry of some of the villages is not satisfied with this procedure, they assess demand (*Jama'*) thereof at the time if the ripening of the crops, by the procedure of *Jarib* (measurement) or *Kankut* and in some of the villages, where the peasants and the cultivators are thought to be distressed and weak, they follow the process of crop sharing (*Ghalla-bakshi*) on the basis of half or one-third or two-fifth or more or less".[35] In this passage, (*Amal-i-Jarib*) does not simply mean measurement, for *Kankut,* which is described, as its alternative, also included measurement; it must be regarded here, at any rate, as equivalent to *Zabt.* It will be seen, then, that from implying, as Moreland supposes, that Akbar's "Regulation System" had come to an end. This passage in the *Farman* suggests that in its essential features, as *Zabt-Nasq* combination, it was more that sixty years after the death of architect, still in force. Moreland's fault, of course, lay not so much in understanding of Aurangzeb's *Farman,* as in that of the meaning of *Nasaq* under Akbar and his too rigid concept of the *Zabt* system.

It should, therefore, come as no surprise that though the *Farman* to *Rasikdas* does not mention *Nasaq* by name, the term remained in official use throughout the 17th century. Mr. Sharma's discovery of its definition in a manual, preserved at Rampur, has already been referred to. Unfortunately, he does not give its text, nor, surprisingly enough, a translation of it, but merely a paraphrase.[36] However, a similar definition of this system appears in a manual of a much more certain date than Mr. Sharma's, and of this I am able to examine the original text. The *Farang-i-Kardana* (1679 AD) describes the *Nasaq* thus: "The first (method of assessment) is *Nasaq, i.e.,* the Amin taking a view of the *muwazana* (equilibrium, balancing) of ten years and the previous year, or averaging the demand (*Jama'*) of ten or twelve years, makes the assessment".[37]

The passage describes two methods comprehended by the *Nasaq.* Our understanding of the first of the two would obviously depend on the meaning we give to the world *muwazana.* Fortunately enough, we have a draft of the *muwazana* in a list of papers to be obtained from the *Qanungo* by the *Amil,* given in the *Dastur ul Aml' Alamgiri,* written in the first year of Aurangzeb's reign. The document is headed "*Muwazana-i-Dah Sala* (the exact term used in the *Farang-i-kardani's* definition) and this is also called *Taq Sim*[38] for the years..." Underneath the heading are two columns, one meant to give a summary of nine years figures and the other for the particulars of the previous years. These latter consist entirely of the figures of the numbers of villages and of the area of land, viz. of land under habitation, tanks, gardens and *nullahs,* and finally, of land capable of being cultivated. In starting lines we have a heading *Taqsim-i-Yak Sala* (the *Taksim* of one year) where under we have spaces for the areas respectively of the land occupied by the peasantry, covered by gardens and held by the artisans. In a parallel column, listing other documents obtained by the Amil, we have registers of revenue balances and, more significantly, the *Dasturn-l 'amals* for the various crops. By the *Muwazana,* therefore, we must understand a record of measured area, on which the assessors applied the *Dasturs.* The first method of *Nasaq,* as defined in our manual, would then be very similar to the system of this name as practiced in the *Zabti* areas under Akbar. For we may, with some confidence, conceive the former to have been practiced in the following lines. The area figures for the last ten years with special reference to that of the previous year, possibly corrected from time to time by occasional actual measurement here and there, are as recorded in the *Muwazana,* summarily accepted for the present year and made to yield the *Jama'* by an application of the *Dasturs.*

The second form of *Nasaq,* namely, of fixing the assessment by averaging the revenue demand of the past ten or twelve years is, on the contrary, more like what we can conceive the *Nasaq* to have been in Bengal and Berar under Akbar—a summary cash assessment without resource to measurement.

Before closing this section, it may not be without interest to note a still later reference to *Nasaq* which shows that even more than a hundred years after the writing of the *Ain,* this term was yet being used to signify a standard appraisement of the cultivable area, representing what the peasants ought to have been cultivating, rather than what they actually did. The *Khulasatu-s Siyaq* (written, 1703-4)[38a] states that the *Karori* or Revenue Collector, "striving after improvements in tillage and having fixed in every village, in accordance with the state of the peasantry, the *Nasaq,* which in common parlance they call *Sir* (Ms. Or. 2026 has 'Si' instead), should strengthen the horsemen and foot troopers so that the peasants may do the sowing in accordance with the *Qarar-dad* (bond) and they may not allow a single cultivable *bigha* and *biswa* to remain uncultivated". I have not been able to identify the Hindi equivalent given here for *'Nasaq'* but it is obvious that we are, again, dealing with *Nasaq* in the form in which it existed in Akbar's time in the *Zabti* areas.

Kan-Kut

The method of assessment known as the *Kan-kut* survived till very recent times and there cannot be much controversy about this nature. However, since little contemporary evidence, beyond the definition of it in the *Ain,* has been brought together either by Moreland or Saran, it may be worthwhile to obtain a picture of this system as it worked in the Mughal period drawn from the sources.

To begin with, the definition in the *Ain's* chapter on "Amal Guzar. If some desire measurement and others accept *Nasaq,* he should keep sending the *Qararnama* (bond) promptly to the court. And he should not make it a habit to take cash and should take corn or produce (*ghalla*) also. And that is done in various ways (*wa an bar chand guna buwad*): *Kamkut-Kan,* in the Hindi language, means corn, and *kut,* appraisement or conjecture. He should measure that total area by *Jarib* (measuring rod) or by counting paces and should weigh the corn (or, produce-*ghalla*) in the balance of his eyes. Men of experience discern it in such a way that little difference occurs between the estimate and actual produce).[39] If any doubt enters his mind, he should, reaping the field three times (respectively, at places) good, middling, and bad, weigh it (the produce) and remove the traces of doubt. Oft times, they size up the land by appraisement and[40] it comes right". The description of sharing (*batai* or *bhaoli*) follows immediately at some length. From the foregoing we can see that *kankut* had three distinctive features: (1) it involved measurement, (2) the *Rai*' or the crop-rate was prepared on the spot, by estimate or sample inspection, for each field separately; and (3) the assessment of the demand was made primarily in terms of kind, not cash.

In the manuals of the next century notably the *Farang-i-kardani* and the *Khulasatu-a Siyaq,* the *Ain's* defintion is so closely confirmed, that their descriptions may safely be relegated to a footnote.[41] What additional information we gain from them is merely that *Kankut* was also known as *Dana-bandi.*

Of greater interest, perhaps, are the drafts of the documents of assessment made according to the *Kankut* in the two manuals, the *Dastur ul Aml-i Narisindagi*, belonging to the closing years of Shah Jahan's reign and the *Khulasatus-s-Siyaq*, written in 1703-4.[41a] The broad principles on which the drafts have been drawn up in both are the same. In both the cases, the first table has six columns, the first giving the name of the *Payees* (*Isami*), the second the crops (*jins*), then the breadth (*arz*) and length (*tul*) of the field, from which the area (*arazi*) is obtained. The sixth or the last column gives the total produce (*ghalla*) in *mans* and *sers.* In his earlier work, the area figures are given in terms of *bighas* and *biswas* but the latter tells us that they should be given in *kanals* and *mandalas* and follows this rule in its tables. In the former, no crop appears twice but in the latter, wheat is rated for one field at 4.0 *mans* to the *kanal,* for another at 4.3 mans, thus confirming the fact that the rates were prepared by estimate for each field separately. The first table is called *khasra* in the *Khulasatu-a Siyaq* and it is followed by another headed *Si* or *Sar* (?): It is this second which carries the heading *khasra* in the*Dastur-L'Amal-i Navisindaqi.* In both the works, the second table totals up the area and produce, listed in the first table, and arranges them according to the crops. Another table follows in the earlier work, particularly the area and produce again, but making two deductions, one for the self cultivated land, *Khud-Kashta* of the 'zamindars' and for another item, whose illegibility prevents us from deciphering.

Finally, there is a table in the *Jama'-bandi* document (in both the works), where the produce is given crop by crop, the revenue share calculated for each in terms of kind and commuted at given price-rates into cash. In the earlier work, the revenue-share in the case of wheat works out at about one-third, in the case of all other crops, it is explicitly set at half the produce (*nisfi*). In the *Khulasatu-S-Siyaq,* the share is one-half in respect of all the crops, including wheat.

That measurement plays a primary part in assessment by *Kankut* is underlined by the fact that *Dastur-l-'Amal-i-Navis indagi* styles, it *Zabt-i-kankut* and the *Khulasatu-s-Siyaq* uses the term *Zabt* for the measurement carried out under it. It is interesting to speculate how from this system the *Zabt* proper might have evolved in the 16th century. Have a standard *Rai'* instead of on-the-spot estimated crop-rates, and you have reached the stage of Sher Shah's *Zabt.* In fact, we have reference, in Akbar's name, to a similar development or distortion of system, bearing its name. In 983 A.H./ 1575-6 AD, in the Bhakkar Sarkar, "Saiyad Muhammad Mir Adl experienced severity in the matter of the peasantry concerning the *Dastur-u-L-'aml.* By the estimate of *Kankut* (*az qarar-i kankut*), he fixed the revenue (mahsul) uniformly at five *mans* per *bigha*".[41b] However, we have no later instance of such deviation and probably as the *Zabt* system became consolidated in its final form, the intermediary forms between it and *Kankut* tended to disappear.

Batai

The process of sharing, *Batai* or *Bhaoli,* in its many forms, especially, the *Ghalla bakshi,* or sharing of produce, was very widely used in Mughal times.[42] Though owing to the administrative inconvenience involved in it, it was not generally encouraged. Sharing is not, properly speaking, a method of assessment and where peasants were in such indignant circumstances as to be unable to bear any risks at all—risks which are involved in any system of assessment-resort was generally had to be made for this method of dealing with them. This is stated explicitly in the preamble of Aurangzeb's *Farman* to *Rasikdas Karori.*[43] A concrete instance of this is, however, provided by the *Mirat-i-Ahmadi* (I, 217-18). In Gujarat, during the reign of Shah Jahan, the peasants are said to have suffered greatly under the administration of 'Azam Khan; owing this he was replaced in A.H. 1052 (1642-43) by Mirza Isa Tarkhan in the office of the Nazim. The new governor, "occupying himself with the affairs of the Suba and the reconciliation of the peasantry, established in the *Parganas* the produce of *Ghalla Bakshi,* which is in the usage of this country, they call *Bhag-batai,* and in a short time, brought the country to prosperity".

On the other hand, the system was also liable to great abuse, not only as Abul Fazl fears (*Ain* I, 286), because the peasants might deceive the revenue officials, but also because in the absence of any check by records as possible under other mehtods, more corn might be ceased from the peasants than the the authorities were entitled to by their regular share of the actual produce. Thus, in Gujarat, where *Ghalla-bakshi* is said to have eased the strain in the peasants in 1642-3, it has assumed an almost monstrous form by the 8th regnal year of Aurangzeb's reign. A *Farman* issued this year recites that owing to the high price of corn, the revenue demand (*Jama'*) had reached the maximum (*kamal*) everywhere. The Jagirdars and officials, keeping their eyes on that (maximum) demand (*Jama*) make the *Jama-bandi* (assessment) by force. If they followed the system of the sharing of half (the produce) (*bata-wai-i-nisfi*), then they, by supposing (Hind-Persian: *kaltar karda*) (the produce to be) two hundred and fifty *mans* instead of (the actual) one hundred *mans* of corn, seize both the parts of the produce (*har do Sar-i mahsul*) and for the payment of the excess of twenty five *mans* (the peasants) having worked themselves to death the whole year, they obtain it out of their wages (*wajh-i mazduri*).[44] We do not know how far the injunction made in the *Farman* that the revenue demand should henceforth be made on the basis of land and state of actual cultivation (*ba qarar-i-hast-o-bud*) and in an accurate manner (*az qarar-i-waqia*), was, in the actual fact, followed. What it places beyond doubt is that sharing too was a double-edged sword and that though preferred by the peasants in its pure form, it could really become a scourge under the manipulating hands of their oppressors.

References

1. From a note in the *Agrarian System,* p. 89, it appears that he had seen some of the manuals, but surprisingly enough, he failed to realize their general relevance as a source material for his studies.
2. *Ain,* I, pp. 296-303, 347; *Akbar Nama,* III, p. 282.
3. *Ain,* I, pp. 304-347; Except Malwa. The identity of the figures for the years appears greater still in the MSS. Add 7652 and Add 6552 in the British Museum, which I have used to check Blochmann's text and tables.
4. The regional price-scales and crop rates had replaced the previous single price-scales and standard crop rates is also implied in two statements made elsewhere by Abul Fazl. Thus *Akbar Nama* (II, 282) says that till the 24th year "reports of prices were sent from every region (*har nahiyat*)". The *Ain* (I, 297) says referring to the "Rai" of Sher Shah that less than it "they do not today demand in all the provinces", which means that the provincial Rai's varied, in favour of excess, from the standard Rai'.
5. *Akbar Nama*, II, p. 270; *Ain*, I, p. 347; See, for the detailed explanation of the terms *Taqsim* and *Muwazana,* section under Nasq.
6. *Ain*, I, p. 296; A.N., II, pp. 118-119; "One bigha by the hempen rope (*tanab-i-San*) is smaller than the *bigha* by the bamboo-rod (*tanab-i-bans*) by two *biswas* and 12 *biswanasa,* as in every hundred *bighas,* the difference comes to 13 *bighas.* Although the hempen rope was also of sixty *gaz* (in length), yet in being twisted, it used to come to fifty-six *gaz* (only). And the *bigha* of the *Ilahi gaz* is larger than the *Sikandri gaz* by one *biswa,* twenty (eight *Hasht* (8) and *bist* (20) without dots have the same shape) *biswansa,* thirteen *biswansa,* eight *tapwansa* an four *answansa.* In a hundred *bighas,* it comes from both causes to twenty two *bighas,* three *biswa* and seven *biswansa*". (*Ain,* I, 297). It is clear that the difference between the two sizes of the *Sikandri bigha,* one measured with rope and the other with bamboo, is given in terms of the latter. The second difference is probably in terms of the *Illahi-bigha.* Abul Fazl, by adding up the two figures, has, then, made a slight slip in arithmetic. If the second difference is also really in terms of the bamboo-measured *Sikandri bigha,* the increase form the *Illahi gaz* would be 9% of it, not 10.1%. The overall increase would similarly be 25.4% instead of 26%. However, in either case, the difference is so small as to be negligible for our purpose.
7. John Marshall in *India—Notes and Observations in Bengal, 1668-72,* edited S.A. Khan, London, 1927, p. 420.
8. I am painfully aware of the fact the figures in Blochmann's edition are by no means perfect in point of accuracy. So far an inspection of almost of all the known early manuscripts of the *"Ain"* available in England has revealed, Mss. Add. 7652 (of which 1.0.6 is an unrevised copy) and Add. 6552 in the British Museum are by far the most carefully written. They belong, at the latest, to the early years of Mohammad Shah's reign and are independent of each other as two good manuscripts of the same work can possibly be. I have

carefully collated the tables as preserved in these two manuscripts with those of Blochmann and usually make use of only those instances where the variations among them are nil or only slight. In the case of the few variants, I take the heading, which would be most favourable to Moreland's hypothesis.

9. Add. 7652 puts 170 *d* and 106 *d* as the minimum figures under the years 18 and 19 respectively, in the tables of Awadh. However, Add. 6552 agrees with Blochmann in having just 200 *d* throughout.

10. The exceptions are the Kabuli gram and ajwain.

11. "...and further the withdrawal of some of the price-reporters (*nirkh-navisan*) from the path of rectitude gained notoriety (*A.N.*, III, 282). This passage is placed under the 24th year and gives an account of the *Jama Deh Sala* and the causes that led to its preparation.

11a. *A.N.*, III, p. 282

12. *Nezmal* in Add. 6552, *harmal* in Add. 7652 and *har Sal* in Blochmann's text only. Moreland, who discusses these variations, prefers for good reasons, the reading *nezmal* over *har Sal.*

13. Ch. Jarett who translates from Blochmann's text only: "The best crops were taken into account in each year and the year of the most abundant harvest accepted as the table shows". (*Ain,* tr. II).

14. Ch. 1. For this word, *Bahar-i-Ajam,* Nawal Kishore, ed., p. 81; the *Ghiyasn-i-Lughat* (Nawal Kishore, ed., p. 26); Steingan, p. 72.

15. The word *Jins-i-Kaml* (as a synonym for *gazin Jins,* select crops) is used in the *Ain,* I, p. 285. We find it also in the *Insha-i-Abul Fazal,* Nawel Kishore, ed., p. 160. Thereafter, it is very often met with in the revenue literature. For a definition of the word, as contrasted with *Jins-i-adna,* see an interesting Persian dictionary of revenue terms, written probably in the latter part of the 18th century, British Museum, Ms. Add. 6603, f. 57a.

16. It may be noticed that I have followed Moreland's reading of the initial words instead of that of Blochmann, *i.e.,* reading *nezmal* in place of *har sal.* If the latter were accepted, the sentence would have to be translated thus; "And every year (the particulars of) the high priced crops exhibited reliability".

17. *Akbar Nama,* III, pp. 117-118. In case the reading *har sal* is preferred over *nezmal* in the first sentence, we may perhaps take it to indicate that now, following new collection of data, the particulars about the high-grade crops available to the Revenue Ministry became more and more reliable with each passing year.

17a. *A.N.*, III, p. 459.

18. Abul Fazl, referring to *Ilan,* says that often revenue exacted there "exceeds one-half and owing to habit of cruel mindness, it does not seem (to them) to be bad". (*Ain,* I, 293). An order issued by Aurangzeb in his 8th regnal year sets the demand at half of the produce in Gujarat (*Mirat-i-Ahmadi,* I, 263). In his *Farman* to Muhammad Hashim (1668-9) this is considered the normal share. (*Ibid.,* 269). In the subsequent official manuals and documents, there

is no paucity of statements to this effect. Thus the *Nigarnama-i-Munshi* (14-18 regnal years of Aurangzeb), Br. M. Ms. Or. 1735, ff. 77 b, 102 b, 119 a, 128 a, 188 b; *Durr-l-ulum* (1100 A.H./1688-9 AD) Bod. Ms. Walker 104 ff. 42b-43a, 55a; *Khubasatu-s Siyaq* (1115 H.H./1703-4), Br. M. Ms. Add. 6588, f. 21b.

19. Ch. *Ain,* I, 288: the *Bitikchi* sends the record of *Zabt,* which in Hindi they call *Khasra* to the court.
20. Definition of *Zabt* on p. 69. Prof. Rashid's copy.
21. British Museum Add. 6588, ff. 75a-75b for the tables discussed in the following paragraphs. Or 2026 is really a copy of this manual, but sought by the plagiarist to be passed off as an independent work. It is useful to compare the two manuscripts in cases to textual obscurity.
22. The totals obtained for each crops are added together to yield the total *Jama'* for the village and this is put at the top. It may also be noted that the area and revenue figures for the crops are distributed between *asal* (previously cultivated) and *izafa* (newly brought under cultivation).
23. In the *Ain's* rates for the Lahor Suba, the highest rates belong to the *Dastur* of Lahor and the surrounding *Parganas.* We give below the rates of this *Dastur* and the rates of the *Khula-s-Siyaq* converted into *dams.*

Wheat	**Dastur for Lahor and in the Ain**	**Dastur used in the Khulasaat-u-s-Siyaq**
	55*d.* 25 J. (as in Add. 7652 & 6552)	200*d*
	50*d.* 25 J. (in Blochmann)	
Gram	35*d* 20 J.	160*d*
Barley	46*d*	140*d*

24. British Museum Ms. Add. 6641, ff. 150-95. In this manual, Shahjahani weights are mentioned, not Alamgiri, the list of *subas* include Qandahar, but not Bijapur and Golkunda; and the name of Shah Jahanbad occurs at least thrice. I think these facts are sufficient for us to fix its period with confidence. The tables discussed in the *Pargana* are given on ff. 182a-185a.
25. The rates are:

Tabacco: 12 annas per *bigha*

Sugar Cane: 8 annas (20 dams) per *bigha*

Brinjal: 5 annas per *bigha*

Sugar Cane, which alone of the three appears on the *dasturs* of the *Ain,* never bears a rate of less than 100 dams per *bigha.*

26. *Ain*, I, p. 300; Ch. Moreland a Yusuf Ali in *J.R.A.S.*, 1918, p. 26.
27. Scholars who objected, only orally according to Moreland, on the ground that *Nasq* (lit. order, method) is not given such a meaning in any dictionary, might have reflected over the use made of the word in a part of Iran. Prof. Lambton's glossary defines it as a term common in Arak for the "capacity of a village in plough lands". (Landlord and Peasant in Modern Persia, p. 436).

27a. *Ain*, I, p. 278; *JRAS*, 1918, pp. 29-30; Saran, P., *Provincial Government of the Mughals*, pp. 301-309, 453-457.

28. The words in the original are: *"Nasq ba kalan-taren-i-deh na-kunad"*. Saran appeals to Jarett whose version is: "He should not entrust the appraisement to the headmen of the village". (*Ain*, Tr. II, 45). Jarett was obviously confused by *Nasq*, which he did not regard as a technical term. It is unavailing to produce, as D. Saran does (pp. 305-6), a whole paragraph of confused to support an obviously bad piece of translation. (Jarett took it for appraisement—a wrong translation).

29. *Ain*, I, 285-6. The passage is translated and discussed further in the section under *Kankut*.

29a. *A.N.*, II, pp. 333, 381-382; *Ain*, I, pp. 285-287.

29b. *Ain*, I, p. 417.

30. Moreland and Y. Ali (*J.R.A.S.*, 1918, pp. 29-30), while admitting that Mss. do not show any variation from the word *beshtar* still suggest that we should read peshtar' (formerly) instead and invite us to interpret to sentence as meaning that *Nasaq* and "little measurement" were both things of the past. They should have, however, reflected that in that case we should also have to read *rafte* instead of *ravad* at the end.

31. The next known change in Gujarat came about during the term of office of Mirza Isa Tarkhan, 1052-4 A.H/1642-5 AD, who instituted crop-sharing (*Mirat*, I, 217-18). From a *Farman* issued by Aurangzeb in the 8th regnal year, it appears that by then this system had deteriorated into an on paper only (see the section under *Batai*); it was also coexistent with a summary method whereby the peasants were compelled to cultivate a certain area of land as determined by the authorities (*Mirat*, I, 263). This latter we can readily identify as a sort of *Nasaq*.

32. *".....paimudan an baz na goyand"* (Bloch.). In Mss. Add. 7652 and 6552, we have *az* instead of *dar*, which, however, does not alter the render above given. I cannot understand how Jarrett managed to translate this sentence as "measurement is not insisted upon" though both Moreland and Dr. Saran have followed him.

33. T. Rai Chaudri, *Bengal under Akbar and Jahangir*, pp. 24-25.

34. An interesting manual written in the later years of Aurangzeb simply entitled *Dastur-l-Aml*, British Library, Fraser 86, f. 60 a, shows that in its item out of 1,12,788 villages in the province of Bengal, only 1,538 villages (with a total area of 8,30,755) had been measured.

34a. Saran, op. cit., pp. 302-303.

34b. *Ain*, I, p. 478.

35. Ms. I.O. 1146, f. 1 b; 1.0.1566, f. 23a. Text edited by J.N. Sarkar, *J.A.S.B.*

36. *Indian Culture*, III, pp. 544-5.

37. P. 69 of Prof. Rashid's copy. *"Awwal Nasaq astki Ami nazar bar muwazana-i-dah Sala wa Sal-i-Guzishta wa paiwasta numuda ya Jama-i-dah do-az-dah sala ra sarasari karda Jama bandi mumayad"*.

38. B.M. Ms. Add. 6598. f.36b. *Muwazana* and *Taqsim* are also put down as synonyms in the *Khulasatu-s Siyaq,* Add. 6588, f. 73 b- 74 a. For *Taqsimat-i-Mulk* mentioned in the *Ain,* see the section under *Zabt.*

38a. B.M. Ms. Add. 6588 f. 796-80a.

39. *Ain,* I, pp. 285-286; Jarett, "The experienced in these matters say that this comes little short of the mark". (*Ain,* tr. II, p. 44).

40. Blochmann omits *wa* (and), but it is given by both Mss. Add. 7652 and 6552.

41. *Farang-i-kardani,* Prof. Rashid's copy, p. 69: "The third (method of assessment) is the procedure of *Dana bandi* or *Kankut,* viz., the Amin going to every part of the cultivated land, village by village, calculates, *baqi numayad* produce by estimate and makes the assessment of demand (*Jama-bandi*) on its basis".

"*Khulasatu-s Siyaq,* Add. 6588, f. 76a. *Kankut* is another name for *Dana Bandi.* In the language of India, they call corn (*ghalla*) *kan* and appraisement *kut.* Having brought the land under measurement (*ba zabt dar awurda*) he (the Amin) should, by conjecture, fix the produce by weighing it in the balance of his eyes; and this is done properly (lit. comes right) under the Indian system of measurement (*Zabt-i Hindi*) which is by *kanal* and *mandla...*"

Add. 6603 (probably late 18th C.), f. 71b also gives an accurate definition of *Kankut.* "*Zabt-i-Dana bandi, i.e.,* whenever the Amin, together with the *Sal* is (third party, impartial arbiter) and other staff, prepares the *Kasra* after having measured the land and estimated the produce (ghalla), they call it *Zabt-i-Dana Bandi*".

41a. B.M. Ms. Add. 6641 ff. 182a-185a and Add. 6588 ff. 75a-76b respectively.

41b. *Tarikh-i-Ma'sm,* p. 245.

42. See for sharing and its form: *Ain,* I, 286 as well as Add. 6603, ff. 50 b- 51 a.

43. Ms. 1.0. 1146, f. 1b; 0.1566, f. 23a; ed. Sarkar, J.A.B.

44. *Mirat-i-Ahmadi,* I, 268. What the *Farman* means to say is that when the actual produce is 100 *mans,* the revenue sharing ought to be 50 *mans.* But the *Jagirdars* and officials calculate the produce at 250 *mans* and so expect a revenue of 125 *mans.* In the first instance, they seize the whole of the 100 *mans*—both their legal share as well as the peasants. For the 25 *mans* still left, they compel the peasants to work for them and obtain this amount out of their wages.

Chapter 8

Organisation of the Agrarian Structure and Practices in North India from the Ancient to the Medieval Age—Pre Mughal Era (Elements of Continuity and Change)*

Ever since ancient times, India has par excellence been an agricultural country and its socio-economic structure till at least the pre-industrialised phase in the recent past has been dominantly governed by the agrarian economy. This accounts for the paramount importance of the agrarian system mutual relations amongst various sections of the rural society and the magnitude of the agricultural surplus forming main income of the communities and the state from one phase to another. Even though the economic historians working on the ancient and medieval periods of Indian history have dealt with many an aspect of the agrarian system, not much attention has been paid so far to the elements of continuity and change in this regard.

The recent archaeological evidence (gathered both in Pakistan and India)[1] points to the fact that even in the pre-Harappan phase in the Indus plains, the agricultural processes on the part of the farming communities involved cultivation of the crops and domestication of animals. With the introduction of cotton and *Qats* along with the existing crops like wheat and barley, the use of plough, the bullock cart, the twin crop pattern diversified and intensified the agriculture, which along with cattle rearing formed the main economic base. This may as well have brought in the tribal relationship the social division of labour and community life. The archeological evidence further testifies the overlapping and co-existence of the pre-Harappan and Harappan cultures wherein agriculture continued to form the primary economic base. The evidence clearly shows the cultivation of both the *kharif* and the *rabi* crops *viz.* rice, pulses, wheat,

* Presented at the Symposium on Transition from Ancient to Medieval Periods. Problems of Economic and Social Organisation of the Society (India and the Territories of USSR), 11th-13th April, 1985.

barley, sesame and cotton as well as irrigation through tanks, life irrigation channels. The economy expanded with the growth of the towns, inland as well as sea-borne trade with West-Asian countries. The Harappans equally developed commercial and cultural contact with Central Asia. The village settlements were more homogenous in racial character than the towns, though both were characterised by the hierarchical social pattern. In many a region of North India, the village settlements were marked by both Harappan elements as well as pre-Harappan traditions. The *Bara* culture exhibits sizeable villages with both mud and mud brick house, use of lime for storing the grains and *tandoors* for cooking food, the cultivation of cereal crops like rice and barley as well as tending of the cattle.

The real break-through in the agrarian economy and rural social structure comes in the Iron age and the innovation of glass technology with improved craftsmanship. The use of iron for agricultural implements, cutting the jungle wood and for other purposes along with the continuance of copper use provided settled agrarian economy, comparatively large sized village settlements, small-scale specialised crafts, inter-regional trade along with the fostered process of urbanisation. It equally led to stable agrarian society and social stratification. This culture of the people (Painted Grey Ware—P.G.W.) has been identified with the later Vedic Period (800-350 B.C.) However, with the beginning of the historical era associated with the Northern Black Polished Ware (N.B.P. 500 B.C. to 1st century B.C.), the iron technology gave further impetus for abundant production of implements on mature basis both for agriculture and craftsmanship, more especially during the Indo-Greek and Sunga phases.

For the Mauryan age, the *Arthasastra* reveals a fairly developed stage of agrarian structure and economy.[2] It deals with the nature of tenures, survey and assessment of the land revenue in the settled villages, topographical survey, record of rights in respect of agrarian lands in the villages, their boundaries, the cultivated and uncultivated lands, agricultural fields, well irrigated lands, gardens, irrigation works and forests. It clearly draws distinction between the crown lands and private owned lands. In the latter category, the cultivating families may even own self developed means of irrigation with proprietary rights for mortgage or sale. The *Arthasastra* recommends that the land revenue assessment on the holdings of the cultivators should be based on the classification of agrarian lands *viz.* upland and lowland soils, the available means of irrigation rendered through overflowing of rivers, river-channels, tanks or wells and that the State share might range between 1/5th to 1/3rd of the gross produce dependent upon the labour necessary for the cultivation of the particular crops. A further distinction is also made between the grain crops assessed in kind and some cash crops assessed basically on cash rates (*hiranya*) and there is every possibility that the incidence of State demand may have varied for these two categories of crops. The assessment was based on actual survey and measurement of the land. Based on similar principles, later on, Manu puts the normal State share at varying rates between 1/12th to 1/6th of the produce and at 1/4th of produce in times of war and other public calamity.[3] This theoretical enuciation is by and large maintained thereafter by the *Dharmasastra* and some legal texts. Apart from it, a peasant had also to pay some extra local cesses (*Kars, bali*) on cattle and other livestock, on dairy produce, pasture land and piscary.[4] However, the *Shukraniti*—a medieval work, emphasised on the variation in the incidence of the State demand governed by nature of soil and means of irrigation, *i.e.,* 1/6th of produce from the barren cultivable land while 1/3rd to 1/4th from the lands irrigated by tanks, canals and wells and 1/2 from the land dependent on rainfall.[5]

The *Jatakas, Arthasastra* and the later grants clearly bring out the varying methods of land revenue assessment viz. division of produce on the thrashing ground (*Kalabhiksa*), appraisement of the standing crops, assessment according to the ploughing capacity of the plough-oxen (*kula*) the seed-capacity of the agricultural fields (*kulyavapa*) in relation to the total respective yields of the crops as well as collective assessment (*pindakara, samksepa*).[6] For the purposes of measurement of the land, a linear sized reed (*nala*) was improved and standardised in the course of the centuries more especially from the early medieval age onwards under the Gujar-Prathiharas, the Katachuri Rajputs of Awadh (11th century) with *naluka* as the assessment area unit and the Sena dynasty of Bengal (12th century) with *drona* as the area unit.[7] The role of cash nexus which was limited in character in the early phase got impetus from the Gupta period onwards, more especially for the valuation of the villages for the purposes of revenue assignment to the religious persons and institutions as well as to the state officials. The available epigraphic evidence shows that in the 12th century it got wider operation, specially in Marwar (Rajasthan) and Bengal.[8]

Both in the ancient and early medieval periods, the Hindu rulers made land grants and revenue assignments for secular and religious purposes. Of the latter category, the main beneficiaries were the Brahman families, the Hindu temples, Buddhist monastries and the various priests and attendants. Grants could be made from waste culturable land as well as from the revenues of the settled villages to an individual family or as collective to numerous families or the institutions and were rather perpetual and hereditary in character. In addition to the land revenue, the grantee was usually bestowed all other items from the assigned villages. Except when granted revenue from the villages of the crown lands, the grantee had no proprietary claim to the agrarian lands of the revenue paying peasant families who continued with their ownership rights over their lands. Some of the grants were conditional while others made by the Pala kings in Bihar are conspicious by their detailed nature. A few 11th-12th centuries grants (*prasadapatta*) favour the assignees with cultivated fields, wells, houses and householders together with a village with its bipeds, quadrupeds, fields and householders.[9] Such grants did not involve the transfer of the cultivators or resident artisans to the assignees as the latter's slaves or serfs. This implied the assignment of all income due to the state from the cultivators or artisans in the villages and did not in any way involve either the persons or the landed and commercial rights of the residents of the villages. This was equally a matter of phraseology used in the grants, which were invariably more detailed in description when granted by the local chieftains, vassal states than those by the royal courts. Apart from the fiscal rights, some of the Pala grants bestowed even the administrative rights for the maintenance of law and order to the assignees. However, the *Pratihar* and the later grants given by the Rajput rulers in the 11th and 12th countries are not so detailed in description.

The assignation of the revenues of the villages and the revenue-free land grants on perpetual basis created a hereditary landed class of priesthood. There is no denying the fact that with the conferment of the fiscal and landed rights on the priestly class, some parasitic attitude was bound to develop and this remained a marked trait of this class throughout ancient and medieval ages. However, it is equally feasible that the Brahmans when assigned revenue or waste cultivable land in the rural areas and more especially in the backward regions or amidst the aboriginal tribes carried on their work on behalf of both the Hindu religion and the state and thereby became the main stronghold of Hinduism in the social life of rural India.

In the background of tribal organisation of the Aryans, it is surmised that in its earliest stages, the concept of ownership of agrarian land was communal and land was regarded as the collective property of the clan. However, the progressively evolutionary stages of the notions governing proprietary rights developed from the communal ownership of the tribe further divided into clans to village community ownership, joint family holdings and the individual rights in the course of the centuries.[10] The communal *vesh, i.e.,* periodic redistribution of land amongst various branches of clan or the practice of redistribution and readjustment of land within a single village or periodic exchange of certain ancestoral lands within a single family were traced in many a village in North Western portions of North India during the second half of the 19th century. But with the gradual improvement of land in particular villages and holdings of the families both through human labour and the development of the artificial means of irrigation, the concept of ownership on the part of severalty gradually gained ground. There were two important factors, social and political which gradually undermined the communal concept of the ownership over agrarian lands. Socially within the tribal order, the village communities entrenched their rights against the tribal control and in their own turn the households and, wherever possible, the land owing families did the same thing. Politically speaking, the constant mutual warfare amongst various Aryan tribes, the tribal chiefs representing the regional and communal concept of authority gave place to the growing phenomenon of a strong and absolute monarchy. The growing conflict between the royal claim over lands and the old concept of communal ownership is quite apparent during the period of the Brahmanas. The monarchy was the true inheritor of the authority of the tribal chiefs and their communal orders. It is no surprise that Megasthenese declared that all land was the property of the crown and no private person was permitted to own it.[11] Significantly the *Arthasastra* is completely silent on the theoretical question of ownership of land. But at the same time, it asserts that the king had the right to evict the defaulting peasants and confiscate the holdings if they were left uncultivated.[12]

Though in its chapter on the inheritance of private property the *Arthasastra*[13] says nothing about the inheritance of land rights, the occupancy rights of the cultivating families in the settled villages were undeniably recognised. The *Arthasastra* does mention the sale of lands to kinsmen and neighbours and the delimitation of the property in the presence of village elders. It lays down the rules that tax payers and the Brahman holders of revenue-fee lands should sell or mortgage only to their respective classes. At the same time, it allows full rights of sale and mortgage to the founders and restorers of irrigation works. But it cannot be stated with certainly if the right of sale or mortgage on the part of tax-payers applied only to urban property, home steads with small fields, orchards or it equally applied to the possessors of the agrarian property in old settled villages. It does seem in the context that the State did permit the ownership of land with rights of sale and mortgage to such families who may have developed their own means of irrigation. This implies two-fold aspect of land ownership viz. the land personally owned by the king who could dispose them as he pleased and secondly such lands over which the king did not claim any proprietary rights but only enjoyed their revenue as the head of the State. As in the Hindu polity, there was hardly any distinction between the position of the king and the state, the king being the head of the State claimed royal ownership over the crown lands from which he derived his personal income. Manu enunciates the theory of land being the property of the first clearer.[14] With growing population and the need for increase in the State revenues, the extension of the cultivable land through the clearance of jungles and reclamation of waste lands continued throughout the ancient Indian period. This could be undertaken only by the families rather than a single individual. A land owner could equally mortgage his land and may be arrears of land revenue. Such a right would prevail only in such regions where the agrarian land may have acquired saleable value. The right of sale was subject to the consent of the village clansmen and before his transfer to outsiders or persons of other castes, the right of pre-emption lay with the near kinsmen, neighbours and creditors. Such a limitation upon the free transfer of land inherited from the original communal rights of the tribe continued to persist in many a part of North India throughout the medieval age, and in fact, medieval period, a land owing family could transfer the land to the tenants though the responsibility for the land revenue payment lay with land owner.[15]

Notwithstanding the evolution of the above mentioned rights of the land owing families, it is remarkable to note that with the establishment of a strong empire under the Guptas, the royal theory of ownership of land is again asserted. This was not only the verdict of Fa hien, the Chinese traveller but also of Katyayana, a late Gupta law giver.[16] The royal claim to land ownership was definitely qualified and limited by the landed rights which the peasant families had acquired in the course of the centuries. After the break up of Harsa's empire and with the establishment of a congeries of Rajput kingdoms in North India, the established land rights of the peasant families were bound to be strengthened. The concept of family ownership of land became strongly entrenched. The later *Smritis* not only emphasise more possession of land but accord clear title to undisputed permanent possession constituting ownership in land.[17] Moreover, with the growing use of money in the eleventh and twelfth centuries, the private rights of ownership comprising mortgage could be still more effective. Al-Biruni (11th century A.D.) justifies the royal share in the produce "in recognition of the protection and their families—Further, trading business, too, pay a tribute for the same reason".[18] Thus to Al-Biruni, the peasant's right to merchandise, though both enjoyed proprietary rights over their respective possessions was subject to the payment of taxation in lieu of the protection afforded by the State. The emphasis is as much, if not more, on the royal share being the first charge on the land as on the preprisetary possession of the peasant on his holding. Al-Biruni's statement was derived either from his study of the Hindu jurisprudence or was based on an eye witnessed situation of the contemporary agrarian relations. The fact that his analysis was meant for the Muslim world before the establishment of the Turkish rule in North India is all the more significant. The commentaries written by the Hindu theorists during the 11th and 12th centuries propounding the royal ownership of land based on the interpretation of *Narashinha Purana* or *Arthasashtra* covered only theoretical aspect and were not even applicable to their own age when the agrarian land rights had undergone considerable change in the course of the centuries. However, the Hindu rulers independent or semi independent, continued to assert royal ownership of land within their territories throughout the medieval age.

Politically speaking, the institution of the monarchy and the concept of the empire underwent a considerable change from the late Gupta period onwards. In proportion to the extent of the Empire, the directly administered territories were much limited. The later Gupta rulers acquiesed to the idea of getting their recognition as the overlords of the vassal states rather than bringing the latter under direct administration. The assumption of 'Great king of kings' and high sounding epithets of the overlordship (viz. *Paramabhattaraka, Parmesvara* and Maharajadhiraja) adopted by the later Gupta rulers and then by the Pala and Pratihara kings do not point towards the centralisation of the authority and uniformity of the empire but merely indicate the assertion and exercise of overlordship over the lords, chiefs and princes owing allegience to them.[20] The vassal chiefs came to be designated by various graded epithets viz. *Mahasamanta, Mahasamntadhipatis, Maharaja, Raja, Ranakar* and *Rajarjankas* etc. The transformation of the term *Samants* meaning hitherto 'neighbour' or 'neighbouring king' into a vassal chief of the overlord monarch is quite significant. At times, the vassal chiefs had their further vassals in the *rajas* or small chieftains. The exact terms of relationship and the extent to which the overlord monarch could interfere or have any effective control in the internal revenue administration of the vassal chiefs cannot be determined. It can be well imagined that these vassal chiefs would have paid tribute to the overlord in proportion either to their revenues or in accordance with the terms of submission. They had also to render military service to the overlord. They may have have as well struck coins in the name of the suzerain. In fact, Harsa made a successful bid to create a personally administered centralised empire. He exercised the prerogative of issuing land grants in the territories of the vassal chiefs and such grants issued by him bear directions given to them for the compliance of the royal order.[21] After Harsa, a number of independent and semi-independent states sprang up in different regions of North India. The kingdoms of the Palas and the Pratihars were comparatively smaller ones but a number of graded vassal chiefs owed allegiance to them. Usually, the latter were vanquished and reinstated local chieftains who undertook to pay fixed tribute and render military service to the overlord. The vassal chiefs had the authority to make religious land grants to the deserving priestly families or institutions.[22] Where the overlord exerted greater control, a vassal chief had to take the approval of the former or the royal officials for making a religious grant in his own territory or else he would make the grant on his own authority. Most likely, the exercise of such power on the part of the vassal chiefs depended either upon personal equation of mutual strength with the overlord or the terms of submission. Very few secular grants for the early medieval period can be traced. For any meritorious services, the overlord could reward the vassal chief with a land grant in the share of the assignation of the revenue from a certain territory.[23] The vassal chief was fully responsible for the realisation of the revenues and the administration of such an assigned territory. From the agrarian viewpoint, more important than the polity of the kingdoms, which is a history of the hegemonies over the vassal chiefs, were the tribal and the clannish landed interests imposed on the caste ridden settled villages during the early medieval age. The conquering tribes and clans always apportioned territories and villages for the realisation of the revenues. In the wake of the Huns, the Gujars came from Central Asia and settled in various portions of North India. The conquering clans usually disposed or suppressed erstwhile clans and established their own intermediary rights of collection and a share in the revenues as their emoluments. The intermediary landed classes were named by various local designations from time to time but the basic traits of their relation to the villages comprising peasant families of the suppressed clans and castes remained the same. The members of the suppressed clans were mostly reduced to the status of the cultivators. Some dispossessions of the previous land owing families may as well have taken place but this was rather a rare phenomenon. Many members of the conquering clans did as well take to colonisation or reclamation of the jungle and waste lands attached to the settled villages and became the peasants under the rule of their own clannish authorities. This was rather inevitable with the growth of the clannish population and the pressure on the settled villages.

The imposition and reimposition of the intermediary rights of the conquering clans is a recurring phenomenon which persisted through out the medieval ages. The Rajput clans ruled over the last Hindu states which fell before the Turkish onslaughts. They ruled over North India from the 7th or 8th century to the end of the 12th century before the establishment of the Turkish rule. What specially distinguished the Rajput polity was the imposition of the clan aristocracies and hiearchial order of landed intermediaries between the peasants of the settled villages and the ruler. At the top, the polity was governed by the same old Hindu idea of establishing hegemony over each other through mutual clannish warfare extending the territories of the conquering state at the cost of the vanquised and imposing tribute and military service on the vassal chiefs. Within the state, a ruler usually assigned the revenues of the settled villages to his own kinsmen and clansmen on the condition of rendering military service. He also made grants to his officials in lieu of their salaries. Religious grants were also made to the Brahmanas in shape of assignation of the villages or revenue free grants of lands. The grantee served as the intermediary and below him were Headmen of the villages who may as well belong to the ruling clan and would collect the revenues after having reserved their own collection charges. The Headman was usually a land owner in his village. The grantees or the Headman had to maintain law and order, possessed a right to alienate waste cultivable lands and to introduce new cultivators on behalf of the ruler but the ruler could never claim rights of ownership on the agrarian land of the peasants in the settled villages. The Rajput families may own lands in the colonised or old villages and as well may enjoy revenue free grants of land but usually they belonged to the intermediary classes and had no clannish or families ties with the peasants in the settled villages. It is only when some of the Rajput families took to cultivation either in the settled or in the colonised villages that a clannish bond can be said to have subsisted between the ruler and cultivating families. The Rajput socio-political structure does bear greater resemblance to a feudalised set up than the preceeding Hindu social orders.

India and the Arab people of West Asia have had intimate commercial relations from times immemorial. Even after the birth of Islam, the Muslim Arab traders kept up the tempo of trade with India in the early medieval age. However, right from the first century of the *Hijrah,* the Arab Islamic state, especially with the establishment of the dynasty of the Ummayides, under the Khalifs pursued the policy of imperialism and expansion towards Persia, Makran, Sindh and Hind. The underlying idea of the Khalifs was to annex the territories so far as possible or else to establish its suzerainty and realise revenues from them. As Islam was a proselytizing religion, the *Khalifs* were equally interested in its spread and extracted *Jiziyah* from such people who did not opt for conversion to Islam. It was in 712 A.D. that Muhammad Kasim approached Sind from the Arabian sea and occupied the territories of Sind after having defeated Raja Dahir of Daybal and other local chiefs.

After the conquest of Sind, the imprisoned soldiers were executed but the artisans, traders, cultivators and common folk were spared after the war. While encouraging the local people to bacome Muslims, *Jiziyah* was imposed upon the Hindus who declined the conversion to Islam and this gave them the status of *Zimmis* in the Isalmic state. The mechanism of the Islamic polity gave rights of citizenship to the *zimmis.* The Hindus as *zimmis* were given freedom of worship. The maintenance allowance of the Brahmans were confirmed and they were permitted to repair their temples. The *Chach Namah* makes it clear that in the rural areas the headmen, village chiefs as *Zimmis* were reinstated by the Arab government with *status quo.*[24] They were shown the reverence as before and the management of the local administration and revenue collection was left in their hands. The instructions of Hajjaj to Muhammad Kasim underline the Arab policy of taxation towards the conquered people of Sind.[25] They emphasize that beyond the *jiziyah* and usual tax, the government had no right whatsoever to interfere with the lives or property of the *Zimmis* and that they may even be permitted to build their temples for worship of course. The converts to Islam were exempted from the payment of *jiziyah* whereas it was imposed upon the *Zimmis* in accordance with the "rules laid down by the Holy Prophet of God". The incidence and classification of *jiziyah* rates are also spelt out. All the same they emphasize that kindness and leniency may be shown in revenue matters so that craftsmen and agriculturists may carry on their professions freely and diligently. As regards incidence of taxation, *ushr* (1/10th) was to be imposed upon the property and the land produce of the converted Muslims whereas the *Zimmis* were to continue to pay usual taxes from the income of their handicrafts or cultivation. However, in view of the later evidence available from *Insha-i-Mahru* (14th century),[26] it is difficult to concede that apart from the imposition of *jiziyah* upon the Hindus (*Zimmis*), the distinction between the latter and the Muslims in respect of incidence of assessment rates in the agricultural lands based on the *shariat* was actually carried out in practice or maintained in the course of the ensuing centuries.

Sind remained a part of the Bagdad *Khilafat* till around 879 A.D. The revenues from the local chiefs and tribes continued to be realised through the Governors. With the decline of the political power of the Khalifs, two principal independent kingdoms of Mansura and Multan came to be established though both of them continued to recognise the spiritual authority of the khalif of Bagdad by reading *khutba* in his name. However, with the decline of the Abbassid Caliphate, the kingdoms of Multan and Mansurah lost link with Baghadad and became independent local states side by side with the other Rajput kingdoms in the North. As a consequence of Mahmud of Ghazni's raids (early 11th century), Punjab was annexed to the Ghaznwid Empire. The Ghazwid Empire was ended by the Seljuqs and the Ghazwid rulers took refuge in the Punjab which henceforth remained their sole possession. From the close of the 12th and the beginning of the 13th centuries, the major portions of Northern India came under the domination of the Turkish rule of the Delhi Sultanate.

For the fiscal, organisation of the State, the early Mamluk rulers of the Delhi Sultanate were obliged to adopt the Turkish ideas of administration, within the limitations imposed by the socio-economic and political structure of pre-Turkish India. It is rather significant to underline the elements of continuity and change in the agrarian relations and structure in North India from the pre-Turkish to the Turkish and the Afghan phases till the incorporation of these territories by the Mughal state. It cannot be conceded that with the establishment of the Ghaznavid rule in the Punjab and the Turkish rule in the other territories of North India, the agrarian set up and administration came to be governed by the Islamic theory of land laws and fiscal administration. As a matter of fact, during the medieval age even in the West Asian countries, the *shariat* principles of agrarian administration, pure and simple were never rigidly enforced.[27] The divergent prevailing proprietary concepts, land tenures and revenue practices in the conquered territories equally affected the Islamic polity. This is particularly true of Sawad in Iraq, Persia and Afghanistan wherein the social class division consequent upon the concept of private property, landed structure and fiscal administration cannot be essentially analysed in terms of the Islamic legal texts.

In India, even after the Turkish conquest the land owing and other agricultural communities, unless recalcitrant, retained their lands, privileges and rights so long as they continued to pay the *khari.* After submission, for payment of the revenues to the State, the restoration of lands to the erstwhile agricultural communities was taken for granted. Of course, Persian terminology, which the Turkish ruling class was used to, came to be applied to various revenue practices and institutions. The rural areas were inhabited by different tribess and clans in different regions and the village communities were governed by the regional and tribal practices undergoing changes from time to time. In the ancient and early medieval ages (pre-Arab and pre-Ghaznavid), the tribal conquests by the Huns, the Gujars and the Rajputs led to the reshuffling in the clannish landed interests imposed on the settled villages, new relationship between the dominant clans with the intermediary landed rights and the other cultivating families in the villages, the colonisation of the new villages settled purely by the families of the dominant clans or with the help of the cultivating families of the other castes, the settlement of villages by the religious assignees and concentration of the professional non-agricultural castes adept in certain crafts in the particular villages and on regional inland trade routes. During the Ghaznavid and the Sultanate periods, where the Hindu chiefs were completely suppressed, they assumed the role of landed intermediaries as dominant clans of the rural society. In the course of centuries, the descendants and branch sects of the erstwhile ruling families were reduced to the position of the petty Zamindars. Many dominant clans accepted Islam and continued to possess *Zamindari* rights. On the Turkish conquest, some of the Rajput families fled from the plains and set up new chieftainships in the sub-Himalayan ranges and other portions of North

India. Even though the term Zamindar or *Zamindari* came into vogue during the Turkish rule, it can be well maintained that the institution of *Zamindari* with its indigenous socio-economic features can be well traced to the pre-Ghaznavid period in North India. However, the institution of *Zamindari* with its manifold aspects found acceptance during the Sultanate period and the Mughal age.

For the Sultanate period, the letters of 'Ain-ud-din' Abulah Mahru, who remained the governor (naib) of the *shiqs* of Lahore and Multan during the reign of Mahammad bin Tughluk and Firuz Tughluk (14th century), emphasise the pragmatic agrarian policy of the State. Mahru justifies the heavier incidence of *kharai* (texation) then permitted by the Shariat and vehemently argues that the existing *kharaj* imposed on the *riaya* since long standing period (*qadimulayam*) could not be waived. The extra *sharai kharai* (taxation) could be covered under *figure* as expounded by Mohammd bin Mohammad al Marazi in *Kafi-al Kafi fil figue.* Mahru argues that the incidence of *mahsul* (realisation) cannot be determined purely from the Shariat angle and that it has to take customary into cognisance the continuting customary practice of the territory. He outlines the guidelines on which revenues could be realized by the principal *rava* (*dumbal, dakhin we Zamindaran*). There is no indication of any divergence in the rate of assessment of the *Kharai* in respect of the lands owned by the non-Muslims (*zimmia*) and the Muslims. Mahru also spells out the rights and privileges of the *muqtas* and *madad-i-maseh* assignees. He argues that the latter should be assigned only half of the revenue paying and half fallow cultivable land (*kahl*) and that *jiziya* could not belong to them or owners of the villages (*malik deh*) which had to be deposited in the State treasury. It may be observed that this policy continued even later on throughout the Mughal age. While underlining the State policy towards the development of irrigation, Mahru takes a stand on the past policy and practice under Caliph Umar to the effect that even though the digging of main canals may be the responsibility of the *baitulmal,* in case the latter is not in a position to bear the expenses for digging and repair of certain types of canals, expenses may be charged from the people (*kaalg*). He spells out the nature of such irrigation canals and emphasisee that even the religious assignees (*ulma wa mashaikh*) availing of such irrigation of the lands of their villages could not be exempted from sharing the expenditure involved therein as this was not the sole responsibility of the *baitul-mal.*

The Delhi Sultanate laid considerable emphasis on the organization of the military-cum-revenue machinery for the collection of the land revenue from the conquered territories in North India. Apart from this, it is very doubtful if the Sultanate rule (excepting Sher Shah's reign) brought about any fundamental changes in the existing pre-Turkish revenue practices and the Hindu principles of agrarian administration either with regard to the incidence of State demand (excepting Alauddin Khalji's reign) or methods of assessment prevailing in different regions of North India. As already explained, a detailed Islamic theory of taxation had been worked out even before the Turkish conquest of North India. But it may be really wondered if all these Islamic fiscal ideas relating to State demand and methods of assessment were really enforced in actual practice even in such regions of North India which were under the direct control of the Sultanate. It has been suggested that the Muslim ideas of the agrarian administration were identical with the local existing Hindu revenue practices and, as such, the latter could be easily continued though the Islamic revenue terminology with Persian and Turkish conotations was adopted. Undeniably, some broad similarity and parallelism could be drawn between the Islamic and the Hindu theories of agrarian administration in respect of the State claim over the revenues, the measurement process and certain modes of assessment of land revenue. The identity of the fiscal ideas was not a matter of simple fortuitous coincidence and could be explained both on historical and geographical factors in the process of agrarian civilization in the South-Asian countries.

Apart from this, there still remained various aspects of land administration in which the Islamic fiscal ideas would not fall in exact line with the Hindu notions of revenue administration. Unlike the Hindu theory, the Hanafite School of the Islamic law did not make any theoretical claim over the ownership of the agrarian lands. Even in the non-Islamic conquered territories, the Muslim theory recognised the ownership of land on the part of the peasants subject to the payment of *Kharai* and *jiziye.* After the Turkish conquest, the ancient practice of two fold aspects of landownership, *viz.,* State owned lands or personally owned by the king and the agrarian lands of the peasants could not work any longer. The main division of lands under the (Turkish) state was on the basis of the utilisation of the revenues, which were either reserved for the State Exchequer (*Khalisa*) or assigned to the administrative and military officials (*iqtas*). There is every probability that the personal lands of the suppressed chiefs remained their personal property and their families and future descendants in the course of the centuries claimed them as exclusively privately owned *Zamindari* villages which stood quite distinct from such villages in their *Zamindari* jurisdiction wherein the land was owned by the primary Zamindars and the *khud kashts riaya* peasant families and the Zamindars claimed only *Zamindari* perquisites (*hqqug*) for the collection of the revenues on behalf of the State. In line with the Hindu practice, the Turkish state also made assignation of the revenues and land grants (*milk, inam, waqf* etc.) to the religious assigness but their resumption under Allauddin Khalji shows that they did not carry the same name of proprietary rights which the Hindu theory and practice had emphasised.

As regards the State demand, both the Muslim and the Hindu theories adopted the differential scale of assessment governed by the nature of the soil, means of irrigation and the labour necessary for cultivation. Whatever be the theoratical concept, the Hindu states had claimed between 1/2 and 1/3rd of the gross in accordance with the above explained principles. The Muslim theory demanded between 1/5th to 1/3 of the gross produce on the *kharaji* lands and between 2/5 to 1/10th on the *ushri* lands. But in actual practice, the Turkish government in Persia had even demanded the differential scale of land revenue at the rate of 1/3rd of the gross produce as the normal demand. Apart from it, both the Hindu and the Muslim states levied various types of cesses on the agriculturists. It also seems that on the eve of the Turkish conquest, the concept of social relationship between the racially and politically dominant classes with the tax paying and protected classes in the Turkish administered South Asian countries was not very much different from the Hindu society in India. During the Sultanate period, it cannot be stated with certainty that in actual practice, distinction in respect of land holding and taxation was made between the Hindu and Muslim agricultural communities.

The earliest statement made by Fakhruddin Mubarak Shah that Qutbuddin ordered the abolition of all taxes except the *shari* ones which in some cases were fixed at 1/20th, most likely refers to the *zakat* on the produce of the lands owned by the Muslims in the Punjab. This equally shows that in the Punjab, which had been under the Ghaznwid rule, the Muslims had been subjected to taxation policy, which was not entirely in accordance with the *Shariat* principles. The reference made in the statement about the fixation of *Kharai* at 1/5th is only a theoretical enunciation of the *Shariat* and does not indicate that it was enforced by the Sultan. Moreover, Qutbuddin's period is too early to assert any taxation policy for other portions of North India which had not been even fully conquered so far. Except for Barani's statement of raising of the State demand to 1/2 of the gross produce by Alauddin Khalji under abnormal circumstance, there is no other unambiguous statement in any of the Persian Chronicles which would throw light on the normal State share during the Sultanate period. It seems that 1/2th of the gross produce was claimed only in respect of cereal crops and not in respect of *jins-i-kamil* (cash expos). It goes without saying that this maximum State share could find justification within the theoretical framework of the *Shariat* though it was the financial exigency rather than theoretical concept, which guided the State policy in this regard.

There is no justification in maintaining that the Sultans of Delhi claimed 1/5th of produce as the normal State share in accordance with the Islamic principles. A 16th century evidence shows that in the territory in Multan, the normal State share was 1/4th of the produce. As it was based on long standing practice, status-quo was maintained by Sher Shah even after the incorporation of Multan in his Empire. In fact, there is every justification to suppose that by and large, the pre-Turkish notions of State demand prevalent in the other portions of North India continued to persist during the Sultanate period.

It may be asserted with still greater vehemence that for the assessment of land revenue, the revenue officers and assignees in the Sultanate period simply followed the principles and practices of the (pre-Turkish) period. The Hindu method of assessment viz., the sharing of the produce (*batao*), appraisement (*kankut*), a standard rate of demand per unit area based on actual measurement and according to the crop sown, fixation of demand based on measurement and assessment on the agrarian land based on rough and ready method of measured land in accordance with the cultivable capacity of the plough even (*hala*) continued to prevail in different regions of North India throughout the Sultanate period. Though these assessment methods continued to be known in the local terminology and dialect, the Persian Chronicles designate the *batai* as *hukm-i-hasi,* appraisement as *hukm-i-mushahde* and assessment according to measurement as *hukam-i-mishat.* The lump sum assessment of the villages also traceable during the Hindu period was known as *muqtai.* The assessment on the lands according to the cultivable capacity of the plough even or the seed capacity do not find any mention in the Chronicles but their continued existence throughout the medieval age is confirmed by the *Ain-i-Akbari* and other Mughal sources. In fact, it is only in the sharing method that a true parallel could be found in the *Kharaj-in-mugasimah* of the Islamic theory. The other Islamic methods, *i.e.,* the *Kharali-muazzafah* or *wazifah* and *kharaj-in-mutatah* despite apparent similarities, differed from the above mentioned Hindu methods of assessment in matters of technical detail. In actual practice, the Turkish Kingdom in South Asian countries, especially in Persia and Afghanistan had mostly known two methods of assessment *i.e., muqasmat* and *misahat.* The *muqasamat* involved sharing method assessable only on the cultivated crops. In contrast to it, the *misahat* was based on the measurement of land and would cover only the area actually sown. Here, the assessment rates would vary according to the nature of the soil, means of irrigation and the type of the crops grown. It seems that the Persian procedure of assessment based on measurement (*misahat*), as known to the Turkish rule in India, was in a more developed stage than the indigenous pre-Turkish Indian practice of measurement. In both the cases, *muqasmat* and *misahat,* revenue was reckoned on the actual produce and the cultivated area. In major portions of Persia, the method of *misahat* was applied and in Shiraz, which was a highly irrigated region, separate rates per area unit (*harb* based on *jarib* and *gaz*) were applied to irrigated and unirrigated tracts yielding cash crops like melons and other horticultural fruits.

In the early medieval age, the Hindu theory has also stressed the imposition of revenue on such cultivable fields, which a landlord or his tenants left fallow out of negligence. This links the assessment of the revenues on the land under occupation than on the actual produce. The process of measurement and an assessment based on differential scale of rates of assessment had been known ever since the time of the *Jatakas* and the Mauryan age and had been practiced in various regions throughout ancient and early medieval times under the Hindu rule. After the Turkish conquest throughout the 13th century, status queue was maintained. However, in the early 14th century, in order to augment his financial resources, Alauddin Khalji stressed the adoption of assessment method based on measurement of land (*be hukam-i-misahat wa wafa-ibiswa*). It seems in the context that the waste land or uncultivated land in possession with the *riaya* was not included in the measurement for the purposes of assessment. Of course, a *biswa, i.e.,* 1/20th part of a *bigha* formed the unit of measurement in this regard. Though Barani has also used technical Turkish terms, the *mishat* method for the assessment of the revenue did not preclude from its process the margin to be given for such cultivated areas and crops, which may have either fully or partially failed to mature due to any calamity. However, in actual practice under dishonest revenue officials or any weak Government this rebate for the immaturity of the sown crops could be denied to the peasants. This accounts for the fact that the peasants always preferred the sharing method based on actual yield to the measurement method. Ghyasuddin Tughluk reverted to the sharing method based on actual turnover of the crops and ordered that full margin of the immature crops and natural calamities should be afforded to the peasants. In fact, Alauddin Khalji was the first Turkish ruler who laid an emphasis on the system of measurement though it seems that like his other revenue measures, this was enforced only in the limited territories of the Sultanate. Later on, Muhammad Tughluk too favoured measurement and enforced it in the Doab region. The practice of simple land measurement for the purposes of assessment of revenues continued in some regions with a limited scope. However, its continuance under the Lodhis is confirmed by the fact that Sikander Lodhi adopted a uniform yard of forty-one digits as a standard unit of measurement. Before Sher Shah's reign, the practice of land measurement was not very common either. The *Ain's* statement about the supercession of the lump sum assessment of the villages (*muqtai*) by Sher Shah shows that this may have been quite in vogue before his reign. There is every probability that along with the practice of farming out larger territories either by the Government itself or by the *Intadars,* the process of assessing the revenues of the villages in a lump sum manner (*mugtai*) without involving either the measurement of land or taking into consideration the individual holdings of the cultivators and further farming them out to any other local landed intermediary gained sufficient currency from Firoz Tughluk's reign and persisted throughout the 15th and first few decades of the 16th centuries.

As regards the mode of payment of land revenue, Barni's version of Alauddin's market control system in Delhi and the enforcement of payment in kind rather than in cash in the *Khalisa* territories, Doab and Delhi clearly shows that cash nexus was quite well known in the rural areas in the 13th century. In fact, the numismatic evidence shows a considerable use of coins and the development of cash nexus and rural trade in the 11th-12th centuries, which continued throughout the 13th century. The practice of making the revenue payment—both in kind and cash—depending on the regional economic situation persisted throughout the Sultanate period.

Looked from the viewpoint of the State, Alauddin's attack on the Hindu landed intermediaries who exempted their own agrarian lands from revenues and defied the revenue regulations can be well appreciated. But the heavy incidence of State demand and the additional cesses must have been extremely harsh on the peasantry. Barni's criticism against Alauddin's revenue policy is not without foundation. For the increase of the State revenues, the Tughluks emphasised the increase of the agricultural lands and produce. Ghyasuddin Tughluk gave remissions of land revenue on account of natural calamities. He was also the first Muslim Sultan to provide irrigation facilities through the opening of canals on a small scale. Mohmmad Tughluk initiated the famine relief policy by advancing *sondhar* (loans) for the sinking of the wells and providing the peasantry with elementary means of production. He also opened a new branch in the revenue department (*diwani kohi*) for the reclamation of waste lands and colonisation as state territories under the direct administration of the Central Government. Later on the canal work was extended by Firoz Tughluk in the East Punjab and two canals *Rajiva* and *Alaghkhani* were opened up. This was an important step in the agrarian policy of the Sultanate. It led to the extension of the agricultural lands in the Parganas of Hissar and Firuzabad and led to the growth of superior crops like wheat, sugarcane, lentil and the growth of superior quality of orchards. Firuz charged water tax (*haq-in-shirb*) over and above the land revenue from the canal irrigated areas.

All these measures undertaken by the Tughluks are reminiscent of the pre-Turkish practices. However, the initiation of the advancement of the *taqavi* to the agriculturists is a distinct contribution in the formulation of the agrarian policy during the Sultanate period.

It may be well realised that taking a rounded picture of the entire Sultanate period from the beginning of the 13th century to the first quarter of the 16th century, effective agrarian steps were taken only in the 14th century under the rule of the Khaljis and the Tughluks. Though Alauddin's Imperial policy was successful in suppressing the Hindu chiefs and weaning them around the Delhi Court, his agrarian policy proved completely ephemeral in nature. Some of the agrarian measures undertaken by the Tughluks were of constructive nature but their military inability, administrative limitations and the extension of the farming system led to the disintegration of the Sultanate. Taking the entire Sultanate in the round, the 13th century represents the Sultanate in the making, the 14th century covers some agrarian experimentation but from the closing year of the 14th century down to its submergence in the Mughal Empire, the Sultanate is characterized only by more or less sterile agrarian policy. This is not to belittle the administrative achievements of the Delhi Sultanate but the agrarian set up of North India in the pre-Akbar medieval age has to be viewed in the socio-economic background and the nature of the political hold that the Turkish and Afghan rulers were from time to time able to exert on the local Hindu chiefs and the petty landed intermediaries (all designated as Zamindars) who formed the backbone of the agrarian society during the medieval age. Throughout the Sultanate period, the prevailing Hindu revenue practices and the socio-economic structure based on landed intermediaries played a dominant role. In general, this is true not only of the Delhi Sultanate, but also of the contemporary Sultanate in Kashmir and other independent states like Gujarat, Malwa, Jaunpur and Bengal which sprang up from the late 14th century onwards on the disintegration of territories of the Delhi Sultanate.

In fact, from the viewpoint of agrarian administration, the hitherto accepted version, the division of North India into the territories under the direct control of the Delhi Sultanate and its further administrative divisions into provinces (*wailayats*) and the regions under the domination of the independent or semi-independent tribute paying Hindu rajas does not portray the correct picture of rural India. Quite distinct from the independent Hindu states, the so-called directly administered territories comprised regions of the erstwhile Rajput ruling chiefs and the latter's vassal chiefs—both Rajput and non-Rajput. On conquest, some of families of the Rajput ruling chiefs fled to safer places in the sub-Himalayan ranges, Rajasthan and well protected regions in Awadh. A few families may have been even completely exterminated. But usually on submission, whether forced or voluntary, the families of the ruling chiefs were allowed to maintain their territories on the condition of the payment of the revenues to the Delhi Sultanate. The landed intermediaries in the territories of the suppressed chiefs were also permitted *status-quo* on similar condition. For want of any archival evidence, it is not possible to suggest if the families of the suppressed chiefs were granted any revenue free villages for their maintenance or they were required to pay tribute (*peshkash*) which approximated to the revenues of their territories after having left them and their further landed intermediaries maintenance allowance and perquisites. It seems that the complete suppression of the ruling chiefs worked to a much greater degree in the North Western portion of India, *i.e.,* Sind, Multan and the plains of the Punjab where the Arabs and the Ghaznawids had ruled even before the 13th century Turkish occupation as well as in the territories of Delhi and Doab where the Turkish rule was enforced quite rigorously during the 13th and 14th centuries. Even in such territories where the rule of the former Rajput chiefs became extinct, the landed intermediaries like the petty chiefs (*Khuts*), *Chaudharies* and *Muqaddams* continued with *status-quo.*[56] Besides this, there were also village communities based on tribal and clannish character and in certain portions of North-West of India still governed by the communal concept of agrarian possessions and paying revenues to the State through their tribal chiefs who enjoyed the perquisites in lieu of collection of the revenues. In other territories of the Sultanate, the erstwhile rulers were mostly accepted as suppressed chiefs (Zamindars). Thus the concept of agrarian administration and the collection of the State revenues of the centrally administered provinces (*wilayats*) basically rested on the local agency of the suppressed Hindu rajas, petty chiefs, the *Chaudharies, Muqaddams* (all designated as Zamindars in general lànguage) as well as the tribal chiefs of the village communities. Both the *Khalisa* revenue collectors and the *iqtadars,* even though with their separate territorial jurisdictions, had to collect revenues from the above mentioned intermediaries.

Throughout the 13th century, the Turkish revenue machinery in the directly administered territories remained par excellence an agency of the revenue collection from the suppressed or half recalcitrant Hindu *rajas, Rais* and petty Zamindars. The easiness and rapidity with which the Turks occupied North India due to the internecine warfare and lack of military strategy on the part of the Rajput chiefs by no means put the Turkish government in saddle for the consolidation of the agrarian administration. Of course in the conquered territories under direct administration it gave fatal blow to the authority of the Hindu *rajas* to claim any suzerainity over the vessal chiefs for this role of sovereign power was in fact claimed by the Sultans themselves. Many of the lower caste chiefs (in certain regions named as *Ranas* and *Thakurs*) who had been suppressed to submission by the Rajput rajas now owed direct allegience to the Sultanate as its Zamindars. The Turkish government had its own establishment of military and civil administration in important cities of the provinces and exerted consistent military pressure on the local chiefs and the petty zamindars for the exaction of the revenues. There were regions in which the Hindu chiefs were completely suppressed while in others the recalcitrant Rajput chiefs if unable to fight pitched battle against the Turkish army would flee and come back to mobilise their resources in the rural areas and put up a defiant attitude for the payment of the revenues. In such regions which were away from the main Turkish military centers, the Rajput clans remained not only politically active but also ran their own administration based on established Hindu notions prevalent in these regions. The picture known from the rhetoric statements of the Persian chronicles for the imposition of the Turkish rule and the conquest of Islam in North India is rather too general, it if not superficial. It may be that the Turkish Sultans and the Hindu chiefs were both animated by the religious fervour for aggression or defence, but there were more important issues at stake, which were essentially political and economic in character. The recalcitrance or open rebellion on the part of a Hindu Chief was mostly actuated by his interests to continue with his political hold in his territory as well as to enjoy the surplus produce of the peasants through the local intermediaries. At times, he still wanted to continue his political and economic hold over the suppressed lower caste chiefs who owed him allegience before the Turkish domination. In his recalcitrance against the Turkish state, he was mostly supported by the Brahmanical order which enjoyed the surplus produce through the religious revenue free grants of land and at the same time exercised considerable influence on the local landed intermediaries and the general Hindu population.

Not only the Hindu chiefs, at times even the tribal chiefs and zamindars of the converted Muslim communities evaded payment of land revenue and offered persisting resistance to the Sultanate. There were various lower caste Hindu tribes who had been traditionally recalcitrant against any established authority and even when converted to Islam continued in their habitual attitude of defiance for the payment of revenues. Thus forced by the political situation in 13th century and its own administrative expediency, the Turkish government was constrained to continue *status-quo* in the land revenue practices in the rural territories and to confine its role as the collector of the revenues through the *Muqtas* and his subordinates as well as the *Iqtadars*. It is only in the early 14th century during the reign of Alauddin Khalji that the policy of imperialism was aimed not only at an expansion without but even consolidation of the rule within the centrally administered territories. For the first time in the history of the Sultanate, the government machinery came in intimate contact with rural areas. The recalcitrant Hindu chief were reduced to submission. According to Barani, the Hindu intermediary zamindars viz., the *Khuts* (petty chiefs) *chaudharies* and *muqaddams* were not only completely subordinated for the payment of the State revenues but even shelved of their usual perquisites (*haquq*) for the revenue collection.[57] They were required to pay revenues on their personal lands which hitherto they had evaded and in the assessment of revenue had unduly imposed heavier demand on the poor *Riaya.*[58]

In matter of assessment and payment of revenues, as a storm administration, Alauddin did not permit the slightest distinction to be made between a village *Muqaddam* and a poor ordinary cultivator (metaphorically put by Barni as *bilahir*)[59] and there was uniform law for all in the exaction of the *kharaji.* It seems from Barani that Alauddin's revenue measures were not extended to all the centrally administered empire but were confined to limited territories. It can be well imagined that the recalcitrant Hindu chiefs and the petty zamindars were reduced to revenue paying classes but it is difficult to understand a situation as to how long the iron hand of administration could deny the legitimate perquisites (*haquq*) of the intermediary zamindars who were responsible for the revenue collection.

In the medieval agrarian society, a strong government might keep this agency under proper control for the payment of the revenues on their own lands and those collected from the other *Riaya* but could never run a normal peaceful revenue administration by denying them their usual collection charges and perquisites. Perhaps Barani has given an overdrawn picture about such an administrative measure of Alauddin Khalji. Alauddin Khalji also crushed the tribal converted communities in Mewat (the *Meos*, popularly known as *Mewatis*) but after him, their submission remained of imperfect nature right till the end of the Delhi Sultanate. However, Alauddin's measures proved too harsh and short-lived so as to leave any permanent imprint on the agrarian administration. According to Barani, this rigid policy was surrendered by Ghyasuddin Tughluk who once again exempted the *Khuts* and *Muqaddams* from payment of land revenues on their own cultivated lands and cesses on the grazing lands and allowed them all their legitimate dues provided they collected only legal revenues from the *Riaya.* The Tughluks also made a strong attempt to keep the Hindu chiefs and the petty zamindars under control and to maintain contact with the rural areas. It is difficult to say as to what extent they were successful though it seems that they could operate well only within limited territories of the Sultanate. After the death of Firuz Tughluq, the process of disintegration had already started. Timur's invasion in 1398 AD gave a further edge to the political anarchy and in the early 15th century, the independent kingdoms of Malwa, Gujarat, Jaunpur and Khandesh were established. Not only did the Rajasthan chiefs assume complete independence but the Rajput chiefs within the Delhi kingdom became equally recalcitrant. The active role of the Rajput chiefs during the 15th century is reminiscent of their attitude throughout the Sultanate period except under Alauddin Khalji. During the rule of the Sayyids and the Lodhis, most of the Rajput chiefs of Katehar, Etawa, Chandwar, Bayana and Gwalior remained constantly defiant with regard to the acknowledgement of suzerainty and the payment of the revenues or *peshkash* to the Delhi state. This state of affairs continued right till the Mughal occupation of the North India. Thus it may be argued that right from the beginning of the 13th century till the end of the Delhi kingdom, the Rajput chiefs and the petty zamindars in the rural territories of the Sultanate, even when forced to submission, were never reduced to unarmed importance either by the Turks, excepting the short period of Alauddin Khalji and a part of the Tughluk regime and the Afghans.

The problem of agrarian administration did not rest simply upon the direct relationship between the Delhi kingdom on the one hand and the Rajput chiefs and the petty zamindars on the other. A microsopic study of some of the rural regions of North India would show that by and large, the Delhi Sultanate was ineffective in stopping private clannish warfare amongst the Rajput clans themselves, between the Rajput and lower caste Hindu agricultural tribes and above all Rajputs and Muslim tribal communities who had settled around their territories. The main issues in such conflicts were the disputed villages and *pargana* settlements, acquisition of lands or imposition of the *Zamindari* rights on the suppressed clans. At times, a stronger Rajput clan would push out another weaker Rajput clan from a certain village or might drive out a lower caste Hindu tribe or a Muslim tribe from a certain region. It world also forcibly impose its *Zamindari* or *Chaudharie* rights over other Hindu or Muslim clans in the settled villages. At times, a powerful Muslim clan overpowered a Rajput clan and acquired a few villages or the *Zamindari* of a disputed pargana. The 'leit-motrif' of social action and regional conflict was not essentially religion. Bloody feuds based on clannish rivalry might continue for generations and the disputed villages and the *Zamindari* rights of dominant clan might also change hands after the victory of one clan over another. The revenue collectors of the Sultanate posted in the *walayats* and *shiqs* had no option but to accept the regional reshufflings in the agrarian possessions and the *Zamindari* rights provided the State revenues were paid by the Zamindars to established authority.

In the independent and semi-independent states of North India, the traditional Hindu land revenue practices continued. As such, the sub-

Himalayan states in the Punjab, Kumaon, Tahri and the Eastern Himalayan ranges and Assam, Rajasthan and some portions of Gujarat and Orissa remained completely uninfluenced by the Turkish concept of administration. Even though some of these regions were invaded by the Turkish armies at some intervals for getting the recognition of the suzerainty of the Sultanate, the local socio-economic and political order remained unchanged. The epigraphic and literary evidence available for the Punjab hill states and more especially for Rajasthan throws considerable light on the contemporary Hindu system of land revenue administration during the medieval age before the Mughal occupation of these territories. In both these regions, not only the old Hindu states continued but many a Rajput family fleeing from the plains after the Turkish invitations settled and carved out new states by suppressing the local non-Rajput chiefs and indigenous tribes. They were considerably helped by the geographical features of these regions to withstand the Turkish penetration and were able to continue their independence till Akbar's age. In line with the past Hindu tradition, the Raja asserted a theoretical claim over the land ownership (known as *prathvipal, bhupal, adeshatu*)[62] though, in practice the hereditary and transferable rights of the peasants were fully recognised.

The agricultural lands were possessed and cultivated by the joint families. The Raja claimed complete ownership over the waste lands and jungles and could alienate them as he pleased. The Raja also made both secular and religious revenue-free grants of land. In Rajasthan, a sovereign Raja claimed military service and tribute from the vassal chiefs. The process of the establishment of the new Rajput states, subduing the weaker rulers of the Rajput clans as vassal chiefs through mutual warfare, at times fighting the Muslim states of Malwa, Gujarat and Delhi Sultanate; the suppression of the lower caste Hindu chiefs as well Muslim tribal chiefs and communities on the part of the Rajput Rajas for the extension of their own states continued throughout the medieval age[63] till the merger of these territories in the Mughal Empire under Akbar. Within the State, the revenue-free grants (*sasan*) of the villages were made to the Brahmans, the Bhats, the temples and their attendants (*charnas*).[64] The revenue-free grants of the waste cultivable lands were also made to the above-mentioned beneficiaries. In line with the old Hindu tradition, these grants were regarded as hereditary and perpetual in nature. The donees possessed full right of alienation. The assignment of lands were made in terms of measured units of land against the cultivable capacity of plough-oxen (hals).[65]

On the secular side, small scale grants of villages in *bhum* were made to the Bhumias who paid small quit-rent (*bhum barrar*) and rendered local services to the State.[66] The caste groups played important role in the socio-economic life of the villages. The communities (*gosthi, shersthi, sangh*) based on clannish character and casteism were well organised. The main agricultural classes were gujars, jats and patels. At times even Vaishyas and Brahmans cultivated lands. The village headman (*mandapika*) functioned on behalf of the ruler for the fixation of land revenue assessment and collection of the revenues.[68] The village headman worked under other revenue officials of the State. The Government always gave due consideration to the elders of the village community and the revenue assignments or revenue free grants of waste cultivable land were made in the presence of few village elders.[69] The assessment of the joint family holdings was based on sharing and appraisement *lata* methods.[70] The land was often measured through the *hala* method. The exact incidence of State demand for this period cannot be traced but it is clear from the epigraphic sources that differential scale of the State share was based on a detailed classification of the agricultural lands in accordance with the means of irrigation. Besides the land revenue, the State also claimed various cesses from the agriculturists.

•

References

1. For details, see A. Gosh, *Indian pre-history,* Poona, 1964; R.E.M. Wheeler, *The Indus Valley Civilisation,* Cambridge, 1968; L. Possehl Gregory (ed.), *Harappa Civilisation,* Cambridge, 1968; D.P. Agrawal, 1967-68: *Protohistoric Chronology & Technology and Ecological Factors: A Synthesis,* Purattatva No. I; R.S. Sharma, Purattatva No. 8, New Delhi, 1975-76; B.D. Chattopadhyaya, *Indian Archaeology and the Epic Tradition,* Purattatva No. 8, New Delhi, 1975-76.
2. R. Shamasastry, *Kautilya's Arthasastra,* (translation) 5th edition 1956, pp. 46-193. (henceforth *Arthasastra,* tr. s.).
3. U. N. Ghoshal, *The Agrarian System in Ancient India,* (hecneforth Ghoshal), pp. 75-76; Manu, Chapter VII, pp. 118-139.
4. *Sukranti,* tr. B. K. Sarkar, Allahabad, 1925, pp. 147-48. Sarkar thinks that *Sukranti* belongs to the late medieval period. Also Ghoshal, p. 23.
5. Ghoshal, pp. 9-77; Meyer, *Jaṭaka Tales,* Vol. II, p. 366; *Jatakas,* Vol. IV, p. 169.
6. *Arthasastra,* p. 66; Ghoshal, pp. 17-18.
7. *Ibid.,* pp. 65, 158; *Ibid.,* pp. 6-16, 45-77.
8. *Ibid.,* pp. 194-95; Fleet, *Epigraphica Indica,* (henceforth *E.I.*) 7, 155-160; II 52-53; V/VII, pp. 304 ff., 11.39-46; I.E. XXIX, No. I, B. 11.26-44 (pala grants in Bihar and Bengal respectively); IV, No. 11.34.35; Ghoshal, pp. 51-52.
9. However against this view, see R.S. Sharma, 'Feudal Elements in the Pala and Prathihara Polity, 750-1000', *Asian History Congress,* New Delhi, 1961.
10. For details, see M. de. Laveleye, *Primitive Property,* (English translation, R.R.L. Marriot), p. 3; C.L. Tupper, *Punjab Customary Law,* II, Statement of Customary Law in different Districts (extracted Chiefly from the Settlement Reports), Introduction, pp. 1-98.
11. Mcrindle, Megesthenes and Arrian, pp. 41-42.
12. *Arthasastra,* (Tr. s.), p. 46.
13. *Ibid.,* pp. 181-95.
14. Manu, Chapter VII, pp. 143-47, Ghoshal, p. 86.
15. Ghoshal, H.R.S., pp. 191-92.
16. P.V. Kane, *Katyayanasmrti,* tr. verses 16 and 17; Ghoshal, pp. 97-98.
17. Ghoshal, pp. 85, 118, f.n. 15-20.
18. Al-Birunis, Tr. Sachau, Vol. II, p. 149.
19. Narasinha Purana, Quoted by M.A. Buch, 'Economic Life in Ancient India', 11, 24, f.n.
20. Also see details, R.S. Sharma, *op. cit.,* f.n. 9.
21. E.1.7. 1556-60 (Land grant of Harsa issued in 25th R.Y.).

22. Of the various available land grant Plates, a couple of them may be quoted e.g. E.I.X., No. I, A. 11. 1-20 (A village grant made in 893 A.D. by Balavarman, a Calukya vassal in Kathiwad); I A xii; p. 195, Plate II, 11. 1-24 (a village grant) dtd. 914 A.D. made by Dharanivarha, a vassal in Eastern Kathiawad).
23. E.I., III, no. 36, 1.4. (This indicates that the district of Vamsapotaka in Gurjjaratrabhumi was conferred on a Gujara vassal of the pratiharas).
24. *Chach Namah,* tr. Mirza Kalich Beg, Karachi, 1900, pp. 164-169.
25. *Ibid.*, pp. 173-74.
26. *Insha-i-Mahru* (Persian text), ed. Sh. Abdur Rashid, Lahore, 1965, vide f.n. 28.
27. Lambton, A.K.S. *Landlord and Peasant in Persia.* (London), 1969 (henceforth Lambton), pp. 15-128.
28. *Insha-i-Mahru, op. cit.*, f.n. 26, Letters Nos. 28, 30-31, 114, pp. 61-63 68-73-80, 204-205 respectively.
29. Moreland, W.H., *The Agrarian System of Moslem India,* Cambridge, 1929, pp. 17-20; Quresi, I.H., *Administration of the Sultanate of Delhi,* Lahore, 1942, pp. 100-103, 106-110.
30. Lambton, pp. 28-30.
31. B.R. Grover, 'Nature of *Dehat-i-Taluqua* (*Zamindari* villages) and the Evolution of the *Taaluqdari* System during the Mughal Age, *Indian Economic and Social History Review',* Vol. II, no. 2, April 1965; Vol. II, no. 3, July 1965, pp. 166-177, 259-288 respectively; Also, B.R. Grover, 'Elements of Continuity and change in Land Ownership and Rights from the Mughal Age to the Early British Administration in India', *Proceedings of the Indian History Congress,* Presidential Address, Medieval India Sectioon on 37th session, Calicut, 1976.
32. *Zia-nd-din* Barani, *Tarikh-i-Firoz Shah,* (Ed.) Sir Sayyid Ahmad Khan, Bib. Indica, Calcutta, 1862 (henceforth Barani), pp. 283-96. The many of the *milk, inam* and *waqaf* grants had been resumed by the State in the pre-Firuz Tughluk period is confirmed by the fact that Firuz after verification restored many religious endowments to the original assignees, *Sirat-i- Firoz Shahi,* fols. 71 b-72 a.
33. See for details, Afhnides, N.P., *Mohammedan Theories of Finance,* New York and London, 1916.
34. Lambton, pp. 17-30.
35. *Tarikh-i-Fakhr-ud-din Mubarak Shahi* (tr. & edited by E.D. Ross), pp. 33-34.
36. Barani, pp. 283-87.
37. *Tarikh-i-Sher Shahi,* (Habib Ganj Collection, Ms. Maulana Azad Library, A.M.U., Aligarh, fol 99-100a); *Tarikh-i-Makhzan-i-Afghana,* Ms. British Museum, Add. 21, 911, fols. 132 a-b.

38. Barani, pp. 290-296.
39. *Ain-i-Akbari,* tr. Jarrett, II, p. 66.
40. Lambton, pp. 17-30; also f.n. 41.
41. Ms. Orient, fol. 3177, Berlin, fols. 44 a-b. This is a transcribed copy of an original Ms. Written in A.H. 380/963 A.D during the Samanid period. It gives details of the geography, revenue taxation, the methods of assessment and the land rights of the peasants.
42. Barani, p. 287.
43. *Ibid,* pp. 429-30.
44. *Ibid.,* pp. 482-83, 497-99.
45. *Ain-i-Akbari, op. cit.,* p. 39.
46. *Ibid.*
47. Barani, pp. 305-306.
48. *Ibid.,* pp. 288-89.
49. *Ibid.,* pp. 429-30.
50. *Ibid.,* p. 442.
51. *Ibid.,* pp. 482-83.
52. *Ibid.,* pp. 497-99.
53. *Ibid.,* pp. 567-71; Shams-i-Siraj Afif, *Tarikh-i-Firoz Shahi* (henceforth Afif), p. 92; *Sirat-i-Firoz Shahi,* fols. 37 a-b, 105b-106a.
54. *Ibid.*
55. Afif, pp. 129-31.
56. Barani, pp. 287-91.
57. *Ibid.*
58. *Ibid.*
59. *Ibid.*
60. *Ibid.,* pp. 429-30.
61. Hutchison and Vogel, *Punjab Hill States,* 2 vols., Introduction and Historical Survey, Vol. I, pp. 1-98; 269-77, 283. Cunningham, *Antiquities of Chamba State,* R.A.S.I., A.G.I. cover numerous sources from V.S. 1190 to V.S. 1593. For Rajasthan, *Vir Vinod,* Udaipur, Vol. II.
62. *Ibid.*
63. *Vir Vinod,* II. For expansion of the Bhatti's of Jaisalmer towards Multan and Sind, Amarkot Inscription (Sanskrit) dated 3rd Vaishakha (bright half) V.S. 1561/16th May, 1504 AD; Jain Inscriptions, III, No. 2487.
64. E.I, (Vol. XXVI, pp. 90-106 Bijoliyan Inscription dated 3rd of Phalgun, dark Malf, V.S. 1226/5th February, 1170 AD; Ajmer Museum Copper plate, dated 15th Asadha, dark half, V.S. 1494/31st August, 143 AD.
65. O.D.R., Udaipur, Thakrada plate (Sanskrit) dated V.S. 1212; plate No. 1725 (Sanskrit) dated V.S. 1589.

66. Also G.D. Sharma, *Rajput Polity,* New Delhi, 1977, pp. 1-24.
67. Jain Inscriptions, Vol. I, No. 807, p. 198, Osia Inscription dated 5th Phalgune, bright half, V.S. 1245/4th February, 1188 AD.
68. *Ibid.,* I No. 389, p. 207, Nadol Copper plated, dated V.S. 1218.
69. O.D.R., Udaipur, plate No, 285, dated 11th Magh (Bright half) V.S. 1494 describes the grants of ten *halas* of land by Maharana Kumba in Village Kheroda in the presence of Purohit Bhikla and Shah Shahana, the two elders of the village.
70. *Ibid.,* No. 866 Bokrahedi grant, dated 15th Sarvana (dark half) V.S. 1593; No. 193 (3) dated V.S. 1785.

Chapter 9

Integrated Agrarian Society During the Mughal Age—A Note

I. During the medieval age, an overwhelming majority of the population lived in the villages and India was predominantly an agrarian society. Indeed, this has continued to be a marked feature of the Indian society right to the present day. Any comprehensive review on the socio-economic and cultural life of the two religious communities viz. the Hindus and the Muslims is bound to take into perview the role and the mutual relationship of the two communities in the agrarian setup.

After the establishment of the Turkish rule in North India, the Muslim ruling classes led a purely urban life. The Turks and the Muslims who came to India were urban minded and took little interest in agriculture as a vocation. The territories which continued to be governed by either independent or autonomous Hindu chiefs on the payment of fixed *peshkash* to the Muslim ruler remained more or less unaffected by the infiltration of the Muslim population in the agrarian society.

II. In the territories under the direct administration of the Muslim rule, two factors gradually affected the agrarian society, viz. the religious land grants and the conversion of the local Hindu population to Islam.

(a) Religious land grants viz. *milk, inam, waqf,* etc. were known as *'madad-i-maash'*. This helped some of the ascetics and families with missionary purpose to settle in the rural areas. *Waqfs* were also given to institutions and the revenues came from the assigned villages. This established contact between the assignees and the Hindu agrarian community.

(b) The Conversion Factor: Whatever the reason, the local Hindu agrarian population was converted to Islam in many a region. The main were (i) political coercion; (ii) patronage; (iii) missionary; and (iv) economic pressure, *i.e.,* the levy of *jizya.* It cannot be stated if the conversions were only on individual basis or even on tribal basis. For want of contemporary documents, we are obliged to rely mainly on sociological studies that proves even the tribal conversions.

III. (a) There has been a controversy about whether or not *jizya* was land revenue or in the nature of a religious tax, levied on Hindus only.

(b) As regards distinction between the two agricultural communities for the purposes of assessment—**Whether Shariat principles were applied or not?** It seems so far as possible, distinction in assessment was made between Hindus and Muslims as is evident from *Tarikh-i-Firoz Shahi.* But for want of contemporary records, no definite opinion can be expressed.

B. Mughal Society

I. Many of the converts continued with their old Hindu ways of life—in manners, customs, food and other aspects of life. An example of Rajauri can be cited from Jahangir's Memoirs. It is known from *Rajatarangini* that there were Hindu Rajas of Rajauri up to a much later date than 1193. In his Memoirs, Jahangir states that the family became Muhammedan in the time of Firoz Shah Tughlak (1356-88). In Jahangir's rule, Tagud-din Khan was the Zamindar of Rajauri. (Rajauri: Kashmir was attached to the Jammu faujdari during the Mughal period). Jahangir, who visited Rajauri many times while going to or returning from Kashmir, notes in his Memoirs:

> "On Friday, the 8th (AD 1620) Rajauri was the camping ground. The people of this country were in old times Hindus and the land holders were called Rajas. They still have the marks of the times of ignorance. One of these is that just as some Hindu women burn themselves along with their husbands, so these women are put into the grave, along with their dead husbands. I heard that recently they put alive into the grave a girl of ten or twelve along with her (dead) husband who was of the same age. Also, when a daughter is born to a man without means, they put her to death by strangulation. They ally themselves with Hindus, and both give and take girls. Taking them is good but giving them, God forbid, I gave an order that hereafter they should not do such things, and whoever was guilty of them should be capital punished."

Another example can be found in Elliott in Awadh in 19th century.

II. **Impact of *'Madad-i-maash'* Policy from Akbar Onwards:** Large scale assignments were made to Muslim families. Various categories of families deserving subsistence were settled in rural areas. Thus scattered holdings in different villages brought them in touch with Hindu agrarian population. As villages were Hindus, *Muqaddams* and Zamindars were also Hindus but the assignees were Muslims (of course, some were Hindus also). Gradually, there was consolidation villages in a *Pargana,* centers of Muslim culture were established. This was ultimately bound to develop into either acrimony or appreciation of both of cultures and the religions of the two communities. There was evidence of harmony also.

III. **Zamindari in Villages:** According to the picture one gets from the *Ain,* on a tribal or caste basis, depending on regional character, there were both Hindu and Muslim Zamindars.

(b) A question is raised whether the *zamindari* and all the *Ryots* and the tenants etc. belonged to the same clan or religion or the *Ryots* could belong to different clan and religion. Evidence is available for both types. There were some purely tribal areas like Meos in Sindh. On the contrary, in Rajasthan, in some places like Ajmer sarkar, the Zamindar and his *Ryots* could belong to different caste and even different religions.

(c) **Impact of Fragmentation of Zamindari:** The fragmentation of zamindari led to the sale of zamindari, sale of *muqaddami* and transfer in the second half of the 17th century on inter-caste and inter-religious basis. The previous balance was disturbed and the reshuffling started composite villages.

(d) For all boundary disputes in a village, the evidence of both the Hindus and the Muslims was taken regardless of the fact of the religion of the parties to dispute.

(e) The Ryots and the *'madad-i-maash'* assignees made a common stand against the zamindars or all the three parties stood up against the Jagirdars due to common economic interest. In revolt, there were territorial, tribal and economic factors.

IV. **Akbar's Approach towards Finance:** In this regard, there was no discrimination between communities. No invidious distinction was made in matters of assessment of land revenue. Even if such distinction did exist in the past, it was not there during the Mughal age. Aurangzeb did re-impose *jizya* but the revenue documents do not show any distinction in matters of assessment and land revenue practices. Aurangzeb's Islamic policy and Farman to Mohammed Hashim was theorctical so far as land revenue practices were concerned. There was distinction in *'madad-i-maash'* grants, horticulture, octroi etc. Imposition of *jizya* was a disastrous policy in the 18th century.

"Madad-i-maash" documents lying with the Punjab University, Chandigarsh, include Farmans from Akbar onwards; Farman of Akbar given to Ananth Nath, a *jagir* of *Pargana* Paithan (Pathankot); Farman of Jāhangir and Shahjahan to the same Jogi family—assignment of land (**Persian Word**) in terms of bighas; Aurangzeb's letter asking the

descendant of the same family for herbs and awarding cash grant as well as robes.

Importance of the Farmans—Some Indications

(i) *'Madad-i-maash'* grant was given to a Hindu medicant family.

(ii) Even though no *Farman* of Aurangzeb is on record, the family continued in possession of the grant and the *Farmans* of the later Mughals and even Ranjit Singh are on record. This shows the continuity of the grant within the same family even though no formal *Farman* of Aurangzeb was issued. The grant must have been continued by the local officials. The fact that Aurangzeb wrote a letter shows that the grant could not have been resumed by the State.

(iii) The assignment of land in terms of measured land shows that the *Pargana* Paithan must have been brought under measurement or may be even rendered *amli.*

(iv) The *Pargana* of Paithan was under the jurisdiction of a Chief Zamindar. This shows that the Mughal State could make grants in the territories of the Chief Zamindars.

Chapter 10

Elements of Continuity and Change in Land Ownership and Rights from the Mughal Age to the Early British Administration in India*

Mr. President, Fellow Delegates, Ladies, and Gentlemen,

I am deeply indebted to the members of the Indian History Congress and its Executive Committee for the honour they have done for having invited me to preside over the Medieval Section of the Calicut Session of the Indian History Congress. More than anybody else I am fully conscious of my own limitations and shortcomings in comparison to the distinguished historians who have held this chair in the past. It seems that my long association with the Congress as an ordinary member and then as an office bearer has influenced my colleagues for offering me this chair. I regard it a privilege and am extremely obliged to my colleagues for the affection shown to me.

The choice of the subject on an aspect of the agrarian problem covering nearly two and a half centuries looks rather over ambitious. For a student of economic history of Medieval India, it may look rather presumptuous to encroach upon the field of historians of the Modern Indian History. All the same the choice has been deliberate, partly because we are still not clear as to when the medieval features of the Indian agrarian society come to a close and also due to the fact that so far the historians specialised in Medieval or Modern India have stuck to their fields based upon their respective source material. The historians of Modern India have relied on the English source material and the English understanding of inherited

---

* Presidential Address, Indian History Congress, Medieval India Section 37th Sesion, Calicut, 29-31 December 1976.

agrarian features from the Mughal rule and other regional states. As such, the limitations of the English writings have been faithfully reflected in the works covering the 18th and the first half of the 19th centuries Indian agrarian society. I have the least intention to cast any reflection on the scholarly works of the specialists on the agrarian history of Modern India. My only purpose is to initiate dialogue with the scholars on modern economic history and to bridge the gulf between the writers on Medieval and Modern Indian history by highlighting the elements of continuity and change in the concept of land ownership and rights from the Mughal era to the early phase of the British administration in India.

The importance of the subject cannot be underestimated in a state of society where during the medieval ages the overwhelming majority of the people subsisted on agriculture and the agricultural surplus formed the bulk of the income of the State. The vastness of the Indian sub-continent with its divergent geographical features, social organisations and village communities based on tribal and cast ties as well as customary practices makes the subject all the more intricate. It is a technical and difficult subject and any reliance on fragmentary source material would be unsystematic and easily liable to misinterpretation. For the last two decades, the access to vast archival source material has enabled us not only to work on regional basis but also to coordinate and organise the common features with clearer perception.

The agrarian problems were highlighted by the early British administrators as they were interested in probing into the land rights during the Mughal Age. From the late 18th century to the middle of the 19th century, different patterns of land settlements were introduced in India. The English administrators and revenue officers surmised on the nature of the land ownership, and rights in regard to the various strata of the agricultural classes during the pre-British period. Notwithstanding the changes in land tenures brought about by them for many a region, they thought that they were mostly continuing the traditional pattern inherited from the pre-British era. For the Mughal age they tried to bank on the Muslim jurisprudence, the Mughal *Farmans* and *Sanads,* the *Ain-i-Akbari* and some other chronicles. During the last two decades, revolutionary change has occurred in the methodology of historical research in the Medieval Indian history. The emphasis on the documentary study relating to the agrarian structure of the Medieval Indian society in coordination with the chronicles and various other categories of contemporary sources has obliged us to reconsider the views expressed hitherto merely on the basis of inadequate interpretation of the technical and terse passages of the chronicles. In early 1961, the present speaker took the initiative of reopening the question on the subject[1] and thereafter scholarly works both on all India and regional level have been produced by Irfan Habib, S. Nurul Hasan, Satish Chandra, Noman Siddiqi and a few other young scholars.[2] However, the problem requires further probing on the basis of various categories of the documents available for different regions of India.

In order to appreciate the rights of the land owners and other classes of the agriculturists during the Mughal age, it is imperative to understand the contemporary concept of ownership and varying rights, privileges and interests in land. In fact, concept of property is as heterogeneous as the societies within which it is found and in the social process of a community it reflects the institutionalized values of the people at a given time. Both in the west and India, the values and property institution have been undergoing changes from one age to another and, as such, different meanings may be attached to the word property in different situations. The private claim to property in land may be recognised subject to the community and the State control for the customs and conventions of the social structure of every people limit the opportunities which property affords and disburse ownership amongst the individual families, and community and the State. During the medieval ages in a settled state in India, the private ownership is qualified by the rights of the community and paramount ownership of the State. Even when due to economic factors in a developed region, the community control over private family ownership becomes negligible or non-existent, the State control implicit in the paramount ownership remains intact. Thus it involves a graduated ownership of land with a graduated group of persons and the State. The pyramiding of ownership characterises the nature of properietorship in land.

It is doubtful if the Islamic theory of land laws in the *dar-ul-harb* was enforced in India at all. Though the Delhi Sultanate laid considerable emphasis on the organisation of the military-cum-revenue machinery for the collection of the revenues from the conquered territories in India, it may really be wondered if at all the theoretical Islamic fiscal ideas relating to the State demand, methods of assessment and the nature of land tenures were really enforced in actual practice even in such regions of North India which were under the direct control of the Sultanate. It could not have been enforced in India, a primarily agricultural country which possessed its own agrarian pattern based on its practices evolved in accordance with the regional geographical features and the clannish customs of the peoples settled in different parts of the country. During the medieval age even in the West Asian countries, the *shariat* principles of agrarian administration pure and simple, were never rigidly enforced. In the West Asian countries, after the Arab conquest, even though Islamic theory affected the conception and development of landed property and land tenure in its own turn, it was modified by the complexity of circumstances and the divergent prevailing customs in the conquered territories. With the relaxation of the rigidity of the Islamic law, the divergence between the theory and practice is clearly marked specially in Persia and Sawad in Iraq. In practice, the landed structure and fiscal administration under the Seljuk Turks, the Mongols and the Safavids in Iran cannot be interpreted in terms of the ideal Islamic law enshrined in the legal texts.[3] Under the Delhi Sultnate and the regional Sultanates under the Muslim rulers, of course, the religious revenue-free grants like *milk, inam* and *waqf* to individuals or institutions were made for the benefit of some charitable object. Even though lands immobilised for *milk* and *waqf* were reckoned as heritable proprietary estates in nature, in practice the amount of revenues or the extent of land thus granted was always subject to alteration or even confiscation by the State. The Indian land owning and other agricultural communities retained their lands, privileges and rights so long as they paid the *kharaj.* The Delhi Sultanate was essentially concerned with the realisation of the revenues for the maintenance of the State and without any involvement into the fineness of the arguments over the nature of land rights of the conquering Muslim communities and the conquered non-Muslim agricultural population, it accepted the *status quo.*

In fact, the concept of agrarian administration as well as the collection of the State revenues of the centrally administered territories *(wilayats)* basically rested on the local agency of the supressed Hindu Rajas, petty chiefs, *Chaudharies, Muqaddams* (designated as Zamindars in general language) as well as the dominant clans and castes of the village communities. After submission for payment of the revenues to the State, the restoration of lands to the erstwhile agricultural communities was taken for granted. Once the State accepted *peshkash* of the revenues from the Zamindars and other agricultural communities, it gave the latter a *de-jure* recognition. The reference to such settlements between the Sultanate and the chief Zamindars can be well understood from the statement of the chronicles, but unlike the Mughal age there is no documentary evidence to show that the landed intermediaries and the primary Zamindars were granted *sanads* for the continuation of their land rights. In the independent and semi-independent states of North and South India, the regional agrarian structure based on varying practices continued.

By the 16th century, the agrarian structure in different regions was based on socio-economic pattern and polity inherent in the Indian situation. The Mughal state having adopted the existing landed structure replenished further with new features for the realisation of the revenues. In order to increase its revenues, it urged maximum coverage of the cultivable land under tillage. As such, it claimed not only revenues from its territories but equally asserted its sovereign power over the control of land. However, it did not enunciate any theoretical claim to the State ownership of the land, nor did it make *Shariat* as the basis of the property concept, land holding and revenue administration. The Indian Muslim jurists remained divided over the issue of the landed property in India. Some scholars upheld the view that the land in India being *Kharaji* was the property *(malkiyat)* of the existing possessors of lands *(maliks)* even though major portion of the land was possessed by the non-Muslims.

Another school of thought considered that the land being property of the *baitul mal* (Muslim State treasury), the State had further right to alienate it to the new grantees with proprietary rights. Keeping in view the vested interests of the *madad-i-maash* assignees for getting full proprietary rights in land, Jalaluddin Thanesari in *Risala-dar-bai Arazi* reviewed the question of the land ownership in India from the theoretical *Shariat* angle.[4] Having analysed the *Hanafite,* and the *Shafite* schools and numerous *fatawas* of the Indian Muslim jurists, past as well as contemporary, Jalaluddin Thanesari argued that there was no evidence to show that at the initial stage of the conquest of India by Islam, the land was either distributed amongst the victors or restored to its original owners. Even when it may be that the land was restored to the original owners, the land changed hands due to political changes and natural calamities. New dominant caste groups and agricultural communities had either expelled the erstwhile land owners or suppressed them to the status of mere cultivators. He substantiated his contention with the case study of the dominant land owning clans in the region of Thanesar (pargana Thanesar, Sarkar Sirhind, Subah Delhi) to which he belonged. As the present possessors and proprietories were not the direct descendents of the original land owners and were in possession without the sanction of the ruler, their possession was unlawful and their lands may be regarded as ownerless. After having divided the lands in India into several categories, he maintained that major portion belonged either to the waste or ownerless category resumable by *baitul-mal* (State treasury) as its property. As such, the State was entitled to alienate proprictary rights to new grantees as land owners. Even if the *Shafite* law were to be followed, the present land owners would be suppressed to mere cultivators of the Muslim community. Such a revivalist contention as that of Jalaluddin Thanesari never struck any chord with the Mughal State. In its chapter on *Rowai Rozi* (currency of Means of Subsistence) of the *Ain-i-Akbari,* Abul Fazl upholds the rights of possessors of property *(khudawandan-i-mal)* who held their lands in the cultivated areas by ancestral descent. In the matter of right to property, he condemns the illicit seizure of property of persons of a different faith. He calls it "a suggestion of the evil one, a phantasy of the dreams of the avaricious and unfit for the ears of the good".[5] For the introduction of the Islamic principle into the

Mughal agrarian administration, Aurangzeb's *Farman* to Muhammed Hashim, (the *Diwan* of *Subah* Gujarat) seems apparently of great significance.[6] As distinct from the land revenue practices since Akbar's age, the *Farman* demands an indoctrination of the *Shariat* principles evolved in other Islamic countries into the Indian agrarian administration. In essence, the *Farman* pronounces the same agrarian principles which were compiled and recorded by Sheikh Nizaum and other learned scholars in *Futawa-i Alamgiri.* The *Farman* is couched in revenue terminology deduced from Muslim commentaries *(fatawas)* of the Islamic countries and cannot be in toto easily aligned with the Mughal revenue system and Indian agrarian life. It may be accepted that despite differences in terminology, some of the Mughal Indian revenue practices were already quite in line with the practices in Islamic countries though in others they were distinctly dissimilar in context. The feasibility of enforcement for such aspects hitherto unknown to Indian agrarian life is rather remote and these clauses of the *Farman* are rather superfluous. In consonance with the Mughal policy, the *Farman* aims at the extension of the cultivable land, reclamation of the fallow land, advance of *taqavi* loans to the needy cultivators and also refers to the remission of land revenue on account of natural calamity, enforcement of the measurement unit of Shahjahani bigha and the legal existence of the revenue-farmers *(Mustajirs)*. The *Farman* also recognises the proprietary rights of some classes of *riaya* (peasants) in land. But above all in consonance with the *Shariat* principle, it makes distinction between the Muslim and non-Muslim *riaya.* The land rights and obligations for payment of the revenue on the part of the cultivator in his holding are determined by his religion and the particular mode of assessment to which his holding is subjected. The distinction between Muslim holding named *Ushri* land subject to the payment of *ushr* (one-tenth) and a non-Muslim holding named *kharaji* land subject to the payment of *kharaj* (land revenue) and even distinction between a Muslim and a non-Muslim revenue-farmer *(ijara ghir)* subject to *ushri* and *kharaji* assessment is rather against the Mughal practice. More important than the theoretical enunciation of such *Shariat* principles is the fact of their implementation in actual practices. The Mughal revenue documents of Aurangzeb's reign do not show any such distinction between the Hindu and the Muslim *raiyat* in the matter of land revenue assessment and collection. Nor do they point towards any separate existence of the *Ushri* land as distinct from the *kharaji* land. They do not take note of any of the methods of assessments expressed in Islamic terminology as the assessment continued to be made according to varying regional methods. The Mughal records clearly show assessment and collection of the land revenue in accordance with the Mughal institutions rather than based on Islamic principles. It is very doubtful if the *Farman* had any effect whatsoever on the working of the agrarian administration under Aurangzeb. Such of the clauses which fitted in the pattern of the Mughal administration were simply of the confirmatory nature whereas those underlining *Shariat* principles hitherto unknown to the Indian agrarian life remained merely with theoretical significance. This is equally confirmed by *waqai-i-Rantambhor* which narrates a significant clash between the *Qazi, Karori* of the pargana Merot *(Subah* Ajmer) over the implementation of the *Shariat* principles in the fiscal policy of the State.[7] Qazi Mohammed Akram of Pargana Merot *(Subah* Ajmer) complained to the Provincial authorities that Sadulla, the *Faujdar, Amin* and *Karori* was not realising the revenues according to the law of the *Shariat.* The *Karori* defended himself on the plea that in accordance with the higher orders, he had continued the traditional pattern of revenue administration and had realised the *sair* (cesses) which benefitted the State finances. He retorted that the Qazi was immature and inexperienced in State affairs and unduly interfered in the financial administration. He upheld that he was independent of the *Qazi* in the administrative matters and that the collection of the revenues purely on *Shariat* principles would render the administration chaotic and would cause ruination of the State revenues. The enquiry officer (agent of *waqai nawis*) confirmed that the *Qazi* could be justified in reporting against the realisation of illegal cesses, if any, and that the *Qazi* could not interfere in the financial administration and the *Faujdari* affairs of the pargana.

The European travellers who visited India during the 16th and 17th centuries upheld that all the land was owned by the State. They evaluated the position of the *tankhwah jagirdars* of the Mughal nobility in comparison to the landed nobility in Europe. Their main attack was on the concept of property in India and the West Asian countries and they considered that the absence of right to private property in India led to agrarian sterility and the sad plight of the peasantry. This was the main thesis even with Bernier though he did concede that in respect of "some houses and gardens", the Mughal King sometimes permitted "his subjects to buy, sell and otherwise dispose of among themselves".[7a] The *tankhwah jagirdars* under the Mughal system were entitled only to the revenues of the assigned territories and were not the owners of the land. The European travellers did not appreciate the institutional implication of this system against the agrarian and political set-up of the country. But the most surprising aspect of the problem is that the ownership rights, howsoever qualified on the part of the Zamindars and certain categories of the other *riaya,* did not attract the notice of the European travellers. Howsoever biased they may be in the evaluation of the Indian agrarian society as against the European society, it seems that in their erroneous judgement they were equally misled by the assertion of the paramount rights of the State in the effective control of the agrarian land. The ownership title of an individual family to an urban land (main cities as well as *qasba* towns) is sufficiently confirmed by the sale deeds available for the 17th and 18th centuries.

The Indian scholarship has well analysed the position and role of the Zamindars as the landed intermediaries for the collection of the revenues and the nature of the perquisites involved therein. Under the Mughals, the institution *zamindari* covers the wide range of landed interests from the chiefs of the princely territories *(zamindaran-i-umda)* to the petty intermediaries.

Broadly speaking there is two-fold division of *lands, i.e.,* unappropriated state owned and appropriated lands vested with the *riaya* for the purposes of habitation and cultivation. The State claimed revenues from all the territories under its control and was the proprietor of all the jungle, unreclaimed and unappropriated waste lands termed as *khas sarkar zamin.*[8] The appropriated land for the purposes of agriculture and habitation was owned by certain categories of the *riaya.* It may as well be appreciated that the terms *riaya* and *raiyat* were synonymous and covered all the cultivating families paying revenues to the State. Thus the *riaya* denoted village *zamindari* families of varying categories with self-cultivated *(khudkashta)* and other *raiyati* lands, the *khudkashta* cultivator without enjoying any *zamindari* or *muqaddami* status, the *muzarian* with occupancy or periodical land tenures and the *paian* or *paikashtkars.* The revenue-free grantees *(aimma* etc.) even when cultivating families were not termed *riaya* or *raiyat.* For the purposes of the fixation of assessment and possession of holdings, all cultivating families of the *riaya* excepting the *paikashtkars* were reckoned as *asamian* (cultivators liable for assessment and payment of revenue). The primary zamindars of the villages like the *Khuts, Chaudharis, Muqaddams* and at times even the semi-officials *Qanungoes* belonged to tue *zamindari* families. Some of the 17th century documents relating to *Subah* Awadh reveal the existence of khuts—a significant landed class exercising *biswadari* rights. Though with the present evidence in hand it is difficult to define the precise nature of the *khuti* land rights, it seems that they were similar to that of a *Chaudhari* with primary *zamindari* rights. The *Muqaddams* even though in lineage belonged to the *zamindari* families, always constituted the principal *riaya* of the villages.

There were two categories of villages, *i.e., zamindari* villages *(dehat-e-Taaluqa)* and *raiyati* villages *(dehat-e-raiyati).* Though the revenues of both the *taaluqa (zamindari)* and *raiyati* villages were assessed by the State, the ultimate responsibility for the collection rested with two different categories of officials. In the *taaluqa* villages the collection was made by Zamindars who were usually the *Muqaddams* and more especially *Chaudharies* in a *pargana.* The performance of *Zamindari* service *(khidmat-i-zamindari)* was regarded as an official service to the State. In lieu of his services, the Zamindar was entitled to *nankar, i.e.*, revenue-free grant of land and customary charges named *rasum-i-zamindari* and *haquq-i-zamindari.* The assignment of the *nankar* was made within the jurisdiction of a *zamindari.* In various parts of India, the *nankar* instead of being given as land grant assumed the shape of payment in kind (grain) or cash known as the *rasum-i-zamindari.* A *Muqaddam* may be given *inam* as a revenue-free grant for the discharge of similar duties. The right of revenue collection on behalf of the State and the entitlement of perquisites was considered hereditary claim based on the idea of ownership *(malkiyat).* Thus the Zamindar or a *Muqaddam* were considered *maliks* responsible for the realization of the revenues of the *zamindari* villages and to enjoy *malikana* and other perquisites *(haquq* and *rassum)* in lieu thereof. Such heritable *zamindari* and *muqaddami* rights and shares being transferable could be mortgaged or sold. With the hierarchical pattern of the landed intermediaries, the *muqaddami* and the *zamindari* families in a *pargana* would claim parallel ownership *(malkiyat)* and other rights *(haquq)* on the same set of villages. The *raiyat* of the *raiyati* villages paid revenues either directly to the State treasury or through the village officials and the *Chaudharies* who were also entitled to remuneration *(dastur)* for the collection of the revenues. A *Chaudhari* by himself may be a Zamindar having jurisdiction over the *taaluqa* villages, but at the same time he may be responsible for the realization of the revenues from the *raiyati* villages. It seems that during the Mughal age, there was no permanent division between the zamindari and the *raiyati* villages. Far from converting the *zamindari* into *raiyati* villages, at times the Mughal government, in order to ensure regularity of revenue collection, created new *zamindaries* over the hitherto non-zamindari villages. The number of the *raiyati* villages may differ from one region to another and from one province to another. In fact, the number of the *raiyati* villages was far less in number and overwhelming majority of the villages were under the *zamindari* jurisdiction. This is because it suited the Mughal policy to employ the hereditary institution of the *zamindari* so long as the Zamindar accepted the responsibility and exerted his influence on the other *riaya* of his territory for the payment of the State revenues. In order to appreciate the concept of ownership and rights in land in *zamindari* (*taaluqa* village) it is essential to bear in mind that the above-mentioned proprietary rights *(malkiyat)* on the part of a zamindari or a *muqaddami* family were essentially of usufruct nature. Same is the case with the *deshmukhs, deshpandyas* or their counterparts, in other portions of South India. Their such usufruct rights were by no means incompatible with the land rights of the *riaya* within the village.

The lands in *a zamindari* village may be divided into two categories, *i.e., kadeemi* or *khudkashta* and *raiyati.* During the medieval ages, the primary Zamindars, *Muqaddams* as well as other *riaya* of different categories in a village constituted the cultivating classes. In the old settled villages, the ancestors of the *zamindari* families belonged to the conquering clans or were introduced by the State for revenue collection and the maintenance of law and order, or were the pioneer colonizers of the settlements. They all owned personal lands for cultivation *(khudkashta).* Thus the *khudkashta* lands were owned by the *zamindari* and *muqaddami* families and peasant proprietor *riaya,* who usually belonged to the dominant and privileged groups of the agricultural community of the village. The peasant proprietor or the *khudkashta riaya* in stock belonged to the original *zamindari* families and would trace their descent to the ancestral *Zamindars, Muqaddams* or *Chaudharies* etc., but of their own did not enjoy any such official status. They were the kith and kin of the *zamindari* and *muqaddami* families and owned ancestral self-developed lands. A *Muqaddam* failing to pay the revenues punctually may as well be denegrated to the position of simple *khudkashta* riaya. The descendents of the pioneer colonizing families, who in the course of historical development were suppressed by the new dominant clans or groups as well as the descendents of the erstwhile *zamindari* and *muqaddami* families who were deprived of the *zamindari* and *muqaddami* status due to any non-fulfilment of the obligations for further development of land and payment of revenues continued in possession of their ancestral *khudkashta* lands. Such *khudkashta riaya* may be termed as peasant proprietors. This class was named variously in different parts of India *viz,* usually *khudkashta* in most parts of North India, *riyaytis* with *gharuhala jot* as *gavetis* in Rajasthan, *thalazadas, thalkari, mirasdar,* in Deecan, Tamil and and some other parts of South India.

In the old settled villages, the lands in possession with the above catagories were named as *kadeemi* lands. Such lands may be reserved by the pioneering families even in the newly developed villages. Under the revenue regulations, they were assessed on fixed or concessional rates of assessment. The *khudkashta raiyati* families were required to cultivate their personal lands of their own or with the help of the hired agriculturists. In practice, the primary zamindari families and the peasant proprietors with large holdings did not cultivate the entire land of their own. They let out lands to the tenants on sharing basis, usually at half the produce or less. They would also give the lands to the tenants on periodical lease. It was considered that this did not create any interest of the tenant in the land so let out and was coverable by the connotation of hired labour, the share of the produce being taken by the tenant as remuneration of wages. However, they were not expected to let it out to the *raiyat* with occupancy rights. They were essentially permanent residents of the village and possessed their ploughs, oxen and means of cultivation. They claimed ownership over the *khudkashta* lands which could be bequeathed, mortgaged or sold. A few interesting documents reveal that even the concept of sale was limited in character as the sale was effected only for a limited period of seven to nine years. However, this does not rule out the practice of the sale on permanent basis as well. A *khudkashta riaya* was assessed for the payment of the revenues only for the lands under actual tillage. Even when he deserted his village, he could reclaim the land on the payment of the arrears after a long period. They constructed their own wells and shared expenses for the construction of the tanks and embankments for irrigation purposes. They formed the core of the village community and had customary rights for the usage of the village waste lands for getting fuel from the jungle either completely free or on the payment of the nominal cesses to the State. The exact proportion of the *khudkashta* land as against the land with other categories of the *raiyat* would, of course, vary from village to village. In view of the evidence in hand, it is possible to work it out for some regions as case studies.

As distinct from the *khudkashta* lands, *raiyati* lands in a village were earmarked for the *raiyat* comprising *Muzarian* and the *Paikashtkars*. As normal rates of assessment were applicable for the developed lands of this category, their possession could not be acquired by the *khudkashta riaya* as *khudkashta* lands. Notwithstanding the malpractice on the part of the *zamindari* and *muqaddami* families, the official practice remains the same right till the end of the 18th century. The *Ain-i-Akbari* in its chapter on the instructions to the *Amil Guzar* gives clear instructions to the latter to see that in case of *suyurghal* lands (charitable assignments), the *madad-i-maash* assignees should not get the *khudhashta* lands cultivated with the help of the cultivators of the *raiyat kashta* land.[9] Jahangir also forbade the malpractice of the dispossession of the *raiyat kashta* land by the *Karories* and the *Jagirdars*.[10] For the late 18th century Deccan, *Hukam Nama-i-Tipu Sultan* instructs that the *Patels* should not appropriate the lands reserved for the other *riaya* and should cultivate only their own lands.[11] In case they employed the *riaya* (of the *raiyati* land) for the cultivation of their personal lands, they would have to deposit the revenues of the entire land with the State treasury.

The *raiyati* land in the village was cultivated by the tenants who at one stage or another in the evolution of the agricultural development of the village were introduced by the primary Zamindars and the *khudkashta riaya* for the further tillage of the land. At the early stage of the development of the village, such tenants were essentially outsiders and came from the neighbouring *zamindaries* or *qasbas*. They were named variously but the usual term applicable to them was the *Paikashtkars* or *Pahis* in North India, *Uparis* or *Rayat* in Deccan and *Pyacarries* in Tamil land and some other portions of South India, *Patomkars* in Malabar and *Chalie Guenies* in Canara. With this legacy even till the 18th century, such a broad classification into twofold categories of the cultivators, *i.e.,* the original settlers *(Kadeemi Khudkasht)* and the later outside settlers *(Paikashtkars* etc.) lingered on. However, it is discernible from the documents covering 16th to 18th centuries that in practice in many a region of North India, the social concept of the peasantry in the villages had changed. In view of the paucity of the agricultural labour, it was always to the interest of the *khudkashta rajyat* to induce the *Paikashtkars* to settle in the villages permanently. In some regions there was so much scarcity of agricultural labour that *Paikashtkars* had to be taken on loan from other villages. Thus those of the *pais* who opted to settle in the villages in due course of time came to hold even occupancy rights. In the Mughal documents along with the other temporary tenants they are also put as *Muzarian.* For many a region of North India, the documents insist on distinguishing the settled *Muzarian* from the *Paikashtkar Muzarian* who were now considered as outsiders and introduced on the land for a limited period of either of the crop season *(kharif or rabi),* or for full one year or even for a period of two to three years. Clearly, in the course of centuries the social concept and nomenclature of such *raiyat* as against the *pais* had changed. In Rajasthan they were named as *Gaveti Ralyati* or *Paltis.* In some portions of *Subah* Delhi they were named *Karsanan (Muzarian) Kadeemi* while in other portions of North they were generally known as *chahaparbandi* cultivators. However, in the *Subah* of Gujarat the original *pais* who had settled since long were still regarded as *paikashtkars.* In Deccan unless they purchased the *mirasi* rights they continued to be known as the *Uparis.* In Tamil land two fold distinction was made between the *Pyacarries.* The temporary tenants and strangers admitted to the village from year to year were known as *Paracoodi Pyacarries,* while those who became permanent tenants and acquired hereditary rights through prescription were known as *Oolcoody Pyacarries.* Thus both in the North and the South such old settled tenants, by whatever nomenclature they may be called, had acquired hereditary *(marusi)* character. They were considered as the regular *asamis* for the purposes of assessment. In some regions of North India they could even mortgage and sell their land while in the south the *Oolucoody Pyacarries* did acquire transferable right but they could not sell the land.

Apart from this there was the leasee class which took the lead for a limited period for cultivation. However, in comparison to the *khudkashta riaya,* the tenant class *(Muzarian)* had moderate means for cultivation *(raiyat-i-raiza, gharib raiyat* etc.). They had to pay normal rate of assessment on their holdings in accordance with the regulations of the State.

The control of the State over the *raiyati* land in possession with the occupancy, periodical tenure and the *Paikashtkars* was more effective even though exercised through the Zamindars and the *Muqaddams* considered as the *maliks* (owners for enjoyment of perquisites) of the villages. For late 18th century Deccan, *Hukam Nama-i-Tipu Sultan* mentions the *raiyati* land as *zamin-i-sarkar* having been appropriated to the *raiyat.*[12] The power of the State to appropriate the *non-kadeemi* land, *i.e., raiyati* land for the purposes of the development was always exercised. Where new villages were developed, the lands may be fully covered by the colonising land owning families or the colonising families would appropriate some portions of land as *(khudkashta)* self cultivated and alienate the other land to the occupancy or *paikashtkar riaya.* On the contrary, where there was partial desertion of the land *(qulba* holdings), the *zamindari* and *muqaddami* families were obliged to introduce new tenants as *asamis* for keeping up the cultivation of the land in the villages. However, where villages grew desolate, as a first step the State would insist on the Zamindars to rehabilitate the villages with the help of the *Paikashikars* and then to introduce regular tenants as *asamis.* In case the Zamindar failed in his obligation to develop the deserted village, as a last resort the State could withdraw the *zamindari* possession and bestow it upon another person for the development of the land. In such new *zamindari,* the land with the *zamindari* or *muqaddami* families for self-cultivation *(khudkashta)* and the land to be cultivated by the other *riaya* introduced would be clearly demarcated.

The number of cultivating classes in a village would, of course, vary from one circle of villages to another or even from one village to another. There were villages where the *Khudkashta Riaya* and the *Paikashtkars* formed the village agricultural community but invariably in the settled *(kadeemi)* villages, the *Khudkashta Riaya* and the *Muzarian* (tenants) as well as the *Paikashtkars* composed the agricultural community of the villages. The 17th century documents of a few parganas of *Subah* Delhi clearly also bring out the stratification of the peasantry in the settled villages.[13] This may be taken as a case study. The documents show the stratification of the land holding and cattle wealth of the *asamis* (revenue paying cultivators) which comprised both the *khudkashta* and the other *riaya.* As the *Paikashtkar* was not an *asami,* the extent of the holding of the *Paikashtkars* is not shown. The documents reveal that the position varied from village to village. In some villages, there was only one class of *asamis* with uniform holdings, in others two classes and still in others three to five categories of holdings. This gives only a tentative analysis as many of the *asamis* had holdings in different neighbouring villages. The documents also record the number of cattle in possession with the agricultural families. They reveal that the oxen holding had a high relation with the average cultivable land holding and the cultivated land per *asami*. The *asamis* had as much holding of the cultivable land and proportionate oxen as they could have cultivated. It is also clear that with the change in the average holding of the cultivable land per *asami*, there was a corresponding change in the average holding of oxen per *asami* and cultivated area per *asami*. The holdings of the cultivable land and oxen per *asami* were in proportion and consequently the land was also proportionately cultivated. The average oxen holding was high in the bigger villages. This indicates that there was a separate holding of oxen for cartage and other purposes in addition to the oxen needed for cultivation purposes.

During the Mughal age the maintenance grants by way of exemption of the revenues on the land, assignation of the revenues of the cultivated lands or cash grants were bestowed upon different kinds of beneficiaries. The 17th century chronicles refer to both *madad-i-maash* and *suyurghal* but in general use they were considered as *aimma* grants. The difference between the *madad-i-maash* and *aimma* lay in the fact that whereas the former comprised only land grants, the latter could cover either land grant or assignation of revenues from the *aimma* lands or for giving cash salary to the religious persons or subsistence allowance to needy persons. The *madad-i-maash* and the *aimma* were both conditional and unconditional in character. All maintenance grants were governed by the Imperial regulations rather by the religious tenets of the *Shariat*. Ordinarily, the Hindus were given the *muafi* and *altamgha inam* but at times they were also given *madad-i-maash* grants. The *madad-i-maash* assignment could be made in the *khalisa, jagir* or *paibaqi* lands and ordinarily land grants were made after proper survey and measurement. The State transferred its right over the revenues of the area thus alienated in grants. Legally, the assignees enjoyed the revenue grants at the State's pleasure and good behaviour. The Mughal State reserved its rights to cancel, resume, decrease or expand the original grant. Technically, such grants were made for the personal life of an assignee but in practice, the hereditary claim for the renewal of grants was conceded. All land grants, unless otherwise specifically mentioned in the original *Farmans,* which were rather rare, were subjected to confirmation by every succeeding monarch and periodical verification. In case of desertion of land or the extinction of the male and female line of inheritance, the *madad-i-rnaash* land reverted to the *khalisa ispo-facto.* Invariably, the fresh grants did not renew all the lands in *madad-i-maash* held previously by the assignee families and a portion of the previous land grant was resumed to the *khalisa.* A study of a few of the renewed *Farmans* by Akbar shows that varying with every case, a slash of 1/4th to 3/5th of the original grant was made for reversion to the *khalisa.* Rules by later rulers also continued to be framed and enforced for the curtailment of the original grant on the demise of the assignee. Since there had been discrimination in the enforcement of these rules by the *sadrs,* Aurangzeb's general *Farman* conceded that all grants already made should be declared hereditary and that the holdings would be continued in the name of the heirs of the deceased, assignee without any change or diminution. Such heirs who already held other grants were also considered valid and additional ones.

For the *madad-i-maash* land grants, the Mughal State always paid due consideration to the fiscal division of a reasonable proportion between the waste cultivable lands and those already under cultivation with the *riaya.* In small holdings, the *madad-i-maash* grant was usually given from the waste arable land of the villages. But where the grants were larger, considerable portion would be given from waste arable land and the balance from the cultivated lands already in possession with the *riaya.* Regulations were made from time to time for the assignment of the waste cultivable and other lands from the settled villages. It is clear from the documents that the practice of alienating the greater share from waste cultivable land was followed right till the 18th century. The assignment of a village in *madad-a-maash* would not always carry full exemption from the payment of the revenues. Only a partial exemption may be conceded and the assignee would be required to pay fixed stipulated amount as against the total revenue of the village. Similarly, he may be required to make fixed payment per bigha of land thus assigned. Such assignment involved payment of revenues on concessional rates as against the full value of the rate of assessment. The *madad-i-maash* assignees were also exempted from the payment of miscellaneous types of cesses ordinarily imposed upon the agricultural *riaya.* The *madad-i-maash* lands were consolidated and concentrated in certain villages *(aimma-i-uzom)* and were distinguished from the villages in the *khalisa* or *tankhwah jagir.* But grants could also be made in the villages which were not totally assigned in *aimma.* In the settled villages where the revenues were granted to the *madad-i-maash* assignees, the land rights of the *riaya* were never distributed. The *malkiyat* rights of the assignees for the revenues and the land ownership rights of the self-cultivating *riaya* co-existed. In case an assignee tried to interfere with the latter's rights, his assignment was liable to be transferred. Where the assignee developed the waste land, he would retain the land even when the total or partial exemption from the payment of the revenues was withdrawn due to any reason.

On the self-developed waste land, the *madad-i-maash* assignees may cultivate the land of their own or they may get the land cultivated from the hired agricultural labour or the tenants *(Muzarian)* on sharing basis. Such tenants on the *madad-i-maash* holdings may continue even on hereditary basis so long as they regularly paid the stipulated share (usually half) to the assignees. The *aimma* lands were always granted within the jurisdiction of a *zamindari.* Of course, the Zamindar or *Muqaddam* would not realise cesses or *malikana* from the grantees totally exempted from the payment of the land revenue and the cesses. But the Zamindar or the *Muqaddam* claimed perquisites on the portion of the revenues withdrawn from revenue free assignment or on the share of revenues paid by the assignees when not totally exempted. However, when the Zamindar sold a share of his zamindari, he may alienate his *biswadari* and *malikana* right over the revenue paying lands to the vendee but he may reserve his lien on the lands in possession with the *madad-i-maash* assignees.

It seems that during the 16th and the 17th centuries the *aimma* lands, though in practice acquired hereditary character, were not transferable. When the *malkiyat* rights of the *madad-i-maash* assignees in practice assumed the saleable character, there is no contradiction involved with the rights of the *Zamindars* and the *Muqaddams.* In such cases of alienation on the part of the *madad-i-maash* assignees, only their own *malkiyat* rights were involved. Of course even in the course of the 17th century, many a *madad-i-maash* family purchased *zamindari* rights in their own villages or other villages. Such assignees claimed hereditary and transferable rights on the *madad-i-maash* lands and *malikana* rights on the shares of the *zamindaries* purchased by them. The *madad-i-maash* families who founded and developed new villages on the assigned *madad-i-maash* waste lands and built houses, wells and mosques etc., with the permission of the State claimed hereditary and transferable rights on it. When in due course of time the *aimma* lands acquired transferable character, the *zamindari* families who purchased the *madad-i-maash* lands acquired the *malkiyat* rights of the vendors along with the continuation of their *malikana* rights over the same villages.

The Mughal government made *waqf* (endowment grants) to the establishments attached to the mosques and tombs *(darghah)* of the Muslim saints and religious heads, *takiyas* (monastic quarters) of the *takiyadars* and the mendicants (*Fakirs*). Such endowment grants made to the Hindu temples and dharamshalas were not named *waqf* but were put under other categories of the revenue free grants viz., *muafi* and *madad-i-maash.* The shares of the *madad-i-maash* grants made to religious institutions were clearly marked for expenditure on the *urs* and *roshanai* etc., the share for the religious head of the institution and for the salary *(tankhwah)* of the attendants *(khadims)*. The members of the *darghah* establishment, *i.e., mujawars* (holy persons) and the *khadims* (attendants) could be granted collective or individual land grants in *madad-i-maash*. It seems that such lands did not acquire an alienable trait. The grant for the maintenance of the holy shrines or tombs, mosques and the schools attached to them were always renewed by State though like any another *madad-i-maash* grant they were subject to transfer, increase or decrease at the discretion of the ruling monarch. The grants conceded to the individuals attached to the institutions were essentially of *madad-i-maash* character and were even so termed in the details of the *Farmans*. As such, they were strictly subject to *madad-i-maash* regulations in respect of verification, succession, renewal and escheat. The Hindu chief Zamindars *(zamindaran-i-umda)* used to grant even hereditary *pattas* for revenue free grants to the Brahmins in the *watan* jagirs of their *zamindaris*. The other Zamindars also gave such grants named *brahmotar* or *nankar* which were resumable by the donors at their discretion. When a *Mansabdar* gave revenue-free grants, i.e., *madad-i-maash* or *aimma* to religious or needy persons in his *tankhwah* jagir, such grants lapsed with the transfer of the *Jagirdar* unless confirmed by his successor at his discretion.

During the course of the 18th century the question of land ownership continued to attract the attention of the Muslim *ulema* and jurists as well as other writers. In *Ahkam-ul-Arazi*, Qazi Muhammad Ala Thanwi examined the concept of landed property in India from the viewpoint of the *Shariat*.[14] He contended that considering the actual agrarian practices in India, the land was neither *ushri* nor *kharaji* and that it was neither ownership of the Zamindars (here Rajas) nor of the *riaya* but was the property of the *baitul mal* (State treasury). Land in India was mostly in the possession of the non-Muslims who had never been evicted by the Muslim conquerors. It was neither *ushri* nor *kharaji* because the Muslim and non-Muslim agricultural communities in India were not governed by the assessment rates prescribed by the *Shariat*. During the pre-Turkish Hindu rule, notwithstanding the actual position of virtual land ownership on the part of the *riaya* (peasantry), the latter of their own considered themselves only as tenants and workers *(Muzarian; Akkaran)* and had never claimed rights of ownership, which were erroneously deemed to be vested with the Zamindars (Rajas). But after the Turkish conquest, even though the possession of the land continued with the existing families, the Sultanate based on expediency never recognised the land ownership of the zamindars (Rajas) either. In case of any desertion of land by the *riaya* (peasantry), the Zamindar was not obliged to pay the revenues of the deserted land and as such under the *Shariat* law could not be treated as the primary revenue payer and the proprietor of the land. The office of the Zamindar was resumable at the discretion of the State. The relations between the State as land owner and all *riaya* (peasants) were governed by the *Shariat* concept of lease and cultivation *(muzariat)* and fixed rent *(ujart)* based on informal deed. Apparently Qazi Muhammad Ala Thanwi considered the position of only the Chief Zamindars and higher dignitary landed intermediaries *(rausa)* and ignored the position of the primary *zamindari* and *muqaddami* families. He did not distinguish between the different categories of the *riaya* and put them all as the tenants *(Muzarian)* cultivating the land of the State. His concept is too theoretical to be accepted. After the assumption of the Diwani rights by the East India Company in Bengal, Bihar and Orissa (1765), tremendous revenue literature was produced on the subject. It comprised not only the reports, memoranda and minutes of the English administrators but also commentaries in Persian by the Indian revenue experts. It was not only the English administrators who took different stand on the concept of property and the nature of land rights exercised by the State and the Zamindars. The most interesting feature of the problem is that even the Indian revenue experts also expressed divergent views.[15] Some of the Indian writers upheld the land ownership on the part of the ruler, others vested with the Zamindars and still others tried to appreciate the position of land rights of the other *riaya* as well. It should be essentially borne in mind that all this revenue literature belongs to Eastern India. Varying factors were responsible for the contradictory position taken up by the Indian writers. Some Indian writers wrote commentaries on the revenue practices in order to suit the predilections of the Indian administrators with whom they were accredited. A few writers tried to generalise the agrarian problems based on their knowledge of the eastern regions. Most of these writers tried to trace the agrarian practices since the age of Akbar. Many of these writers could not take cognisance of the change, if any, in the revenue practices and land rights which had taken place especially during the course of the 18th century. All the same, it is very useful revenue literature as some intelligent writers analysed the position rather correctly and with a clear perception of the varying land rights of the State, the Zamindars and different categories of the *riaya*.

The controversy amongst the English administrators Warren Hastings, Phillip Francis, James Grant, John Shore, Thomas Law and Cornwallis over the concept of proprietary rights in agrarian land in Bengal is too well known to be narrated. Their Minutes are full of contradiction. Though broad similarities could be drawn between the English pre-capitalist concept of property and the pre-British Indian concept of property, there are still marked differences based on the respective concept of the land laws and practices in the agrarian life of the two countries. Even John Shore, who was the shrewdest of the administrators, could not easily trace any vital analogy between the English and Indian proprietary rights and found the situation singularly confused. He commented that "the relation of a Zamindar to government and of a Rayat to Zamindar, is neither that of a proprietor nor a vassal, but a compound of both The former performed the act of authority, unconnected with proprietary right; the latter has rights without real property; and property of the one, and rights of the other are in a great measure held at discretion".[16] With the best of probing, John Shore and even other administrators were unable to understand the Indian concept of land ownership and the comparative land rights of the State, the Zamindars and the other categories of the *riaya*.

The introduction of the Permanent Settlement (1793) in Bengal, Bihar and Orissa was as much influenced by the financial and political considerations on the part of the East India Company as the latter's policy of not ending the institution of *zamindari* and the usage of the realisation of the revenues *i.e., Jama muqarari* or *Jama muqarari istamrari*. It is clear from the zamindari records that both according to the assertion of the Zamindars and the English understanding, the above revenue terms, even though distinct from each other, were considered to be denoting permanently fixed revenues.[17] Subject to the payment of the revenues, the State assumed to itself and made over to the Zamindars its own supposed absolute proprietary rights to the soil. The property in the soil was formally declared to be vested in the land holders and the revenue payable to the government from each estate was fixed for ever. The conferment of the proprietary rights on the Zamindars was more of an imitation of the English system of landed property. All the same unlike the English concept in order to avoid discretionary and arbitrary fixation of rates upon the raiyats by the Zamindar, the State reserved its right to regulate the terms by which the Zamindar was to let his lands to the raiyats though, in practice, such significant right was not exercised for a long time. All this implied a complete revolution in the agrarian structure and ownership of the estates which formed the subject of the settlement.

There is vast revenue and legal source material of the late 18th and the 19th centuries, which throws light on the working of the institution of the *zamindari* and land rights of the *riaya* both for the pre and the post-Permanent Settlement periods. The untapped zamindari records preserved at the States' Archives of Bengal, Bihar and Orissa and in possession with the private *zamindari* families offer a serious challenge to the historians for the construction of a reliable picture of the agrarian society of Eastern India. No less significant are the judicial proceedings and judgements of the Privy Council and the High Courts for the analysis of the land rights of the proprietors and varying classes of the *raiyats* in different parts of India. The coordination of the revenue and the legal sources gives a clearer perception of the working of the land system in India. The *zamindari* document of the Bihar State Archives covering the 17th and 18th centuries right till the enforcement of the Permanent Settlement clearly bring out the significance of the *Jama muqarari, muqarari peshkash* and the *muqarari istamrari peshkash* assessed on the lands of the Zamindars.[18] The terms *jama muqarari* and *peshkash muqarari* associated with the *peshkashi* (revenue paying) Zamindars were synonymous. After the deduction of the amount of the entitled remunerations (*muqaddmi, nankar, rasum-i-zamindari* or *rasumi rajgi* in respect of a Chief Zamindar) of the Zamindar from the assessed revenues of the villages or *parganas* of the *Zamindari,* finally calculated revenues *(jama muqarari)* were to be realised from the Zamindar. The revenues thus fixed were to be regularly paid by the zamindar on the basis of actual returns. In practice, however, the revenues may be fixed periodically. All the same depending on the geographical and political situation, the personal recognised status of the Zamindar, the State may or may not concede the right to the Zamindar to make payment of the revenues on periodically fixed assessment rather than on annual returns. Strictly speaking, the term *peshkash muqarari istamrari* never meant fixation of the revenues in perpetuity. The term *istamrari* implied only a long term rather than perpetual. When an ordinary tenant *(muzaraih)* took *istamrari* lease, ordinarily it was conceded for the maximum period of ten years. The revenues of the *zamindaries* in the *amli* and even in the *ghair amli* territories based on the principle of *peshkash muqarari istamrari* were liable to be revised after a reasonable span of period. The documents reveal that ordinarily in a large *amli zamindari,* only a few villages or a couple of *parganas* would be earmarked for *istamtari* settlement whereas revenues of the remaining portions of the *zamindari* jurisdiction would be based on the principle of annual assessment. Where continuous records of a particular *zamindari* family for the 17th and the 18th centuries are available, it is clear that the revenues of the villages or parganas were revised at times annually and at times after two or five years. In respect of *istamrari* villages or *parganas* at every settlement, the *Zamindar* will have to request the Government for retaining the previously fixed revenues for that year and for future as well. It was the discretion of the Government to accept or to reject the demand. At the same time, the Government may concede such request only partially. It may retain fixed revenues in respect of some villages or *parganas* while for others the revenues may be revised. The documents show that in respect of the same family for some *istamrari* villages and *parganas,* the assessment remains fixed for a considerable length of time or even constant while for others, it is revised even after two to five years. Since such a concession for regarding the territory in *istamrari* was conditional upon continuous loyalty and service to the State, the extent of the special concession was essentially governed by the political relationship between the State and the *Zamindar*. In the initial stages after the conquest of a *zamindari,* revenues may have remained fixed for some period but they were revised when the state had consolidated its position. However, a *Zamindar* having some portions of his zamindari on *istamrari* basis was in general terminology ranked as *muqarari peskashi istamrari* zamindar. The possibility of such *istamrari* settlements cannot be ruled out both in the amli as well as *ghair amli* territories of the *Zamindars*. This was specially marked in some portions of Bengal and such territories of Orissa where *Mughalbandi* operations did not take place. During the 18th century, Murshid Quli Khan (1700-1727), the Governor of *Subah* Bengal screwed up the machinery of the zamindari institution and reassessed the revenues *(peshkash)* of the *Zamindars* after a long period. This assessment remained in force until it was revised by the East India Company especially on the eve of the enforcement of the Permanent Settlement. For the 19th century, a judgement of the Privy Council is on record where the *pattahs* of the *muqarari istamrari riaya* on fixed rates of assessment were not regarded perpetual in character. The judges gave a clear verdit that unless such expressions as *bafarzahdam* or *naslan ba naslan* (hereditary or generation after generation) or similar terms were used, the words *istamrari* and *muqarari* did not of themselves denote that the State grant was an estate of inheritance.

The application of English theory of rent equally affected the agrarian relations in India. The Regulations of the Permanent Settlement claimed revenue as the share of produce of every bigha of cultivated land in line with Mughal practice. They did not use the word rent with reference to the annuity payable by the *Zamindar* but used the word revenue. Later on, a distinction was made between revenue and rent. The term revenue was understood to mean the amount paid by the superior land owners to the State while rent was the amount payable to the superior land owners by those who held under him whether they were the actual occupants or intermediate holders. Later on, the word rent was broadly defined in the Tenancy Acts enforced in different provinces of India. Now the relationship between the *Zamindars* and the *riaya* was essentially that of between the landlord and the tenant. However, even though the theory of Ricardo and Malthus and later political economists was modified by the customary practices, it had revolutionary legal effect of the transfer of property in the soil by means of grants in perpetuity and meant a change of ideas even from what the early British administrators entertained in India. The landlord or the rent receiver was the owner of the land and the rent payer even when he was in occupancy, paid for the use and occupation only of the land. This implied a complete change from the Mughal concept of property and agrarian relations.

However, this was not incompatible with the traditional right of the *Zamindar* to *malikana* which now stood as an allowance for proprietary right to a person who was owner or proprietor. *Malikana* was not rent. Nor did it have the elements which would constitute the rent. The innovation of auctioning the zamindari shares by the Government for the clearances of the arrears of the revenue introduced by the East India Company in the last three and a half decades of the 18th century was continued in the post-Permanent Settlement period.

The growth of subnifeudation and subdivisions of the lands in many a *zamindari* and *taaluqdari* is a new phenomenon in the agrarian structure of the permanently settled territories during the first half of the 19th century. For easy and punctual realisation of rent, the *Zamindars* and the *taaluqdars* granted leases of small territorial units *(patni taaluq)* in perpetuity and fixed rent to a large number of intermediaries who were considered as the proprietors in the same sense as the lessor *Zamindar* or *taaluqdar.* The *de facto* position was legally recognised by the Regulation VIII of 1819. The Regulation not only recognised the saleable character of the *patni* tenures on account of the execution of the money-decrees, but also admitted the right of the *patnidars* to gift, mortgage and to create similar subordinate tenures. The division of the *patni* tenure into second line *(dur patni),* third line *(seh patni),* the fourth line *(chahar patni)* created under-tenures in an hierarchical manner. There were, of course, some *patnis* which were granted for life only. Apart from the *patni* tenure comprising an entire village or a few villages, the lands within a village were alienated at fixed rent to another class named *muqarari* which was not essentially an intermediary tenure. A *muqarari* tenure could be for life or hereditary *(maurus muqarari)* and could be further alienated on similar lines unto second line *(darmaurusi, darmuqarari)* and third line *(seh-muqarari, seh-maurusi).* The establishment of the *patni* tenure down to the village level and the *muqurari* tenure of a defined portion of a village created a new proprietary class not only of rent but also of the land in the same manner as the Zamindars were considered the proprietary owners. So long as the paucity of agricultural labour persisted, the assessment rates continued to be based on regional customary practice. But gradually they drifted towards an arbitrary fixation by the land owner. The worst hit class was that of the *Paikashtkars.* It was not until 1859 and 1885 that the Government regulated the assessment rates and redefined the rights of the occupancy and non-occupancy raiyats.

As the Permanent Settlement combined the rent receiving right with the ownership of land, the village headmen *(Mandals)* who did not purchase *patni* shares and the *khudkushta* riaya having lost their ownership rights were reckoned as occupancy raiyats on their respective holdings. Invariably, the village headmen *(Mandals)* purchased the *patni* shares. In the *zamindari* territory permanently settled, the distinction between the tenemental lands and the personal lands *(nij-jot* or *nij* or *khamar* in Bengal; *zirat, nij, sir* or *kamat* in Bihar) was always maintained. This seems to be more or less in continuation with the Mughal tradition.

As distinct from the *Zamindari* territories, a *khas mahal* was declared as an estate in the private possession of the Government as proprietor. Even though the position varied from *mahal* to *mahal,* in a few *mahals* land ownership remained vested with *mandals* and *pattah* holders, in others with the rent-receiving *taaluqdars* and still others with the Government itself. The revenue-free *(la kharaj)* land grants like the *milk, altamgha, aimma, madad-i-maash* and *waqf* based on the Mughal *Farmans* were continued provided the grantees had been in possession since the pre-Diwani period *(i.e.,* previous to 12th August, 1765). However, previous distinctions between one or the other category were done away with. They were all considered perpetual but inalienable grants. Different rules were framed for the land grants which were not based on the royal *Farman (non-Badshahi).* Later on, the Bengal Tenancy Act (1876) included the revenue-free grants in the definition of estate and the owners were considered as the proprietors.

During the early 19th century, it was realised that the Permanent Settlement in Bengal had ignored the land rights of the cultivating raiyats and left them completely at the mercy of the *Zamindars*. Moreover, the state had frozen its revenue claims on the *zamindari.* The British revenue administrators with their experience in the Ceded and Conquered Provinces considered the problem of land ownership and revenue settlement from the viewpoint of the cultivating peasant communities which would as well ameliorate their economic condition. Such a concept was quite in line with the economic thinkers who wanted to create a free market in India for the British manufactured products. In 1827, McCulloch advocated the transformation of the cultivating tenantry into peasant proprietors or, failing that to give them long-termed leases of land on moderate rates.[19] Jones argued that the Permanent Settlement—an exercise in the imposition of a different English model to Indian conditions—was against the feelings and habits of the people and that the decaying village system involving group responsibility for discharging revenue obligations to the State being more traditional in character should be reconstructed.[20] It is not intended here to suggest that the creation of property in land was the British innovation because of the impact of the contemporary economic thought upon the administration of the East India Company in India. However, it cannot be denied that the practical considerations for land revenue settlements in India preceded the contemporary thinking in moulding and crystallising the character of the peasant proprietary bodies of the village communities claimed to have been discovered during the first half of the 19th century. The early settlement officers traced the existence of cultivating proprietors in an eclipsed state. The settlements (1801-1822) made with the revenue-farmers, *Taaluqdars* and *Zamindars* entitled *Malguzars* recorded the coparceners in a *zamindari* merely as "under-tenants". It was strongly felt that great injustice had been done to the peasant owners whose rights were being undermined and destroyed. Notwithstanding growing sympathy with such class, the concept of property right in the land as understood in the English phraseology was adhered to. In the pre-British system, the undertaking on the part of a *muqaddami* or primary *zamindari* family was not incompatible with the land owning rights of the coparceners *(sharikan)* of the *zamindart* and the self-cultivating *(khud kashta) riaya.* Even when a *zamindari* was held in abeyance, a zamindar may forego his perquisites *(nankar)* but he was entitled to *malikana* and would continue to own his self-cultivated lands. Under the British, a right holder (a person possessing permanent rights in the soil) entitled to engage for the payment of the land revenue would be deemed to have a proprietary right in land. This was clear English innovation in the concept of agrarian property which had far reaching effects upon the land owning classes. In accordance with the Bird and Thomson school of thought, where more than one proprietor existed in the same set of villages, two-tier proprietary rights were recognised with the superior and the inferior proprietors.[20a] The *Taaluqdars* and the big zamindars were the superior proprietors while the primary zamindars, headmen and the village proprietary bodies were the inferior proprietors. The Government could form settlement with either of them and mere allowance would be paid to the non-engaging party. Rules were framed regulating the proprietary rights of both the parties.

The village communities were characterised by communal *zamindari, pattidari* and *bhaichara* owned lands. They were generally large co-parcenary societies or corporations—each constituting a number of separate proprietors who either held the land in common, dividing what escaped of the rents when all charges had been paid or divided the lands and each family collected and defrayed the rent and charges in severalty; or held some of the lands of the same property in common and others severally. They were regulated by the joint responsibility for the payment of the revenues. Both the *pattidari* and *bhaichara* estates were of perfect and imperfect nature. But the distinction of the ancestral and customary shares was more superficial than real. There were regions in which mere communal *zamindari* lands existed and the role of the village communities was extremely limited. The communal *zamindaries* and *pattidari* shares can be well traced to the 17th and 18th centuries. The *bhaichara* features may as well be pre-British but the joint responsibility of the payment of the revenues was not a favoured mode of assessment in North India during the Mughal age. As the main interest of the British Government lay in the stability of the realisation of the revenues, as a matter of policy it encouraged 'market property in land' and the joint responsibility of the payment of the revenues. It is in this respect that the contemporary economic thought influenced the land policy in India. The English Government being alien to the Mughal agrarian system could not easily prepare a detailed record-of-rights of the complex land interests of different persons for the realisation of the revenues in severalty. Moreover, despite some reduction in the assessment made in 1822 and 1833, the magnitude of rent imposed on land remained high and led to accumulation of the arrears which could not be easily cleared. It was considered that the joint responsibility for the revenue payment on the part of the cultivating communities would be the best course for realising the maximum revenues.

The proprietary right in land, as generally enforced in the North Western Provinces (excepting Awadh) being simultaneously enjoyed by the individual families *(taaluqdari* and *zamindari)* and the village communities, was graduated in character. None of the proprietors was vested with full ownership except where the land revenue was redeemed. The right holding with title to use and occupation of the land was regarded heritable and transferable subject to customary practice of the village community. Unless a right holder undertook the engagement for the payment of the revenues, he could not be vested with proprietary rights in land. The non-proprietary cultivators with prescriptive right on their respective fields and governed by fixed rates of assessment were considered as occupancy tenants while others not covered by these characteristics were treated tenants-at-will. The occupancy rights, though heritable, were not alienable without the consent of the proprietors. The occupancy tenants could not dig wells, plant gardens or locate labour on their holdings. The *paikashtkars,* whose prescriptive right was recognised, were also declared occupancy tenants while others remained tenants-at-will.

Though apparently the new landed structure had broad similarities with the pre-British pattern, in the ultimate analysis in the concept of land rights, it was rather different. The division of proprietary classes into superior and inferior was rather arbitrary. According to the pre-British concept they were only higher or superior *Zamindars* with *taaluqdari* rights and the primary village zamindars and both shared the customary perquisites in lieu of collections done in their *taaluqdaris*. Neither of them was a proprietor of the land in the absolute sense. The *muqaddami* and the primary *zamindari* families with self-cultivating *(khudkashta)* rights formed the backbone of the agricultural communities. But the new connotation of proprietorship in land rendered them inferior proprietors as against the higher landed intermediaries vasted with superior proprietorship.

In Awadh, as in the case of Bengal, the title to the proprietary right to the soil (excepting estates of six persons) was deemed to be vested with the British Government (1858) to be further disposed at its discretion. Two distinct interests in land exercised by the *Taaluqdars* as superior holders and the primary *Zamindars* as inferior holders were created. The term associated in the earlier summary settlement (1856) with the latter class as 'subordinate proprietors' was withdrawn *ex-officio*. The inferior holders were to make payment of the revenues through the *Taaluqdars* and were entitled to fixed sum in respect of their profits, the cost and risk of collection. They had permanent and heritable right in the land subject to the regular payment of the revenues. The decision for the *taaluqdari* settlement influenced by aristocratic reaction as an aftermath of the Great Rebellion (1857) was essentially political with considerable weightage for the recognition of the *de facto* pre-British position held by the *Taaluqdars*. It was not enforced because of its instrinsic superiority as against the concept of the village communities. There is no denying the fact that in the pre-British system as well, where *taaluqdari* based on socio-economic and political factors was evolved, district interests in the land for sharing the *malikana* and other perquisites were claimed by the agreeing landed intermediaries as proprietary rights *(malkiyat)*. In Awadh, the position was all the more intricate as due to political and economic factors, apart from the ordinary *Zamindars* and small *Taaluqdars (taaluqdaran-i-mufassalan)*, the high dignitary *Zamindars* entitled Rajas *(zamindaran-i-umda)*, many of whom during the Mughal age held *mansabs* and *tankhawh jagirs* had also assumed the role of the *Taaluqdars* under the Lucknow Government during the later half of the 18th century. They even acquired *sanads* from the Government. Such *Zamindar-Taaluqdars* held *watan-jagir* (patrimony), *nankar* and, at times, *inam* in lieu of service to the State, the appended *zamindaries* with sharing *malikana* rights and their personal land *(seer)*. The 18th and early 19th centuries revenue documents and the *Dasturul aml* (Code of Revenue Regulations) of Nawab Saadat Ali Khan (1798-1814) spell out the concept of land ownership and respective land rights of the *taaluqdars*, big and small, primary *Zamindars*, *Pattidars*, coparcenary *zamindari* families, *Muqaddams* and Tenants *(Muzarian)*.[21] Where the land was shared by many *Zamindars* or the *Taaluqdars* in the hierarchal pattern, the settlement was made with the biggest of the *Zamindars* (also entitled *taaluqdars)* whom the other co-sharers appointed as their representatives. If the priority for settlement with the state was not acceptable to the *Taaluqdar,* it may be offered to an appended *Zamindar* or failing any settlement even to the *Pattidar* or the *Muqaddam* who would assume the role of the *Zamindars*. If the offer was not acceptable to any of the parties, the revenues may be realised directly by the Government *(tahsil kham).* If a co-sharing *zamindari* family wanted to withdraw from a joint settlement, it was free to apply to the Government for the partition of the *zamindari* lands and could make separate settlement with the Government for the payment of the revenues. In case of refusal for engagement by a *Taaluqdar* or *Zamindar*, he may surrender his ownership *(malkiyat)* rights for the collection of the revenues and enjoyment of *malikana* but he would continue to possess his personal *zamindari (jot khas)* lands. The *zamindari* and *taaluqdari* shares were transferable though such waste lands which were not assessed for the revenues could not be sold without the permission of the Lucknow Government. The *taaluqdari* institution, which had been well recognised by the Mughal State, continued to operate in Awadh during the 18th and 19th centuries. But at the same time in line with the Mughul practice, the Lucknow Government effected revenue settlement with the *Zamindars*, as representatives of co-sharing families, *Muqaddams* and even revenue farmers *(Mustajirs).* The revenue of various territories of the Awadh State were realised directly by the State officials from the *Zamindars* and *riaya* as *tehsil kham.* It is true that in the three decades preceding the annexation of' Awadh (1856), the powerful *Taaluqdars* taking advantage of the turbulent period extended their *taaluqas* through both legitimate and coercive means and, at times, even mitigated the demarcated line of the commended villages or completely suppressed them so as to incorporate them in their own *zamindari* villages. But their object in suppressing the *zamindari* and petty *taaluqas* was to increase the income of their estates through *malikana* realisation. They never asserted rights of ownership in the absolute sense. In the disturbed regions, eyen at the village level, the land rights of the self-cultivating *(khud kashta) riaya* and the tenants *(muzarian)* were sufficiently blurred and were not sought after. All the same, in principle, the traditional concept of the ownership of land and the land rights of the varying *riaya* classes in the *zamindari* and *taaluqa* villages persisted right till the annexation. Whatever may have been the British understanding about the concept of the Indian property at the time of the enforcement of the Permanent Settlement, at this stage it clearly comprehended the position of the *Taaluqdars* in Awadh. Though the restoration of the Revenue Settlement with the superior holders of land and chiefs (entitled *Taaluqdars)* was quite in line with the pre-British practice, it differed in a two-fold manner. Firstly, the *taaluqdari* settlement was enforced throughout Awadh whereas under the Nawabi rule, notwithstanding the consolidated position of the big and Raja *Taaluqdars,* there were territories where the State made settlement directly. Secondly, the most important institutional change was the conferrment on the *Taaluqdars* the proprietary right in the soil. It was a natural corollary of the fact that the British Government has assumed all the proprietary right in the soil and then granted to the *Taaluqdars.* The British Government was quite clear about the land rights exercised by the *Taaluqdars* but as a matter of policy, it granted the *taaluqdaries* with permanent hereditary and transferable proprietary rights. This is confirmed by the fact that the six estates which had been previously spared the general confiscation of all the lands in Awadh after the Great Rebellion (1857) were later found to be in disadvantageous position. It was realised that with mere *status-quo ante,* they enjoyed only land rights and privileges based on usage but they could not claim ownership of the soil of the *taaluqdaries* as they had never done before. So this anomalous position was subsequently remedied. However, it was clarified that the inferior *Zamindars* entitled under-proprietors and other holders of subordinate interests would be effectually protected from wrong and would not be left at the mercy of the *Taaluqdars.* The amount of proportion to be paid by the former to the latter was to be fixed and recorded after careful and detailed survey. It was considered that such safeguards would help in the maintenance of the rights of the village communities. Previously under normal circumstances the sharing of the perquisites by the landed intermediaries was based on regional and customary practice. But now the *taaluqdari* institution with new concept of land ownership brought significant change in the land rights of the primary *Zamindars* and the *riaya* in the *taaluqas* of the *Taluqdars.*

At the time of introducing the rayatwari settlement in the Madras Presidency, Munro believed that it was 'no innovation' and was in continuation with the pre-British institution, customs and revenue practices of the people. He thought that according to the pre-British concept, the Sovereign had at all times been regarded as the sole landlord and that great mass of tenants were all tenants-at-will.[22] He considered that the term *zamindari* was generic comprising the hereditary Rajas, *Poligars, Deshmukhs, Despandyas, Desais, Patels, Karnums* and even talliaries of the villages. Even though they held hereditary *inam* lands in lieu of discharging the official duties, they were not propertly landlords.[23] The *Zamindars* and *Poligars* who possessed great estates were tributary in character and some of them may be independent princes.[24] The hereditary *inam* land holding held by the higher or the lower categories of the *Zamindars* could not be gifted or sold and was resumable at the will of the State.[25] The *Kulwar* or rayatwari system involved settlement with every cultivator directly who paid rent to the Government. The cultivators were severally responsible for the payment of the rent without the intervention of any intermediary. They and the patels were jointly responsible for the payment of the rent of the whole village.[26] As according to the British concept of property, the revenue settlement made with any landholding class would also render to as the owner of the land, in contrast to the *zamindari* settlement done earlier in Bengal, Munro preferred to make settlement with the rayats. The land holdings of the rayats assessable directly by the State were to be considered their property held of the East India Company which in due course of time would also acquire saleable character.[27]

Munro's main object was to avoid the defects of the *zamindari* settlement of Bengal which has concentrated land ownership in few hands at the cost of the cultivating classes. But, in principle the rayatwari system was not totally in continuation with the pre-British patter which was essentially characterized by the landed intermediary classes.[28] Munro himself concedes the existence of different categories of the zamindars but he could not distinguish the nature of ownership rights of these classes on their personal lands and the *inam* lands held by virtue of being landed intermediaries. However, Munro's assertion of the State claim for periodically raising the magnitude of the revenues to be realised from the poligars instead of getting only fixed unalterable *peshkash* is quite in line with the Mughal practice. Whereever the poligars held *inam* lands, they were continued subject to the payment of revenues assessed and fixed periodically. The British claim to resume the *inam* lands or to alter the amount of fixed revenues from the *inam* lands was equally traditional in character. In the prevailing political situation, Munro did not like to vest the ownership rights with the landed intermediaries and preferred to recognise the rayats as proprietors who would have no armed followers and could not form any combination to disturb the publicd tranquility. Having acquired property, they would rather be indebted and would stand by the system. It is a fact that in the regions where the rayatwari system was enforced, even in the pre-British era the assessment on the holdings of the *riayas* was done directly by the state and the cultivators reckoned as *asamis* were severally responsible for othe payment of the revenues. But the reveneus were collected through the agency of the landed intermediaries like the patels, deshmukhs and the poligars etc. The patels, karnums and other landed intermediaries were given hereditary *inam* lands which involved partial or total exemption from the payment of the revenues on a part of their self-cultivated (*khudkashta*) land or they may be assigned separate lands for this purpose. The *inam* lands may be alterable at the discretion of the State but as distinct from such lands, the self-cultivated (*khudkashta*) land of the *riaya* as well as the landed intermediaries was always regarded as their ownership. The ownership rights were equally exercised on the orchard and valuable trees like *sandal, sagwan* and coconut. The owners, of course, had to pay revenues on the trees and exemption was given only on such trees which were planted within the premises of the houses. The development of the wasteland was done through the agency of the Patels and the other landed intermediaries who had distinct interest in such developed lands. Under the rayatwari system, the mitigation of the rights of the self-cultivating *(khudkhshta) riaya* in the Madras Presidency was a deviation from the pre-British practice. In the method of the assessment, even though there appears to be striking resemblance of the rayatwari system with the fluctuating assessment of the lands done previously, in the matter of detailed operation, it was not in complete conformity with the pre-British method. The reshuffling of the nature of land rights and the high incidence of rent implicit in the rayatwari system caused severe socio political strains and agrarian tensions in the territories of its operation, However, the maintenance land grants *dharmadayam (khairati, bhattavritti)* as well as endowed grants *(devadayam)*, which had acquired hereditary and transferable character, were continued and were considered as the private property of the assignees. Later on in the Ceded Districts (1831, 1845), the East India Company forbade the transfer of such land by gift or sale and confined the assignment to the life time of the grantee only.

In Ajmer-Merwara, the British government inherited varying nature of land rights claimed by the land holders. It seems that during the course of the 18th century, the Marathas had imposed stipulated amount *(mamla* or *ain)* without disturbing the prevailing revenue practices and landed structure. The British government gave a due recognition to the existing pattern without going into the detail of the original nature of the title of the land holders. The territories of Ajmer-Merwara may be broadly divided into three categories *viz.*, the *khalisa*, the *istamrari* tenures and the maintenance lands granted and endowed to the individuals and religious institutions. In the *khalisa* villages where the revenues were realised directly by the State, the irrigated lands were owned by the *Biswadars* who exercised the *biswadari* rights like the self-cultivating *(khudkashta) riaya.* Having permanently improved land they had right to transfer, by sale, mortgage or gift. The British Government also created new *biswadari* holdings for the development of land. This system transformed the cultivating communities into *shamlat* or *bhai-chara* proprietary bodies. Each member possessed permanent rights in the land improved by him. However, the State claimed its ownership over the waste land defined within the village boundaries but in 1850 it surrendered its ownership rights in favour of the *Khewatdars* who were regarded as the owners of the improved land. Apart from the continuation of the traditional *biswadari* rights of the self-cultivating *riaya* at individual family level, the British policy emphasised the creation of fresh proprietary rights within the concept of the brotherhood of the cultivating communities.

The *Zamindars* (chiefs) who held *mansabs* and conditional *tankhwah jagir* during the Mughal age, the other *Zamindars* (*Thakurs*, etc.) with conditional service *jagir* and the *Taaluqdars* having assumed the *role of istamrardars* claimed to make the payment of the revenue on perpetually fixed basis. Despite the authoritative enquiry report by Cavendish (1829-30)[29] and later reports (1839 and 1841) contrary to the asserted position by the *Istamrardars,* the British Government did not interfere until 1873 when the institution of the *istamrardari* was recognised as in perpetuity on the payment only of *mamla* and subject to certain restrictions against transfer. As such, the ownership of the *Istamrardars* was of limited nature. In the *istamrardari* estates, the cultivators who had improved the land by sinking wells and construction of embankments etc. were provided only a certain amount of security of tenures. But they were not conceded the land rights enjoyment by the *biswadari* cultivators in the *khalisa* lands. The cultivators of the unimproved lands were treated as tenants-at-will. The *Istamrardars* also created another petty land holding class of *guzaredars* who were their kith and kin and held similar rights of ownership as of grantors.

The bhomia *(non-bhomi-chara)* had existed in this region of Rajasthan since the Mughal age or even earlier. They exercised *khudkashta* rights of ownership over the land.[30] As privileged class of the peasantry, they paid only a portion of the assessed revenues *(bhom*-bab*)* to the State. Their rights for holding land for discharging police duties on a small scale were continued. At times, a person possessed both *istamrardari* and *bhom* rights. Later on, the British Government having modified its policy abolished the quit-rent of the *bhomias.*

The maintenance land grants to the individuals, the endowment grants to the religious institutions made by the earlier Governments, the Mughals and the Marathas were continued. The British government also made similar land grants which though hereditary were not alienable in character. However, *muafi* grants which did not previously carry total exemption of the revenues were renewed on similar condition and revenues were realised in respect of the unexempted portion (usually one-fourth) of the assessed revenues. The self-cultivating *riaya* of the assigned villages which had traditionally enjoyed *khudkashta* rights were now deemed to possess *de facto* ownership of land.

In the Punjab during the Sikh rule, though some changes were brought about in the machinery of the revenue collection, the Mughal concept of the *malkiyat* and land rights was maintained. Of course, in some parts of the Punjab considerable reshuffling of the *malkiyat* rights of dominant class and groups took place in the process of the consolidation of the Sikh regime. It is clear from the revenue documents of the Sikh Period and the early English reports that varying types of land holdings and land tenures were prevalent in different regions of the Punjab.[31] The assessment was done on distinct family holdings measured in terms of land possession determined by the cultivating capacity of the plough *(hal* or *qulba)* or a well *(chah)* or block of land *(chak)* or other local units. The assessment was made after taking into consideration the detailed classification of land, the nature of proprietary land, the clannish and caste structure of the land owning classes and, at times, other regional factors and customary practices. The methods of assessment in vogue were more conducive to the payment of the revenues in severalty than on a joint basis. The role of the village communities for the determination and payment of the revenues was limited in character and served only as an agency for the local land revenue administrative machinery. The *zamindari* features of individual ownership, communal and coparcenary shares in the villages along with the individual family responsibility for the revenue share were quite marked. In fact, village communities were more suitable to the settled villages and not where significant portion of the waste cultivable land and specially new tracts of virgin soil were being developed by variety of tenure based on the local practices. Of course, the village communities of the *bhaichara* type were favoured by the hardy Jat communities in the Doab region (East Punjab) and in the territories of Delhi (Haryana and Cis-Sutlaj not under Sikh rule) which were later on transferred to the Punjab in 1858. In the *bhaichara* villages, the practice of the share of the land to be cultivated by the owners and the sharing of the common profits and expenditure may vary from the *pattidari* villages, but in either case it involved the division of fiscal responsibility undertaken by an individual family. The joint responsibility for the payment of the revenues was by no means its basic characteristic.

The British rule in the Punjab more or less adopted the proprietary concept and rights of the agricultural classes as enforced by Bird and Thompson in the North-Western Province. However, the North-Western and South-Western portions of the Punjab as well as the hilly tracts of Kangra were equally influenced by the traditional practices.[32] In the initial stages, the British administration tried to graft the village communities of the type of North-Western Provinces even in such regions which were alien to such concept. But the experiment was not always successful and was surrendered. Ordinarily, the communal *zamindari* lands and when further split into *zamindari* possessions were held in severalty for payment of land revenue on separate individual family holdings rather than on joint basis. In the communal *zamindari* estates, the occupancy tenants owned individual responsibility for the payment of the revenue and *malikana* on their respective holdings. Even in the regions where the village communities prevailed the concept of *pattidari* and *bhaichara* itself underwent a change from the North-Western provinces to the Punjab. In some village communities there were owners *(malik kabaza)* of certain fields with complete proprietary title *(malkiyat makbuza)* who did not belong to the village brotherhood and did not share the joint rights, profits, and responsibilities of the members of the village communities. The division of the *proprietary* right of the superior *(ala malik),* the inferior *(adna malik)* and title holders was on the same pattern as in vogue in North-Western Provinces, though the regional names given to such proprietors were not uniform. In line with the practice of the North-Western Provinces, the settlement was invariably decided in favour of the inferior proprietors and the share of the allowance of the superior proprietors was fixed in accordance with the regulations. The occupancy tenancy was also framed on the same lines except that in the *bhaichara* villages of certain regions based on the traditional practice the occupancy tenants *(muzarian maurusi)* who possessed rights of mutation in holding, mortgage and sale as well as right of grazing their cattle on the waste land but without claim to share the profits of the *shamlat,* were confirmed with ownership rights within certain limits. In some cases, they were recorded even as inferior proprietors *(adna maliks).* On the other hand, in certain regions, under certain circumstances, they were liable to enhancement of the revenue rates.

References

1. B.R. Grover, "Nature of Land-Rights in Mughal India" paper read at the Indian Economic History Seminar, Delhi, April, 1961, *IESHR*, i, (1963), 1-23; "Nature of *Dehat-i-taaluqa (zamindari villages)* and the Evolution of the *Taaluqdari* System during the Mughal Age", *IESHR*, ii, no. 3, (1965) 166-77, 259-88; "The concept of Village Community in North India during the Mughal Age and the pre-British Era", Seminar paper, Indian Institute of Advanced Study (Simla, 1964).

2. Irfan Habib, *Agrarian System of Mughal India*, Bombay, 1963 ; S. Nurul Hasan, "The Position of the Zamindars in Mughal Empire", *IESHR*, iv, 1964, 107-19; "Three Studies of the Zamindari System", *Medieval India: A Miscellany*, Bombay, 1968, 233-9; "Aspects of Zamindari System in Deccan", *IHC*, 1969, pp. 262-6; *Thoughts on Agrarian Relations in Mughal India*, New Delhi, 1973; Satish Chandra, "Indian Economy Before the Industrial Revolution in Britain: The Village Society", paper presented at Seminar on Colonization of Indian Economy, A.M.U., Aligarh, 1972; "Some Aspects of Indian Village Society in Northern India during the 18th century, The Position and Role of the *khud-kasht* and *pahi-kasht"*, paper read at the International Congress of Orientalists, XXIX Session, Paris, 16-22 July 1973; Satish Chandra and Dilbagh Singh, "Structure and stratification in the society in Eastern Rajasthan", *IHC*, Muzaffarpur 1972. N.A. Siddiqi, *Land Revenue Administration under the Mughals (1700-1750)*, Bombay, 1971; G.D. Sharma, "Some Land Revenue Grants of the Time of Ajit Singh and Abhay Singh of Marwar", *IHC*, Varanasi Session, 1969; "Nature of Bhom Rights during the 17th century Marwar", *IHC*, Jadavpur, 1974; Dilbagh Singh, "Caste and the structure of village society in Eastern Rajasthan during the 18th century; *The Indian Historical Review*, II, ii, January 1976, pp. 299-311; Muzaaffar Alam, "Some aspects of the changes in the position of the *Madad-i-Maash* holders in Awadh, 1676-1772, *IHC*, Jadavpur, 1974.

3. Lambton, A.K.S., *Landlord and Peasant in Persia*, London, 1969, pp. 15-128.

4. *Risala-dar-bai'-Arazi*, MS. Maulana Azad Library, A.M.U. Aligarh, Shaifta Collection, *Fiqh, Arabia*, No. 24/26. I have also gone through the translation of this work by Zafarul Islam, Centre of Advanced Study, Department of History, A.M.U., Aligarh. I am extremely obliged to him for this courtesy.

5. *Ain-i-Akbari*, MS. Hamiltan I, Berlin, fols. 122a-124b; tr. Jarrett, p. 54.

6. Ali Muhammad Khan, *Mirat-i-Ahmadi*, Bombay, 1889, I, *Farman* No. 14, pp. 268-272; *Farmans* No. 16-17, pp. 283-88.

7. *Waqai-Ranthanbore*, No. 2411, Asafia Library, Hyderabad Deccan, *Waqai* dated II *Rabi* II, 22nd R.Y. (Aurangzeb), pp. 207-208.

7a. Bernier, *Travels in the Mughal Empire 1656-68*, tr. A. Constable and revised by V.A. Smith, London, 1916, p. 204.

8. Rajasthan Archives Bikaner, *Akhbarat Darbar Maulla*, dated 10th Rabi I 10th R.Y. Aurangzeb.

9. *Ain-i-Akbari,* MS. Hamilton I Berlin, fols. 120a-121a.
10. *Tuzk-i-Jahangiri,* MS. Orient Oct 101, Berlin, Regulations (Dasturulaml) of Jahangir, clause No. IX. fols. 30a-30b.
11. A copy of *Hukamnama-i-Tippu Sultan,* State Archives, Hyderabad, dated 1216 Fasli.
12. *Ibid.*
13. Rajasthan Archives, Bikaner, *Yaddasht haqiqat qulba hai muwaze pargana Rewari (Subah Delhi)* dated A.H. 1067-1073/1656-63 AD; *Haqiqat Arazi mazruat wa uftada muwaze pargana Rewari,* dated A.H. 1013/1663 AD.
14. Qazi Muhammad Ala Thanwi, *Risala Akham Arazi,* MS. A.M.U., Aligarh. I have gone through the Persian portion of the manuscript lent to me by Zafarul Islam, Aligarh. I am indebted to him for this courtesy.
15. B.R. Grover, "Some Rare Persian Manuscripts and Documents on India (16th-18th centuries) in the German Libraries", *Max Mueller Bhavan Publications,* 1964 Year Book, New Delhi, pp. 59-73.
16. Harington's Analysis, Vol. III, p. 397. Appendix to the Fifth Report, No. 6.
17. Bihar State Archives, Patna, *Zamindari Records* pertaining to the *Subahs* of Bihar and Allahabad.
18. *Ibid.*
19. McCulloch, "Revenue and Commerce of India", *Edinburgh Review* (March 1827), p. 354.
20. Jones, *A Short Tract on Political Economy, Including Some Account of the Anglo-Indian Revenue Systems* (as reprinted by Whewell in the *Literary Remains,* p. 273).

20a. J. Thomason, *Directions for the Settlement Officers,* 1844; Settlement of N.W.P., Calcutta Review, December 1849; *Selections of Papers Relating to the Directions for Revenue Officers Regarding the Settlement and Collection of Revenue,* 1849, *Parliamentary Papers.* No. 999, 1853; *Selections from the Records of the Government North-Western Provinces,* Mr. Thomason's Despatches, Vol. I, Allahabad, 1855; Letter of J. Thomason, Lt. Governor, N.W.P., Agra, the 31st January, 1844 to Lord Ellenborough, G.G. of India, paras 1-44.

21. The documents available with U.P. State Archives, Allahabad and Lucknow and National Archives of India, New Delhi, covering the 18th and 19th century Awadh are significant in this respect.
22. Tamil Nadu State Archives (TNSA), *Madras Board of Revenue Consultatians, 26 September, 1805,* Thomas Munro to William Petrie, President and Members of the Board of Revenue, 25 August 1805; also *Selections from the Records of Bellary District-Political, Revenue and Agricultural Matters, 1800-1853,* ASO (D) Vol. 73, Munro to the President and Members of the Board of Revenue, 30 November 1806.
23. T.N.S.A., *M.B.R.C., 26 September 1805,* Munro to the Board of Revenue, 25 September 1805; For the position of the poligars, J.C. Dua, "Poligars: Their Rise in the Ceded Districts," *IHC,* XXXIII, 1972, pp. 467-474.

24. T.N.S.A., *Selections from the Records of Bellary District,* ASO (D), Vol. 72, Thomas Munro to Archibald Obins, Esquire, Private Secretary to the R.H. the Governor of Madras, 20 June 1806.
25. *Op. cit.*, f.n. 22.
26. T.N.S.A., *Selections from the Records of Bellary District—Political Revenue and Agricultural Matters—1800-1856,* ASO (D) Vol. 73 and 76, Circular issued by Thomas Munro, 10 August, 1801; *Bellary Records,* 397/79, Munro to the Board of Revenue, 3 November 1802; also J.C. Dua, "Position of Patels and Karnums in the 'Ceded Districts' During the first quarter of the nineteenth century", *I.H.C.*, XXXIV, 1973, pp. 104-18.
27. *op.cit.*, fn. 22 & 23.
28. *op. cit.*, f.n. 23.
29. Cavendish Enquiries (3 vols. in Persian), District Record Office, Ajmer (Rajasthan). The evolution of the *istamdarari* rights in the course of the 18th and early 19th centuries can be well analysed from the family records of the Rajas of Binai and Masuda and the Thakur of Kharwa (District Ajmer, Rajasthan).
30. Also see G.D. Sharma, "Nature of Bhom Rights during the 17th century in Marwar", *op. cit.*, f.n. 2.
31. *Jamabandi* Records of the Punjab under the Sikh rule available at Punjab Secretariat Records Office, Lahore (Pakistan), of which some are also available with Punjab Secretariat Record Office, Chandigarh, Punjab; Administration reports including the Cis and Trans Sutlej States 1849-50 and 1850 and 1850-51 with accompaniments dated 1851:
    (a) Panjab; H. M. Elliot's note on the revenue and resources of the Punjab (1847 A.D.). (For. Department MS No. 351);
    (b) Supplement to the above note by H.M. Elliot (1849 AD); Settlement Reports of the Districts of Punjab.
32. G.G. Barnes, *Report on the settlement in District of Kangra (in the train Satlaj States),* Lahore, 1855, paras, 107; 109-135; 227-232; 250-255; 332-431.

Glossary of Revenue, Administrative and Other Terms Used in the Sources of the Mughal Period

A

Abad-Beshi: آبادبیشی	P	First assessment of newly settled or cultivated land.
Abkari: آبکاری	P	Business of the distillers; distillery; duty on the manufacture and sale of spirituous liquor; excise duty levied on eating shops, gaming houses; itinerant tumblers, jugglers and the like in some parts of the south of India.
Abwab: ابواب	A	(*Bab* means door, a section, a chapter; *abwab* is plural of *bab*) Heads or subjects of taxation or the taxes imposed during the Mughal period by the Government in addition to the regular assessement on the land. Miscellaneous cesses, imports and charges levied by zamindars and the Government officers.
	(1)	*Abwab-i-faujdari*: taxes imposed on zamindars, in communication of fees which had been payable to the office of the *faujdar*, q.v.
	(2)	*Abwab-i-thanadar*: Taxes impsed on retailers of spirituous liquors and other articles put

Abbreviations: A= Arabic; H= Hindvi; M= Mongolian; Mar= Marathi; P= Persian; S= Sanskrit; T= Turkish; Tel= Telugu; A.P.= Arabic, Persian; H.A.= Hindvi, Arabic; H.P.= Hindvi, Persian; P.A.= Persian, Arabic; P.H.= Persian, Hindvi.

for sale in markets attached to police or military stations and payable to the *kotwal*, q.v.

Abwab-i-Mamnua: A ابواب ممنوعہ Unauthorised taxes or cesses; charges levied by revenue officers illegitimately, without the proper sanction of the Government.

P Court of land and justice: under the Mughal kingdom there were four *adalats* as enumerated below: *Nizamat:* The Supreme Coutr of Criminal Justice, normally presided by the *Nazim/Subadar/Viceroy* of the province. This was sub-divided into the:

Roz-Adalat (i-a)or court held once in a week by the *Nazim* or *Subadar* for the trial of capital offenders.

Adalat-ul-Aaliyat (i-b) The high court in which quarrels and cases regarding personal property were tried. This court was normally presided by the deputies of the *Subadar* or the *Nazim*.

Adalat-i-Diwani (ii) The court deciding civil cases and was presided by the *Diwan.* q.v., the chief officer in charge of the revenue of the principality.

Adalat-i-Faujdari (iii) The court of the *Qazi*, q.g., the chief judge of a town or a district in civil cases and questions regarding the Muslim religion. Under him the *Muhtasib* held a court for the adjudication of offences against morals, i.e., gambling, drunkenness.

Adh-Batal: H ادھ بتائی Division of produce of land in equal shares between the landlord and the sub-tenant.

Adhia: ادھیا	H	Division of produce of land between two parties in equal proportions; one party furnishing the land and seed and the other the labour. The payment of half the annual assessment by the cultivators to the person who is responsible to the government for the revenue at the vernal and autumnal harvests.
Ahad-Dar: عہددار	P.A.	(*Ahad*: agreement; *dar* one who has) one who makes an agreement. An officer of the Mughal government, who for a percentage on the collection, engaged for the revenue of a district or a *pargana*, q.v.
Ahadi: احدی	A.P.	One of the class of *sawars*, q.v. in the Mughal cavalry. They were not under any *mansabdar* and had direct connection with the Emperor in their individual capacity. These *ahadis* brought their own horses at the time of employment and as such were paid high salaries in comparison to others. In case of death of their horses, the Government was obliged to replace them free of cost.
Ahal Kar: اہل کار	P	Agent; a clerk of the Zamindar or the Government.
Ahan: آہن	P	(*Ahan* means iron). A tax on the blacksmith.
Ahsham: احشام	A	Plural of *hashm*; followers, attendants, retinue. In Carnatic and the Deccan, a kind of irregular troops or militia employed chiefly as garrisons and as an armed police force.
Aimma: ائمہ	A	Land granted by the Mughal Government, either rent-free or subject to a small quit-rent, to learned and religious persons of the Muhammadan faith, or for the religious and charitable purposes in relation to Islam.

Aimma-Baz-Yaft: ائمہ بازیافت P Lapsed *aimma* grants or such grants subsequently assessed.

Aimma-Baz-i-Zamin: ائمہ باززمین A Land held rent-free or at a quit-rent under an *aimma* grant.

Aimma-Dar: ائمہ دار P Holder of land granted for religious or charitable uses or to religious or learned Muslims.

Aimma-Mauza: ائمہ موضع A.P. A village given as a charitable endowment to learned and religious persons.

Ain (C): ع ع A (The Arabic letter). The official counter-mark of the Wazir upon a royal mandate for an assignment of revenue under the Mughal Governments.

Ajir: آجر A A hired servant or labourer, a bondsman, a bond slave; one who has entered into an engagement for a stipulated sum to serve another for a specific term.

Akhbar-Nawis: اخبارنویس P In Mughal administration, there were three types of intelligencers who were charged with writing new letters to the Imperial directly or through certain channels. They were *harkara, waqai nawis,* and *waqai nigar*. All of them were called alike *akhbar-nawis.*

Akhir: آخر A The last assessment, the rate at which the revenue was last fixed.

Akhir-i-Sal: آخرِسال A.P. (*Sal* means year) The end of the revenue year.

Akhir Jama Tumari: آخرجمع طوماری A.P. Improved revenue from that fixed originally; applied especially to the revenues of provinces in the time of Muhammud Shah, as contrasted with those fixed during the reign of Akbar the Great.

Akhir-i-Hisab-Kharch آخر حساب خرچ	A.P.	Adjustment of the cultivators at the end of the year, showing the amount of revenue assessed, paid, and in arrears, with the items of deduction for expenses.
Akhir Jama Wasil Baqi آخر جمع واصل باقی	A.P.	Final settlement of the accounts of land owners or villages, crediting profits and receipt; debiting all disbursement and payments of revenue and adjusting the balance.
Al-Abd العبد	A	Form of counter-signature by subordinate officer or clerk (lit. Al; the and *Abd* means slave).
Al- Tamghah التمغہ	T	(*al* red and *tamgha*, a stamp or impression). A royal grant under the seal of some of the mughals of India and recognised by the State authorities as conferring a title to rent-free land in perpetuity, hereditary and transferable.
Amala عملہ	A	Ministerial offices; workers; clerks and remaining staff of a civil court collectively.
Amal-Dar عمل دار	A.P.	(*Amal,* business, authority and *dar*, one who has) A manager; an agent, a governor of a district; a collector of the revenue.
Amanat امانت	P	Office of the *Amin.*
Amani امانی	P	A term applied especially to the collection of revenue direct from cultivators by officers of government upon removal or suspension of an intermediate claimant or *zamindar* (landlord).
Amil عامل	A	An officer of government in the Department of Finance, especially a Collector of Revenue on the part of the Government, or of the

farmer of the revenue; also himself a farmer, or a contractor for; the revenue under the Mughal system; and invested with supreme authority, both civil and military, in the district which he formed.

Amin: امین A Trustee; revenue officer appointed to take charge of estate or for particular purposes of local investigation or arrangement.

Amir: امیر A (from *amr*, a command) A Mohammadan of high rank in the Mughal administration.

Amir-Al-Umara: امیر الامرا A Chief of Chiefs (a title of a *persona qrata*).

Anna: آنہ A An anna was usually equal to four paisas; A rupee during the Mughal period was equal to sixteen annas.

Arsath: اڑسٹھ H A monthly account of receipt and disbursement.

Arsatta: اڑسٹا H Estimates; a monthly treasury account of receipt and expenditure made up frpm the daily entries of register maintained in the Treasury.

Arz Begi: عرض بیگی P An office who presents and reads letters; representations to a king or great personage; an Usher.

Arz Dasht: عرض داشت P A written petition; letter addressed to the Emperor; an *Arzdasht* is more elaborate in form than an *Arzi.*

Arzi: عرضی A.P. Petition or humble representation, either moral or written; the technical term for a request to a superior from the side of an inferior.

Arzi Dawa: عرضی دعویٰ	P	A petition of complaint; the plaint; the first pleading in a law-suit.
Arz-i-Muqarrar: عرض مقرر	P	(*Muqarrar* mean established) A petition representing the circumstances of a case; a representation to the royal authority of the proceedings taken in respect of a grant of revenue or a *zamindari*.
Asalatan: اصالتاً	A	In person, personally; anti-thesis to *wakalatan* (i.e., through the *wakil* or agent).
Asami: آسامی	P	A cultivator; a non-propreitary cultivator, a defendant in a law suit.
Asami-Shikmi: آسامی شکمی	P	One who cultivates the land of another person and pays him a fixed rent.
Asami-Maurausi: آسامی موروثی	P	A hereditary farmer or cultivator; one who although not a proprietor, cannot be dispossessed as long as he pays a stipulated rent of land.
Asami-Pai Kasht: آسامی پائے کاشت	P	A man who cultivates land in a village without any hereditary right, a tenant at will.
Ashrafi: اشرفی	P	A gold coin (after the anem of a king named Ashraf) weighing about a *tola*. Different weights were assigned to this gold coing in different periods. During the reign of Farrukh Siyar, the weight of an *Ashrafi* was 11-1/2 *mashas,* i.e., less half *masha* in a *tola*., q.v.
Asli: اصلی		(From *asl*; original) original applied to a registered village under the Mughal system in opposition to *Dakhili* (one who was occupied subsequently).
Asl Dastawez: اصل دستاویز	P	an original document or record in contradictions to a copy.

Asl Jama: اصل جمع A — The original rent or revenue charged upon the lands of an estate or village or district, without any *abwab* (or extra cesses). q.v.; also the amount taken as the basis of a revenue settlement.

P — A party pleading his own case, the main party in a law suit.

Asl Tumar-Jama: اصل طومار جمع P — The original rent roll of the assessement of the land revenue in the Mughal provinces according to the register of Raja Todar Mal, in the reign of Akbar the Great.

Asmani-Farman: آسمانی فرمان P — A term used in deeds and leases, providing for any incidents or injuries arising from calamitous seasons or unjust exactions of the Government which, if affecting the land owner, the *ryots* engaged to make good.

Aurang: اورنگ P — Place where goods were manufactured; factory; also throne.

Awarja: اوارجہ A — A diary; a day book; an abstract account of receipt and disbursements. In Mughal revenue records, it denotes a revenue account, specifying, first and unproductive lands of a village, and then those paying revenue; field, jagir by jagir, arranged under the names of the occupants, with a specification in separate columns of the number of each field or jagir in the filed book, the quantity of land and kind of cultivation; the total rent or revenue paid by each occupant being also summed up. The *awarja* was to be submitted for the persual of the Emperor or Diwan at the time of granting land or jagir to a Mansabdar with a view to ascertain whether there is actually some paibaqi (q.v.) land left over for such assignment.

Awarja Jama Kharch: اوارجہ جمع خرچ — An account of receipt and expenditure.

B

Badar Navisi: بدرنویسی — P — Writing off items of an account which are objectionable or excessive. Audit of an account.

Badia: بادیہ — A — A tract of land, arable or otherwise, in desert, owned by some cultivator or not.

Badraqah: بدرقہ — A — A guide; a guard; an escort; safe conduct; also a charge for convoy formerly levied on mechandise (normally at the rate of one percent, as the expenses of keeping the highways and rivers safe from robbers). Offices into which the Government's duties were paid.

Bagar: بیگار — P — Compulsory labour generally without payment.

Baha-i-Khilat: بہائے خلعت — P.A. — (*Baha* (P) means cost, value, and *khilat* (a) means a dress of honour) a cess or tax added at so much percent to the ordinary revenue to defray the cost of the complimentary dresses or robes of honour granted by the Mughal emperors or Governors to persons whom they deemed proper so as to distinuguish.

Bahali: بحالی — Re-instated; re-established; restored to or replaced in; a former condition; restored to a situation or appointment.

Bahali-Sanad: بحالی سند — P — A grant restoring to a person possession or privileges of which had had been deprived, or confirming him in their enjoyment.

Bahangi: بہنگی — H — A stick or a pole with strings at both ends for carrying baskets, boxes etc. on shoulders.

During Mughal period, customs was levied as a whole on a bahangi full of load of commodities.

Bahangi-Bardar: بهنگی بردار H.P. The man who carries baggage etc. on *bahangi*, q.v.

Bahi: بہی H.P. A book of accounts. A journal, a diary, a ledger. This word in the Persian Records is commonly used to describe the volumes of copies of Persian letters. Thus *Bahi-i-huzuri* represents issues, and *Bahi-i-amadani* receipts.

Bahr-Dar: بہی دار A.P. A harbour master, an overseer of boats; a collector of port duties.

Bai Bil Wafa: بیع بالوفا A (Bai meant sale) conditional sale, sale depending for its completion on the consent of the seller. Aslo, the nominal sale of an article or land in lieu of a debt, to be returned when the debt is paid, or upon condition that the debt shall be paid by a given term, in default of which, the article or land becomes definitely the property of the purchaser.

Bai-Miadi: بیع میعادی A.P. Conditional or eventual sale.

Bai-Nama: بیع نامہ P.A. A deed of sale.

Bai-Sultani: بیع سلطانی P Sale of land or other property by the order of the Government.

Baiz: بیض A (A *sord* of cypher or monogram formerly affixed to a written paper in place of a signature by Mughal functionaries and persons of rank.

Baizana: بیضانہ A Fee paid to a magistrate or public officer for affixing his cypher to a deed or legal document.

Bajgir: باج گیر P — Tax collector, a collector of tribute or revenue.

Bajguzar: باج گذار P — A zamindar or land owner who was required to pay revenue of the land in his possession.

Bakhshi: بخشی P — Pay master in Muhammadam armies; general, commander-in-chief, an officer who kept an account of all disbursments connected with military tenures. It is originally a Mongolian word, under the Mongol system frequently one with the Commander-in-Chief.

Bakhshi-i-Aazam: بخشی عاظم P.A. — A title given to four Bakhshis in immediate attendance on the Emperor.

Bakhshi-al-Mulk: بخشی الملک P.A. — The Bakhshi of a province.

Bakhsh Bandar: بخشی بندر P — A harbour or custom master. Also, a custom house.

Bakhshi-al-Mumalik: بخشی المما لک P.A. — The Bakhshi of all the provinces. Usually this title was given to the Amir al-Umara, q.v. (i.e., the Prime Minister).

Banda-Wala-i-Bargah: بندہ والا بارگاہ P — (Slave of the exalted court) A noble man under the Mughal system charged with the diwani or revenue administration of a province and holding a jagir for his personal and official expenses.

Band-i-Jama: بندِ جمع — Distribution of the assessed lands among cultivators so as to allot to each an equal proportion of good and bad lands, and to make him responsible for a fixed proportion of both.

Band-o-Bast: بندوبست P — Settlement of revenue to be paid by zamindar, renter, or farmer to the government or by the tenant to the Zamindar.

Bando Bast Dawami: بندوبست دیوامی	P	Permanent or perpetual settlement.
Daul Bando-Bast: دول بندوبست	P	Particular statement of the manner in which the rental of an estate or district is subdivided.
Bando-Bast Miadi: بندوبست میعادی	P	Temporary settlement, one for a presecribed time.
Bangah: بنگاہ	P	Followers, suiters and baggage of an army.
Banjara: بنجارہ	H	Grain and cattle merchants who move about to different markets for transacting their business.
Baqaya Tajih: بقایا توجیہہ	P	An account of arrears of revenue for any given period of former years.
Badi-Dar: باقی دار	P	A person declared defaulter by the revenue department who is in arrears.
Baqi-Jama: باقی جمع	P	Statement of revenue after deducting the balances of former years.
Baqi-Zamin: باقی زمین	P	The balance of the land revenue after deducting any deficit from the preciding year.
Barani: بارانی	P	Applied to land, it signifies that which is watered by rain, not by irrigation.
Barat: برات	A	A record, a register, an assignment or order on the revenue.
Barawurd: برآورد	P	An estimate, a bill of salary. A monthly statement, submitted to Government of the revenue and village establishements of the sums payable to each person, and the increase as compared with preceding months. A statement of disbursments of the district.
Bardasht: برداشت	P	Stores, supplies, furnishing porters and provisions to Government officers and troops.

Barq Andaz: برق انداز	A.P.	A match-lock man but commonly applied to a person armed with sword and shield who acts as a door keeper or escort.
Batnan Bad Batnan: بطناً بعد بطناً	A	Generation after generation; a term inserted in a grant to denote its descent in the direct male line; it is understood to imply the right of perpetual descent to heirs general without restriction.
Battah: بٹہ	H	Weight. Difference or rate of exchange. In revenue matters it applies to the amount added to or deducted from any payment according to the currency in which it is paid as compared with a fixed standard coin. Discount on un-current or short-weight rupees. A cess or charge imposed to make up for any probable deficiency in the value of the coin.
Baz-i-Jama: بازجمع	A.P.	Miscellaneous revenue. Aggregate of revenue realized from sources other than the mal (revenue) and sair (customs and excise; as from fine for petty offences, fees, cesses etc.).
Baz-i-Khurch: بازخرچ	A.P.	Miscellaneous expenses. An item in revenue accounts for sundry charges not included in the fixed regular disbursement. A deduction in accounts of the revenue allowed to land owners to cover their claims, for compensation of expenses incurred in collection of the revenue, repairs of roads and bridges, including some thing additional by way of remuneration for their public services.
Baz-i-Zamin: باززمین	P	Land exempted from assessment. Any land paying no revenue or a light quiet-rent only to the government held under different tenures.

Bel Dar:	بیلدار	P	A digger, a miner.
Beopari:	بیوپاری	H	Merchant, dealer, trader.
Bhat:	بھاٹ	H	Learnerd man, scholar, philosopher, a title of Maratha Brahmans.
Bidahand:	بدہند	P	A superscription of assent by the Emperor on a petition for an assignment of revenue.
Bigah:	بیگھ	H	Measure of land varying in extent in different parts of India. Standard bigha is equal to 3025 sq.yds. or 5/8ths of an acre.
Bila-Bandi:	بلابندی	P	Doing anything, as cultivating land, pending the final adjustment of the conditions.
Bila Shart:	بلاشرط	P	Or Bila mashrut; unconditional, absolute; a grant of land or mansab without any condition, as of service etc. being attached to it.
Bilah-Bandi:	بلہ بندی		An account of the revenue settlement of a district, specifying the name of each mahal, the farmer of it and the amount of the rent.
Biswa:	بسوہ	H	Twentieth part of a bigha.
Bisli:	بستی	P	(or bisi) twenty.
Biyutat:	بیوتات	A	(plural of bait, a house). A term applied to lands that were originally assigned to the members of the royal family, but had come under general cultivation.
Bud-Na-Bud:	بودنہ بود	P	(or basb-na. bud) Remission of rent on failure of crops.

C

Cachehri:	کچہری	H	A court, an office, a public place where any public business is transacted.
Cash	کاش		A copper coin of low value current in south India, eighty of which made one fanam.
Chabutra:	چبوترہ	H	Custom house, a market place.
Chahi:	چاہی	P	Land irrigated from wells.
Chakla:	چکلہ	H	A large division of a province comprehending a number of parganas; first introduced as a recognised local division in the reign of the Mughal Emperor, Shahjahan.
Chakla Nawis:	چکلہ نویس	P	The accountant of the revenues and charges of a *Chakla.*
Chalan:	چالان	H	An invoice, a voucher, a pass, à document sent with goods or treasure.
Chaudhri:	چودھری	H	A headman or a caste or a village—a holder of a landed property classed with the Zamindar and *Taalluaqadar.*
Chuk:	چوک	H	A quadrangle, a courtyard; an open place in a town where the market is held.
Chatr:	چتر (چھتر)	P	Literally an umbrella, a costly umbrella used by the *kings* and emperors of India.
Chaubdar:	چوب دار	P	A male bearer. An officer who carries a silver or gold staff and whose business is to announce the arrival of a visitor (Chaub=stick; dar=bearer).
Chauki:	چوکی	H	Station of police or customs.

Chauaki-dar چوکی دار H.P. (Dar P.) Watchman. A peon of the police or customs department.

Chauth: چوتھ S An assessment equal to one fourth of the original assessment or generally to one-fourth of the actual government collections demanded by the Mahrattas from the Mughal and Hindu princes of India as the price of forbearing to ravage their countries.

Chehra: چہرہ P Descriptive roll of a royal servant or army man.

Chittha: چٹھا H A rought journal or daybook. Register of pay of royal employees. Particular statement of the measurement of a landowners' estate founded on actual measurement. It also applies to an account of all the lands in a village, divided numerically into *daghs* or shares, showing the quantity of land in each, the type of cultivation and the name of the cultivators. Also, a field book, more usually termed *Khasra*, an account of all the lands of a village, according to their allotment, in the order in which they have been measured.

Chiraghi: چراغی P (Chiragh mean lamp) An allowance or tankhwah for keeping a lamp or lamps constantly burning at the tomb of a Muslim saint or for the purpose of illuminating a place of worship.

Chungi: چنگی A handful of grain levied as a tax or fee for weighing or as a compensation for the use of market convenience as bags booths.

D

Dadani: دادنی P Paying in advance. Advancing pay to labourors or manufacturers; any additional grant or allowance.

Dafadar:	دفعہ دار	A.P.	Officer commanding a small body of cavalry or infantry; head of a party of police constables.
Daftar:	دفتر	P	A book, volume or register; also any office.
Dagh-i-Tashiha:	داغِ تصحیحہ		The office where the horses of the mansabdars were mustered and branded. The officer had to issue a tashiba nama to each mansabdar that he brought his horses for the purpose of verification. On the productioon of such certificate, the jagir or tankhwah was continued to the assignee otherwise it was confiscated till such certificate was procured by the mansabdars and submitted for the persual of the Diwan of the suba.
Dagh:	داغ	P	A spot, a mark with hot iron, a brand, especially such a mark stamped on the necks of horses belonging to the mansabdars of the Mughal reign so as to avoid any double crossing by them at the time of their verification by the competent authority for the purpose of ascertaining the fact whether they actually maintained the number they were asked to at the time of the grant of the mansab.
Dak:	ڈاک	H	Post or transport by relays of men or horses.
Dakhnian:	دکھنیاں	H	(Dakhkhan means south) those who belong to the south, i.e., the Marathas.
Dakhl:	دخل	A	Taking possession, occupancy. The terms is used to denote that the entry has been made in the register of revenue accounts.
Dakhl-Nama:	دخل نامہ	P	A deed of possessioon. A document giving right of occupancy.

Dakhil: داخل A Entry of an item in a deed or register. Inclusion of a minor in a major parcel of the land.

Dakhil-Kharij: داخل خارج P (or Madakhil o Makharij) Entering and ejecting, erasure of an entry. Removal of the name of old landowner and insertion of the new proprietor's name in revenue registers at the time of transfer of land or property.

Dakhil Daftar: داخل دفتر A.P. Entered upon the record which is equivalent to being laid on the table or postponed indefinitely.

Dakhili: داخلی P Included: applied especially to villages which have become induced in the revenue list of villages paying revenue, having branched off from, and being dependent upon; those on which the assessment was originally levied; and which are therefore termed *asli*, q.v. (original) in position dakhili, the subordinate or included.

Dallal: دلّال A A broker; an agent between buyers and sellers.

Dam: دام H.P. A copper coin or a measure of money. In the days of Akbar the Great, a rupee could be divided into forty dams whereas during the reign of Alamgir, 46/1/3 dams, at a later period 80 and 90 are in the proportionate rates which appear to have been liable to great fluctuations.

Dam Dari: دام داری P A branch of revenue arising from fowlers, players, musicians etc.

Dam-i-Wasilat: دامِ واصلات Gross assets of a village.

Damrhi: دمڑی H A nominal coin of the value of 3-1/8 or 3-1/4 dams or from eight to twelve kauris.

Daramad: درآمد	P	(In its present sense it means imports) An account of fees paid for serving a process, the return of a process.
Darbandi: دربندی	P	An item in the village accounts, statements of proportianate rates of revenue payment.
Darbar: دربار	P	A court of the Emperor. A hall of audience.
Dar-Bast-i-Aimma دربست ائمّہ	P	Grant of the whole of the lands, constituting a rent free estate.
Dargah: درگاہ	P	A court of the Emperor. It is more usually applied to a Muslim shrine or the tomb of some reputed holy person, and the object of worship and pilgrimage.
Dar Hawala: درحوالہ	A.P.	Sub-tenure, holding a farm on lease from a landowner or lessee.
Dar Ijara: دراجارہ	A.P.	A sub-lease or farm.
Dar In Wala: درایں ولا		A phrase heading official papers in the Mughal revenue records in the south of India, implying in this case or this time, by these presents.
Darkhawst: درخواست	P	A petition, an application. In revenue matters, the representation of the proprietor of an estate as to the amount of the revenue he is able to pay or proposal for renting or farming an estate or any branch of the government revenue.
Dar Mustajir: درمستاجر	P	(Mustajir means a tenant) A sub-lessee, or tenant holding of a farmer, not of the land owner (Zamindar).
Dar-o-Bast: درو بست	P	Entire, whole. The whole of a district of estate as opposed to *qismat* (or portion of it).

Darogha: داروغہ	P.M.	It is a Mongolian word used in Persian known as Superintendent, Manager or Inspector of police and revenue departments.
Darogha Arz-i-Mukarrar: داروغہ عرضِ مکرّر	P	An officer under the Mughal government, whose duty was to draw up an abstract of papers which required the assent of the emperor, and present them for confirmation and signature. He was mainly charged with the superintendence of the assignments to the *mansabdars*, for the horses, they maintained by virtue of the *mansab* assigned to them.
Darogha Dagh-i-Tashiha: داروغہ داغ تصحیحہ	P	Officer in charge of the Daftar Dagh-i-Tashiha.
Dastak: دستک	P	Passport; permit or license.
Dastak Talah-i-Zar: دستک طلب زر	P	Warrant issued against defaulters of revenue, demanding payment and subjecting them to the expenses of maintaining the officer who serves it until the amount is paid.
Dastawez: دستاویز	P	Any legal paper, a bond, a title deed. Anything in writing produceable in evidence or by which a person may be bound in law. A certificate of any kind.
Dastbar-Dari: دست برداری	P	A petition for withdrawl of a suit from a court of law.
Dast-Baqi: دست باقی	P	Balance in hand, money collected but not brought to account, whether referring to balances in the hands of revenue collectors or the collections made and embezzled by them.
Dast Gardan: دست گرداں	P	A loan without any voucher.
Dastur: دستور	P	A commission or percentage on the collections of the revenue allowed by the Mughal government to the zamindars.

Dastural-Aml: دستورالعمل — A — A body of rules and regulations for the guidance of revenue officials.

Daul or Dawal: دول — A — Estimate, valuation. A statement of the particulars of the gross revenue levied from an estate or district. An estimate of the amount of revenue which a district or estate may be expected to yield.

Daul Nama: دول نامہ — P — Extract from the general particulars of an estimated assessment, for the information of the person paying, supplied to him as a *patta* or lease.

Deshmukh: دیش مکھ — A hereditary native officer under the Mughal government exercising chief police and revenue authority over a district, containing a certain number of villages, and responsible for collecting revenue and depositing it into the treasury.

Des Kulkarni: دیس کلکرنی — Mar — The district accountant. One who prepares a general account of various statements of accounts of the villages under the supervision of the district concerned.

Deshpanday: دیشپانڈے — Mar — The hereditary revenue accountant of a district or sarkar or a certain number of villages holding office by hereditary tenure and paid by lands.

Desh Mukhi: دیش مکھی — Mar — The fees levied by a *desh mukh* or his account, The office of a *desh mukh.*

Dih: دیہہ — P — A village, comprehending not only the actual village but the lands belonging to it.

Dihat: دیہات — A.P. — (An Arabic plural to a Persian noun dih, q.v.) villages collectively, as opposed to towns.

Dihati Jama: دیہات جمع — P.A. — Village assessment, revenue assessed upon any number of villages forming a local division.

Dih Bandi: دیہہ بندی — P — A detailed statement of the villages in any particular district and of the revenue assessed on each; such statements were to have been prepared by the *Qanungos* at the time of the decennial settlement and deposited in collector's offices.

Dirah: درہ — A — A dirah is equal to a yard.

Disai: ڈیسائی — Mar — The superintendent or ruler of a pargana or province, the principal revenue officer of a district. This office was hereditary and frequently recompensated by grants of land.

Diwan: دیوان — P — A minister, a chief officer of state. Under the Muhammadan government, the title was especially applied to the head financial minister, whether of the state or of a province. In the latter case, its owner was charged with the collection of the revenue, and the remittance of it to the Imperial treasury, and was invested with extensive judicial powers in all civil and financial cases. The title also denoted the head officer of any revenue or financial department.

Diwani: دیوانی — P — Office of the Diwan; the right to collect and receive the revenue of the country.

Diwani Adalat: دیوانی عدالت — P — Civil court.

Diwan Khanah: دیوان خانہ — P — (Khanah, a house). The court or office of diwan; a court of civil or revenue jurisdiction; a hall of audience.

Doury

(Dhori) (Deorhi): دیوڑھی H — Service land or lands granted rent free by zamindars to village servants, to poor relatives, or religious mendicants. Lands for the queen and others of the royal household.

F

Falus: فلوس P — A small copper coin of varying weight and value and sometimes applied to paisa of Hindustan.

Fanam: فنام — (Originally falam but more properly phalam). It was anciently a gold coin, but latterly of silver, or sometimes of base gold. It bore various local values but according to the old Madras monetary system, prevailing till 1818, forty two fanams went to one star pagoda.

Fara: فرعہ P — A term used in the Mughal revenue record for the increased revenue derived from new taxes. (lit. above, over).

Fara Faujdari: فرعہ فوجداری A.P. — The produce of the *faujdari* or criminal court arising from fines and confiscations (*zabti*) carried to the credit of the government.

Fard: فرد A — A single thing or individual, a sheet of paper, a list or statement, a long slip of writing containing a list, a catalogue, etc.

Fard-i-Haqiqat: فردحقیقت A.P. — A statement of circumstances. A return made by the officers of the government to a requisition for information.

Farid-i-: فردسوال A.P. — (Lit. a petition, an application). The recommendation report of a revenue officer in favour of the grant of a *zamindari sanad* to the person named in the application, and specifying the districts to be granted.

Term	Origin	Meaning
Fard-i-Tashkhish: فرد تشخیص	A.P.	(From Tashkhish; settlement). Recorded of a revenue settlement.
Farigh Khati: فارغ خطی	A.P.	A written receipt and acquittance, a deed of release from all demands, a deed of dissolution of partnership or of parcenership, a bill of divorcement.
Fariq-i-Awwal: فریق اول	A.P.	The first party in a suit.
Fariq-i-Sani: فریق ثانی	A.P.	The second party in a suit.
Farmaish: فرمائش	P	A royal commission to execute any work.
Farman: فرمان	A	Royal grant or charter.
Farzi: فرضی	A	By way of proposition, fictitions. It is applied especially to a person who is either altogether an imaginary party in a suit or purchase, or to one who, although the ostensible, is not the real principal, or to a suit or purchase conducted by or effected under an assumed or fictitious name.
Farzi Muddai: فرضی مدعی	A.P.	A fictitious plaintiff or prosecutor.
Farzi Muqaddama: فرضی مقدمہ	A.P.	A fictitious suit or prosecution; one set on foot by other ostensible parties than those really interested.
Faslana: فصلانہ	A.P.	Relating to the harvest or the crop; a fee or perquisite derived from it.
Fasl: فصل	A	(Lit. to divide). In revenue records it means a section of the year pertaining to a crop or harvest. There are still two principal harvests in the year spring and autumn, to which a third is sometimes added.

Fasli Fuslee, corruptly,

Fassily, Fusly: فصلی A.H. Belonging to the harvest, or season when cultivated, or lands, productive of crops assessed according to the value of the crops, or frequency and abundance of the harvests. The harvest year—a mode of computing time prevailing throughout India, and one of the forms used in giving a date to all public orders and regulations. The era originated with the emperor Akbar, who, finding different eras current, thought to simplify the existing chronology by introducing a new mode of computing time. In fact, however, he only aggravated the confusion, by adding to the number; the old eras still continuing to be current along with the new. According to Akbar's directions the year of the Samvat, corresponging with the Hijra year 962=A.D. 1555, and which was therefore Samvat 1612 (1555+57), was arbitrarily shown of 649 years, and called the Fasli year 963, the name as the Hijra. Startling from this point, it has since gone on concurrently with the Samvat, or luni-solar year of the Hindus; so that by adding 649 years to the fasli year, we got the Samvat year; and by adding 592-93, the difference of the Christian date. The Fasli year began on the 10th of the lunar month Aswin, corresponding to the 10th September 1555: if more than four months of the year have expired, the addition is 593. Thus, the date of Reg. i., 10th February 1833, corresponds with the 1st of Phalgun 1889 (1833+56) Samvat, and with the 1st of Phalgun 1240 (1833-593) Falsi. In the Dakhin, the Fasli year is reckoned somewhat differently, being two years later than the same year in Hindustan, having been introduced by Shah Jahan. The addition to the Fasli therefore, to convert it into the

Christian year, is only 590; thus, the Bomb. Reg. dated Fasli 1239 is equivalent to A.D. (1239+590) 1829. The Tamil year of Fasli, 1257-58, corresponds with 1848 (=1258-590). The Madras government fixed its commencement to the 12th July. Its subdivision are little attended to, as its sole use is its application to revenue matters; and the year only is specified, not the months.

Fasil-i-Bhadonwi: فصل بھدونوی — This is an intermediate harvest of occasional cultivation, consisting of grains of quick growth as millet and different sorts of pulses which may be sown at the commencement of the rainy season, and gathered in the month of September. This is, however, commonly included in Kharif crops.

Fasl-i-Kharif: فصل خریف — A.P. — The autumnal harvest, consisting chiefly of rice, or grains requiring irrigation. The seed is sown at the beginning of the rainy season, and the crop is usually reaped after their close, or in months of October and November.

Fasl-i-Rabi: فصل ربیع — A.P. — The spring harvest, which yields dry crops as wheat, barley, different kinds of pulse and grain that do not require irrigation or much water. The seed is sown towards the close of the periodical rains or in the months of September, February and March.

Fatwa: فتویٰ — A — A judicial decree, sentence or judgement, a notification of the decision of the Muslim law particularly one delivered by a *Mufti* or a doctor of law; q.v.

Faujdar: فوج دار — P — (Fauj, army and dar, one who has). An officer under Mughal rule, who was invested with the charge of the police and jurisdiction in all criminal matter; a Mughal commander of army.

Term	Origin	Meaning
Faujdari: فوج داری	P	The office of a faujdar.
Fauj-Sar Anjam: فوج سرانجام	A.P.	Lands or revenue exclusively assigned for the maintenance of troops or of police force and forts.
Fauj Sih Bandi: فوج سہ بندی	P	The troops of the faujdar, provincial troops or militia employed in garrisoning forts, escorting treasure, and in revenue and police duties.
Fauti: فوتی	A	(From faut, death). A person deceased, or one who is legally defunct, from profligacy or any legal disqualifications. The property of one who dies intestate and without legal heirs, which therefore reverts to the Emperor.
Fauti Farari: فوتی فراری	A.P.	A list or register containing names of cultivators, officers, armymen etc. who have died or have deserted their homesteads.
Feringhee: فرنگی		Term usually applied in early days to Portuguese settlers in India; later used for all Europeans generally.
Fihrist: فہرست	P	A list, an inventory, a catalogue.
Fotah: فوطہ	P	A bag of money, tax, revenue, land tax, annual rent of cultivated land.
Fotah Dar: فوطہ دار	P	A banker, a cash keeper, a money changer; An officer for weighing money and bullion and examining and valuing coins—(In Hindi Fotah dar is called Pod-dar).
Fotah Dari: فوطہ داری	A.H.	Office of the fotah-dar where cash was accumulted.
Fotah Khana: فوطہ خانہ	P	A banking house, treasury, a money changer's shop.

Furuz:	فروض	A	(Plural of farz) shares, portions, the portions in which the property is divided among those entitled to inherit.

G

Ganda:	گنڈہ	H	A money of account equivalent in reckoning to four kauris or the 20th part of an anna.
Ganj:	گنج	P	A mart; a market.
Gaz:	گز		A measurement of length equal to 3 feet or 36 inches. It had 16 girahs, q.v.
Ghair Band-o-bast:	غیر بندوبست	P	Unsettled; applied to those lands which are not included in revenue settlement.
Ghair Jama:	غیر جمع	P	Land not paying revenue or rent-free.
Ghair Mashrut:	غیر مشروط	P	Unconditional; applied to those lands which are granted to persons or mansabdars etc. without any stipulations of service, or the like being attached to them.
Ghat:	گھاٹ	H	Landing place on the bank of a river. A quay, a wharf where customs are commonly levied.
Girah:	گرہ	P	A measurement of length. A girah is equal to a nail. 16 girahs were equal to a gaz (yard) and a girah is equal to about 2 inches.
Girdawar:	گرد آور	H	A patrol, a watch, a guard, a superintendent or Inspector of Police, or customs or forests.
Golandaz:	گولنداز	P	A gunner, cannonier, bombardier.
Goshwara:	گوشوارہ	P	An embroidered cloth worn by Mughal chiefs as ornament over the sides of a turban. An abstract statement, giving the substance of

different documents, the abstract or sum of a village or zamindari account, showing the total quantity of land, its distribution, as waste, cultivated, follow, productive etc. made up from chittas (q.v.). An index, a summary of statements etc.

Gumashta: گماشتہ — P — An agent, or representative appointed by zamindar or Jagirdar to collect his rent or by a merchant to carry on his trade in different places where he did not reside.

Gaon-Nisbat Inam: — P — Land granted rent-free by the village out of its own lands; the loss or deduction thence accruing to the government assessment being made good by the village community-there were many kinds of such grants.

Gunjaish: گنجائش — P — (Lit. profit, gain). In revenue terms, it is applied to the capabilities of a village particularly with reference to a proposed increase in revenue. Excess of the real over the recorded area of a *zamindari*.

Guzar-Ban: گزربان — A — An officer appointed to take both on highways (roads) and at ferries in the river and sea.

H

Had-o-Bast: حدوبست — P — (Also *had bandi*) settlement and demarcation of boundaries.

Hafiz-i-Daftar: حافظ دفتر — A.P. — Keeper of records, a servant or officer who has charges of the books of daftar or an office.

Hal: حال — A — State, condition, present or actual condition. In revenue accounts, the actual state of the collections.

Hali: حالی | A | (Literally; present, actual new) as applied to coins, current.

Hal-i-Hasil: حالِ حاصل | P | The actual produce or revenue of any tract of land.

Hal Hasili: حال حاصلی | P | Actually productive, land yielding revenue varying with the crops growing upon it.

Hal-i-Haqiqat: حالِ حقیقت | P | Statement of the actual condition of an estate, an account showing the amount of revenue to be paid by each cultivator to government or landowner and the items of which it consists.

Hal-i-Jama: حالِ جمع | P | The actual rent or revenue payable to the government.

Hal-i-Taujih: حالِ توجیہ | P | An account of the revenue collections for the current period.

Harkara: ہرکارہ | H.P. | Harkaras wre also public intelligencers. They were posted in a province for reporting news of all sides and occurrences to the governor of the Suba and to send letters closed in envelopes for being despatched to the imperial court with the provincial post. These harkaras also kept their agent in the offices of nazim, subadar, faujdar, thanadar, etc.

Hasb-Al-Hasil: حسب الحاصل | A | According to the produce; land paying revenue according to the kind and value of the crops.

Hasb-Al-Hukm: حسب الحکم | A | According to command. The initial words and thence the title, of a document issued agreeably to royal authority, by the Wazir (Minister) or other high ranking officer of the government.

Hasb-Al-Wusul: حسب الوصول		(Literally according to collections or receipts): The term formerly used in revenue accounts to designate items of an uncertain value, of which no estimate can be computed, and which are entered only after their actual receipt.
Hasbul Hukm: حسب الحکم	A	The initial words and thence the title, of a document issued agreeably to royal authority by the wazir, diwan, or other high officers of the government.
Hasil: حاصل	A	Produce, profit, especially as a revenue term, the amount derived from the government. Share of the produce of the soil, and from any other source of taxation or import; revenue, tax, duty.
Hasil Zamin: حاصلِ زمین	A.P.	Land in cultivation and paying revenue.
Hast-o-Bud: ہست و بود	P	(*Hast,* is, and bud, was). A comparative account showing the present and past produce of an estate; an examination of the asserts or resources of a country made before the harvest, and sometimes after measurement of the lands; a detailed statement of any land yielding revenue; the rent roll of a village signed yearly by the village *mutasaddi* (accountant); the common form is an abstract of each cultivator's account, specifying his tenure, the amount of revenue payable by him, the quantity of land in or out of cultivation, and the amount of revenue realized or in arrear.
Hat: ہاٹ	H	A market. A moveable market, one held only on certain days in a week.
Haq-dar: حق دار	P	(*Haq* means right and *dar* means one who has). The holder of a right, a person vested with any property or priviledge, the holder of a share (of the revenue or the crops) a government or the village officer who claims

		prescriptive rights or fees, one who makes a claim or demands a right, a claimant.
Haq-i-Havala Dar: حق حوالدار	A.P.	Right of the *Havala dar*, an officer appointed either by the land owner or the government). A portion of grain given to the officer of the landlord employed to collect the revenue from sub tenants usually at the rate of seer and a half per maund (of forty seers).
Haq-i-Intifa: حق انتفاع	A.P.	Revenue profits on payment of the government demand).
Haq-i-Raaya: حقِ رعایا	A.P.	The right of the farmer of a land, his right of occupation while paying the demand of the government, or the land owner and his right to the established share of the crop.
Haq-i-Shufa: حق شفع	P	Right of pre-emption in a person whose possession adjoin those for sale.
Haqiqat: حقیقت	A	(From *haq*) statement of accounts or revenue; representation of circumstances as they are.
Haqiqat-i-Jama Tumar: حقیقت جمع طومار	A.P.	(From *Jama*) aggregate and *tumari* (registered)—particular account of the public revenue agreeably to the recorded rates.
Haq-i-Zamindar: حقِ زمین داری	P	The right or dues of a zamindar agreeably to the sanad by which he holds his lands or his engagements with the government.
***Hawalah dar* (Hawaldar):** حوالہ دار	A.P.	(From Hawala, trust, dar, one who has). An officer of the Imperial forces.
Haweli: حویلی	A	A house, habitation. The tract of country adjacent to a capital town and originally annexed to it for the supply of the public establishments.

Hazari: هزاری P (From hazar, a thousand). A commander of thousand either nominally or actually; in later case it was an honorary military title at the Imperial court of the Mughal, borne by civil as well as military functionaries.

Hazrat-Firdaus Aram Gah: P حضرت فردوس آرام گاه Posthumous title of Muhammad Shah.

Hijra: ہجرا H.A. Literally. Departure from one's country, separation of friends or lovers; whence it gives name to the departure of flight of Mohammed from Mecca to Medina, which, in the Khilafat of Omar, was constituted as the commencement of the Mohammadan era; this event took place on the night of Thursday the 15th of July, A.D. 622. The usual era therefore reckons from the dawn of the 16th of July. The Mohammadan year is strictly lunar, consisting of twelve months, each of which should count from the actual visibility of the new moon; but chronologically the months are completed at 30 and 29 days alternately, making the year consist of 354 days; but eleven times in a cycle of thirty years one day is added to the year, which makes the average length of the Mohammedan lunar year 354-11/30 days, or 354d. Shrs. 48 min., and the average length of the months 29d. 12 hrs. 44 min. The intercalary years of the cycle are the 2nd, 5th 8th, 10th, 13th, 16th, 19th, 21st, 24th, 27th and 29th. To ascertain if any given year be an intercalary year, it is to be divided by 30, when one of the specified numbers will be the remainder; thus A.H. 1137 divided by 30=37, leaving 27, and it will be therefore the 27th year of the cycle. The rule given by Major Jervis, from Professor Carlysle, for finding the corresponding years of the Hijra and the Christian era, is only an approximation: "Multiply the centuries of the year by 3, and add to the product for the years over the century as many times as it may be divided by 33, deduct the total from the whole number, and add to the remainder 621; thus. Required the year of our Lord corresponding to the year Hijra 1396; then 13X3=39, to which add 2, the quotient of 96 divided by33, making 41; then 1396-41=1355+621=A.D. 1976. That this is not correct in cases where the number in excess of the centuries, is a trifle less than 33, or a trifle more than any of its multiples is evident from a comparison with the standard tables: for instance, the year 1132 should be, according to this rule, A.D. 1720, but it begins 14th November 1719 according to the tables: so 1198 should be 1784, but in the table it begins 26th November 1783. The result, however, is near enough for general purposes, requiring correction only as to the period at which the year commences. Another rule for the same is—Multiply the Hijra year by 970203, cut off six decimals, add 622. 54, and the sum will be the year of the Christian era, and decimal of the day following, in old style; thus, A.H. 1215 X 970203=1178.796645, leaving 1178 + 622.54 = 1800.54. The Hijra year commences on the 25th May; so that this again is only an approximation. A more simple form and one which also shows the day on or about which the concurrence of the Mohammadan and Christian year commences, is the following: Multiply the Hijra year by 2.977, the difference between 100 solar and as many lunar Mohammadan years; divide the product by 100, and deduct the quotient from the Hijra year; add to the result 621.596 (the decimal being the equivalent of the 15th July, *plus* 12 days for the change of the Kalendar); and the quotient will be the Christian year from the date at which the Mohammadan year begins; thus, Hij. 1269 X 2.977 = 3778, which divided by

100 = 37.778 and 1269-37.778 = 1231.222 + 621.596 = 1852.791, or to 9 months and 15 days, i.e., the 15th of October, which is the commencement of the Hijra year 1269. The reverse formula for finding the corresponding Hijra year to a given Christian year is thus laid down; Subtract 622 from the current year; multiply the result by 1. 0307; cut off four decimals, and add. 46; the sum will be the year, which when it has a surplus decimal, requires the addition of 1: thus, 1852-622=1230; 1230 X 1.0307 = 12 7.7610 + 46 = 1268.22; add therefore I, and we have the equivalent Hijra year 1279. Comparative tables of the Christian and Mohammadan years are to be found in 'Art de verifier less dates," "Playfairs' Chronology," "Prinsep's Useful Tables," Calcutta, and "M'Cudden's Oriental Eras", Bombay, 1846; but they are not always quite correct. The months of the Mohammadan year, and the number of days in each, are the following:—

1.	Muharram	days 30
2.	Safar	,, 29
3.	Rabia-ul-awal..	,, 30
4.	Rabia-us-sani..	,, 29
5.	Jumadi-ul-awal..	,, 30
6.	Jumadi-us-sani..	,, 29
7.	Rajab..	,, 30
8.	Shaban..	,, 29
9.	Ramazan..	,, 30

10.	Shawal..	,, 29
11.	Zilkade, or Zulkata..	,, 30
12.	Zilhijja, or Zulhijja..	,, 29

except in the intercalory years, when this last month has also 30 days. The Mohammadans in India commonly employ the Persian names of the days of the week, which are, for the first five only, the numerals prefxed to the work Shamba, "a day"; or sometimes the Arabic names which are similarly composed with *Yaum.* "a day", and the numerals as far as five: the sixth and seventh have special denominations; as,

Sunday	Ey-shamba	Yaum-ul-ahad,
Monday	Do-Shamba	------ul-isnain,
Tuesday	Seh-shamba	------us-salasa,
Wednesday	Chahar-shamba	------ul-arbaa
Thursday	Panj-shamba, or Jumarat	------ul-khamis,
Friday	Juma, (the day of assembly or prayer)	------ul-juma,
Saturday	Shamba, or Hafta, (the 7th)	-----us..sabat, (the Sabbath).

Hijri: ہجری H Relating to the Hijra, or Mohammadan era.

Hudu-i-Arba: حدودارلع A Boundaries of the four sides of a land or landed property.

Hukm: حکم Orders issued by the Emperor.

Hun: ہن

It is a common term used by Muslim writers for pagoda. It signifies gold in the old Carnatic language. The hun was subdivided into *fanams* or *panams* and 'cash' or 'kas'. The old *faman* was of gold only and was 1/60 of a *hun*. The division adopted by the English was word two. '*Kas*' may be a corruption of the Sanskrit word *'Karsha'*. Eight '*kas*' made one *fanam*. The accounts were formarly kept at Madras in Pagoda, *fanams* and '*kas*'.

Hundi: ہنڈی H Bill of exchange (also *hundawi*).

Huzur Tahsil: حضور تحصیل

(Or *Tahsil-i-huzur*-tahsil means collection of revenue) Collection of revenue by the Chief fiscal officer appointed by the Government, without the intervention of a third party.

Huzuri: حضوری A

Relating to the chief authority, to the local or central government, under the Mughal Government the term was sometimes applied to such lands as paid revenue to the Diwan or financial representative of the Imperial government in opposition to the *Nizamat* lands which paid revenue to the Nazim or the *Vice-ray Sub-a-dar.*

Huzuri Taalluq: حضوری تعلق A.P.

A certain district called a *taaluq* (an estate, a dependence) paying revenue direct to the Government, usually known as independent talluq, that which is not held of any other owner or revenue payer.

I

Ibra Nama: ابرانام A.P.

A written acquittance or relinquishment of a claim by a man who holds title over it.

ID: عید A

Muhammadan festival. Two important ids of Muslims are Id al-fitr and Id-al-zuha. Id al-fitr is celebrated after the end of month of Ramzan during which Muslims keep fast. In this Id, new clothes are worn and grains are distributed among the poors in charity. On Id al-zuha, Muslims sacrifice animals and distribute the meat in poors, etc.

Iharah: احاره — A — A contract; a monopoly; price, profit; especially employed to denote a lease or form of land held at a defined rent or revenue, whether from government direct, or from an intermediate payer of the public revenue; a farm or lease of the revenue of a village or pargana or mahal also of customs or collections of any description, as of customary fees or allowances; any items of revenue, letting lands on farm or lease; the lands so let.

Ihtimamdar: اہتمام دار — A.P. — A superintendent, a supervisor, a manager; the holder of a trust, the officer charged with the realisation of a stipulated revenue for a certain district or pargana under the Muslim government, a zamindar; also an agent or a deputy of the zamindar (land-lord) appointed by him to realise the revenue of any portion of his zamindari.

Ijarah-Dar: اجارہ دار — A.P. — A farmer of any item of public revenue, whether from land customs, or any other source; the renter of a village or estate at a stipulated rate.

Ijmali Mahal: اجمالی محال — P — (From mahal; an estate). An un-divided estate, one held in parcenership by the heirs of a common ancestor.

Ikhrajat-i-: اخراجات اورنگ — P — Expenses of the *aurang* (factory or commercial firms). In the accounts of the salt revenue, the term included the expenses incurred in the manufacturing, storing and transport of the salt.

Ilahi-Gaz: الٰہی گز	P.A.	The standard yard of forty one fingers. It was instituted by Akbar the great.
Ilaqa-Dar: علاقہ دار	P	The person who engages, either on his own account or as the representative or others, for the payment of the assessed revenue upon a district or a village.
Imam-Barha: امام باڑہ	H	Building in which Muharram (q.v.) is celebrated and services are held in commemoration of the death of Ali (fourth Khalifa) and his sons Hassan and Husayn.
Inam: انعام	A	(Literally, a gift). A gift from superior to his inferiors. In southern and central India, the term was especially applied to grants of land held rent-free and in hereditary and perpetual occupation; the tenure came in time to be qualified by the reservation of a portion of the assessable revenue, or by the exaction of all proceeds exceeding the intended value of the original assignment; the term was also vaguely applied to grants of rent free land, without reference to the perpetuity or any specified conditions. The grants are also distinguishable by their origin from the ruling authorities, or from the village communities and are again distinguishable by peculiar reservations or by their being applicable to different objects. They are first calssed as: *Sanad-i-inam* or *Gaon-nisbat-inak.*
Iqrar-Nama:	اقرارنامہ	A deed of of agreement or acknowledgement.
Isma Navis: اسم نویس	P	The officer charged with the duty of writing names of all the zamindars of a district.
Istambar: استمرار	A	(Continuance, perpetuity). A farm or lease granted in perpetuity by the government or the land owner at a stiuplated rent and exempt from *abwabs,* q.v. such a lease granted in charity at a quit rent.

Istardad: استرداد — A — Demanding or ordering restitution of anything, whether given, pledged or sold.

Itlaq: اطلاق — A — Foes paid suitor on the decision of their cases; also a fee exacted from a defendant as wages for a peon or speoy stationed over him as soon as complaint was preferred against him.

Itlaq Nawis: اطلاق نویس — A — The officer who maintains the accounts of the expense and fees on the issue of summons; during Mughal times he was to serve as the accountant attached to the revenue collector who wrote orders for payment of revenue and other purposes and kept an account of the fees paid to the peons, sepoys, the surplus of which, above their wages, went to the credit of the government.

Ittila Nama: اطلاع نامہ — A.P. — A summon or notice served on the cultivators whenever they fell in arrears asking them to pay their due failing which their lands were to be attached by the government.

Izafa: اضافہ — A — Any increase in the amount of revenue received from a country whether from improved or additional condition or from an enhanced rate of assessment; increase in revenue from any additional source; grant of an entire village granted rent-free as an extra-allowance to the chief hereditary village or the district officer.

Izafa Beshi: اضافہ بیشی — A.P. — General increase in the rate of assessment.

J

Jagir: جاگیر — P — (Ja or Jai, a place or position, and gir, taking or occupying). A tenure common under the Muhammadan government, in which the public revenues of a given tract of land were made over to a servant of the State together with the powers requisite to enable him to collect and appropriate such revenues, and administer the general government of the district. The assignment was either conditional or unconditional. In the former case, some public service as the levy and maintenance of troops or other specified duty was engaged for: in the latter it was left to the entire disposal of the grantee. The assignment was either for a stated term, or more usually for the life-time of the holder, lapsing on his death to the State, although not unusually reveiwed to his heir on payment of a nazranah or fine, and it was sometimes specified to be a hereditary assignment, without which specification it was held to be a life tenure only. A jagir was also liable to forfeiture on failure of performance of the conditions on which it was granted, or on the holder's incurring the displeasure of the Emperor. On the other hand, in case of the inability of the state to vindicate its rights, a jagir was sometimes converted into a perpetual and transferable estate.

Jagir Bilashart: جاگیر بلا شرط — A.P. — (or *Ghair* mashrut*)*. An unconditional or absolute assignment of jagir.

Jagir-i-Ahsaam: جاگیر احشام — A.P. — Lands assigned for the maintenance of ahsham (troops).

Jagir-i-Amal: جاگیر عمل — P — The share of the revenue claimed by the Mughal govt. for the exchequer on certain holders of jagir after deducting the Maratha *Chauth, q.v.,* and another fourth or twenty five per cent for the Faujdar.

Jagir-i-Bakashi: جاگیر بخشی — P — An assignment of land for the support of the Pay Master General or the Commander-in-Chief.

Jagir-i-Tan: جاگیرتن	P	An assignment of jagir for personal support, usually unconditional.
Jagir-i-Zat: جاگیرذات	P	A grant of jagir for personal support usually conditional.
Jagir-Mashrut: جاگیرمشروط	P	A Jagir granted with conditions mentioned in the *sanad* of the jagir.
Jagir Mahal: جاگیرمحال	P	A district or village assigned to a *Jagirdar.*
Jagir Sar Anjam: جاگی سرانجام	P	(An assignment of jagir to a person for a specified duty performed by him.
Jagirdar: جاگیردار	P	One who is the holder of a jagir.
Jaidad: جاے داد		Assignment of land, a place, assets, funds, resources, property; also an employment.
Jama: جمع	A	(Amount, aggregate). Total in general but applied especially to the debit or receipt side of account and to the rental of an estate; also to the total amount of rent or revenue payable by a cultivator or a landlord, including all cesses as well as land-tax.
Jama-Bandi: جمع بندی	P	A register of the village holdings. A statement showing the particulars of the public revenue, its amount and how assessed. Total assessment of land revenue due for a year or a period of years from an estate.
Jama Bandi Asami War: جمع بندی آسامی وار	A.P.	Account of revenue assessment settled with each individual cultivator (Also known as *raiat war jama bandi*).
Jama Bandi Jins War: جمع بندی جنس وار	A.P.	Account of revenue assessed at certain rates, according to the produce or crops raised.

Term	Origin	Meaning
Jama Bandi Tashkish: جمع بندی تشخیص	A.P.	Amount of revenue assessed upon any tract of land agreeably to a fixed standard.
Jama-Dar: جمع دار	P	A commander of (any number of) armed persons. An officer of police, customs or army.
Jam-i-Hasil: جمع حاصل	A.P.	The total of the revenue collected.
Jama Múqarrari: جمع مقرری	A.P.	A fixed or permanent account of revenue. An account maintained by the *Qanungo,* q.v. of lands permanently assessed.
Jama Sadr: جمع صدر	A.P.	The revenue assessment settled with the Government direct by the land owners.
Jama Wasil or جمع واصل یا		
Wasul Baqi: وصول باقی	A.P.	The amount of the collections and outstanding balances; an account showing the particulars of the revenue to be paid, of the instalments discharged and the arrears due.
Jam-O-Kharch: جمع وخرچ	P	Receipt and expenditure.
Jam-O-Wasil Baqi: جمع وواصل باقی	P	Total received balance; an account in 3 columns stating the totals of the revenues expected according to the settlement, the amounts received and the balances outstanding.
Jangal Buri: جنگل بُری	P	Clearing lands of the forests; also applied to a sort of tenure under which waste or forest lands were granted in absolute property to the clearer free of rent or revenue for a certain period at the expiry of which part or parts as were in cultivation were to be liable to a fixed rent and customary imposts.
Jarib: جریب	A	A chain or rope meant for measuring lands.

Jarib Kharch: جریب خرچ	A.P.	Expense of measuring land paid by the tenant to the land owner.
Jins-i-Zabti: جنس ضبطی	A.P.	Produce or crops of a more valuable kind than ordinary such as cotton, tobacco or sugar paying a money rent.
Jizya: جزیہ	A	A capitalition tax authorised by the Muslims of conquest to be imposed on all subjects not of Muslim religion. It was imposed by Aurangzeb Alimgir and also by Bahadur Shah I and Shah Alam I.
Julus: جلوس	A	The year of ancession of an emperor to the throne, regional year.
Jumada I or جمدہ اول **Jumadal Awwal:** جمادی الاول	P	Fifth month of the Muslim lunar year.
Jumad Alsani جمدہ ثانی **or Jumada II:** جمادی الثانی	A	Sixth month of the Muslim lunar year.
Junubi: جنوبی	P	Literally the southerners, i.e., the Marathas (Plural *Junubiyan*).

K

Kachahri: کچہری	H	Court house, an office where any public business is transacted.
Kaghaz-i-Kham: کاغذخام		Rough records of all the villages of a pargana.
Kahar: کہار	H	Palanquin-bearer, water drawer.
Kalam: کلم		Tamil—A measure of land.

Kamil:	كامل	A	(Entire, perfect). In revenue language it means the whole sum raised by a village for the total of its expenses including the demands of the government; also, the largest amount of revenue realized from a village or district. In southern parts of India it means the fixed or standard statement as determined in different places by former governments.
Karkhanajat:	کارخانہ جات	P	Workshops, factories.
Karora:	کرورا	H	Tax-gatherer, inspector, overseer of a market.
Karoh:	کروہ	P	A measure of distance the same as *Kos,* q.v.
Karori:	کروری	H	The possessor or a collector of a Karor or ten millions of any given kind of money. It was specially applied as an official designation to a collector of the revenue to the extent of a *Karor* of *dams* or Rs. 2,50,000/ -Karori was also at various times invested with the general superintendence of the lands in his *pargana* or district and the charge of the Police and as such, his duties were similar to that of a Tahsildar.
Kauri:	کوری		A small shell used as coin. In accounts four Kauris were equal to one ganda, q.v.
Kavalgar & Malayalam:	کول گر		Proptector, guardian, watchman, village watchman who also generally acts as messenger and guide for travellers.
Khalat:	خلقت	A	A robe of honour presented by the ruling or a superior authority to an inferior as a mark of distinction.
Khalisah:	خالصہ	A	(From Khalis, pure, sincere). The exchequer, the office of the government under the Mughal administration in which the business of the revenue deptt. was tranacted, and

which was continued during the early period of the British rule; as applied to lands, it means those of which the revenue remains the property of the government, not being made over in jagir, etc., to any other parties. Lands or villages held immediately by government, and of which the state is the manager or holder. It is termed in some official papers as the rent roll of the government meaning the revenue receivable from the government, Khalisah lands.

Khalisa wala Sharifa: خالصہ والا/شریفہ	A	Wala and Sharifa are added to show one's respect to the word Khalisa.
Khan-i-Saman: خانِ ساماں	P	The Khan (Sardar or Great man) of Saman (household). The comptroller of the Imperial household. Also, Mir Saman, q.v.
Kharif: خریف	A	Harvest during the autumn.
Kharita: خریطہ	A	Receptacle, small silk bag in which letters of great man are enclosed.
Khas: خاص	A	Private, peculiar; as a revenue term it is applied to the management of estates and the collection of the revenue thereof by the officers of the government without any intermediate person between then and the cultivator.
Khas Mahal: خاص محال	A	Estate managed by the Government.
Khas Taaluqa: خاص تعلقہ	H	Taluk or certain district placed by order of the Emperor under the direct control and management of the State.
Khawas: خواص	A	A body of favourable attendants of the royal court.
Khazanchi: خزانچی	P	Officer in charge of the State treasury or its branch.

Khizana (Khazana): خزانہ

Treasury. Apart from the Khizana-i-amirah—there were about a dozen type of treasuries during the Mughal period.

1. ***Khizana-i-amirah:*** The grand or general treasury.

2. ***Khizana Andarun-i-mahal:*** The treasury inside the royal place meant for the begams (ladies) and the females.

3. ***Khizana Bagaya*** (arrears): The treasury where arrears of previous years were deposited.

4. ***Khizana Jaib-i-Khas***: The treasury was exclusively meant for supplying Emperor's pocket money, the payments made by him with his own hands.

5. ***Khizana Jaib-i-faiz:*** This treasury for donations of pious nature. This treasury was to keep accounts of expenditure which the Emperor spent annually in charity as well as his weight in silver, gold etc. which were all distributed among the poor section of the people and to religious mendicants on days of festivals and ceremonial occasions.

6. ***Khizana Rikab-i-Sadat:*** This type of treasury always accompanied the Emperor during his marches and was responsible for keeping account of income and expenditure during his journey for pleasure or war purposes.

7. ***Khizana Nazr wa peshkash:*** This type of treasury was responsible for receiving the payments against tributes, gifts, presents, *nazrs* and *nazranas,* q.v.

8. ***Khizana Sarf-i-khas*** (Privy purse). The treasury for imperial household. The amount in this treasury was spent by *Khan-i-jaman,* q.v. and not by the Emperor.

9. ***Khizana, Bait-al-mal:*** The properties of persons dying without heirs were collected by this treasury and also distributed among the needy sections of people. This was entirely public money having no concern with the revenue of the State.

10. ***Khizana-i-sadga:*** This treasury was responsible of collecting from the Muslim population.

11. ***Khizana-i-jizya***: Jizya or poll-tax on non-Muslim population was deposited in this treasury.

12. ***Khizana-i-mutafa***: The treasury for collecting and despositing miscellaneous items.

Khufia Nawis: خفیہ نویس | P | Or secret writer was a most confidential agent of the Mughal court in the provinces of the country. Some Khufia nawis were also posted at courts of kings not directly or indirectly connected with the Emperor. The secret reports on events of the province etc. were despatched direct to the Emperor without any communication with the local authorities, who mostly did not know his name even, officers and the people all alike were in mortal dread of Khufia nawis.

Khuld Aramgah: خلد آرام گاہ | Posthumous title of Jahan Dar Shah.

Khuld Makan: خلد مکان | Posthumous title of Aurangzeb.

Khuld Manzil: خلد منزل | Posthumous title of Shah Alam I Bahadur Shah.

Khutba: خطبہ — A — Sermon delivered from the puppit of the mosque during Friday (noon), Id-al-fitr and Id al-Zuha wherein the name of the present king or Emperor is mentioned. Unless the name of the king not mentioned in the Khutba, he was supposed to be not recognised by the masses as their master or ruler.

Kifayat: کفایت — A — (Surplus; profit; advantage). Profit or increase in the amount of revenue received by the government whether by raising the rate of assessment or imposing additional taxes.

Kifayat-i-Hast-O-Bud: کفایتِ ہست و بود — A.P. — Increase of actual and past assessment founded on a revision of the value of the lands and resumption of illegal or lapsed alienations.

Kifayat-i-Faujdari: کفایت فوجداری — A.P. — Increased assessment on the border lands held by military governors.

Kifayat-i-Sair: کفایت سائر — Increase of the revenue derived from miscellaneous items of taxation whether effected by additional imports or reduction of charges.

Kitab-i-Intiqal: کتابِ انتقال — A.P. — (Kitab means a book and Intiqal means transfer). It was a register containing records of transfers and other changes effected in properties of a village or a pargana.

Kos: کوس — H — Measure of distance approximately of two miles but varying in different parts of India.

Kotwal: کوتوال — P.H. — (In Hindi language, Kot means fort; whereas in Persian, wala or wal means one he has). Kotwal previously was an administrator of the fort establishment. An officer who was different from the commander of the forces in the fort. In later period of the Mughal Empire, he was entrusted with the police duties of a city which was usually surrounded by four walls and was, for all practical purposes, a big fort. The Kotwal was also the superintendent of the market and his duty was to see that the commodities were sold according to moderate rates.

Kul Bandobast: کل بندوبست — P — A complete settlement either that of a whole estate by the landowner or of a district by Government.

Kul Jama: کل جمع — A.P. — (Sum total). Total realisable revenue.

Kulkarni: کلکرنی — Mar — One of the principal village functionaries under the *Patil,* the village registrar and accountant whose duty was to keep accounts between the farmers and the government, as well as those of village expenditure. He had all the village records and revenue papers.

L

Lagan: لگان — H — The rent or revenue charged on a land or estate.

La Khiraj: لاخراج — A — From La which means not and Khiraj meaning tribute. Rent-free land, applied to land exempted for some particular reasons from paying any part of the produce to the Government.

Langar Khana: لنگرخانہ — P — An alms house. The place where langar is distributed.

Langar: لنگر — P — Public kitchen, especially for feeding those who are poor or invalid. These were found in cities etc. during Mughal period.

Lawazma: لوازمہ — P — Necessary papers, documents and vouchers.

Lavazim-i-Sanad: لوازمہ سند — P — The particulars necessary for a grant of a *sanad,* q.v. the vouchers from and to the different officers and departments requisite for the final issue of a grant of land or revenue, which were usually endorsed on the sanad.

Lawazma-i-Huquq: P
لوازمہ حقوق
Necessary papers confirming the rights and titles of an applicant requesting for grant of jagir or tankhwah.

Luqta: P
لُقطہ
In Muslim law, treasure trove, property which a person finds on the ground and takes charge of as a trust until claimed by the owner, calling witnesses to his finding it and announcing his intention of restoring it. If not claimed after a year, he should dispose it off, if of any value, in charity, or he may keep it but still for the owner if the article be durable.

M

Madad-i-Mash: A
مدد معاش
An assignment of revenue for the purpose of supporting pious and learned persons.

Madakhil: P
مداخل
Additions to the revenue etc. of a district either from the annexation of other lands or from the full assessments of lands which had been wholly or partially exempt from the payment of rent or revenue.

Madar Al-Mahamm:
مدارالمہام
Prime Minister.

Mah: P
ماہ
(Or Mahina) means month.

During the Mughal period, three types of months were used in official correspondence. Similarly, there were three types of years, i.e., (1) fasli, q.v. (2) hijri, q.v. and (3) julus, q.v.

In the bulk of revenue records, Arabic and Akbari months were used with fasli year.

Following are the months which were current during the reign of Akbar the great and they were, of course, the outcome of his own mind:

(1) **Sachqail**: In Turkish language, *Suchqai* means rat. The Mughal Emperor issued orders that nobody may hurt or injure rats during this month.

(2) **Udi-il**: UD means cow. The Emperor issued orders that during this month, cow and bullocks should be given special protection and the farmers and cultivators also be given whole hearted co-operation in performance of their usual affairs. They must also be helped by cash and kind, if need be.

(3) **Pars-il**: *Pars* meant an animal smaller than a leopard, a Cheeta. The hunting of this animal was prohibited in this month. It was also advised that the help of this animal be avoided in game of hunting. He should be given complete rest.

(4) **Toshqai-il**: *Toshqai* means rabbit. Hunting and eating of rabbits was strictly forbidden during this month.

(5) **Lui-il**: *Lui* means crocodile. Hunting of crocodiles was not allowed. It was also ordered that fish must not be taken in meals during this month. By and large, lives of all the creatures of water were asked to be given complete protection during the month.

(6) **Eela-il**: *Eelan* means snakes. Killing or hurting of snakes was forbidden during this month.

(7) **Ayat il**: *Ayat* or *Aat* means horse. It was ordered that the horses must not be killed during this month for purpose of eating their meat. On the contrary, it was deemed more vulnerable to give them away in charity to needy persons.

(8) **Qui-il**: *Qui* means goats and sheep that were prohibited to be killed or molested during this month.

(9) **Pachi-il**: *Pachi* means monkey. It was the month of monkeys. They were asked to be looked after with care and it was forbidden to have a catch of them in the jungle. On the contrary, it was advised to release them in forests during this month.

(10) **Takhaqui-il**: *Takhaqu* means cocks. Killing of cocks and hens was prohibited during the month—even cockpitting was also forbidden. They were to remain in peaceful atmosphere.

(11) **Eet-il**: *Eet* means dog. Hunting with the help of dogs was forbidden in this month. It was desired that he should not be molested in anyway. Eet-il was the month of complete rest for dogs.

(12) **Tanguzi il**: *Tanguz* means Pig. Molestation of pigs was not allowed in this month.

Similarly, there were certain instructions attached with each month of the Muslim lunar month with a view to make the lot of people good in general.

(1) During the month of *Muharra*, q.v. molestation of any living being was strictly prohibited.

(2) During the month of *Safar*, q.v. it was desired to release the slave girls.

(3) During the month of *Rabi Al Awwal* (*Rabi I*) q.v., Akbar the Great advised his subjects to give alms at least to thirty poor and needy persons.

(4) The month of *Rabi Al Sani* (*Rabi II*), q.v., was supposed to be the month of sanitation and each person was asked to keep his body clean by taking baths etc.

(5) During the month of (*Jumada I*) *Jumdi Al Awwal*, q.v., attractive and silken clothes were fordden to be used.

(6) During the *Jumadi Al Sani* (*Jumada II*), q.v. leather was forbidden to be touched and used for any purpose.

(7) In the month of *Rajab*, every man of forty years of age was required to help the persons of his age.

(8) In the month of *Shaban*, q.v. molestation of living beings was forbidden.

(9) During the month of *Ramazan*, q.v. every wealthy person was required to give food and clothes in charity to invalid persons.

(10) To remember the name of God for thousand times in quick succession was the order of the month of *Shawwal*, q.v.

(11) During the month of *Zul Qada, Ziqad Ziqada* every one was asked not to sleep in the first half of the night and to behave with the followers of other religions very nicely during each day of the month.

(12) Construction of buildings for the sake of ease and comforts of the people (pro bono publico) was required during the month of *Zul Hijja* or *Zi Hij*, q.v.

Apart from these months, the mention of Persian months is also found in the revenue records of the Mughal Government. These are also enumerated here under:

(1) **Azar**: Also *Azur* means fire. It is the name of the angel who is supposed to be presiding over the realm of fire. *Azar* is the 9th of the solar months whereas by *Azur* is meant the ninth day of any month. Particularly, the 9th day of the fourth month is called *Azur*.

(2) **Dai**: Name of the 10th month of the solar year, winter or the 1st month of it, December. Name of the 9th day of every month. Also, the name of the angel who presides over the affairs of the month of Dai and of the 8th, 15th and 23rd day of every month.

(3) **Bahman**: The middle month of the winter season equivalent to that of the month of January.

(4) **Isfand**: Also, *Isfandyar* is the name of the twelfth solar month and name of the 5th day of every month. It is also the name of the angel who presides over the 12th month.

(5) **Farwardi**: Name of the month and the 19th day of every month. It is also the name of the angel.

(6) **Uirdi-Bihisht**: The 2nd Persian month, mid-spring, April: the third day of every month which the people of Iran celebrated by a festival.

(7) **Khurdad**: Name of the third month.

(8) **Tir**: Name of the fourth solar month of the Persians when the sun is in Cancer. The 13th day of every month. Also, the name of the angel who is thought to be the guardian of the cattle and presides over the said month and the day.

(9) **Amar Dad**: Name of the Persian month.

(10) **Shar War**: Or *Shahr* means the moon. Also, the name of the Persian month.

(11) **Mihr**: The month of September, the 16th day of every month. Also, the name of an angel.

(12) **Aban**: Plural of *ab*. Name of the month of the Persian year during which the sun continues in scorpio. Name of the 10th day of any Persian month.

Mahajan: مہاجن — S — A great man but mostly applied to a merchant; a banker or money changer.

Mahal: محال — A — (Plural of *Mahalat*, but used as a singular noun). A district, a division of a *ta-alluqa* or district yielding revenue according to assessment. Under the Mughal Government, the term was also applied tŏ a department of miscellaneous revenue derived from a tax on some particular class of thing or persons. Place of duty. The land which was assigned to a mansabdar in jagir.

Mahi Maratib: ماہی مراتب — P.A. — The dignity of the fish; the privilege of having carried before a man of rank, the representation of a fish or part of it of metal gilt borne upon a pole with two circular gilt balls similarly elevated; conferred formerly as a mark of distinction by the Kings of Delhi on individuals of the highest order only.

Mahsul: محصول — A — Profit, tax, duty, excise, customs, the produce or return realised from any thing.

Mahwar: ماہوار — P — Monthly stipend, wages, the revenue that is collected in a month.

Mahzar-Nama: محضرنامہ — P — A muster roll, a list of persons present at an assembly, a public attestation.

Maimana: میمنہ — A — Right wing of an Army in the battle field.

Maisara: میسرہ — A — Left winf of an Army in the battle field.

Majmuah Dar: مجموعہ دار — A.P. — (Majmuah means an aggregate or total; and dar one has). A revenue accountant, one who keeps the accounts of the government collections. In some places, he was the revenue accountant of a district subordinate to the *Amil* or manager, and removable at pleasure. He kept accounts of the revenue settlement, audited those of the *Qanungos* (q.v.) and possessed a general power of scrutinizing the revenue accounts and assets of his district. In some parts, he was also the receiver and auditor of the rents paid by the Zamindar (farmer or cultivator actually in possession of the land).

Makharij: مخارج — A — (Plural of *makharj* which means outgoing). As a revenue term, it means deductions from the revenue, alienations, assignments of portions of the claims of the government, remissions of revenue due by the land owners on account of lands dismembered or alienated.

Mal: مال — P — (Wealth. goods, property of any description). In Muslim law, it is sometimes used for personal as opposed to real property or for money as distinguished from goods and chattols. In India, it was used for the public revenue from any source what-so-ever but more especially for that derived from lands, in which sense, as a fiscal term, it is now restricted, or the revenue claimed by the government from the produce of cultivated lands, the wealth of the Empire.

Mal Adalat: مال عدالت — P — A revenue court in which all questions between the government and land owners and between them and their tenants or officers charged with the collection and over which the Collector (Diwan presided, were determined).

Mal-Guzar: مال گذار — P — Landlord; land holder who pays malaguzari, q.v.

Mal Guzari: مال گذاری — P — Land revenue, rent paid in money; the paying of rent and taxes, the state of a renter; assessed land.

Malik: مالک — A — Owner; but an owner of land during Mughal Government was supposed to be the *malik* of the crop etc. over the land. All lands were owned by the king. Similarly, a *malik* of a building was actually the owner of the material and not the land though in case of death of the *malik,* land was usually transferred to his legal successor but it could not be claimed as a matter of right.

Malikana: مالکانہ — P — Proprietary, annual or monthly allowance paid to a land ownew by the person or farmer who occupies his lands for the purpose of cultivation etc. or in case of absconding of an owner of a land, one half of the produce of the crops of the relevant year only was assigned to him as *malikana.*

Mal Wajib: مالواجب — P — Fixed and proper revenue which is requistic or customary to pay (The State took one-third

		of the grass produce in case of grain; but one-fourth to one-eighth in case of opium, sugarcane, vine, plantain and cotton).
Man: من		A measure of weight of general use in India but varying in value in different parts. Usually it contains forty seers whereas a seer contains eighty (and in some places even ninety tolas, q.v.).
Mandawai: منڈوی	Mar	A building into which goods are received from ships in sea-ports, a store, a warehouse etc., a customs house.
Mandi: منڈی	H	A special market for any particular article.
Mansab: منصب	A	Office, dignity, a military title and rank conferred by the Mughal government of Delhi regulated by thc supposed numbers of horses (*sawars*), which the holder of the title could, if so demanded by the imperial officers both military or civil, bring into battle-field or during peace for inspection and verfication. The manasab usually varied from ten to ten thousand. The holder was also paid for the maintenance of *Zat* (Soldiers). Jagirs were assigned for the maintenance of this force, which was in the highest and lowest grades rather nominal than real; the first part of the *sanad* (or grant) in which the titles of the grantee were recited. Also, please see Jagir in this context. The formula of pay or jagir of mansabdar was: Mansab x 2 + sawar x 2 + amount of Khurak dawwab = monthly tankhwah of mansabdar.
Mansab-dar: منصب دار	P	Holder of some rank of office under the State.
Maqta: مقطع	A	According to agreement, fixed, consolidated; applied especially to a tenure by which a ryot holds his land at a fixed rate per plough or

per *bigha* or to the engagement by which his rent is fixed for a given term without liability to enhancement.

Masha: A weight specially for weighing gold. A tola has 12 masha weight.

ماشہ

Mashrut: A Stipulated, conditional as applied to assignment or grants of land revenue importing that the grant was accompanied by certain stipulated terms and conditions.

مشروط

Mashrut Diwani: A.P. Conditional assignments for the remuneration of a fiscal functionary.

مشروط دیوانی

Mashrut Faujdari: A.P. Assignments to the officers charged with the military and police establishments.

مشروط فوج داری

Mashrut Thana Jat: A.H. Conditional assignments for the support of the military or police stations.

مشروط تھانہ جات

Matrukat: Estates, goods or property of a person deceased to which his heirs are legally entitled.

متروکات

Maujudat: Daily account of collection of revenue and cash.

موجودات

Maulavi: (A person learned in and expounder of the Muhammadan law; a teacher especially of Arabic and Persian).

مولوی

Maurusi Asami: A.P. Or Maurusi *rait.* A cultivator in a village holding by hereditary descent. Although not one of the proprietary community, he retains his land as long as he pays the established rent and cannot be dispossessed of it as long as that is paid; he cannot alienate his land by sale or mortgage without the consent of the parties of whom he holds.

مشروط آسامی

Mauza: موضع — A village.

Mauza War: موضع وار — A.P. — (By villages). Assessment of the government revenue or lands comprised within the village limits and dependencies, settled either with the whole community of proprietary villages or an individual representing them, distinguished therefore from a zamindari settlement.

Mazul: معزول — A — Dismissed or removed from an office or appointment.

Mihmani: مہمانی — P — Hospitality or charge of a guest under the Muhammadan government a deduction from the revenue allowed to land holders to defray the cost of their entertaining travellers, pilgrims and strangers in general; also a cess levied in some places by zamindars under pretext of providing for similar purposes.

Mir Saman: میر سامان — P — The Comproller of the Imperial household. Also, Khan-i-Saman, q.v.

Mir Peshkar: میر پیش کار — A.P. — The head of the Department of Accounts. Accountant General.

Mirza: مرزا — P — A title, when prefixed to a name of person, it means some civilian designation such as Mirza Abbas but when following it, means Prince as Abbas Mirza.

Muafi: معافی — A.P. — (Forgiven, remitted). Remission or exemption from the demands of the State; a grant of land free of assessment. The term also designated a particular grant formerly made by zamindars and the revenue officers of the Government which became hereditary and transferable and was also applied to lands which were held free of revenue on the condition of rendering service in lieu thereof.

Muafi Istiwa: معافی استوا — (Istiwa means equal) a tenure by which waste land is held rent-free for a certain period of time and for a further period at a quitrent until the given term is expired.

Muafi Mamuli: معافی معمولی — P — Customary deductions from the government revenue made formerly to the native collectors and farmers on account of charitable allowances or similar remission made by them to their sub-ordinates or to the cultivators.

Muchalka: مچلکہ — A written obligation or agreement, a bond, a deed; it is commonly applied to a counterpart covenant on the part of the proprietors and cultivators of land, agreeing to the rate of assessment imposed by the imperial government; also to an engagement under a penalty to observe the conditions of any deed or grant, or to one exacted from thieves or suspected persons engaging to desist or refrain from any illegal acts.

Mufassal: مفصل — A — Country or opposed to town, country districts and stations as distinguished from head quarters.

Mufassal Jama: مفصل جمع — A.P. — The gross of revenue payable to the zamindar or Malguzar (q.v.) by the subordinate cultivators and through him to the government which is then *Sadr Jama* or State Revenue.

Mufassal Kharch: مفصل خرچ — A.P. — Charges of collection in the provinces.

Mufti: مفتی — A — A Muhammadan Law Officer.

Muhassil: محصل — A — Collector of the revenue; tax collector sometimes appointed on the control basis on varied conditions.

Muharrir:	محرر	A	Clerk-writer.
Muharram:	محرم	A	First month of the Muslim lunar year.
Muhtasib:	محتسب	A	Superintendent of markets and police. An officer appointed to take cognisance of improper behaviour as of indecency, drunkenness, gambling, also of the sale of intoxicating drugs and liqours and false weight and measures.
Mukhtar:	مختار	A	Agent, mostly of a property holder.
Munshi:	منشی	A	Writer; Secretary; interpreter or teacher of *Persian.*
Muqaddam:	مقدم	A	(A Chief, a leader, one who goes before). In India, it has become a revenue term applied to the head-man of a mauza or the village or of a caste or corporation. The Muqaddam in southern parts of India was head of the village who was charged with the realization of revenue and its payment to the Collector or the Diwan of the district. He was also charged with the superintendence of the cultivation, the management of the affairs of the village and the disbursement of its expenses; he was also entrusted, to a certain extent, with jurisdiction in disputes among the farmers and cultivators.
Muqarrari:	مقرری		Relating to whatever is fixed. As a revenue term, it is applied to a tenure held at a fixed and permanent rate of rent when payable to the government.
Muqararridar:	مقرری دار	P	A holder of Muqarrari farm or tenure.
Mushrif:	مشرف	A	An Inspector; an examiner of cash in treasury. An officer of the treasury.

Mustajir: متاجر A Farmer, renter, one who holds land under a proprietor. Also, a farmer appointed by a zamindar to collect revenue on his behalf.

Mustaufi: مستوفی A An examiner or auditor of accounts; a Controller, a head clerk. The Principal officer of the department in which during the Mughal period, the accounts of ex-collectors or farmers of revenue were examined.

Mutaharrifa: متحرّفه P Taxes levied on trades and professions, on the artifacts of a village or their implements, as upon the weaver's loom, upon tradesmen and their shops and stalls and sometimes upon house.

Mutasaddi: متصدی A Accountant or revenue official.

Mutawalli: متولی A An administrator, prosecutor, a trustee, a religious or charitable foundation. A treasurer of a charitable institution.

Muwajial: موجّل A Deferred, as payment.

Muwakkal: موکل A A constituent, one who appoints a deputy, representative or *Wakil,* q.v.

Muwazana: موازنه P Comparison of accounts of produce revenue etc. of various years of a particular village or district.

N

Nagar: نگر H A town, a city.

Najibs: نجیب A Literally noble under Mughal Government—it applied to irregular troops.

Nakhkhas: نخاس A A daily fair or market for selling and purchasing cattle and horse, a tax levied on the sale of horse and cattle.

Term	Origin	Meaning
Na-Khuda: ناخدا	P	The captain or commander of a war ship.
Nal-Bandi: نال بندی		Literally, horse-shoe money; a light tribute exacted order the Muhammadan rule, on the plea of keeping up the cavalry of the State or preventing the horse man (*sawar*) from devastating the crops, farms and lands of cultivators. It was later on converted into a small permanent tribute.
Nama: نامہ	P	A deed, a written document such as *Iqrar-nama* (a deed of assent), *laqsim-nama.* (a deed of partition), etc.
Nankar: نان کار		A gift land to a man for providing means of his sustenance.
Naqdi: نقدی	P	Retainers who received their salary in cash.
Naqdi Jinsi: نقدی جنس	A.P.	Money rent calculated on the value of the produce.
Naqd-Mazkurat: نقد مذکورات	A.P.	Miscellaneous items in the revenue accounts allowed for and settled in money.
Naqid: نقیب	A	A servant or herald whose business was to proclaim the title of the Emperor or King and to introduce those who pay their respect to him.
Naqsha-Juz-O-Kul: نقشہ جزوکل		(*Naqshaa* means map). Details of particulars of small and great, a report drawn up by the revenue officers and surveyors furnishing details of cultivation, the condition of the farmer, the quality and quantity of lands—recorded with a view to guide the officers in charge of lands assessment.
Naqqara: نقارہ		A kettle drum, the use of which was restricted to persons of high rank as a mark of state.

Naslan Bad Naslin: نسلاً بعد نسلاً	A	A term used in the deeds of grant of land to express that it has been granted to the persons and his successors in regular descent or succession.
Nau-Babar: نوبرار	P	Lands recently mode subject to assessment.
Naubat: نوبت	P	An instrument of music or a band playing at the gate way of a great man. This honour was not given to every officer. Those who were specifically granted this privilege could enjoy the honour.
Naubat Khana: نوبت خانہ		A large room over the outer gate of a palace where the drums or musical instrument are sounded, a guard house.
Nau-Roz: نوروز	P	The New Year's Day of the Persians held on the Sun's entrance into Aries. This was also celebrated by the Mughal Emperor of India with great pomp and show and as such was treated as the state function.
Nayab: نایب	A	Assistant or deputy, a lieutenant, a viceroy.
Nazim: ناظم	A	A viceroy, a governor, the superior officer of a province charged with the administration of criminal law and the police. *Suba-dar,* q.v.
Nazir: ناظر	A	A superintendent of accounts; an officer employed in a judicial court; a sheriff; inspector; supervisor; commissary.
Nazr: نذر	P	Ceremonial present generally from an inferior to a superior.
Nazranah: نذرانہ	P	Tribute, present especially to a superior from an inferior. Same as *nazr*, q.v.
Niabat: نیابت	A	The office of a *Nayab* or the deputy.

Nizamat: نظامت — A — The office of the *Nazim* of the Province.

Nuskha: نسخہ — P — A copy of the official paper bearing seal of some high ranking officer.

Nuzul: نزول — A — In revenue language, an escheat, escheated property in gardens and houses and property that is considered to have lapsed to the state. An officc for investigating lapsed claims.

P

Pagoda: پگوڈا — Canterai, cantiroy or Kanthiraya Pagoda so called after the Mysore King Kanthirava Narasa Raja (1638-59) who was the first to his time to establish a mint. Six of these pagodas were held to be equal to five star pagodas, and a star pagoda was equivalent to Rs. 3/8/=. So a Kanthiraya Pagoda was worth Rs. 2/14/8.

Pai-Baqi: پاۓ باقی — H.A. — (Pai-H & bagi A). In Mughal finance, the designation of such lands as were set apart for jagir grants if required; also, the revenue from lands so reserved not yet alienated; and of land which having been alienated, had been resumed and paid revenue until a fresh assignment had been made.

Pai-Bawi Khalisa: پاۓ باقی خالصہ — A.P. — The revenue of resumed or lapsed but suspended alienations receivable in the Public Treasury.

Pai Nam: پاۓ نام — A denomination under the Muhammadan Government of the principal division of a *suba.* (The term is not clear and still requires thorough study which is continued H X P).

Paida: پیادہ — P — Peon. Footman. A warrior who used to fight on foot (without any horse etc.).

Paikar: پائیکار H A dealer or agent; a broker.

Pargana: پرگنہ P Sub-division of the district; a tract of country consisting of many villages. Pargana is also used for tahsil, q.v.

Parwana: پروانہ P Order, letter from an officer of the highest rank to his subordinate officer or to mansabdar, etc. An order assigning the possession of an estate of jagir.

Patil: پاٹل Mar The headman of a village who has the great control and management of the village affairs is head of the Police and exercises, to a limited extent, the functions of a magistrate; he is also the principal agent in the realization of revenue and the chief medium of communication with the officers of the Government.

Pattah: پٹہ H A deed of lease, a document gien by the Diwan to the zamindar (landlord) or by some other receiver of revenue to the farmer or cultivator of sub-tenant, specifying the conditions on which the lands are held paid to the authority or person from whom the lands are held. The term was laxly applied to a variety of deeds securing rights or property in land, also to a deed of gift in general.

Pattah Dar: پٹہ دار H.P. One who holds a lease or engagement for his lands.

Patwari: پٹواری H Village accountant whose duty it is to keep all kinds of land account and submit the same to the revenue officers of the Government.

Pesh-Kar: پیش کار P The personal assistant of a man in power; one exercising in revenue and customs affairs a delegated authority.

Pesh Kash: پیش کش	P	Offering or tribute paid to a superior or the Government. During early Mughal period, it was offered by *Deshmukh, Deshpanday* and other zamindars for acquiring the said offices.
Poligar: پولی گار	Tel	Feudal chief in the southern part of India.

Q

Qabz-Al-Wusul: قبض الوصول	A	A receipt; an acknowledgement. In revenue accounts, it means the recepit which is issued to a cultivator of a land by the patwari for the instalments he paid to him. It was also applied to acquittance roll of the government servants.
Qala: قلعہ	A	A fort. In Hindi, it is called garh or Kot.
Qala-dar: قلعہ دار	A.P.	The Commander of the forces stationed in the fort. He was also responsible for the administration of the qala and was a paymaster. He was entitled to hold jagir from the adjoining place.
Qanungo: قانون گو	A.P.	(*qanun* means law and *go* means one who speaks) An expounder of the laws, but in India during the Mughal period, it applied especially to village and district revenue officers, who under the said period, recorded all the circumstances within their sphere which concerned landed property and the realization of the revenue, keeping registers of value, tenure, extent and transfers of lands, assisting in the measurements and survey of the lands, reporting deaths and successions of revenue payers and explaining, when required, local practices and public regulations.
Qarawal: قراول	T	A game keeper, a hunter.

Qariya: قریہ — A tract of land less in area and population than a mauza or a village.

Qasar, Qasur: قصر، قصور — A — (Defect, deficiency, fault, offence, crime). In revenue language, it means an allowance for difference in the value of coins, a cess formerly levied upon the farmers to cover any difference that might occur between the value of the coins paid by them and the standard currency.

Qaul: قول — A — A word, a promise, an agreement, a contract. This term was used in various deeds granted by superiors to inferiors in which the engagement implies an act of favour. A promise of pardon or of safe conduct to a rebel or offender to induce him to give himself up. In revenue transactions, a *qaul* usually means the document granted by the Collector or receiver of revenues to the subordinate payer of revenue or the actual farmer stating the terms and conditions of the agreement and the amount to be paid and securing him against further demands. It frequently implies also that the contract or lease is granted on favourbale conditions as in the case of cultivation of waste lands for which remission of rent is granted for a given period by a *qaul.*

Qauli or Kauli: قولی، کولی — A — Land held under a *qaul* or stipulated tenure, also waste land brought in to cultivation under a *qaul* from the government.

Qazi: قاضی — A — A judge under the Muslim rule charged with both civil and criminal law.

Qazi Alquzat: قاضی القضات — A — Chief (Qazi) Judge who used to sign the sanad of jagir issued to mansabdar.

Qist: قسط — A — The amount paid as an instalment; the period fixed for its payment; as a revenue term it

		denotes the portion of the annual assessment to be paid at specified periods in the course of the year; such periodical payment is called a *qist*.
Qist Bandi: قسط بندی	A.P.	Settlement of instalments of the revenue both as to time and amount; a document given at the beginning of the year to the revenue payer by the collector or zamindar, in which the time and amount of the instalments to be paid are clearly mentioned; a counterpart statement of the same, kept by the receiver of the revenue, or a district account showing the particulars of the instalments to be received during the year from farmers etc., any document relating to fixed periodical payments of the revenue or of a debt.
Qismat: قسمت	A	(Share, distribution). Applied in revenue matters to a portion of land detached from a large division as from *taalluqa* or a *pargana* particularly when subject to a different jurisdiction.
Qismat Nama: قسمت نامہ	A.P.	A deed of partition or share.
Qism War Gaushwara: قسم وار گوشوارہ	A.P.	An abstract account of lands classed. according to their quality.
Qism War Jama Bandi: قسم وار جمع بندی	A.P.	An account of the assessment of the lands of a village or pargana according to their quality
Qita: قطعہ	A	(A part, a section). A term used in accounts to signify each item that is to be brought under a separate head, also for an item that is set down but of which the particulars appear elsewhere. In revenue language, any tract of land is called Qita Arazi.
Qita Bandi: قطعہ بندی	P	A mode of assessment formed upon an equal distribution among the farmers of the good

and bad soil of a village in like porportion and holding each cultivator responsible for his share of both; also assessment of the cultivator according to the shares of each without advertence to the soil or the cultivation.

Qubuliyat-Nama: قبولیت نامہ P Deed of agreement showing willingness to accept the offer of jagir etc. and to pay rent of the land.

Qurq-Amin: قرق امین P An officer of the court of law employed for the specific purpose of attaching a property for realizing the dues of the government or loan taken by a private party or individual.

Qurq Mahal: قرق محال P An estate under attachment.

Qurq Sazawal: قرق سزاوال P An officer appointed to attach and hold an estate and realise arrears of rent or revenue or to detain goods for debt, a bailiff, a shariff's officer.

Qurq Tahsil: قرق تحصیل P Collection of the revenue of an estate which has fallen into arrears and from which the properties are nominally set aside by the officers of the revenue.

R

Rabi: ربیع A Crops sowed during the spring season.

Rabi Al-Awwal: ربیع الاول A 3rd month of the Muslim lunar year. Also written as "*Rabi* I".

Rabi Al-Sani: ربیع الثانی A 4th month of the Muslim lunar year. Also written as "*Rabi* II".

Rah-Dar: راہ دار P One who held charge of the public roads; one in-charge of the office of the *Rah-dari*.

Rah-Dari: راہداری	P	A passport, a custom's pass or permit; transit duties at inland stations upon grain and other articles, levied by the Government.
Raiyyat: رعیت	A	A subject but especially applied to the population engaged in cultivation of lands; a cultivator; a farmer; a peasant.
Rajab: رجب	A	7th month of the Muslim lunar year.
Rajah: راجہ	H	A Hindu head of a principality or kingdom; the Hindu landlords, big zamindars and kings were called *Rajas;* those who were obeyed by some *Rajas* were called *Maharajas* (i.e., the *Raja* of *Rajas* or the Emperor).
Ramzan: رمضان	A	9th month of the Muslim lunar year. During this month, all the Muslims are required by the Muhammadan law to observe fast during the day.
Ramnah or Ramna: رمنا	H	A park, a preserve for game; used sometimes as the general name of grass lands.
Rao: راو	H	A title given to a Hindu chief or a prince.
Raqba-Bandi: رقبہ بندی	A.P.	(*Raqba* means area of lands). A statement of the area of an estate, village or township; one of accounts that was kept by the village *patwar,* q.v. showing the total quantity of land belonging to the community, the portions that pay or are exempt from revenue and those which are cultivated or uncultivated, or incapable of cultivation.
Ras-Al-Mal: راس المال	A	(*Ras* means head, used technically in application to cattle as *Panj ras Gao*). As the Mughal revenue term, it applied to principal, capital fund for or trading stock, the original price of an article.

Ratib: راتب — A — Daily allowance of food to labour or to animals as elephant etc.

Ratl: رطل — A — A weight, variously rated at 12 to 16 ounces; a pound.

Ratti: رتّی — A weight particularly for weighing gold; 8 *rattis* are equal to a *masha*, q.v.

Rawanna: روانہ — P — A permit issued by the Customs Department to a person to carry the goods written therein to the place of destination.

Razi Nama: راضی نامہ — A.P. — (From *razi,* one who agrees and *namah,* a deed, a document). A written assent, a deed of agreement, document signed by a plaintif at the end of the lawsuit that he is satisfied with the decision; a deed of compromise by which the plaintiff acknolwdges that he has been satisfied by the defendent. During the Mughal period, every *deshmukh* etc. had to submit a *razinama* signed by all the zamindars (farmers) of the mahal concerned wherein they expressed their willingness to accept the *deshmukh* etc. notifying that they had no objection to his appointment as such. This *razinama* was to be submitted together with relevant papers for the finalization of the grant of the *deshmukhi.* A jagirdar was also required to submit a *razi-nama* if his appointment was objected to by the villagers, failing which his jagir was liable to be transferred.

Risalah: رسالہ — A. — A troop of horse commanded by a *risaladar.*

Risaladar: رسالہ دار — A.P. — (From *risalah,* a body of horse). An officer commanding a troop of irregular horse (Cavalry).

Roz Namcha: روزنامچہ — H.P. — A daily account-book, a register in which daily events are recorded.

Rubakar: روبکار — P — Engaged in, intent on, proceeding with, before the constituted authorities as in a court of justice. An order issued by the revenue officers.

Rubakari: روبکاری — P — The written record of a case, stating the particulars and the grounds of the decision drawn up.

Rudad: روداد — A.P. — Narrative or record of proceedings, statement of facts or occurrences; report of a subordinate officer deputed to inquire into any affair; also a return to an official enquiry.

Rupiyah or (Rupee): روپیہ — H — A silver coin, the general denomination of the silver currency of India (and in Indonesia too) and the standard measure of value; the coin was struck by Sher Shah. It was then of the weight of 175 grains troy and was considered to be pure but in the decline of the Muhammadan empire, every petty chief coined his own rupees varying in weight and value, usually bearing the title of the Emperor of India. This practice was observed to the last. In later period, the weight and value of the rupee or *rupiyah* was one tola of silver.

S

Sad: صاد — A — The Arabic letter; the initial of the title of the *Subah-dar* affixed by him as a cypher to *zamindari* grants as their authentication.

Sadr: صدر — A — Chief, supreme. The highest or the foremost of any thing. The chief seat of the government as opposed to the provinces.

Sadr Al Sudur: صدرالصدور — A — The chief judge. During the Mughal period, he was especially charged with the investigation of the cases of all those who applied to the Sovereign for the grant jagir or tankhwah. He was also in charge of religious endowments and the appointments of Qazis, (q.v.) and other law officers.

Sadr Jama: صدر جمع — A.P. — The sum total of the revenue payable to the government direct, exclusive of the charges of collection.

Sadr Daftar: صدر دفتر — A.H.P. — The principal revenue officer of a district of the *suba* (province).

Sadr Kharch: صدر خرچ — A.H. — Expenses of the principal authority or establishment.

Sadr Mal Guzar: صدر مالگذار — A.H. — The chief revenue payer, one who pays it either into the Government treasury, or to the Collector of a district directly, and not through any agency.

Sadr Qanungo: صدر قانون گو — A.H. — The chief of *Qanungos,* q.v.

Sadr Qist Bandi: صدر قسط بندی — A.P. — The engagement for revenue instalment payable to the Government by the principal revenue payer, as distinguished from those entered into with him by his under-payer.

Safar: صفر — A — The 2nd month of the Muslim lunar year.

Safi Nama: صافی نامہ — A.P. — A deed of acquittance, a deed of release or of acquiescence in the terms of a *razi-nama,* (q.v.) of which it is the counter-part; the latter or deed of consent being executed by the plaintiff; the *safi-nama* or deed of acquiescence, by the defendant.

Sahukar: ساہوکار — A banker; a dealer in money.

Saikh: سلخ — A.P. — The last day of a month of 30 days—day of the new moon.

Sail:	سیل	A	A petitioner; one who interrogates; also an examiner.
Sailabi:	سیلابی	A.P.	The land watered by inundations.
Sair:	سائر	A	In its original purport, the word signifies moving or the remainder; from the latter it came to denote the remaining or all other sources of revenue accruing to the Government, in addition to the land tax from a variety of imports as customs, transit duties, licences, fees, house tax, market tax etc.
Sair Dar:	سائر دار	P	The collector of *Sair* (customs) duties.
Sair Jahat:	سائر جہات	A.H.	A tax on boats, an inland toll, the *sair* duties collectively.
Sair Jama:	سائر جمع	A.P.	The total amount of the revenue in addition to the land tax.
Salana Dar:	سالانہ دار	P.H.	One who receives an annual allowance, *tankhawah* or stipend.
Salatin:	سلاطین	A	(Plural of *Sultan* (King). In India and in the Mughal recorded it means the members of the royal family, i.e., princes and not the King.
Sali:	سالے	P.H.	Annual, relating to the year, land taken up for the year; a rate in the cultivator's lease when two or more crops are raised from the soil in the same year, that is to day, when the ground is worked throughout the year, not in one season only.
Saliana:	سالیانہ	P.H.	Annual allowance, salary or pension.
Sanad:	سند	A	A grant, a charter, a patent, a diploma; a doucment conveying to an individual, emoluments, titles, privileges, offices or the

Government rights to revenue from land etc. under the seal of the ruling authority. The Mughal Government had different forms of *sanads* according to the nature of grant.

Sanad-i-Inam: سند انعام — P — It is a grant emanating from the ruling power of the time of the grant, free from all government exactions, in perpetuity and validified by *sanad* or official deed of grant; it usually comprises land included in the village area but which is uncultivated or has been abandoned and it is subject to the *had* or dues of the village functionaries. It may be granted sometimes with a reservation of a half, a third, or a fourth of the government claim.

Sanad Nawisand: سند نویسند — A.P. — A form of word inscribed by the chief authority upon the petition (*arzi*) to him for a grant of revenue after the necessary preliminaries had been completed.

Sanwat: سنوات — A — A rupee which has been current more than one year. Old coin current at depreciated rate after a certain number of years.

Sar Desh Mukh: سردیش مکھ — Mar — Chief of *deshmukhs,* q.v.

Sar Desh Panday: سردیش پانڈے — Mar — Chief of desh pandays, q.v.

Sarapa: سراپا — P — Head to foot; a complete *Khalat* or dress of honour, specially given on appointment to office by the Mughal government.

Sardar: سردار — P — A chief, a head man, a commander of army.

Sarishta: سررشتہ — P — Record office, department; office.

Sarishta Dar: سررشتہ دار — P — Officer who lays petitions before judicial officers, or the head ministerial officer of a law court.

Sarkar: سرکار P A landlord, an administrator of affairs. The Government or the Supreme Administrative body of a country. The tract of a territory under the Mughal Rule comprising some *parganas.*

Sarraf: صرّاف A A money changer, a banker, an officer appointed to ascertain the value of different currencies of various kings current during particular period of a king.

Sazawal: سزاوال P The office or the business of a *Sazawal.*

Sazawali: سزاوالی A special officer to take charge of and collect revenues of an estate from the management of which the owner or partner has been removed; or an agent appointed by a land owner or lessor to compel payment of rent by tenants or lesses. Indian Collector of the revenue.

Sawar: سوار P A horse man; cavalary man during Mughal period, a rider or person mounted, one carried by any conveyance.

Seer or Ser: سیر H A measure of weight varying in different parts of India. A seer is 1/40th part of a *man* (maund) and normally is equal to 80 or 90 tolas, q.v.

Shaban: شعبان A Eighth month of the Muslim lunar year.

Shagird-Pesha: شاگرد پیشہ A A menial servant, also retinue, an attendant

Shah Bandar: شاہ بندر P (*Shah,* King, a *bandar;* port). A port or harbour master, a customs officer, an officer who regulated the port duties and charges; a royal harbour or maritime establishment. In the revenue account of the Mughal government of Bengal, it designated

		especially Dacca and the customs levied there.
Shahid-i-Marhum: شہید مرحوم	P	Posthumous title of Emperor Farrukh Siya.
Shah-i-Qiran: شاہِ قرّان	P	Master of *giran* (a period of 30 years). One who has completed thirty years of reign.
Shahjahanabad: شاہ جہان آباد		Old name of Delhi.
Shawwal: شوال	A	Tenth month of the Muslim lunar year.
Shikmi: شکمی	A.P.	Subordinate, dependent: as a revenue term it applies to a subordinate tenure in which the holder pays his revenue or his share of it through some other person to the Government and not direct; it applies also to the individual cultivating land on such terms; he may be a joint proprietor with the revenue payer, having equal rights or he may be an hereditary tenant; in the former case, the superior cannot sell or mortgage any of land without the concurrence of the *Shikmi-Kasht-Kar* (or cultivator).
Shikmi Asami or Shikmi Kasht-Kar: شکمی آسامی یا کاشتکار	A.P.	A subordinate cultivator; one who paid the revenue to the Government through a superior share-holder and whose name was not entered as the cultivator in the records of revenue.
Shikmi Taaulluqa: شکمی تعلقہ	A.P.	An estate comprised within a *zamindari* and paying the revenue through the zamindar or other revenue contractor or *malguzar,* q.v.
Shiq: شق	A.P.	A certain tract of country forming a collectorate or an aggregate of land from which a certain revenue is collected.

Shiq-dar: شقدار	A.P.	(*Shiq;* a division, a tract of land and *dar,* one who has). A revenue officer or Collector appointed either by the Government or a zamindar (landlord) to collect the revenue from the small tract of country or from an estate; during the Mughal period it was sometimes applied to the chief financial officer of a province, and to the *viceroy* in his financial capacity.
Shuqqa: شُقہ	A	A royal letter or missive, a letter from a superior authority to an inferior or subordinate relating to State business.
Sih Bandi: سہ بندی	P	Irregular soldiers employed in the services of the revenue department as also by the *faujdar* temporarily.
Sih Bandi Fasl: سہ بندی فصل	H.A.	Troops employed for realizing revenue duties.
Mudam Sih Bandi: مدام سہ بندی	H.A.	Permanent establishment of militia.
Sikka: سکّہ	A	A coining die, a royal signet, a stamped coin especially the designation of the silver currency of the Mughal Emperor, without the *Sikka,* and *Khutba,* (q.v.) of the new King, his authority was supposed to be incomplete. It was, therefore, deemed necessary to issue *Sikka* and *Khutba* by every Mughal king just after his accession to the throne.
Sipahi: سپاہی	P	A police officer of the lowest rank; a soldier in the Mugahl army.
Sir Deshmukh: سردیش مکھ	M	He was a zamindar from amongst the Marathas who was invested with the power to realise revenue, on commission basis, on behalf of the Mughal Empire, in the territories of Deccan in addition to *Chauth,* (q.v.). Sir Deshmukh was chief of *Deshmukhs.*

Sir Deshmukhi: سر دیش مکھی	M	The office of a *Sir Deshmukh* (q.v.) or *Zamindar,* (q.v.). The portion of ten per cent exacted by the Marathas in the *Subas* of the Deccan.
Siyaha: سیاہ	H.P.	An account book; an inventory, a list. It is specially applied in India to the daily cash book.
Siyaha Amadani: سیاہ آمدنی	H.P.	A treasury account of the collections received from the cultivators daily.
Siyaha Bahi: سیاہ بہی	H	The day book in which daily receipts and disbursements are entered; it is also applied to a journal or diary in which the orders of a court of justice are recorded.
Siyaha Ahkam -i-Qudsi: سیاہ احکامِ قدسی		The day book containing orders issued daily by the Emperor on receipt of petitions, *arzis, sual,* etc.
Sual: سوال	A	A request; a petition for the grant of revenue.
Suba: صوبہ		Province, viceroy under Mughal Government; one of the largest sub-divisions of the Mughal dominions and the seat of the *Subadar.*
Suba-Dar Suba-Dari: صوبہ دار صوبہ داری	P	Governor of the province; Nazim, *q.v.* Office of the *Subadar.*
Supurd: سپرد	P	(Delivering, giving cover). Relinquishing as part of an estate held on lease from being unable to cultivate the whole.
Supurd Nama: سپردنامہ	P	A deed of handing over the part of a land to another for the purpose of cultivation.
Surat-i-Hal: صورت حال	A.P.	*Surat* means form and *hal* means condition. A representation of report of the facts and

		circumstances of a transaction whether made by an individual before witnesses or by a subordinate officer to a superior office.
Surat-i-Mahal: صورتِ محال	A.P.	A list or register of estates.
Surat Nama: صورت نامہ	A.P.	A written detailed account of an estate or transactions.

T

Taahud: تعہد	A	Agreement, contract, lease or engagement; revenue lease. Engagement with Government for payment of public revenue.
Taahud-Dar: تعہد دار	A.P.	*Taahud* from *ahd* means lease, promise, agreement, contract; in revenue term one who has entered into an engagement for the revenue due on his own share: the holder of a farm or lease.
Taalluqah or Taalluq: تعلقہ/تعلق	A	A district, a division of a province, an estate, applied to a tract of proprietary land usually smaller than a zamindari, although sometimes including several villages. A *taalluq* was sometimes granted by the Mughal Emperor at a favourable assessment as a mark of favour, or on condition of clearing and cultivating waste lands.
Taaullaq-Dar: تعلقہ دار	A.P.	The holder of thc *taalluq,* a collector of revenue from the land farmers either on behalf of the Government or of the farmer of the revenue whose undue exactions it is his duty to prevent.
Taalluqada Dari: تعلقہ داری	A.P.	The tenure, office or estate of a *taalluqdar.*
Taalluqadari Haq: تعلقہ داری حق	A.P.	The dues or allowances payable to the *Taaluqadar* in addition to his stipulated proportion of the assessment.

Taayyul: تیول A Land held in jagir by a member of a royal family, an appanage.

Tabinan: تابینان These were the *sawars* employed by the Mansabdars and, as such, paid by them.

Tablaq: طبلق A.P. A bundle or file of official papers.

Tah-Bazaari: تہہ بازاری P.H. A tax levied on the sellers of the articles in bazaar either in form, cash or kind as the rent of the ground on which their shops or stalls are placed.

Tahsil: تحصیل A (From *hasil*) job, collection of the revenue derived from the land; the revenue collected.

Tasil-Dar: تحصیل دار A.P. A collector of the revenue appointed by the State for collecting revenue of a pargana (q.v.).

Khas Tahsil: خاص تحصیل A.P. The collection of the revenue by the officers of the Government direct from the farmers and cultivators.

Tahvil-dar: تحویل دار P A Cashier. A person who is in charge of the *tahvil* (i.e., treasury or cash).

Tahwil: تحویل P Change, transfer, charge, trust, especially cash in the keeping of a person appointed to take care of it.

Takhfif: تخفیف A A statement or remission of revenue.

Takhsis Jama Bandi: تخصیص جمع بندی A.P. A particular statement of the assessment concluded with the revenue payer.

Takhta: تختہ H.Mar (A plank, a platform). A tabular statement of revenue accounts.

Talab: طلب A (A request, demand, petition) calling or sending for, summons, demand of pay. According to various documents of Inayat Jung Collection by *talab* we understand the pay fixed by the Emperor, or Mir Bakhshi or the *Subah Dar* (Nazim, i.e., Viceroy), q.v. according to the high and low ranks of the *mansabdar.* The *talab-dar* was given the choice to select the *pargana* of the *suba,* where he desired to get his jagir *tankhwah.* If the *pargana* was capable to part with the said amount, he was given pay from the *pargana* of his choice, otherwise he was again supposed to submit his subsequent choices. He sometimes preferred to have a part of his pay from a *pargana* then the remaining amount was termed as the *titamma talab* (balance of his pay) which was assigned to him from some other *parganas* afterwards.

Talab Baoi: طلب باقی A.P. An account showing the amounts due from each payer of the revenue, the sum realised and the balance due.

Talab-Titamma: طلب تتمہ A.P. The balance of the *tankhwah* payable to the *mansabdar* under the circumstances narrated under the head of *talab,* q.v.

Talab Dastak: طلب دستک A.P. (*Dastak* means a note). A summon, a write, a demand for payment of revenue.

Talbana: طلبانہ A Daily pay or fees to a subordinate officer of the the court charged with serving process, issuing summons or writs payable by the parties on whom they are served.

Taliqah: تعلیقہ A An account, note, inventory.

Tamassuk: تمسک H A written acknowledgment or agreement.

Tamassuk-i-Hazir Zamini: A.H.P. As a bond as security for personal appearance, a bond given by landholders to the revenue officers of the Government on receiving the grant of *zamindari* as a surety for their persona l appearance whenever required by the Government or its officers.

تمسک حاضر ضامنی

Tan Daftar: P (*Tan* means body or an individual and *daftar* means the office). An office in which assignments of revenue to individuals were registered.

تن دفتر

Tanga: تنکہ (Or tanka) a gold or copper coin.

Tankhwah: P (*Ta,* body, person and *Khwah,* what is desired) Pay, salary. An order of draft for money, a bill of exchange. An assignment by the ruling authority upon the revenue of any particular locality (*jagir*) in payment of wages, pay, gratuity or pension.

تنکہ

Tankhwah-Dar: P A holder of an order for wages etc. or of assignments by the ruling authority upon the revenue of any particular locality in payment of wages, pay, gratuity or pension, or in repayment of advances, or any specified head of charge.

تنخواہ دار

Tankhwah Dahand: P (*Dahand* means let them give). The form of words inscribed by the *Wazir* (or the minister) upon a written application for an assignment of revenue when complied with; if the sum exceeded 90,000 dams, the signature of the emperor was necessary.

تنخواہ دہند

Tappah: H A small tract or division of country, smaller than a *pargana* but comprising one or more villages, a division of country, for the revenue

ٹپہ

		of which only one engagement is entered into with the Government: a small estate.
Taqavi: تقاوی	A	Loans made to agriculturists for purchasing seed, bullocks or agricultural improvements by the Government.
Taqsim: تقسیم	A	Distribution of the assessment of the revenue upon the several sub-division of an estate or district.
Taqsim-i-Jama: تقسیم جمع	A.P.	The distribution of the whole standard assessment among the different territorial sub-divisions, whether large or small. Also, the apportionments of the revenue payable by a village or estate amongst joint proprietors.
Taqsim-Nama: تقسیم نامہ	A.P.	A deed of partition amongst joint proprietors when ceasing to hold their estate in common.
Taqsim-Pargana War: تقسیم پرگنہ وار	A.P.	Sub-division of the whole assessment according to the district divisions termed as *pargánas*; q.v. accounts of the standard assessment of each *pargana*, extracted from the general rent-roll of the empire.
Tariz: تعریض	A	(Exchange) Statement of particulars of the landed property deposited in the office of the revenue collector.
Tasdiq: تصدیق	A	(Verification,attestation) a counter mark attached to the documents passing through the hands of the Government officer or clerks especially on petitions to the Emperor for assignment of revenue; specification of establishment and expenses; fixed amount or scale of expenditure for any special purpose.
Tashiha: تصحیہ	A	Muster of the horses belonging to the Mansabdars or to the Empire for the purpose of being stamped.

Tashiha Darogha: تصحیہ داروغہ — The office of the Darogha or Superintendent of the examining and stamping of the horses of the State; Assignment of revenue or allowances to the officer in charge of the Department.

Tashkish: تشخیص — A — (Valuation, assessment, corrected assessment). Net standard revenue or the actual or absolute amount of realisable revenue; particular account of such revenue or the available funds which it constitues; (the term is used with some laxity but it always implies a determine or determinable amount of revenue assessment.

Taufir: توفیر — A — (increase; applied in revenue language to an augmentation of the revenue; either from the extended cultivation or the lapse or resumption of alienated assignments; excess above an intended amount of assignment, which, when realised in a jagir, was considered to be the right of the State.

Taufir-i-Mauza: توفیر موضع — A.P. — (*Mauza* means village). A village not originally included in the assessment, a village in excess.

Taurir-i-Zamin: توفیر زمین — A.P. — Lands in addition to or excess of an original grant or measurement.

Taujih: توجیہ — Usually a village account, which was kept by the village accountant, (*patwari*). Also, a register of the estates of a collectorate kept in the collector's office. A Register containing accounts of the Army, showing the name of each payer of revenue, the total amount as it falls due by monthly instalments and the balance outstanding.

Thana: تھانہ — H — A station, a military post, a police station. under the Mughal Empire it was a military post or garrison, a place sometimes with a small fort where a petty officer with a small irregular force was posted to protect the country from high handedness of the law breaker and to extend help and cooperation to the revenue officer for collecting revenue from those land holders who showed their unwillingness to pay it.

Thanah-Dar: تھانہ دار — H.P. — An officer in charge of *thanah* or police station. He was an officer under the faujdar, (q.v.) employed with a small irregular force for prosecuting the country and enforcing payment of the revenue to the authorities appointed by the Government for the purpose.

Tirij: تیرتج — H.Tel. Kar — An abstract account completed from other detailed accounts, an item in a number of items to be added together, a paper or list of items to be added together.

Tirij Asami War: تیرتج آسامی وار — H.P. — (*Asami war,* according to cultivators) one of the village accounts specifying the number of each sub-divisions of the village lands, the name of its occupants, the number of *bighas,* q.v. occupied wihtout particularising the fields and the amount assessed upon the whole land.

Tola: تولہ — A weight; there were 40 seers in a maund, (*Man*) 16 *Chattak* was equal to a seer where as a *Chattak* was of 5 tolas. Gold is still weighed in terms of tolas. 8 *rattis* were equal to a *masha* and 12 *masha* were equal to a *tola.*

Top Chi: توپ چی — T — A conductor of ordance, an officer of the artillery.

Top Khanah: توپ خانہ — T.P. — (*Top*; cannon and *Khana;* house). An arsenal, an artillery park, a foundary for manufacturing cannons, guns and other fire-arms; a place where military stores were kept.

Tughra: طغری — A — The imperial signature, the sign manual on a royal grant of revenue; the royal titles usually pre-fixed to a public document written in ornamental character also called *tughra.*

Tumar: طومار — A — A roll, a record, a register, an account.

Tumar Jama: طومار جمع — A.P. — The sum total of land revenue according to register; the recorded standard assessment of land revenue of the provinces of the Mughal Empire in the reign of Akbar the Great, as settled by his Minister Raja Todar Mal and subsequently revised at different periods down to the fall of the said Empire.

U

Uftada: افتادہ — P — Tracts of fallow land which have not returned to cultivation.

Uhda-Dar: عہدہ دار — A.P. — (*Uhda;* office, rank and *dar;* one who has). An officer, filling either a civil or military appointment. During the Mughal period, the name was also applied to the farmer or contractor of revenue; also to a subcontractor.

Umara: اُمرا — A — (Plural of *amir*; a noble man). The collective name of the top most officers at a Muhammadan Court, especially that of the great Mughal.

W

Wakil: وکیل — An agent of the Jagirdar or liaison officer between the Jagirdar and the royal court; an attorney. Mostly, all the Jagirdars were war lords who were engaged in the war and as such, Wakils were appointed by them to look after their jagir *mahals* and enter into correspondence with the revenue officials on behalf of them.

Wakil-i-Mutlaq: وکیل مطلق | A | A plenipotentiary, a vice-regent or a representative invested with full powers.

Waqai: وقائع | A | Plural of *Waqia.* Events, occurrences, news.

Waqai-Navis: وقائع نویس | A.P. | A writer or surveyor of occurrences in *parganas* and *subas.* He was the more regular reporter than that of *Waqai-nigar.* The *Waqai-navis* was attached to every field Army, province and large towns and was charged to send his reports of occurrences once in each week. He was supposed to appoint clerks in the office of *Faujdar, Kotwal, Diwan, Subadar* for submitting daily reports to him. Important news were then despatched by him to the Imperial court. There was a difference between *Sawanih nigar* and *Sawanish nawis, Sawanish nigar* was advised to submit his reports direct to the Imperial court whereas the contents of the newsletters drafed by *Sawanih nawis* were to be communicated to the *Subadar* or, in case of a field army, to the *Sipah Salar* (the general in command), before being despatched to the Imperial court.

Waqai Nigar: وقائع نگاری | A.P. | (*Waqai,* events and *nigar;* one who writes, records). An officer on the royal establishment under the Mughals who kept a record of the various orders issued by, and transactions connected with, the sovereign in the revenue department: an officer of this denomination was also attached to the provincial governor, who reported to the principal remembrancer at the Imperial court the particular revenue transactions of the province. Head newswriter: any communicator or official intelligence. In the period of Aurangzeb, the *Wagai nigar* was also entrusted with the post of *Bakhshi* q.v. He was to submit his reports eight times in a month.

Waqai Nigar : P — The establishment of news writers employed by the Mughal governments and posted at different places of a Suba for furnishing the Emperor with the day to day reports about the activities of the Subadar in regard to his subject and his attitude towards the King as well. This office was also required to furnish up-to-date reports about revenue affairs.
وقائع نگار

Waqf: P — A bequest for religious or charitable purpose, an endowment, an apportion of property by will or by gift to the service of God in such a way that it may be beneficial to human beings, the donor or testator having the power of designating the persons and purpose to be so benefited.
وقف

Wasil: A — (From *Wasl,* joined connected, attached). As a revenue term, it implies the amount of revenue collected.
واصل

Wasil Baqi: A — An account showing the amount of revenue realised by farmers, Zamindars, etc. and the balance outstanding against the cultivators etc.
واصل باقی

Wasil Baqi Kharch: A.P. — An account maintained showing the amount of revenue assessed, the portion realized, the balance outstanding with the deductions of charges of collection; it was drawn up at the close of the year at the settlement of the revenue accounts.
واصل باقی خرچ

Wasilat: واصلات	A	The proceeds of an estate, profits of land.
Watan: وطن	H.P	(Native country, place of residence). During the period of Aurangzeb, it became a right for *Mansabdar* or *Jagirdar* to apply for *jagir tankhwah* from a place which the applicant made his *watan*. Similarly, *Deshmukhs* etc. were granted *deshmukhi* in their native country.
Watan Dar: وطن دار	H.P.	The holder of a hereditary right, property or office with the privileges and emoluments attached to it.
Wazifa: وظیفہ	A	(Plural *Wazaif*). A pension, a grant of land rent free or at a quit-rent to pious persons or for the officer in lieu of the services they rendered in the past; revenue collected at a stipulated or fixed rate for a certain quantity of land.
Wazir or Vazir: وزیر	A	Literally one who bears a load, a porter. The principal minister in the Mughal Government.
Wizarat or Vizarat: وزارت	A	The office of the Wazir/Vazir.
Wujuh or Wujuhat: وجوہ/وجوہات	P	Salaries, allowances, wages, extra collections of revenue by the landholders for personal expenses.

Y

Yad Dasht: یادداشت	P	Memorandum, a note, a petition; also a certificate.
Yamin: یمین	P	Right wing of fighting Army.
Yarah: یارا	A.P.	(From *yar*) a friend or companion. When applied to revenue term, it means a tax toll or revenue.

Yasal:	يسال	J	Wing of an Army.
Yasaq:	يساق	T	Maintaining a regular force of permanent nature.
Yasar:	يسار	T	Left wing of a fighting Army.
Yasawal:	يساول	T	An officer of parade, one carrying a gold or silver staff; a state messenger.
Yaum:	يوم	A	*Yaum Al-Ahad*—First day of the week, i.e, Sunday. *Yaum Al-Isnain*–Second day of the week, i.e., Monday. *Yaum Us-S-Salsa*–Third day of the week, i.e., Tuesday. *Yaumal-Arba*—Fourth day of the week, i.e, Wednesday. *Yaum Al-Khamis*—Fifth day of the week, i.e., Thursday. *Yaum Al-Jumat*—Sixth day of the week, i.e., Friday (Day of Congregation). *Yaum Al-Sabt*—*Sabbath* day: Seventh day of the week, i.e, Saturday. *Yaum Al-Ashura*—Tenth day of the month of Muharram (Sacred because of being the day when Husain, the son of Ali, was murdered in Karbala (Arabia).
Yaum Al-Fitr:	يوم الفطر	A	The day of breaking fast after the fast of the month of *Ramazan,* q.v.

Yaum Al--In-Qitta: A — The day of cessation, the day on which any thing terminates. In law, the last day on which any one who has become possessed of a property illegally may restore it, more to make compensation to the real owner.

يوم الانقطاع

Yaum Al Qarr: A — The day of rest, the day after the sacrifice of the tenth *Zul-hijja,* when people repose from their labour.

يوم القر

Yaum Al-Nahr: A — The day of sacrifice that is the tenth day of the month *Zul-hijja* or the festival of *Baqr-id.*

يوم النهار

Z

Zabt: P — Occupation, seizure; in law, attachment, taking lands under the management of the officers of the Mughal Empire; land which had been held free but has been subjected to money-assessment.

ضبط

Zabti: P — Attached, applied to lands taken possession of by the Government officers or to rent-free lands which have been subjected to assessment.

ضبطی

Zaif: A — Defective money current but not receivable at the public treasuries.

زیف

Zail: A — Appendix, supplement to a letter or book; the lower margin of a *zamindari* grant in which the names of the land granted are recapitulated.

ذیل

Zamindar: P — *Zamin,* Land and *dar* who has or possesses. An occupant of land, a landholder: the rights of the *Zamindar* have been the subject of much controversy with reference to his character as hereditary owner of the land he

زمین دار

occupies, or as the responsible collector only of the revenues on behalf of the Government. Under the Mohammadan administration, the latter was the capacity in which the Zamindar was ordinarily considered, and the chief authorities never hesitated to exercise the power, when they possessed it, of turning out a *Zamindar* and placing another in the *Zamindari,* whence the one in possession was termed *Sanadi,* or *Ahkami,* the *Zamindar* by patent or command. Whilst managing the lands and realising the revenue, the *Zamindar* was allowed a fee or commission of ten per cent. Upon the total collections, and a portion of the land was exempted from the revenue assessment to the extent of five per cent. on the collections, under the denomination of *Nankar,* being intended for the personal support of the *Zamindar* and his family; further deductions from the stipulated amount of revenue, termed *Mathaut,* were also allowed, to cover various charges borne by the *Zamindar.* On the other hand, he was empowered to levy internal duties and customs on articles of trade passing through his district, and to impose petty taxes, or *Abwabs,* on the cultivators, in addition to the portion of the public revenue demandable from them individually. On his relinquishing the management of the *Zamindari,* or being removed from it without cause of grave offence, it was customary to assign him, as *Malikana,* ten per cent. on the *Sadr* collections, or the same rate on the net collections when held *khas,* or managed by the government officers direct. But although in these respects the *Zamindar* appears to be a representative of the State, employed to realise and transfer to the public treasure nine-tenths of the revenue, and to be nominated or removed at pleasure; yet the practice of hereditary succession, and the right to mortgage and sell, partook more of the tenure of ownership, and extensive tracts came to be held by successive generations of the same family, through more or less protracted periods, in some instances apparently from a date anterior to the fiscal regulations of the Mohammadan governments; in the decline of the latter also, many *Zamindaris* which were held originally under a special grant were converted into hereditary proprietaries, and the *Zamindars,* appropriating by fraud or force very extensive districts, assumed the states of chiefs and princes, and were sometimes powerful enough to resist the authority and withhold the revenues of the State. In the southern provinces, the term *Zamindar* was applied indiscriminately to the local hereditary revenue officers, whether of the districts, as *Deshmukh, Despande,* and others, or of the villages, as the *Patil, Chaughala,* and *Kulkarni.*

Zamindarana: زمین دارانہ — A.H. — The pay of a *Zamindar,* the allowance made to him when set aside.

Zamin-Dari: زمین داری — P — The office and rights of a *Zamindar:* the tract of land constituting the possessions of a *Zamindar.*

Zamindari-Chauki: زمین داری چوکی — H — (*Chauki*), a station). A post at which the officers of the *Zamindar* formerly collected tolls and customs on goods passing through his estate.

Zamindari-Patta: زمین داری پٹہ — H — (*Patta*) a lease; a document granted by Government in recognition of the possessions of a Zamindar.

Zamindari-Jama: زمین داری جمع H.A. (*Jama*). The amount of revenue which the holder of a zamindari engages to pay to the government.

Zamindari-Muchalka: زمین داری مچلکا H.A. (*Muchalka*, an agreement). An obligation entered into by a *Zamindar* on receiving the grant of a *zamindari*, engaging for the due observance of its conditions.

Zamindari-Rasum: زمین داری رسوم H (*Rasum*), Fees. Cesses or fees levied by a Zamindar.

Zamindari-Sanad: زمین داری سند H (*Sanad*) Deed or patent granting a Zamindari.

Zat: ذات A (Possessed of, master, owner, person). A grant of revenue of lands alienated from the Government revenue in favour of the individual either as a personal favour or on the condition of personal service, a personal grant.

Zila: ضلع A A division of a province, a district.

Zila-Dar: ضلع دار A.P. The officer in charge of a *zila*, q.v. In Delhi territory, the title was also given to the head of a village who was chosen to superintend the revenue affairs of several adjacent villages, united under him for the convenience of revenue arrangement.

Zin-Kaff: زین قاف Sepoy or peon.

Zimar: ضمار A In law, anything uncertain as disputed debts, treasuretrove: any property of which the possession or recovery is doubtful.

Zimma: ذمہ A A deed of protection, an authorised assurance of immunity in life and property such as may be granted to infidels under a Muslim Government; a tenure in trust, but which by possession, came to signify a tenure in right in some places, in others an under tenure or a sub-division of an estate, in which the holder is entitled to levy the revenue due by the cultivators, and pay it either to the *Zamindar,* or sometimes direct to the Governmental subtenure, part of a *hawala,* q.v.

Zimmadar: ذمّہ دار — A.P. — A person in charge, the one who holds *zimma.*

Zimmi: ذمّی — A — One living under protection, a client, a dependent especially applied to a subject, of a Muhammadan Government, of a different religion who is allowed to live in peace and without molestation on paying tribute.

Zimn: ضمن — A — The endorsement of a grant, giving an abstract of its contents.

Zimn Navisand: ضمن نویسند — A.P. — (*Nawisand,* let them write) a form of words 'let them write the abstract' formerly inscribed upon a *sanad,* q.v.—granting as an assignment of revenue or *zamindari* which served as authority for the subordinate officers to make out the particulars of the assignment or grant.

Zirarti: زراعتی — A — Cultivable arable lands. Also sometimes assessable lands subject to assessment.

Zubdatut Tashkhis: زبدۃ التشخیص — A — (*Zubdat:* gist and *tashkhis,* valuation, assessment, papers giving an account of the state of land, etc.

Zul-Hijja: ذوالحجہ — A — Twelfth month of the Muslim lunar year.

Zul-Qada: ذوالقعدہ — A — Eleventh month of the Muslim lunar year.

Zunnar Dar: زنّاردار — P — One who wears the sacred thread, *Brahmin,* the highest of the Hindu caste.

Index

Index

P